W9-AYJ-574

Collecting
Little Golden Books

A Collector's Identification and Price Guide

3rd Edition

by Steve Santi

Free Public Library of Monroe Township
306 S. Main Street
Williamstown, N.J. 08094-1727

8 6 3 3 1 ▮

© 1998 by

Steve Santi

All rights reserved. No portion of this publication may be reproduced or transmitted in any form or by any means, electronic or mechanical, including photocopy, recording, or any information storage and retrieval system, without permission in writing from the publisher, except by a reviewer who may quote brief passages in a critical article or review to be printed in a magazine or newspaper, or electronically transmitted on radio or television.

Published by

krause
publications

700 E. State Street • Iola, WI 54990-0001
Telephone: 715/445-2214

Please call or write for our free catalog.
Our toll-free number to place an order or obtain a free catalog is 800-258-0929
or please use our regular business telephone 715-445-2214 for editorial comment and further information.
Little Golden Books® and associated trademarks are the property of Golden Books Publishing Company, Inc.
Wonder Books is a registered trademark of Price Stern Sloan.

ISBN: 0-87341-244-3

Printed in the United States of America

TABLE OF CONTENTS

DEDICATION

To Brian, Christine, and Paul who lost their father to the computer during the making of this book.

ACKNOWLEDGMENTS

A special thanks to some of the many people who have helped to make this guide possible:

John Wharton

Robert Sohl

Scott McAdam

Kim McLynn

Melanie Donovan

Mary Janaky

Rebecca Greason

Clif Erickson

Diane McCue

Linda Terpstra

My wife Charlotte who has been very supportive with my collecting.

NOTE FROM THE AUTHOR

Any questions can be directed to the author by either e-mailing (LGBSTEVE@aol.com), visiting his web page at (http://members.aol.com/lgbsteve), or you can also send a letter with a self-addressed envelope to:

Steve Santi

19626 Ricardo Ave.

Hayward, CA 94541

FOREWORD

I met Steve Santi in late 1987. Since then, I've come to know him as a man who cares…What I mean by that is golden books. What? Golden books? Yes. I'm not sure how long he has been collecting them…since who knows when. I don't consider him a collector, though, but a historian. Think back on how we have been raised on the little golden book—as much as we have been raised on the Disney animated film. He has taken of his time, energy, money, and knowledge to accumulate the history of a treasure—the Little Golden Book. Without him, not even the golden book people, Western Publishing, would know all about the Golden's recorded history.

It has been a pleasure to know Steve, a man with a golden vision…Thanks, Steve.

Ron Dias

Note:

Ron Dias has illustrated or collaborated on many of Disney children's books since getting his first job as an animator/illustrator for the Walt Disney Studios in the late 1950s.

He is credited with illustrating twelve Little Golden Books, but he worked on many before Disney Studios started allowing illustrators to be given name credit.

Ron received national attention in 1956 when he was invited to visit President Eisenhower in Washington, DC. This visit was the result of winning a national contest on designing a "Children's Friendship" postal stamp.

Ron is still very active in the animation industry.

The History of Little Golden Books

One of the largest printers of children's books in the world, Western Publishing Company, Inc., had its start in the basement of 618 State St. in Racine, Wis.

Edward Henry Wadewitz, the 30-year-old son of German immigrants, had been working two jobs—one at a paint store and the other for West Side Printing Company—while taking bookkeeping classes at night. When the owner of the printing company was unable to pay Wadewitz his wages, he offered to sell him the business. With dreams of owning his own business, Wadewitz, with $2,504, some of it borrowed from his brother Al, purchased the West Side Printing Company in 1907.

Wadewitz knew that if the printing company was to make it, he would need someone who was more knowledgeable in the field than he. Roy A. Spencer, a printer with the Racine Journal Co., was one of the first people Wadewitz hired.

West Side Printing Company, with four employees, showed sales of $5,000 at the end of the first year. In 1908, with commercial job sales increasing, the company hired more employees. It also left a $10-a-month rental building and moved into a larger one. The company also purchased a new automatic cutting machine and three new presses that year.

In 1910, after the purchase of the company's first lithographic press, the name was changed to Western Printing and Lithographing Co.

Less than four years later, the company moved into an even larger building—the basement of the Dr. Clarendon I. Shoop Building located at State and Wisconsin Avenue in Racine. Dr. Shoop was famous for bottled medications and tonics.

Western Printing and Lithographing Co. had become so

Western's business started in 1907 in this basement print shop. "Pioneer employees" were (from the left) Roy A. Spencer, Catherine Bongarts Rutledge, E.H. Wadewitz, W.R. Wadewitz, and William Bell. The shop consisted of not much more than two battered presses, a few fonts of worn type, and a hand-powered cutting machine.

successful that when Dr. Shoop retired in 1914, it took over all six floors of the Shoop Building. By its seventh year, sales had topped $127,000 and two new departments were formed: electrotyping and engraving. The company also purchased a new 28" x 42" offset press.

Wadewitz was approached by the Hamming-Whitman Publishing Company of Chicago to print its line of children's

A major sign of growth was the 1929 move to the new main plant in Racine, Wisconsin.

books. What Wadewitz did not foresee was that Hamming-Whitman would soon be going out of business. Unable to pay its bills, Hamming-Whitman left Western with thousands of books in its warehouse and in production. Trying to cut its losses, Wadewitz entered Western into the retail book market for the first time. This was so successful that the remaining Hamming-Whitman books were liquidated.

After acquiring Hamming-Whitman on Feb. 9, 1916, Western formed a subsidiary corporation called Whitman Publishing Company. Whitman employed two salesmen the first year and grossed more than $43,500 in children's book sales.

Sam Lowe, who later owned Bonnie Books, joined the Western team in 1916. Lowe sold Western and Whitman on the idea of bringing out a 10-cent children's book in 1918. Disaster almost followed when an employee misread a book order from S.S. Kresge Company, confusing dozens for gross, resulting in too many books being printed. Lowe was able to sell F.W. Woolworth Company and other chains the idea of having children's books on sale all year round. Until that time,

In 1910 West Side Printing Company changed its name to Western Printing & Litographing Co. and moved to the imposing building seen here, which was owned by Dr. Sharp's Laboratories.

stores usually treated children's books as Christmas items.

Toward the end of 1918, Western was outgrowing the Shoop Building, so another building, which the company named Plant 2, was purchased to house the bookbinding and storage departments. In order to print a 6" x 9" book, Western purchased a 38" x 52" Potter offset press in 1923. This same year, Western started producing games and puzzles. With sales of more than $1 million in 1925, Western decided to add another product, playing cards, to its ever-growing line of merchandise. To be able to handle this, Western obtained the Sheffer Playing Card Company and formed another subsidiary corporation—the Western Playing Card Company.

By 1928, Western had built a new, modern, air-conditioned plant on Mound Avenue in Racine, and by 1929, sales were more than $2.4 million. The print run for children's books exceeded 10 million, playing cards five million, and games and puzzles, one million. As a result, the company had to make plans to expand its new building.

In 1929, Western purchased Stationer's Engraving Company of Chicago, manufacturer of stationery and greeting cards. This was the second operation Western had outside of Racine.

Western was able to keep its plant operational during the Depression years (1929–1933) by introducing a couple of new products. The Whitman jigsaw puzzle became very popular during this time of uncertainty. A new series of books called Big Little Books was also marketed. Brought out in 1932, the 10-cent books became very popular during these years when people were looking for inexpensive entertainment. The first Big Little Book title was *The Adventures of Dick Tracy*. With this line of books, Western was setting the stage for future inexpensive reading material like comic books and Little Golden Books. People love to copy success, and many publishers started bringing out their own books styled after the Big Little Book.

By the end of 1933, the Depression was nearing an end, Disney's Big Bad Wolf had been beaten by the Three Little Pigs, and Western and Walt Disney signed their first contract, giving Western exclusive rights to Disney's major characters. Walt Disney Little Golden Books have been published since 1944, but it wasn't until 1947 that new stories were published quite regularly, and have been ever since. The first three books of the Disney series were published under Wait Disney's Little Library before being changed to A Little Golden Book. The first three stories originally came with dust jackets.

Western, seeing a problem in having its plants and offices so far away from the rest of the publishing industry, purchased a plant in Poughkeepsie, N.Y., in 1934. This event marked the beginning of a close relationship with Dell Publishing Company and Simon & Schuster, Inc. Dell Publishing and Western produced "Color Comics," which contained many of Western's licensed characters, from 1939 to 1962, and "A Children's History" was the first joint effort between Western and Simon & Schuster in 1938. Little Golden Books would be coming out in only four more years!

Western formed the Artists and Writers Guild Inc. in the 1930s to handle the development of new children's books. This company, located on Fifth Avenue in New York, would later have an immense hand in the conception of Little Golden Books.

Western expanded its operations to the West Coast when it opened an office in Beverly Hills, California, sometime in the early 1940s. Being closer to the movie capital of the world was going to make it a lot easier to do business with the studios that owned the characters it licensed.

During World War II, Western did its part to help with the war effort. The company had a contract with the U.S. Army Map Service to produce maps for American soldiers in the fields. Along with the maps and other projects it did for the military, Western also manufactured many of its own products that were sent to the soldiers and the Red Cross overseas, such as playing cards and books.

In 1940, Sam Lowe left the company and George Duplaix replaced him as head of the Artists and Writers Guild.

While the guild and Simon & Schuster were collaborating on a book of Walt Disney's *Bambi*, Duplaix came up with the concept of a colorful child's book that would be durable and affordable to more American families than the children's books being printed at that time. In 1941, children's books sold for between $2.00 and $3.00—a luxury to a lot of families. With the help of Lucile Olge, also of the guild, Duplaix contacted Albert Leventhal and Leon Shimkin, both of Simon & Schuster, with his idea. Leventhal was a vice president and sales manager at Simon & Schuster.

The group decided on twelve titles to be released at the same time. Each title would have 42 pages, 28 in two color and 14 in four color. The book's binding was designed after a side staple binding being done in Sweden. These books were to be called Little Golden Books.

The group originally discussed a 50-cent price for Little Golden Books, but Western did not want to compete with the other 50-cent books already on the market. The group did some more figuring and found that if it printed 50,000 copies of each book instead of 25,000, the books could be sold for 25 cents. In September 1942, the first twelve titles were printed and released to stores in October.

Little Golden Books, with their colorful, bright pages, were designed to be handled by children, and inexpensive enough that children could read or handle their books whenever they wanted. With these qualities and many more, the books became very popular with parents, but not with librarians in these early years. Librarians felt these books did not contain the quality of literature a child should be reading. They did not consider that a book a child could handle was better than a book on a six-foot shelf or that an affordable book was better than not owning one. This attitude has mellowed quite a bit since the 1940s, but surprisingly it is still held by some librarians today.

The first ad to announce Little Golden Books was published in the Sept. 19, 1942, edition of *Publisher's Weekly*. The ad listed the types of stories and the artists doing the first twelve books. The ad stated the books measured 8-1/4" x 6-1/4" and contained 44 pages—30 pages in black and white and 14 in full color. Whether it was because of the war, getting the price down to a quarter, or a printing error in the ad, the books were released with 42 pages and not 44 pages.

The first twelve Little Golden Books:

1   Three Little Kittens
2   Bedtime Stores
3   The Alphabet A-Z
4   Mother Goose
5   Prayers for Children
6   The Little Red Hen
7   Nursery Songs
8   The Poky Little Puppy
9   The Golden Book of Fairy Tales
10 Baby's Book
11 The Animals of Farmer Jones
12 This Little Piggy

Within five months, 1.5 million copies had been printed and the books were in their third printing. They became so popular with children that by the end of 1945, most of the first twelve books had been printed seven times. Simon & Schuster, Inc. published Little Golden Books, while the Artists and Writers Guild produced them and Western Printing and Lithographing did the printing.

When the books were first released, they were sold mainly in book and department stores. From there, they moved into variety stores, toy stores, drug stores, and finally in the late 1940s, something new called the supermarket. Parents did not mind paying a quarter for a book. So, for the first time, a quality children's book was made available to children who normally couldn't have afforded one.

During World War II, there was a paper shortage in the United States. To help ease this shortage, the War Production Board put restrictions on paper use in 1943. As a result, retailers were receiving only one of every ten books they ordered. Some Little Golden Book titles were being printed with less than the original 42 pages. In some cases, the size of the book was also reduced slightly. Books that had been reduced to compensate for the paper shortage stated on the copyright page: "First Printing this edition."

Most of the first thirty-five titles were released with blue bindings. Books that have this binding were published with dust jackets. Book No. 35, *The Happy Family*, was the last book published with the blue binding. The dust jackets of these early books mentioned on their back inside flap the purchasing of U.S. Savings Stamps. One of the characters of each of these books was also used to talk to children about purchasing these stamps.

The following are some of these shorts:

THE THREE LITTLE KITTENS

They found their mittens and they rushed out to say,
"Oh! Mother dear, see here, see here our mittens we have found."
"What! Found your mittens, you good little kittens!
I'll get you all War Stamps today!"
So, you be good kittens, hold on to your mittens, save your pennies the War Stamp way!

BEDTIME STORIES

One day Chicken Little strutted through the woods. Behind her strutted Henny Penny and Ducky Lucky and Goosey Loosey. On the way they met Turkey Lurkey.
"Where are you going?" asked Turkey Lurkey.
"We are all going to buy War Savings Stamps, just as we do every week!"
So Turkey Lurkey joined them and they all hurried off to buy War Savings Stamps. And so should you!

FROM A TO Z

A is for the airplanes which Jimmy's War Stamps buy.
B is for the Bond he'll get to keep them in the sky.
C is for children who save a bit each day.
D is for the dimes they save that help the U.S.A.
You can buy Stamps every week, like Jim.
Soon you'll be buying a Bond, like him.

MOTHER GOOSE

There was an old woman who lived in a shoe.
She had so many children,
She knew just what to do.
She gave them some broth without any bread,
Bought them all War Stamps
And sent them to bed.
Soon she was able to buy them a War Bond.
If you buy War Stamps with your pennies, soon you can buy a Bond too.

PRAYERS FOR CHILDREN

Today our country, which has given us so much, needs our help. It asks all of us, children and grown-ups alike, to put our savings into War Stamps and Bonds.
These Bonds will help to buy the ships and tanks and planes and guns our country needs to win the war quickly.
Then, too, we will get back all the money we invest, and more, later on.
Surely we will all want to buy War Stamps or Bonds every week to help our country!

THE LITTLE RED HEN

This year the Little Red Hen has a Victory Garden. She has extra food to sell to the duck, the goose, the cat and the pig who will not grow their own.

With the pennies she saves, she buys War Savings Stamps every week. Soon she will have enough stamps to buy a War Bond. If you buy War Stamps every week, you will soon be able to buy a Bond too.

NURSERY SONGS

Mary buys War Savings Stamps, Savings Stamps, Savings Stamps, Mary buys War Savings Stamps
To help the U.S.A.
Soon she's going to have a Bond, Have a bond, Have a Bond, Soon She's going to have a Bond.
Why not start yours today?

THE POKEY LITTLE PUPPY

The poky little puppy sat near the bottom of the hill, looking hard at something on the ground in front of him.

"What is he looking at?" the four little puppies asked one another And down they went to see.

There was a War Savings Stamp lying on the grass.

And the poky little puppy hurried home faster than he had ever run before, to paste the stamp in his War Stamp Book. All the five little puppies buy War Stamps every week.

So should you.

THE GOLDEN BOOD OF FAIRY TALES

While the wicked Old Giant was asleep, Jack tucked the magic hen under his arm, and fled down the beanstalk to his home.

Every day the hen laid a golden egg, and Jack sold the gold to buy a War Savings Bond, which is much more valuable.

Even if you don't have a magic hen, your pennies will buy War Savings Stamps and soon you will be able to buy a Bond too!

BABY'S BOOK

Where is Tommy?
Here he is.
He has a new War Stamp.
Soon he will buy a War Bond.
Do you buy War Stamps every week like Tommy?
Of course you do!

THE ANIMALS OF FARMER JONES

All the animals are hungry. But Farmer Jones has gone to town. He is buying War Savings Stamps. He buys War Savings Stamps every week. You should buy War Stamps every week, too.

Soon you will be able to buy a War Savings Bond.

THIS LITTLE PIGGY AND OTHER COUNTING RHYMES

This little piggy goes to market.
What do you think he'll buy?
He's buying some War Savings Stamps.
So do I.
This little piggy cried, "Wee, wee, wee,
Boo! hoo! hoo!
I have no War Savings Stamps."
Is that you?

THE GOLDEN BOOK OF BIRDS

Robin Redbreast's beak is high and he is singing proudly, he has just bought War Stamps for the whole Robin Family.

If you save your pennies and buy War Stamps, you will want to sing, too.

NURSERY TALES

You remember how the kind old shoemaker and his wife made tiny shoes and tiny jackets and trousers and hats for the good little elves who helped them.

(If you don't remember, you can read about them in this very book.)

Well, one night the elves came back. They crept into the shop and left a gift on the shoemaker's workbench.

What do you suppose that gift was? It was a War Savings Stamp Book half filled with War Savings Stamps. These days, a War Savings Stamp is the best gift of all!

A DAY IN THE JUNGLE

All the animals were on their way to visit the mouse. The story had spread that he had something really worth seeing, and all were anxious to find out what this tiny animal could possibly have that was worth looking at. But they all gasped when he showed it to them-a brand new twenty-five-dollar War Bond!

"How," growled the lion, "did you manage to do that?"

"I just kept buying War Stamps," said the mouse, "and pretty soon I had enough for a bond. It was quite simple."

If a mouse can to it, can't you, too?

THE LIVELY LITTLE RABBIT

The red squirrel, was very wise, told all the animals that buying War Stamps was a very fine thing to do. All the rabbits hurried off to take his advice. And who do you think was the first in line? The lively little rabbit, of course.

Then all the other little rabbits, and the squirrel, and the owl, and yes, even the weasels, bought their War Stamps.

And so should you!

THE GOLDEN BOOK OF FLOWERS

If Miss Petunia, The Rose, the shy Violet, the naughty Daisy, the Water Lily, the Goldenrod and all our other flower friends could come right out of this book to speak to you today they would all say: "BUY MORE WAR STAMPS"

HANSEL AND GRETEL

Hansel and Gretel have learned how to provide for the future. Each week they buy War Savings Stamps, and soon they are going to buy a Bond. It's a good way for you to save, too.

MY FIRST BOOK OF BIBLE STORIES

Just as Joseph asked the Egyptians to set aside part of their crop to provide for the years to come, so your Government is asking you to use part of your money to buy War Savings Stamps.

Once the paper shortage was over, the books were again printed with their original 42 pages. Back orders that had piled up during the shortage began being filled and the company found itself with thousands of new customers.

Sales of Little Golden Books were doing so well that in 1944, Simon & Schuster decided to create a new division headed by George Duplaix called Sandpiper Press. Duplaix hired Dorothy Bennett as the general editor. Bennett came to Sandpiper Press after leaving a position as assistant curator at the Museum of Natural History in Washington DC. She was responsible for a lot of the subjects used in Little Golden Books through the mid-1950s. *The Giant Golden Book Encyclopedia* was one of the books she authored. Bennett fought very hard to keep television and movies out of Little Golden Books. She felt the quality and context of the books would be weakened. She hated to see the book *J. Fred Muggs* printed and thought it poetic justice when the monkey, J. Fred Muggs, bit the host and was taken off the show he appeared on. Bennett wanted the books to teach children something of the world they lived in, whether it was history, geography, science, or the experiences a child would have while growing up.

Along these same lines, in the 1940s, Little Golden Books, dealing with good little boys and girls and their experiences of every day things, were approved by Mary Reed, Ph.D., assistant professor of education at the Teacher's College, Columbia University. Reed went on to supervise the subject matter of Little Golden Books until 1961.

Doctor Dan, the Bandage Man, Little Golden Book No. 111, was released in January 1951. The first printing of the book was 1,750,000, the largest first printing on any Little Golden Book to date. Six Johnson & Johnson Band-Aids® were glued down the right side of the title page. Later, girls were given equal time with *Nurse Nancy*. As the *Doctor Dan* stories changed, so did the style of the Band-Aids included with the book—later there were circus and stars and stripes Band-Aids.

In 1952, on the Little Golden Book's tenth anniversary, approximately 182,615,000 Little Golden Books had been sold. *The Night Before Christmas* alone sold more than 4 million copies. In their eleventh year, almost 300,000,000 Little Golden Books had been sold. More than half of the titles printed by 1954 had sold more than 1,000,000 copies each. Little Golden Books were now available almost everywhere in the world except the Soviet Union. With the distinction of being labeled a capitalistic story, *The Poky Little Puppy* was not allowed to be sold, nor were any other Little Golden Books, in the Soviet Union.

May 1, 1954, was the release date of *Little Lulu and Her Magic Tricks*, which had a first printing of 2,250,000. The book had a small package of Kleenex in its front cover and directions for making tissue toys. Such an extensive advertising and promotional campaign was done for the book that it was even shown on the *Arthur Godfrey Show* in May 1954.

Quite a few of the titles in the 1950s showed that children were starting to spend a lot of time in front of their television sets. By the mid-1950s, children's TV shows and westerns were top sellers in Little Golden Books, while in the early 1960s, the books were about Saturday morning cartoon shows. From 1965 to the early 1970s, though, Little Golden Books dropped TV and went back to printing original stories about growing up.

In 1955, Little Golden Books were released in the activity series, which ran until 1961. This series consisted of books with learning wheels, stamps, paper dolls, paper models, paint and coloring books, and even a calendar. This was not a new idea for Little Golden Books. Back in the early 1950s, the company brought out books with masks, puzzles, stencils, decals, tape, tissue, and Band-Aids.

Boxed puzzles, made from cover art of Little Golden Books, were produced in the early 1950s. The boxes were a little smaller than the original books. There were four series. (Value ranges from $15.00-$20.00.)

The first series consisted of:

> *The Lively Little Rabbit*
> *The Five Little Firemen*
> *The Jolly Barnyard*
> *The Poky Little Puppy*
> *The Shy Little Kitten*
> *Tootle*

The second series consisted of:

> *The Alphabet from A to Z*
> *A Year on the Farm*
> *Johnny's Machines*
> *The Wonderful House*
> *The Marvelous Merry-Go-Round*
> *Dr. Dan the Bandage Man*

The third series consisted of:

> *Busy Timmy*
> *Little Black Sambo*
> *When You Were a Baby*
> *Little Yip Yip and His Bark*
> *Happy Man and His Dump Truck*
> *A Day At The Playground*

The fourth series consisted of:

> *Katy the Kitten*

> *How Big*
> *Brave Cowboy Bill*
> *Little Golden ABC*
> *Day at the Beach*
> *Train in Timbuctoo*

There was also a release of tray puzzles by Playskool. These puzzles came in a box of four and each set had to do with a certain subject. The pictures were of Little Golden Book covers or inside art. Each puzzle in the set had a different number of pieces for ages 4 to 8. (Value per set is $25.00-$40.00.)

Puzzle Sets:

80-1 Animal Babies
80-2 Ways to Travel
80-3 Horses and Colts
80-4 Fairy Stories
80-5 Life of a Cowboy
80-6 Indian Pals
80-7 Farms and Farming
80-8 Children and Religion
80-9 Funny Animals
80-10 Workers We Know
80-11 Dogs and Puppies
80-12 Children in Action

In 1958, Western Publishing and Lithographing Co., Inc. and Pocket Books Inc. became joint publishers. The company name then became Golden Press, Inc. But in 1960, Western Printing and Lithographing became Western Publishing Company, Inc. and Pocket Books' interest in Golden Press was acquired in 1964.

Also in 1958, Little Golden Books were brought out in A Giant Little Golden Book. Most of these contained three Little Golden Books of the same subject in one volume.

In 1959, a series of Little Golden Books called a Ding Dong School Book, written by Dr. Frances R. Horwich, was published by Golden Press (See Ding Dong School Books). *Ding Dong School* was a children's television show in the 1950s hosted by Miss Frances.

The Golden Hours Library was produced in 1967. This consisted of a box shaped like a clock, with moving hands,

Examples of Little Golden Activity Books with paper dolls

which contained 12 Little Golden Books in miniature. (Value is $45.00.)

The books were:

How To Tell Time
Heidi
The Big Little Book
Old MacDonald Had A Farm
Four Little Kittens
Rumpelstiltskin
Hop Little Kangaroo
Four Puppies
The Littlest Raccoon
Tommy's Camping Adventure
Colors Are Nice
Little Cotton Tail

In 1972, Golden produced an 11-1/2" x 14" four-tray puzzle boxed set. Each set contained four puzzles about a Little Golden Book, with the condensed story printed on the box's inside top flap. The two titles were *The Poky Little Puppy* and *The Lively Little Rabbit*. Scuffy the Tugboat Game was also produced in this series.

In 1974, Little Golden Books were published in the Eager Reader series. These books were printed with large type for beginning readers (see Eager Reader Series).

In 1977, Western Publishing developed A Little Golden Game for children ages 5 to 8, which were games based on Little Golden Books. The boxed covers were duplicates of the Little Golden Book the game depicted. Three books that were produced as games were *Old MacDonald Had a Farm*, *Jack and the Beanstalk*, and *The Three Little Pigs*.

Little Golden Books have been printed in more than forty-two countries. Most of these countries release the same titles as the United States, although a few have had original titles of their own (see Foreign Little Golden Books).

In 1982, Little Golden Books were forty years old and more than 800,000,000 books had been sold. On Nov. 20, 1986, the one billionth Little Golden Book was printed, *The Poky Little Puppy*. Australia celebrated the printing of the 200 millionth Little Golden Book in February 1988.

Little Golden Books were numbered numerically in the beginning, starting with No. 1, *The Three Little Kittens*, in 1942, and ending with 600, *Susan in the Driver's Seat*. But just because they were numbered does not mean they were published in sequential order. For instance, book 205 was published two years before 204, and some numbers never had a title. In 1971, new releases began to be numbered by going back to 105. Later, 102 through 104 were redone. One possibility for the renumbering not continuing past 600 could be that 615 through 630 had already been given to My First Golden Learning Library in 1965. This was a series of books with different colored foil spines and letters of the alphabet broken down in a dictionary-type format. They were illustrated by William Dugan and written by Jane Werner Watson.

The books of the 1970s had no chronological order of publishing—the books were published in the 100, 200, 300, and 500 numbers. The only similarity I noticed in these different numbers was that the two books redone in the 500s did not have to do with science fiction.

In 1979, Western changed its numbering again to the new numbering system; for example, 101-42, where 1 indicates assortment, 01 indicates category, and -42 indicates position in category. I recommend that if you are a collector trying to collect by book numbers, collect the first edition and forget the numbers because the categories' subject matter may change each year.

The price of these books has changed quite a bit since 1942, when they sold for 25 cents. Twenty years later, the price increased to 29 cents. This was followed by 39 cents in 1968, 40 cents in 1974, 59 cents in 1977, 69 cents in 1979, 89 cents in 1982, and 99 cents in 1986. Books printed today no longer have a price printed on the cover.

How to Tell Editions

1. The edition number will be mentioned on the first or second page of the book.

2. Look on the last page of the book in the lower right hand corner by the spine. There will be a letter which tells the edition. For example, A=1st, Z=26th, AA=27.

3. On the bottom of one of the first two pages, you will see something like A B C D E or a b c d e. The first letter to the far left is the edition.

4. Books printed since late 1991 no longer have the letters of the alphabet designating editions on the title page. Now, the books, besides having the copyright date, will also have a printing date in Roman numerals. If a book from this period does not have a Roman numeral date, it is a first printing, and it was left off by mistake. If the letter "A" precedes the Roman numerals, the book is a first edition, and if an "R" precedes the Roman numeral, the book is a (R)evised edition of an earlier Little Golden Book. If there is no letter preceding the Roman numeral, the numerals themselves state when the book was printed.

For those of you not familiar with Roman numerals, "MCMXCI" is 1991. When reading Roman numerals, you subtract the number on the left from the one the right when the one on the left is smaller: M=1000, C=100, X=10, VIII=8, VII=7, VI=6, V=5, IV=4 (or 5-1), III=3, II=2, I=1; so with the number "MCMXCI," you have "M"=1000, "CM"=900 (1000-100), "XC"=90 (100-10), "I"=1 for 1000 + 900 + 90 + 1 = 1991.

5. If none of the above can be used, it is probably a first edition. You can also take the last book number listed on the back of the book and look up its copyright date in this guide and compare it with the copyright of the book you are not sure of.

The Golden Hours Library

How to Determine the Value and Condition of a Book

There isn't an easy way of putting a condition on a book. What is good to one might be fair to another. In this book, I will give you guidelines to assist you in putting a value and condition on your books. The prices given in this book are also only meant to assist you in valuing or paying a fair price.

The prices listed in this book were compiled from dealings with different people throughout the United States. The prices may be a little high or low depending on the area in which you live. Dust jackets are not priced and add 25 to 200 percent to the value of the book.

Percentage of listed value	Condition	Comments
100%	Mint	No marks of any kind on book. Should look like it just came off the store shelf.
75%	Fine	Clean, tight book. May have some light pencil marks. Name may be written on inside cover in space provide. A little of the cover luster may be gone. Overall condition of the book should be one that was read but well cared for.
50%	Good	This is your average book. May have some light soiling or chipping on front cover. No tears or scrapes on the cover. The inside pages may have small creases or folded corners, could have small tears no more than 1/4" long. No tape. Some of the spine cover may be missing or chipping. The book is well read but still in complete condition.
25%	Fair	The spine is getting loose. The cover is soiled. No crayon scribbling or ink that distracts from any part of the book. There may be some tape on pages. A well-read and not taken care of copy.
0%-10%	Poor	A damaged book. Crayon, ink on pages, missing pages, chewed pages, missing activities. The book probably looks like it just came out of the trash.

Values on the following pages are for first editions in very fine + or better condition.

Little Golden Books—By Book Number

No. 1
Three Little Kittens
Illus.: Masha
1942   42 Pages   **$40.00**

No. 2
Bedtime Stories
Illus.: Tenggren, Gustaf
Author: Misc. Authors
1942   42 Pages   **$40.00**

No. 3
Alphabet From A-Z, The
Illus.: Blake, Vivienne Leah
1942   42 Pages   **$40.00**

No. 4
Mother Goose
Illus.: Elliott, Gertrude
Author: Fraser, Phyllis
1942   42 Pages   **$40.00**

No. 5
Prayers For Children
Illus.: Dixon, Rachel Taft
1942   42 Pages   **$40.00**

No. 6
Little Red Hen, The
Illus.: Freund, Rudolf
1942   42 Pages   **$40.00**

No. 6
Little Red Hen, The
(2nd Cover)
Illus.: Freund, Rudolf
1942   28 Pages   **$20.00**

No. 7
Nursery Songs
Illus.: Malvern, Corinne
Author: Gale, Leah
1942   42 Pages   **$40.00**

No. 7
Nursery Songs
(2nd Cover)
Illus.: Malvern, Corinne
Author: Gale, Leah
1942   42 Pages   **$15.00**

No. 8
Poky Little Puppy, The
Illus.: Tenggren, Gustaf
Author: Lowrey, Janet Sebring
1942   42 Pages   **$40.00**

No. 9
Golden Book Of Fairy Tales, The
Illus.: Hoskins, Winfield
1942   42 Pages   **$40.00**

No. 9
First Little Golden Book Of Fairy Tales, The
Illus.: Elliott, Gertrude
1946   42 Pages   **$16.00**

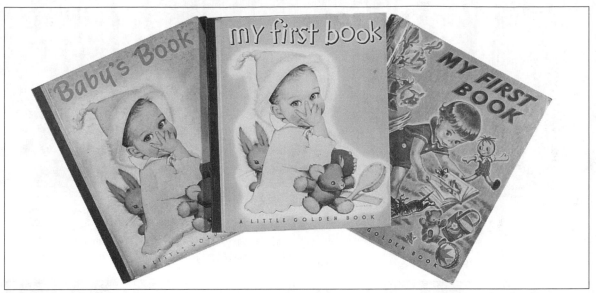

No. 10

Baby's Book
Illus.: Smith, Bob
Author: Smith, Bob
1942   42 Pages   **$75.00**

No. 10

**My First Book
(2nd Cover)**
Illus.: Smith, Bob
Author: Smith, Bob
1942   42 Pages   **$40.00**

No. 10

**My First Book
(3rd Cover)**
Illus.: Smith, Bob
Author: Smith, Bob
1942   42 Pages   **$20.00**

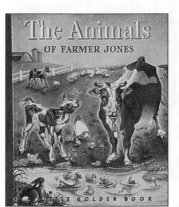

No. 11

Animals Of Farmer Jones, The
Illus.: Freund, Rudolf
Author: Gale, Leah
1942   42 Pages   **$40.00**

No. 12

**This Little Piggy Counting
Rhymes**
Illus.: Paflin, Roberta
1942   42 Pages   **$50.00**

No. 14

Nursery Tales
Illus.: Masha
1943   42 Pages   **$25.00**

No. 12

**Counting Rhymes
(2nd Cover)**
Illus.: Paflin, Roberta
1947   42 Pages   **$16.00**

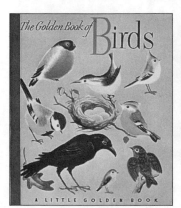

No. 13

Golden Book Of Birds, The
Illus.: Rojankovsky, Feodor
Author: Lockwood, Hazel
1943   42 Pages   **$25.00**

No. 15

Lively Little Rabbit, The
Illus.: Tenggren, Gustaf
Author: Ariane
1943   42 Pages   **$25.00**

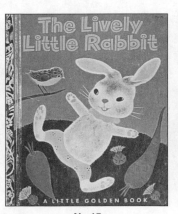

No.15

**Lively Little Rabbit, The
(2nd Cover)**
Illus.: Tenggren, Gustaf
Author: Ariane
1943   28 Pages   **$11.00**

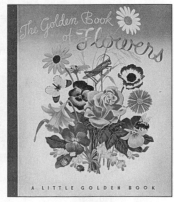

No. 16

Golden Book of Flowers, The
Illus.: Hershberger
Author: Witman, Mabel
1943   42 Pages   **$30.00**

No. 17

Hansel And Gretel

Illus.: Weihs, Erika
Author: Bros. Grimm
1943 42 Pages **$25.00**

No. 17

**Hansel And Gretel
(2nd Cover)**

Illus.: Weihs, Erika
Author: Bros. Grimm
1943 28 Pages **$14.00**

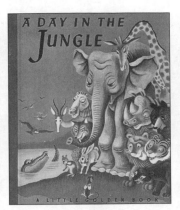

No. 18

Day In The Jungle, A

Illus.: Gergely, Tibor
Author: Lowrey, Janet Sebring
1943 42 Pages **$30.00**

No. 19

My First Book Of Bible Stories

Illus.: Ferand, Emmy
Author: Walton, Mary Ann
1943 42 Pages **$35.00**

No. 21

Tootle

Illus.: Gergely, Tibor
Author: Crampton, Gertrude
1945 42 Pages **$25.00**

No. 22

Toys

Illus.: Masha
Author: Oswald, Edith
1945 42 Pages **$25.00**

No. 23

Shy Little Kitten, The

Illus.: Tenggren, Gustaf
Author: Schurr, Kathleen
1946 42 Pages **$25.00**

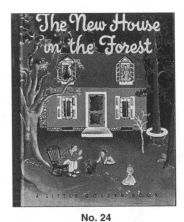

No. 24

New House In The Forest, The

Illus.: Wilkin, Eloise
Author: Mitchell, Lucy Sprague
1946 42 Pages **$40.00**

No. 20

Night Before Christmas, The

Illus.: Dewitt, Cornelius
Author: Moore, Clement C.
1946 42 Pages **$25.00**

No. 20

**Night Before Christmas, The
(2nd Cover) (Gilded pictures)**

Illus.: Malvern, Corinne
Author: Moore, Clement C.
1949 28 Pages **$14.00**

No. 20

**Night Before Christmas, The
(3rd Cover)**

Illus.: Malvern, Corinne
Author: Moore, Clement C.
1949 24 Pages **$6.00**

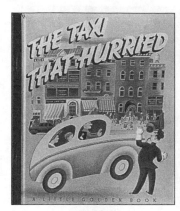

No. 25

Taxi That Hurried, The

Illus.: Gergely, Tibor

Author: Mitchell, Lucy Sprague; Simonton

1946   42 Pages   **$25.00**

No. 26

Christmas Carols

Illus.: Malvern, Corinne

Author: Wyckoff, Marjorie

1946   42 Pages   **$18.00**

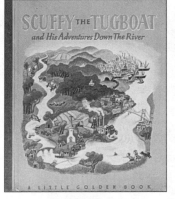

No. 26

Christmas Carols (2nd Cover)

Illus.: Malvern, Corinne

Author: Wyckoff, Marjorie

1946   28 Pages   **$9.00**

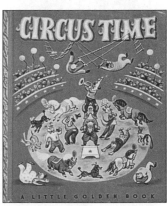

No. 27

Story Of Jesus, The

Illus.: Lerch, Steffie

Author: Alexander, Beatrice

1946   42 Pages   **$25.00**

No. 28

Chip, Chip

Illus.: Carbe, Nino

Author: Wright, Norman

1947   42 Pages   **$25.00**

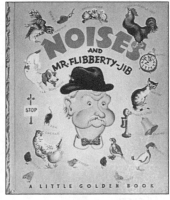

No. 29

Noises And Mr. Flibberty-Jib

Illus.: Wilkin, Eloise

Author: Wilkin, Eloise

1947   42 Pages   **$35.00**

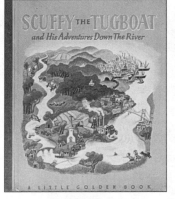

No. 30

Scuffy The Tugboat

Illus.: Gergely, Tibor

Author: Crampton, Gertrude

1946   42 Pages   **$25.00**

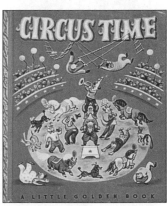

No. 31

Circus Time

Illus.: Gergely, Tibor

Author: Conger, Marion

1948   42 Pages   **$20.00**

No. 32

Fix It, Please

Illus.: Wilkin, Eloise

Author: Mitchell, Lucy Sprague

1947   42 Pages   **$27.00**

No. 33

Let's Go Shopping!

Illus.: Combes, Lenora

Author: Combes, Lenora

1948   42 Pages   **$14.00**

No. 34

Little Golden Book Of Hymns, The

Illus.: Malvern, Corinne

Author: Werner, Elsa Jane

1947   42 Pages   **$14.00**

No. 35

Happy Family, The

Illus.: Elliott, Gertrude

Author: Nicole

1947   42 Pages   **$30.00**

No. 36

Saggy Baggy Elephant, The

Illus.: Tenggren, Gustaf

Author: Jackson, Kathryn and Byron

1947　42 Pages　**$20.00**

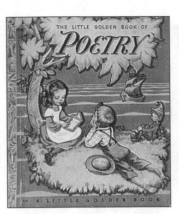

No. 37

Year On The Farm, A

Illus.: Floethe, Richard

Author: Mitchell, Lucy Sprague

1948　42 Pages　**$20.00**

No. 38

Little Golden Book Of Poetry, The

Illus.: Malvern, Corinn

1947　42 Pages　**$14.00**

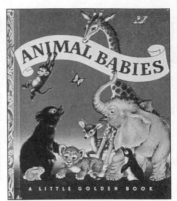

No. 39

Animal Babies

Illus.: Werber, Adele

Author: Jackson, Kathryn & Byron

1947 4　2 Pages　**$14.00**

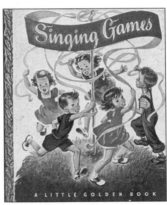

No. 40

Little Golden Book Of Singing Games, The

Illus.: Malvern, Corinne

Author: Wessles, Katheryne Tyler

1947　42 Pages　**$14.00**

No. 41

New Baby, The

Illus.: Wilkin, Eloise

Author: Shane, Ruth & Harold

1948　42 Pages　**$30.00**

No. 41

**New Baby, The
(2nd Cover)**

Illus.: Wilkin, Eloise

Author: Shane, Ruth & Harold

1948　28 Pages　**$15.00**

No. 42

Little Red Riding Hood

Illus.: Jones, Elizabeth Orton

Author: Jones, Elizabeth Orton

1948　42 Pages　**$16.00**

No. 42

**Little Red Riding Hood
(Puzzle Edition)**

Illus.: Jones, Elizabeth Orton

Author: Jones, Elizabeth Orton

1948　28 Pages　**$100.00**

No. 43

Little Pond In The Woods

Illus.: Gergely, Tibor

Author: Ward, Muriel

1948　42 Pages　**$20.00**

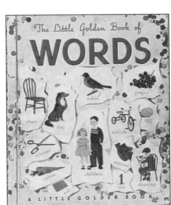

No. 44

Come Play House

Illus.: Wilkin, Eloise

Author: Oswald, Edith

1948　42 Pages　**$27.00**

No. 45

Little Golden Book of Words, The

Illus.: Elliott, Gertrude

Author: Chambers, Selma Lola

1948　42 Pages　**$15.00**

No. 46
Golden Sleepy Book, The
Illus.: Williams, Garth
Author: Brown, Margaret Wise
1948   42 Pages   **$20.00**

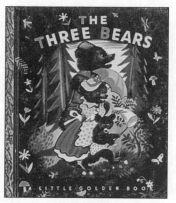

No. 47
Three Bears, The
(First cover only had one printing)
Illus.: Rojankovsky, Feodor
1948   42 Pages   **$60.00**

No. 47
Three Bears, The
(2nd Cover)
Illus.: Rojankovsky, Feodor
1948   42 Pages   **$10.00**

No. 48
Year In The City, A
Illus.: Gergely, Tibor
Author: Mitchell, Lucy Sprague
1948   42 Pages   **$20.00**

No. 49
Mr. Noah And His Family
Illus.: Provensen, Alice and Martin
Author: Werner, Jane
1948   28 Pages   **$16.00**

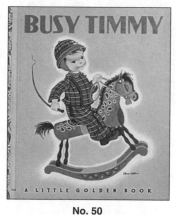

No. 50
Busy Timmy
Illus.: Wilkin, Eloise
Author: Jackson, Kathryn and Byron
1948   28 Pages   **$30.00**

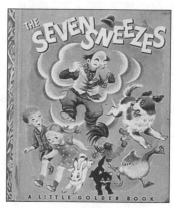

No. 51
Seven Sneezes, The
Illus.: Gergely, Tibor
Author: Cabral, Olga
1948   42 Pages   **$20.00**

No. 52
Little Pee Wee or, Now Open
The Box
(1st edition)
Illus.: Miller, J.P.
Author: Kunhardt, Dorothy
1948   42 Pages   **$17.00**

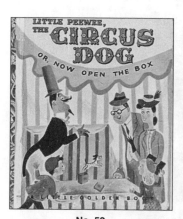

No. 52
Little Pee Wee, The Circus Dog
or, Now Open The Box
Illus.: Miller, J.P.
Author: Kunhardt, Dorothy
1948 42   Pages   **$25.00**

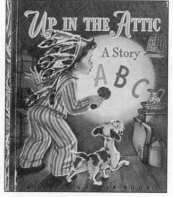

No. 53
Up In The Attic
Illus.: Malvern, Corinne
1948   42 Pages   **$16.00**

No. 57
Little Black Sambo
(42 page edition)
Illus.: Tenggren, Gustaf
Author: Bannerman, Helen
1948   42 Pages   **$150.00**

No. 57
Little Black Sambo
(28 page edition)
Illus.: Tenggren, Gustaf
Author: Bannerman, Helen
1948   28 Pages   **$100.00**

No. 57
Little Black Sambo
(24 page edition)
Illus.: Tenggren, Gustaf
Author: Bannerman, Helen
1948   24 Pages   **$60.00**

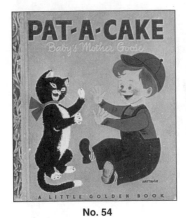

No. 54

Pat-A-Cake

Illus.: Battaglia, Aurelius

Author: Mother Goose

1948   28 Pages   **$14.00**

No. 55

Name For Kitty, A

Illus.: Rojankovsky, Feodor

Author: Mcginley, Phyllis

1948   28 Pages   **$14.00**

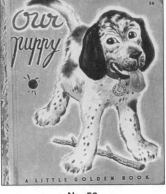

No. 56

Our Puppy

Illus.: Rojankovsky, Feodor

Author: Nast, Elsa Ruth

1948   28 Pages   **$14.00**

No. 58

What Am I?

Illus.: De Witt, Cornelius

Author: Leon, Ruthelius

1949   28 Pages   **$14.00**

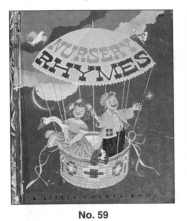

No. 59

Nursery Rhymes

Illus.: Elliott, Gertrude

1948   28 Pages   **$14.00**

No. 60

Guess Who Lives Here

Illus.: Wilkin, Eloise

Author: Woodcock, Louise

1949   28 Pages   **$30.00**

No. 61

Good Morning, Good Night

Illus.: Wilkin, Eloise

Author: Werner, Jane

1948   42 Pages   **$30.00**

No. 62

We Like To Do Things

Illus.: Lerch, Seffie

Author: Mason, Walter M.

1949   42 Pages   **$14.00**

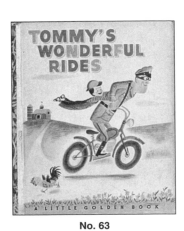

No. 63

Tommy's Wonderful Rides

Illus.: Miller, J.P.

Author: Palmer, Helen

1948   42 Pages   **$15.00**

No. 64

Five Little Firemen

Illus.: Gergely, Tibor

Author: Brown, Margaret Wise

1948   42 Pages   **$20.00**

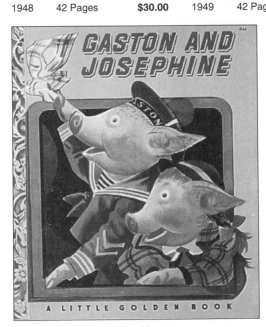

No. 65

Gaston And Josephine

Illus.: Rojankovsky, Feodor

Author: Duplaix, George

1949   42 Pages   **$25.00**

Free Public Library of Monroe Township
306 S. Main Street
Williamstown, N.J. 08094-1727

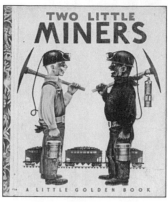

No. 66
Two Little Miners
**(Richard Scarry's first
illustrated book)**
Illus.: Scarry, Richard
Author: Brown, Margaret Wise
1949   42 Pages   **$25.00**

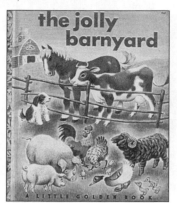

No. 67
Jolly Barnyard, The
Illus.: Gergely, Tibor
Author: Bedford, Annie North
1950   28 Pages   **$14.00**

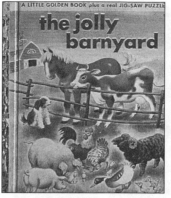

No. 67
**Jolly Barnyard, The
(2nd edition) (Puzzle edition)**
Illus.: Gergely, Tibor
Author: Bedford, Annie North
1950   28 Pages   **$100.00**

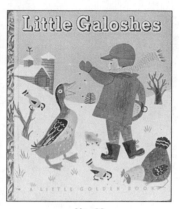

No. 68
Little Goloshes
Illus.: Miller, J.P.
Author: Jackson, Kathryn and Byron
1949   42 Pages   **$20.00**

No. 69
Bobby and His Airplanes
Illus.: Gergely, Tibor
Author: Palmer, Helen
1949   42 Pages   **$16.00**

No. 70
When You Were A Baby
Illus.: Malvern, Corinne
Author: Eng, Rita
1949   42 Pages   **$14.00**

No. 71
Johnny's Machines
Illus.: De Witt, Cornelius
Author: Palmer, Helen
1949   42 Pages   **$14.00**

No. 72
**Bugs Bunny
(Copyright by Warner Bros.
Cartoon, Inc.)**
Illus.: Warner Bros.
Author: Mckimson, Tom
1949   42 Pages   **$14.00**

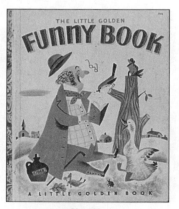

No. 73
Little Yip Yip And His Bark
Illus.: Gergely, Tibor
Author: Jackson, Kathryn & Byron
1950   42 Pages   **$16.00**

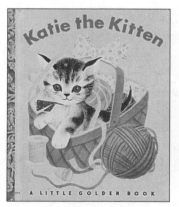

No. 74
Little Golden Funny Book, The
Illus.: Miller, J.P.
Author: Crampton, Gertrude
1950   42 Pages   **$14.00**

No. 75
Katie The Kitten
Illus.: Provensen, Alice & Martin
Author: Jackson, Kathryn & Byron
1949   42 Pages   **$15.00**

No. 75
**Katie The Kitten
(2nd edition) (Puzzle edition)**
Illus.: Provensen, Alice and Martin
Author: Jackson, Kathryn and Byron
1949   28 Pages   **$100.00**

No. 76
Wonderful House, The
Illus.: Miller, J.P.
Author: Brown, Margaret Wise
1950   42 Pages   **$16.00**

No. 77
Happy Man And His Dump Truck, The
Illus.: Gergely, Tibor
Author: Miryam
1950   42 Pages   **$20.00**

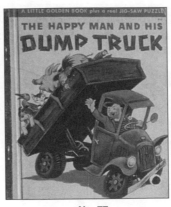

No. 77
Happy Man And His Dump Truck, The (2nd edition) (Puzzle edition)
Illus.: Gergely, Tibor
Author: Miryam
1950   28 Pages   **$100.00**

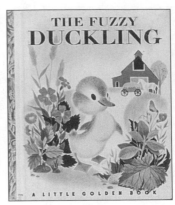

No. 78
Fuzzy Duckling, The
Illus.: Provensen, Alice and Martin
Author: Werner, Jane
1949   28 Pages   **$14.00**

No. 79
Little Trapper, The
Illus.: Tenggren, Gustaf
Author: Jackson, Kathryn and Byron
1950   28 Pages   **$14.00**

No. 80
Baby's House
Illus.: Blair, Mary
Author: Mchugh, Gelolo
1950   28 Pages   **$15.00**

No. 80
Baby's House (2nd edition) (Puzzle edition)
Illus.: Blair, Mary
Author: Mchugh, Gelolo
1950   28 Pages   **$100.00**

No. 81
Duck And His Friends
Illus.: Scarry, Richard
Author: Jackson, Kathryn and Byron
1949   28 Pages   **$14.00**

No. 81
Duck And His Friends (Puzzle edition)
Illus.: Scarry, Richard
Author: Jackson, Kathryn and Byron
1949   24 Pages   **$100.00**

No. 82
Pets For Peter (1st edition) (Puzzle edition)
Illus.: Battaglia, Aurelius
Author: Werner, Jane
1950   28 Pages   **$100.00**

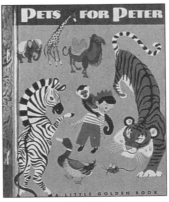

No. 82
Pets For Peter
Illus.: Battaglia, Aurelius
Author: Werner, Jane
1950   28 Pages   **$14.00**

No. 83
How Big
Illus.: Malvern, Corinne
Author: Malvern, Corinne
1949   28 Pages   **$20.00**

No. 83

How Big
(2nd Cover)
Illus.: Malvern, Corinne
Author: Malvern, Corinne
1949   24 Pages   **$11.00**

No. 84

Surprise For Sally
Illus.: Malvern, Corinne
Author: Crowninshield, Ethel
1950   42 Pages   **$20.00**

No. 85

Susie's New Stove
Illus.: Malvern, Corinne
Author: Bedford, Annie North
1950   42 Pages   **$30.00**

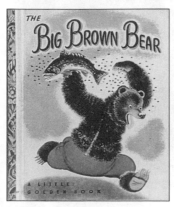

No. 86

Color Kittens, The
(1st edition)
Illus.: Provensen, Alice and Martin
Author: Brown, Margaret Wise
1949   28 Pages   **$25.00**

No. 86

Color Kittens, The
(Puzzle edition)
Illus.: Provensen, Alice and Martin
Author: Brown, Margaret Wise
1949   28 Pages   **$125.00**

No. 87

Marvelous Merry-Go-Round, The
Illus.: Miller, J.P.
Author: Werner, Jane
1949   42 Pages   **$14.00**

No. 88

Day At The Zoo, A
Illus.: Gergely, Tibor
Author: Conger, Marion
1949   42 Pages   **$14.00**

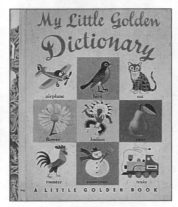

No. 89

Big Brown Bear, The
Illus.: Tenggren, Gustaf
Author: Duplaix, Georges
1947   42 Pages   **$25.00**

No. 90

My Little Golden Dictionary
Illus.: Scarry, Richard
Authors: Reed, Mary; Oswald, Edith
1949   56 Pages   **$14.00**

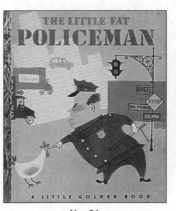

No. 91

Little Fat Policeman, The
Illus.: Provensen, Alice and Martin
Author: Brown, Margaret Wise
1950   42 Pages   **$16.00**

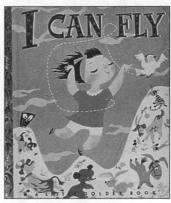

No. 92

I Can Fly
Illus.: Blair, Mary
Author: Krauss, Ruth
1950   42 Pages   **$25.00**

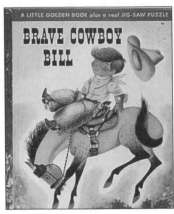

No. 93
Brave Cowboy Bill
(1st edition) (Puzzle edition)
Illus.: Scarry, Richard
Author: Jackson, Kathryn and Byron
1950　　42 Pages　　**$125.00**

No. 93
Brave Cowboy Bill
(Puzzle missing)
Illus.: Scarry, Richard
Author: Jackson, Kathryn and Byron
1950　　42 Pages　　**$18.00**

No. 94
Jerry At School
(Puzzle edition)
Illus.: Malvern, Corinne
Author: Jackson, Kathryn and Byron
1950　　42 Pages　　**$100.00**

No. 94
Jerry At School
Illus.: Malvern, Corinne
Author: Jackson, Kathryn and Byron
1950　　28 Pages　　**$14.00**

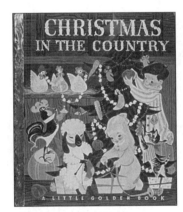

No. 95
Christmas In The Country
Illus.: Worcester, Retta
Author: Collyer, Barbara; Foley, John R.
1950　　28 Pages　　**$20.00**

No. 96
When I Grow Up
(1st edition) (Puzzle edition)
Illus.: Malvern, Corinne
Author: Mace, Kay & Harry
1950　　42 Pages　　**$100.00**

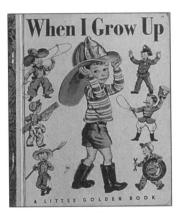

No. 96
When I Grow Up
Illus.: Malvern, Corinne
Author: Mace, Kay and Harry
1950　　28 Pages　　**$14.00**

No. 97
Little Benny Wanted A Pony
(Mask in back of book)
Illus.: Scarry, Richard
Author: Barnett, Olive O'Connor
1950　　42 Pages　　**$60.00**

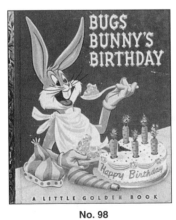

No. 98
Bugs Bunny's Birthday
(Copyright by Warner Bros. Cartoon, Inc.)
Illus.: Warner Bros.
Author: Warner Bros.
1950　　28 Pages　　**$14.00**

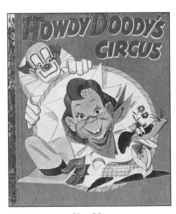

No. 99
Howdy Doody's Circus
(Copyright by Robert E. (Bob) Smith)
Illus.: Dauber, Liz
Author: Gormley, Don
1950　　28 Pages　　**$25.00**

No. 100
Little Boy With A Big Horn
Illus.: Battaglia, Aurelius
Author: Bezchdolt, Jack
1950　　42 Pages　　**$15.00**

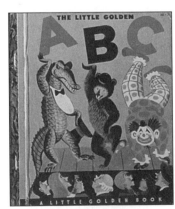

No. 101
Little Golden A B C, The
(1st edition) (Puzzle edition)
Illus.: De Witt, Cornelius
1951　　28 Pages　　**$100.00**

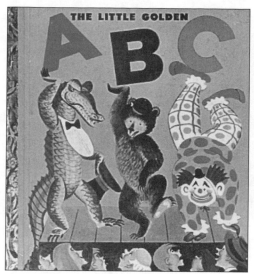

No. 101
Little Golden A B C, The
Illus.: De Witt, Cornelius
1951   28 Pages   **$8.00**

No. 102
Ukele And Her New Doll
(1st edition) (Puzzle edition)
Illus.: Grant, Campbell
Author: Grant, Clara Louise
1951   28 Pages   **$125.00**

No. 102
Ukele And Her New Doll
(Puzzle missing)
Illus.: Grant, Campbell
Author: Grant, Clara Louise
1951   28 Pages   **$20.00**

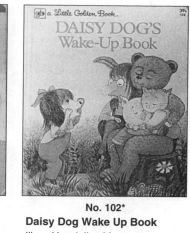

No. 102*
Daisy Dog Wake Up Book
Illus.: Vogel, Ilse-Margaret
Author: Vogel, Ilse-Margaret
1974   24 Pages   **$6.00**

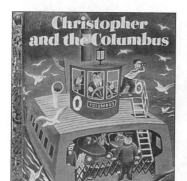

No. 103
Christopher And The Columbus
Illus.: Gergely, Tibor
Author: Jackson, Kathryn and Byron
1951   28 Pages   **$11.00**

No. 103*
Fritzie Goes Home
Illus.: Augistiny, Sally
Author: Emerypogue, Kate
1974   24 Pages   **$6.00**

No. 104*
Just Watch Me
Illus.: Aloisel, Frank
Author: Daly, Eileen
1975   24 Pages   **$6.00**

105*
Never Pat A Bear
Illus.: Seiden, Art
Author: Watts, Mabel
1971   24 Pages   **$6.00**

No. 106*
Magic Next Door, The
Illus.: Stang, Judy
Author: Swetnam, Evelyn
1971   24 Pages   **$6.00**

No. 107
Kitten's Surprise, The
Illus.: Rojankovsky, Feodor
Author: Nina
1951   28 Pages   **$11.00**

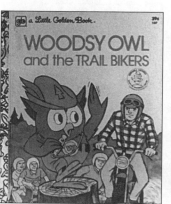

No. 107*
Woodsy Owl And The Trail Bikers
Illus.: McSavage, Frank
Author: Graham, Kennon
1974   24 Pages   **$6.00**

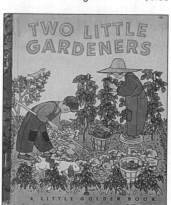

No. 108
Two Little Gardeners
Illus.: Elliott, Gertrude
Author: Brown, Margaret Wise
1951   28 Pages   **$15.00**

No. 108*

A B C Is For Christmas

Illus.: Augistiny, Sally

Author: Watson, Jane Werner

1974   24 Pages   **$6.00**

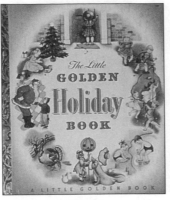

No. 109

Little Golden Holiday Book, The

Illus.: Wilkin, Eloise

Author: Conger, Marion

1951   28 Pages   **$25.00**

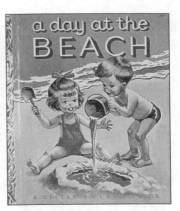

No. 109*

Noah's Ark

Illus.: Gergoly, Tibor

Author: Hazen, Barbara Shook

1969   24 Pages   **$6.00**

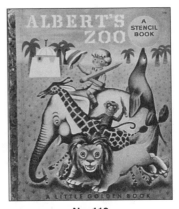

No. 110

Day At The Beach, A

Illus.: Malvern, Corinne

Author: Jackson, Kathryn and Byron

1951   28 Pages   **$25.00**

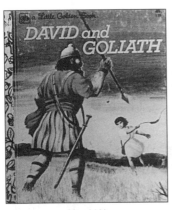

No. 110*

David And Goliath

Illus.: Lee, Robert J.

Author: Hazen, Barbara Shook

1974   24 Pages   **$6.00**

No. 111

Dr. Dan The Bandage Man

(Band-Aids pasted to title page)

Illus.: Malvern, Corinne

Author: Gaspard, Helen

1950   28 Pages   **$100.00**

No. 111*

I Think About God Two Stories About My Day

Illus.: Cassan, Christine; Hyman

Authors: Val, Sue; Smaridge, Norah

1974   24 Pages   **$6.00**

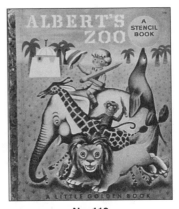

No. 112

Albert's Stencil Zoo

(Unpunched)

Illus.: Scarry, Richard

Author: Werner, Jane

1951   28 Pages   **$80.00**

No. 112

Albert's Stencil Zoo

(Complete but used)

Illus.: Scarry, Richard

Author: Werner, Jane

1951   28 Pages   **$20.00**

No. 112*

Book Of God's Gifts, A

Illus.: Schreter, Rick

Author: Hannh

1972   24 Pages   **$6.00**

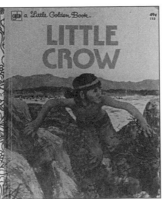

No. 113

Little Golden Paper Dolls, The

(Uncut)

Illus.: Miloche, Hilda; Kane, Wilma

Authors: Miloche, Hilde; Kane, Wilma

1951   28 Pages   **$125.00**

No. 113*

Little Crow

Illus.: Aldrich, Andy

Author: Mcdermott, Caroline

1974   24 Pages   **$6.00**

No. 114

Pantaloon
(Die Cut Window)
Illus.: Weisgard, Leonard
Author: Jackson, Kathryn
1951   28 Pages $20.00

No. 114

Pantaloon
(Without die-cut window)
Illus.: Weisgard, Leonard
Author: Jackson, Kathryn
1951   28 Pages $20.00

No. 114*

Stories Of Jesus
Illus.: Forberg, Ari
Author: Richards, Jean H.
1974   24 Pages $6.00

No. 115*

My Home
Illus.: R.O. Fry
Author: Bartowski, Renee
1971   24 Pages $6.00

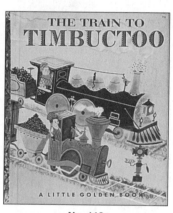

No. 116

Laddie And The Little Rabbit
Illus.: Gottlieb, William P.
Author: Gottlieb, William P.
1952   28 Pages $11.00

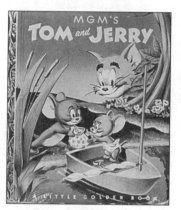

No. 116*

Where Did The Baby Go?
Illus.: Wilkin, Eloise
Author: Hayes, Sheila
1974   24 Pages $11.00

No. 117

Tom And Jerry
(Copyright by Leow's Inc.)
Illus.: Eisenberg, Harvey; Maclaughlin, Don
Author: MGM
1951   28 Pages $14.00

No. 117*

Pano The Train
Illus.: Giannini
Author: Holvaes, Sharon
1975   24 Pages $7.00

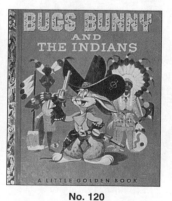

No. 118

Train To Timbuctoo, The
Illus.: Seiden, Art
Author: Brown, Margaret Wise
1951   28 Pages $20.00

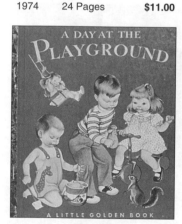

No. 119

Day At The Playground, A
Illus.: Wilkin, Eloise
Author: Schlein, Miriam
1951   28 Pages $25.00

No. 119*

Wizard Of Oz, The
Illus.: Turner, Don
Author: Jason Studios Carey, Mary
1975   24 Pages $8.00

No. 120

Bugs Bunny And The Indians
(Copyright by Warner Bros.
Cartoon, Inc.)
Illus.: Kelsey, Richard
Author: Bedford, Annie North
1951   28 Pages $14.00

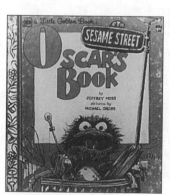

No. 120*

Oscar's Book
(Copyright by Children's
Television Workshop)
Illus.: Gross, Michael
Author: Moss, Jeffery
1975   24 Pages $6.00

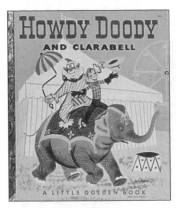

No. 121

Howdy Doody And Clarabell
(Copyright by Kagran
Corporation)
Illus.: Seiden, Art
Author: Kean, Edward
1951   28 Pages   **$25.00**

No. 121*

Santa's Surprise Book
Illus.: Winship, Florence
Author: Elwart, Joan Rotter
1966   24 Pages   **$6.00**

No. 122

Lucky Mrs. Ticklefeather
Illus.: Miller, J.P.
Author: Kunhardt, Dorothy
1951   28 Pages   **$25.00**

No. 122*

Road Runner, The 'A Very
Scary Lesson'
Illus.: Delara, Phil; Totten, Bob
Author: Schroeder, Russel
1974   24 Pages   **$6.00**

No. 123

Happy Birthday
(Only American 35 cent LGB)
Illus.: Worcester, Retta
Author: Nast, Elsa Ruth
1952   28 Pages   **$40.00**

No. 123*

Remarkably Strong Pippy
Longstocking, The
(Copyright by G. G. Communi-
cations, Inc.)
Illus.: Turner, Don; Jason Studios
Author: Hogan, Cecily
1974   24 Pages   **$14.00**

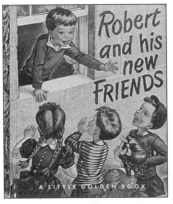

No. 124

Robert And His New Friends
Illus.: Malvern, Corinne
Author: Schneider, Nina
1951   28 Pages   **$11.00**

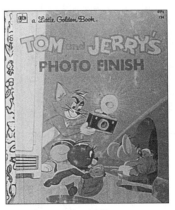

No. 124*

Tom And Jerry's Photo Finish
(Copyright by Metro-Goldwyn
Mayer, Inc.)
Illus.: Andersen, Al
Author: Lewis, Jean
1974   24 Pages   **$10.00**

No. 125

Boats
Illus.: Combes, Lenora and Herbert
Author: Lackman, Ruth Mabee
1951   28 Pages   **$8.00**

No. 125*

Barbie
(Copyright by Mattel, Inc.)
Illus.: Biesterveld, Betty
Author: Biesterveld, Betty
1974   24 Pages   **$9.00**

No. 126

Gingerbread Shop, The
Illus.: Elliott, Gertrude
Author: Travers. P. L.
1952   28 Pages   **$16.00**

No. 126*

Scooby Doo And The Pirate
Treasure
(Copyright by Hanna-Barbera
Productions, Inc.
Illus.: Lorencz, William; Arens, Michael
Author: Lewis, Jean
1974   24 Pages   **$10.00**

No. 127*

Bugs Bunny's Carrot Machine
(Copyright by Warner Bros., Inc.)
Illus.: Totten, Bob
Author: Carlisle, Clark
1971   24 Pages   **$6.00**

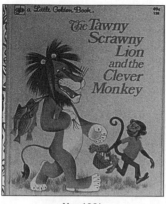

No. 128

Mister Dog
Illus.: Williams, Garth
Author: Brown, Margaret Wise
1952   28 Pages   **$25.00**

No. 128*

**Tawney Scrawney Lion And
The Clever Monkey, The**
Illus.: Jancar, Milli
Author: Carey, Mary
1974   24 Pages   **$7.00**

No. 129

**Tex And His Toys
(Uncut with tape)**
Illus.: Malvern, Corinne
Author: Nast, Elsa Ruth
1952   28 Pages   **$90.00**

No. 129*

**Bouncy Baby Bunny Finds His
Bed, The**
Illus.: Westerberg, Christine
Author: Bowden, Joan
1974   24 Pages   **$6.00**

No. 130

What If?
Illus.: Miller, J.P.
Authors: Tanous, Helen and Henry
1951   28 Pages   **$12.00**

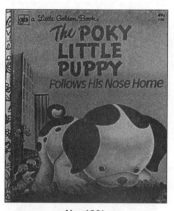

No. 130*

**Poky Little Puppy Follows His
Nose Home, The**
Illus.: Miclat, Alex
Author: Holl, Adelaide
1975   24 Pages   **$6.00**

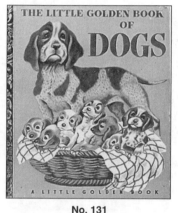

No. 131

Little Golden Book Of Dogs, The
Illus.: Gergely, Tibor
Author: Jones, Nita
1952   28 Pages   **$8.00**

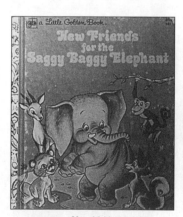

No. 131*

**New Friends For The Saggy
Baggy Elephant**
Illus.: Neely, Jan; Alvarado, Pet
Author: Holl, Adelaide
1975   24 Pages   **$6.00**

No. 132

**Whistling Wizard
(Copyright by Bil Baird and
Cora Baird)**
Illus.: Crawford, Mel
Authors: Stern, Alan; Pray, Rupert
1953   28 Pages   **$18.00**

No. 133

Rainy Day Play Book, The
Illus.: Malvern, Corinne
Author: Pray, Rupert
1951   28 Pages   **$11.00**

No. 133*

**Mr. Rogers Neighborhood 'Hen-
rietta Meets Someone New'
(Copyright by Small World
Enterprises, Inc.)**
Illus.: Jason Art Studios
Author: Rogers, Fred M.
1974   24 Pages   **$6.00**

No. 134

Seven Little Postmen

Illus.: Gergely, Tibor

Author: Brown, Margaret Wise

1952   28 Pages   **$16.00**

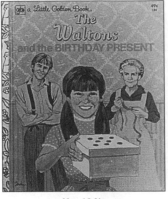

No. 134*

Walton's and the Birthday Present, The

(Copyright by Lorimar Productions, Inc.)

Illus.: Godfry, Jane

Author: Godfry, Jane

1975   24 Pages   **$6.00**

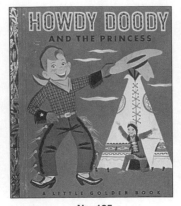

No. 135

Howdy Doody And The Princess (Copyright by Kagran Corporation)

Illus.: Seiden, Art

Author: Kean, Edward

1952   28 Pages   **$25.00**

No. 135*

Underdog And The Disappearing Ice Cream

(Copyright by T. TV & Leonardo Television Pro)

Illus.: Jason Art Studios

Author: Fern, Mary

1975   24 Pages   **$14.00**

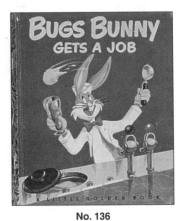

No. 136

Bugs Bunny Gets A Job (Copyright by Warner Bros., Inc.)

Illus.: Strobel, Tony; Maclaughlin, Don

Author: Bedford, Annie North

1952   28 Pages   **$12.00**

No. 136*

Land Of The Lost, The Surprise Guests

(Copyright by Sid an Marty Krofft Television)

Illus.: Irvin, Fred

Author: Graham, Kennon

1975   24 Pages   **$10.00**

No. 137

Puss In Boots

Illus.: Miller, J.P.

Author: Jackson, Kathryn

1952   28 Pages   **$11.00**

No. 137*

Magic Friend-Maker, The

Illus.: Nagel, Stina

Author: Bond, Gladys Baker

1975   24 Pages   **$11.00**

No. 138

Tawny Scrawny Lion

Illus.: Tenggren, Gustaf

Author: Jackson, Kathryn

1952   28 Pages   **$14.00**

No. 139

Fun With Decals

(Complete uncut)

Illus.: Malvern, Corinne

Author: Nast, Elsa Ruth

1952   28 Pages   **$125.00**

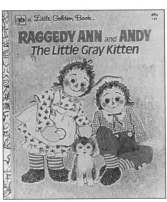

No. 139*

Raggedy Ann And Andy The Grey Kitten

(Copyright The Bob-Merrill Company, Inc.)

Illus.: Goldsborough, June

Author: Curren, Polly

1975   24 Pages   **$6.00**

No. 140

Mr. Wigg's Birthday Party

Illus.: Elliott, Gertrude

Author: Travers, P. L.

1952   28 Pages   **$18.00**

30

No. 140*

Pink Panther In The Haunted House, The

(Copyright by Mirish-Geoffrey DFE)

Illus.: Baker, Darrell; Jason Studios

Author: Graham, Kennon

1975   24 Pages   **$6.00**

No. 141

Wheels

Illus.: Weisgard, Leonard

Author: Jackson, Kathryn

1952   28 Pages   **$14.00**

No. 141*

Tweety Plays Catch The Puddy Cat

(Copyright by Warner Bros., Inc.)

Illus.: Alvarado, Peter; Lorencz, William

Author: Daly, Eileen

1975   24 Pages   **$6.00**

No. 142

Frosty The Snowman

Illus.: Malvern, Corinne

Author: Bedford, Annie North

1951   28 Pages   **$11.00**

No. 143

Here Comes The Parade

(LGB characters appear as balloons)

Illus.: Scarry, Richard

Author: Jackson, Kathryn

1950   28 Pages   **$16.00**

No. 143*

Runaway Squash, The

(Copyright by Alphaventure)

Illus.: Bunky

Author: Wiersum, Gale

1976   24 Pages   **$6.00**

No. 144

Road To Oz, The

(Copyright by Maud Gage Baum)

Illus.: McNaught, Harry

Author: Baum, Frank L.

1951   28 Pages   **$25.00**

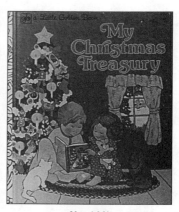

No. 144*

My Christmas Treasury

Illus.: Emrich, Sylvia

Author: Wiersum, Gale

1976   24 Pages   **$6.00**

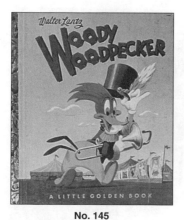

No. 145

Woody Woodpecker

(Copyright by Walter Lantz Productions, Inc.)

Illus.: Thompson, Riley

Author: Lantz, Walter

1952   28 Pages   **$11.00**

No. 145*

Bugs Bunny, Too Many Carrots

(Copyright by Warner Bros., Inc.)

Illus.: Alvarado, Peter; Totten, Bob

Author: Lewis, Jean

1976   24 Pages   **$6.00**

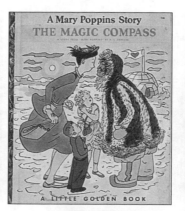

No. 146

Magic Compass, The

Illus.: Elliott, Gertrude

Author: Travers, P.L.

1953   28 Pages   **$18.00**

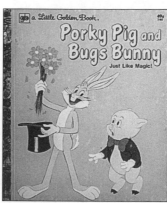

No. 146*

Porky Pig And Bugs Bunny - Just Like Magic

(Copyright by Warner Bros., Inc.)

Illus.: Totten, Bob

Author: Nathan, Stella Williams

1976   24 Pages   **$6.00**

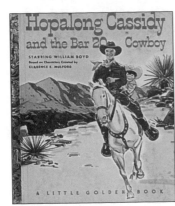

No. 147

Hopalong Cassidy And The Bar 20 Cowboys
(Copyright by Doubleday and Company, Inc.)
Illus.: Sahula-Dycke
Author: Mulford, E.M.
1952　　28 Pages　　**$25.00**

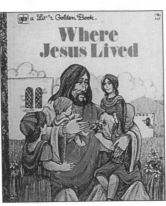

No. 147*

Where Jesus Lived
Illus.: Le Hew, Ronald
Author: Watson, Jane Wernen
1977　　24 Pages　　**$6.00**

No. 148

Uncle Wiggily
(Copyright by Howard R. Garis)
Illus.: Crawford, Mel
Author: Garis, Howard R.
1953　　28 Pages　　**$20.00**

No. 148*

Ginghams, The Backward Picnic, The
(Original Western Character)
Illus.: Koenig, Jo Anne E.
Author: Bowden, Joan Chase
1976　　24 Pages　　**$6.00**

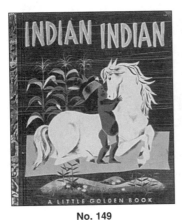

No. 149

Indian, Indian
Illus.: Weisgard, Leonard
Author: Zolotow, Charlotte
1952　　28 Pages　　**$16.00**

No. 149*

Woody Woodpecker At The Circus
(Copyright by Walter Lantz Productions, Inc.)
Illus.: McSavage, Frank
Author: Nathan, Stella Williams
1976　　24 Pages　　**$6.00**

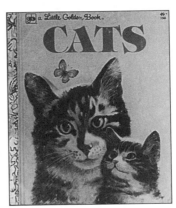

No. 150

Rootie Kazootie
(Copyright by Rootie Kazootie, Inc.)
Illus.: Crawford, Mel
Author: Carlin, Steve
1953　　28 Pages　　**$25.00**

No. 150*

Cats
Illus.: Crawford, Mel
Author: French, Laura
1976　　24 Pages　　**$6.00**

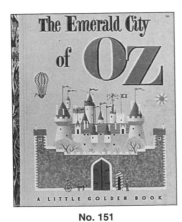

No. 151

Emerald City Of Oz
(Copyright by Maud Gage Baum)
Illus.: McNaught, Harry
Author: Archer, Peter
1952　　28 Pages　　**$27.00**

No. 151*

Wild Kingdom
Illus.: Seward, James; Creative Studios
Author: Meier, Esta
1976　　24 Pages　　**$6.00**

No. 152

All Aboard
Illus.: Malvern, Corinne
Author: Conger, Marion
1952　　28 Pages　　**$14.00**

No. 152*

Big Enough Helper, The
Illus.: O'Sullivan, Tom
Author: Hall, Nancy
1978　　24 Pages　　**$6.00**

No. 153

Thumbelina

Illus.: Tenggren, Gustaf
Author: Anderson, Hans Christian
1953   28 Pages   **$14.00**

No. 153*

Bible Stories From The Old Testement

Illus.: Robison, Jim
Author: Lee, Sing
1977   24 Pages   **$6.00**

No. 154

Nurse Nancy
(Band-Aids pasted to title page)

Illus.: Malvern, Corinne
Author: Jackson, Kathryn
1952   28 Pages   **$110.00**

No. 154*

Animals' Christmas Eve, The

Illus.: Robison, Jim
Author: Wiersum, Gale
1977   24 Pages   **$6.00**

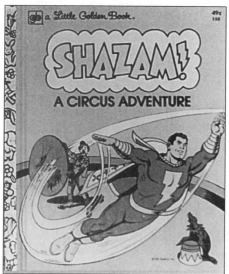

No. 155*

Shazam! A Circus Adventure
(Copyright by DC Comics, Inc.)

Illus.: Shafenburger, Kurt
Author: Ottum, Bob
1977   24 Pages   **$6.00**

No. 155

Little Eskimo, The

Illus.: Weisgard, Leonard
Author: Jackson, Kathryn
1952   28 Pages   **$15.00**

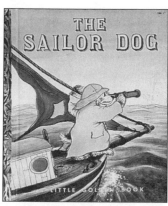

No. 156

Sailor Dog, The

Illus.: Williams, Garth
Author: Brown, Margaret Wise
1953   28 Pages   **$20.00**

No. 156*

Raggedy Ann And Andy Help Santa Claus
(Copyright The Bob-Merrill Company, Inc.)

Illus.: Goldsborough, June
Author: Curren, Plooy
1977   24 Pages   **$6.00**

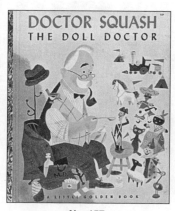

No. 157

Doctor Squash

Illus.: Miller, J.P.
Author: Brown, Margaret Wise
1952   28 Pages   **$16.00**

No. 157*

Big Bird's Red Book
(Copyright by Children's Tele-vision Workshop)

Illus.: Smollin, Michael J.
Author: Cert, Rosanne & Jonathon
1977   24 Pages   **$6.00**

No. 158

Christmas Story, The

Illus.: Wilkin, Eloise
Author: Werner, Jane
1952   28 Pages   **$10.00**

No. 159

Tin Woodsman Of Oz, The
(Copyright by Maud Gage Baum)

Illus.: McNaught, Harry

Authors: Baum, Frank L.; Archer, Harry

1952   28 Pages $25.00

No. 159*

Cookie Monster And The Cookie Tree
(Copyright by Maud Gage Baum)

Illus.: Mathieu, Joe

Author: Korr, David

1977   24 Pages $6.00

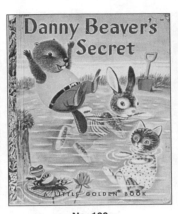

No. 160

Danny Beaver's Secret

Illus.: Scarry, Richard

Author: Scarry, Pat

1953   28 Pages $14.00

No. 160*

Donnie And Marie, The Top Secret Project
(Copyright by Osbro Productions, Inc.)

Illus.: Neely, Jan

Author: French, Laura

1977   24 Pages $6.00

No. 161

Topsy Turvy Circus

Illus.: Tenggren, Gustaf

Author: Duplaix, George

1953   28 Pages $14.00

No. 161*

Bugs Bunny, Pioneer
(Copyright by Warner Bros., Inc.)

Illus.: Baker, Darrell

Author: Brown, Fern G.

1977   24 Pages $5.00

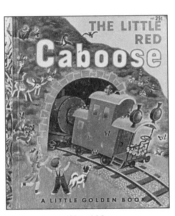

No. 162

Little Red Caboose, The

Illus.: Gergely, Tibor

Author: Potter, Marion

1953   28 Pages $10.00

No. 162*

Superstar Barbie 'The Fairy Princess'
(Copyright by Mattel, Inc.)

Illus.: Robison, Jim; Irvin, Fred

Author: Foster, Anne

1977   24 Pages $7.00

No. 163

My Kitten

Illus.: Wilkin, Eloise

Author: Scarry, Patsy

1954   28 Pages $16.00

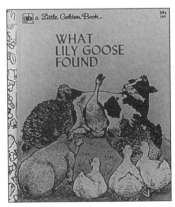

No. 163*

What Lily Goose Found

Illus.: Sumera, Anabelle

Author: Cawley, Lorinda Bryan

1977   24 Pages $6.00

No. 164

Bugs Bunny At The County Fair
(Copyright by Warner Bros. Cartoons, Inc.)

Illus.: Beecher, Elizabeth

1954   28 Pages $14.00

No. 164*

Rabbit's Adventure, The

Illus.: Swanson, Maggie

Author: Wright, Betty Ren

1977   24 Pages $6.00

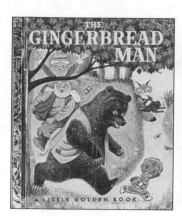

No. 165
Gingerbread Man, The
Illus.: Scarry, Richard
Author: Nolte, Nancy
1953   28 Pages   **$11.00**

No. 165*
Benji 'Fastest Dog In The West'
(Copyright by Mulberry Square
Productions, In)
Illus.: Willis, Werner
Author: Ingoglia, Gina
1978   24 Pages   **$5.00**

No. 166
Wiggles
Illus.: Wilkin, Eloise
Author: Woodcock, Louise
1953   28 Pages   **$30.00**

No. 167
Animal Friends
Illus.: Williams, Garth
Author: Werner, Jane
1953   28 Pages   **$10.00**

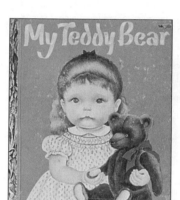

No. 168
My Teddy Bear
Illus.: Wilkin, Eloise
Author: Scarry, Patricia
1953   28 Pages   **$25.00**

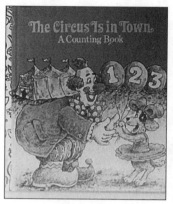

No. 168*
Circus Is In Town, The
Illus.: Ross, Larry
Author: Harrison, David L.
1978   24 Pages   **$5.00**

No. 169
Rabbit And His Friends
Illus.: Scarry, Richard
Author: Scarry, Richard
1953   28 Pages   **$12.00**

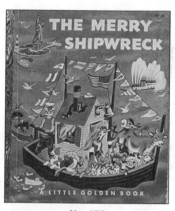

No. 170
Merry Shipwreck, The
Illus.: Gergely, Tibor
Author: Duplaix, George
1953   28 Pages   **$14.00**

No. 170*
Best Of All, A Story About The
Farm, The
Illus.: Cauley, Lorinda Bryan
Author: Hogan, Cecily Rugh
1978   24 Pages   **$5.00**

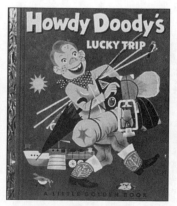

No. 171
Howdy Doody's Lucky Trip
(Copyright by Kagran Corporation)
Illus.: McNaught, Harry
Author: Kean, Edward
1953   28 Pages   **$25.00**

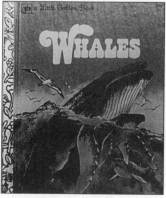

No. 171*
Whales
Illus.: Ruth, Rod
Author: Watson, Jane Werner
1978   24 Pages   **$7.00**

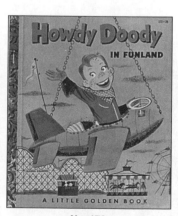

No. 172
Howdy Doody In Funland
(Copyright by Kagran Corporation)
Illus.: Seiden, Art
Author: Kean, Edward
1953   28 Pages   **$24.00**

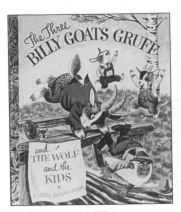

No. 173

Three Billy Goats Gruff, The

Illus.: Scarry, Richard

1953   28 Pages   **$12.00**

No. 173*

Rabbit Is Next, The

Illus.: Powell, Linda

Authors: Leithauser, Gladys; Betmeyer, Lois

1978   24 Pages   **$5.00**

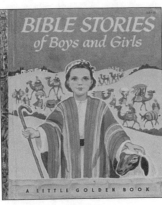

No. 174

Bible Stories of Boys and Girls

Illus.: Dixon, Rachel Taft; Hartwell, Marjore

Author: Werner, Jane

1953   28 Pages   **$8.00**

No. 175

Uncle Mistletoe

Illus.: Malvern, Corinne

Author: Werner, Jane

1953   28 Pages   **$27.00**

No. 175*

Where Will All The Animals Go?

Illus.: Grant, Leigh

Author: Holaves, Sharon

1978   24 Pages   **$6.00**

No. 176

Christmas Manger, The

(Nativity scene to put together)

Illus.: Lerch, Steffie

Author: Werner, Jane

1953   28 Pages   **$18.00**

No. 176*

ABC Around The House

Illus.: Irvin, Fred

Author: Holaves, Sharon

1978   24 Pages   **$6.00**

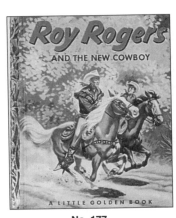

No. 177

Roy Rogers And The New Cowboy

(Copyright by Roy Rogers Enterprises)

Illus.: Crawford, Mel

Author: Bedford, Annie North

1953   28 Pages   **$22.00**

No. 178

Brave Little Tailor, The

Illus.: Miller, J.P.

Author: Bros. Grimm

1953   28 Pages   **$10.00**

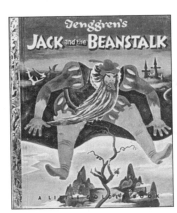

No. 179

Jack And The Beanstalk

Illus.: Tenggren, Gustaf

Author: English Folk Tale

1953   28 Pages   **$11.00**

No. 180

Airplanes

Illus.: Combes, Herbert and Lenora

Author: Lachman, Ruth Mabee

1953   28 Pages   **$10.00**

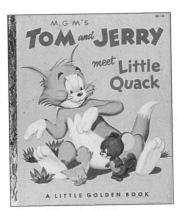

No. 181

Tom And Jerry Meet Little Quack

Illus.: Maclaughlin, Don; Eisenberg, Harvey

Author: MGM

1953   28 Pages   **$10.00**

No. 182*

Gingerbread Man, The

Illus.: Elfrieda

1965   24 Pages   **$6.00**

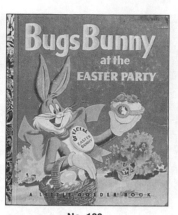

No. 183

Bugs Bunny At The Easter Party

Illus.: Warner Bros.; Strobl, Tony; Kudo, Ben

Author: Hitte, Kathryn

1953   28 Pages   **$14.00**

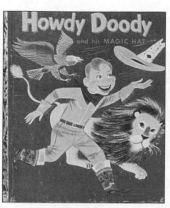

No. 184

Howdy Doody And His Magic Hat
(Copyright by Kagran Corporation)

Illus.: Seiden, Art

Author: Kean, Edward

1954   28 Pages   **$25.00**

No. 184*

Birds

Illus.: Wilkin, Eloise

Author: Watson, Jane Werner

1973   24 Pages   **$7.00**

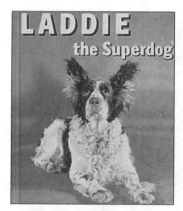

No. 185

Laddie The Superdog

Illus.: Gottlieb, William P.

Author: Gottlieb, William P.

1954   28 Pages   **$10.00**

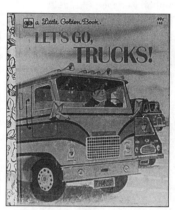

No. 185*

Let's Go, Trucks!

Illus.: Dugan, William

Author: Harrison, David L.

1973   24 Pages   **$6.00**

No. 186

Madeline
(Copyright by Ludwig Bemelmans)

Illus.: Bemelmans, Ludwig

Author: Bemelmans, Ludwig

1954   28 Pages   **$17.00**

No. 186*

Petey And I, A Story About
Being A Friend

Illus.: Irvin, Fred

Author: Conn, Martha Orr

1973   24 Pages   **$6.00**

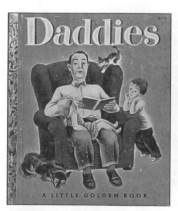

No. 187

Daddies

Illus.: Gergely, Tibor

Author: Frank, Janet

1954   28 Pages   **$20.00**

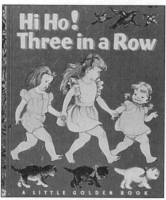

No. 188

Hi! Ho! Three In A Row

Illus.: Wilkin, Eloise

Author: Woodcock, Louise

1954   28 Pages   **$25.00**

No. 189

Musicians Of Bremen, The

Illus.: Miller, J.P.

Author: Bros. Grimm

1954   28 Pages   **$8.00**

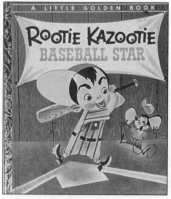

No. 190

Rootie Kazootie Baseball Star
(Copyright by Steven R. Carlin)

Illus.: Crawford, Mel

Author: Carlin, Steve

1954   28 Pages   **$30.00**

No. 191

Party Pig, The

Illus.: Scarry, Richard

Authors: Jackson, Kathryn and Byron

1954   28 Pages $25.00

No. 192

Heidi

Illus.: Malvern, Corinne

Author: Spyri, Johanna

1954   28 Pages $8.00

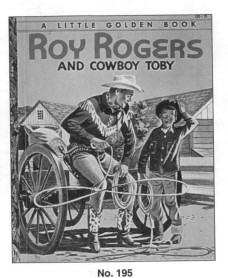

No. 195

Roy Rogers And Cowboy Toby

(Copyright by Roy Rogers Enterprises)

Illus.: Crawford, Mel

Author: Beecher, Elizabeth

1954   28 Pages $22.00

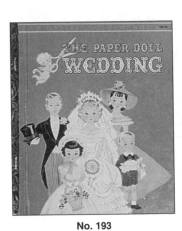

No. 193

Paper Doll Wedding

(Uncut)

Illus.: Miloche, Hilda; Kane, Wilma

Authors: Miloche, Hilda; Kane, Wilma

1954   28 Pages $125.00

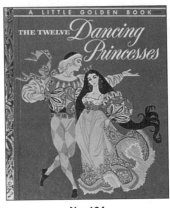

No. 194

Twelve Dancing Princesses, The

Illus.: Beckett, Sheilah

Authors: Bros. Grimm; Werner, Jane

1954   28 Pages $25.00

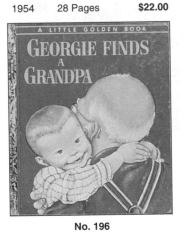

No. 196

Georgie Finds A Grandpa

Illus.: Wilkin, Eloise

Author: Young, Miriam

1954   28 Pages $22.00

No. 197

Tom And Jerry's Merry Christmas

(Copyright by Loew's Incorporated)

Illus.: Eisenberg, Harvey

Author: Archer, Peter

1954   28 Pages $8.00

No. 198

First Book Of Bible Stories

Illus.: Wilkin, Eloise

Author: Werner, Jane

1954   28 Pages $20.00

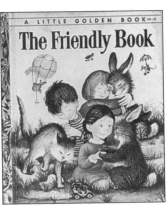

No. 199

Friendly Book, The

Illus.: Williams, Garth

Author: Brown, Margaret Wise

1954   28 Pages $11.00

No. 200

Golden Goose, The

Illus.: Tenggren, Gustaf

Author: Folk Tale

1954   28 Pages $12.00

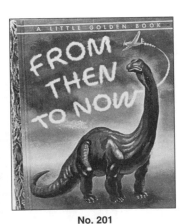

No. 201

From Then To Now

Illus.: Gergely, Tibor

Author: Leventhal, J.P.

1954   28 Pages $10.00

No. 202
Little Indian, The
Illus.: Scarry, Richard
Author: Brown, Margaret Wise
1954   28 Pages   **$14.00**

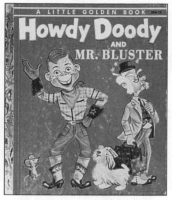

No. 204
Howdy Doody And Mr. Bluster
(Copyright by Kagran Corporation)
Illus.: Marge, Elias
Author: Kean, Edward
1955   28 Pages   **$25.00**

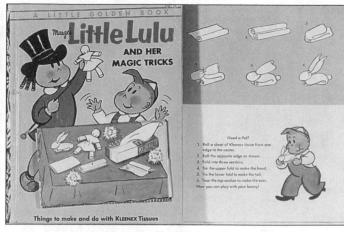

No. 203
Little Lulu And Her Magic Tricks
(Complete with Kleenex)
Illus.: Buell, Marjorie Henderson
Author: Buell, Marjorie Henderson
1954   28 Pages   **$60.00**

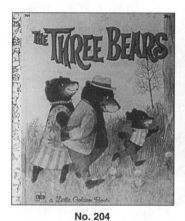

No. 204
Three Bears, The
Illus.: Goldsborough, June
Author: Watts, Mabel
1965   28 Pages   **$6.00**

No. 205
Prayers For Children
Illus.: Wilkin, Eloise
1952   28 Pages   **$7.00**

No. 206
Little Gray Donkey
Illus.: Gergely, Tibor
Author: Lunt, Alice
1954   28 Pages   **$11.00**

No. 207
Open Up My Suitcase
Illus.: Malvern, Corinne
1954   28 Pages   **$20.00**

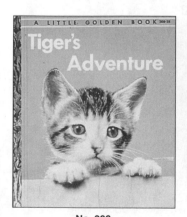

No. 208
Tiger's Adventure
Illus.: Gottlieb, William P.
Author: Gottlieb, William P.
1954   28 Pages   **$11.00**

No. 209
Little Red Hen, The
Illus.: Miller, J.P.
Author: Folk Tale
1954   28 Pages   **$8.00**

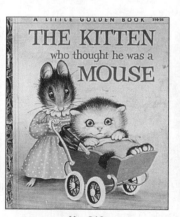

No. 210
Kitten Who Thought He Was A
Mouse, The
Illus.: Williams, Garth
Author: Norton, Miriam
1954   28 Pages   **$18.00**

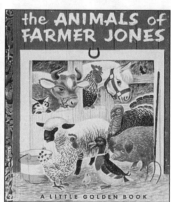

No. 211
Animals Of Farmer Jones, The
Illus.: Scarry, Richard
Author: Gale, Leah
1942   28 Pages   **$7.00**

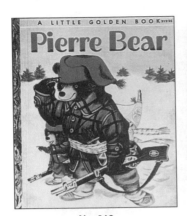

No. 212

Pierre Bear

Illus.: Scarry, Richard

Author: Scarry, Patricia

1954   28 Pages   **$25.00**

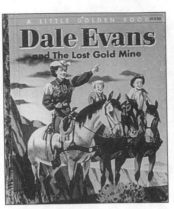

No. 213

Dale Evans And The Lost Goldmine
(Copyright by Dale Evans
Enterprises)

Illus.: Crawford, Mel

Author: Hill, Monica

1954   28 Pages   **$20.00**

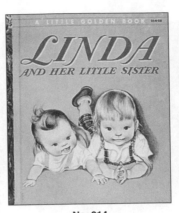

No. 214

Linda And Her Little Sister

Illus.: Wilkin, Eloise

Author: Wilkin, Esther Burns

1954   28 Pages   **$75.00**

No. 215

Bunny Book, The

Illus.: Scarry, Richard

Author: Scarry, Pat

1955   28 Pages   **$8.00**

No. 216

Happy Family, The

Illus.: Malvern, Corinne

Author: Nicole

1955   28 Pages   **$16.00**

No. 217

Hansel And Gretel

Illus.: Wilkin, Eloise

Author: Bros. Grimm

1954   28 Pages   **$7.00**

No. 218

House That Jack Built, The

Illus.: Miller, J.P.

Author: Mother Goose

1954   28 Pages   **$11.00**

No. 219

Giant With Three Golden Hairs, The

Illus.: Tenggren, Gustaf

1955   28 Pages   **$16.00**

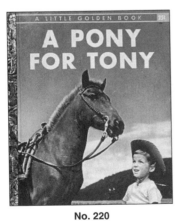

No. 220

Pony For Tony, A

Illus.: Gottlieb, William P.

Author: Gottlieb, William P.

1955   28 Pages   **$12.00**

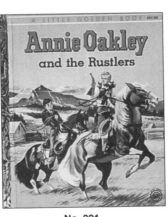

No. 221

Annie Oakley And The Rustlers
(Copyright by Annie Oakley
Enterprises, Inc.)

Illus.: Crawford, Mel

Author: Mcgovern, Ann

1955   28 Pages   **$20.00**

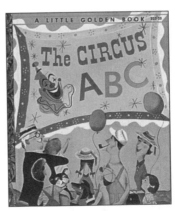

No. 222

Circus ABC, The

Illus.: Miller, J.P.

Authors: Jackson, Kathryn and Byron

1955   28 Pages   **$18.00**

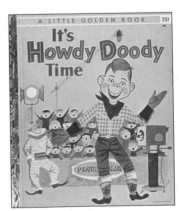

No. 223

It's Howdy Doody Time
(Copyright by Kagran Corporation)

Illus.: Seiden, Art

Author: Kean, Edward

1955   28 Pages   **$25.00**

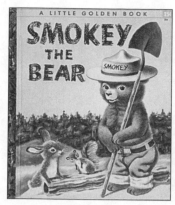

No. 224
Smokey The Bear
Illus.: Scarry, Richard
Author: Werner, Jane
1955   28 Pages   **$20.00**

No. 225
Three Little Kittens
Illus.: Masha
1942   28 Pages   **$7.00**

No. 226
Rootie Kazootie Joins The Circus
(Copyright by Steven R. Carlin)
Illus.: Crawford, Mel
Author: Carlin, Steve
1955   28 Pages   **$25.00**

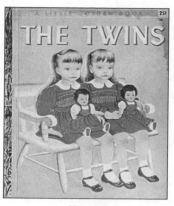

No. 227
Twins, The
Illus.: Wilkin, Eloise
Authors: Shane, Ruth and Harold
1955   28 Pages   **$75.00**

No. 228
Snow White And Rose Red
Illus.: Tenggren, Gustaf
Author: Folk Tale
1955   28 Pages   **$12.00**

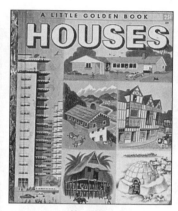

No. 229
Houses
Illus.: Gergely, Tibor
Author: Werner, Elsa Jane
1955   28 Pages   **$10.00**

No. 230
Gene Autry
(Copyright by Gene Autry)
Illus.: Crawford, Mel
Author: Fletcher, Steffie
1955   28 Pages   **$22.00**

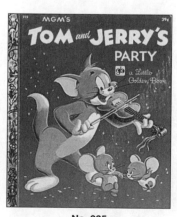

No. 231
Roy Rogers And The Mountain Lion
(Copyright by Frontiers, Inc.)
Illus.: Crawford, Mel
Author: Mcgovern, Ann
1955   28 Pages   **$22.00**

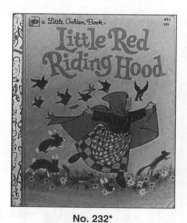

No. 232*
Little Red Riding Hood
Illus.: Watts, Mable
Author: Grey, Les
1972   28 Pages   **$5.00**

No. 232
Skyscraper, The
(Never Printed)
24 Pages

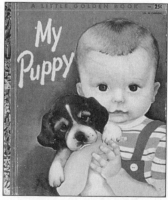

No. 233
My Puppy
Illus.: Wilkin, Eloise
Author: Scarry, Patsy
1955   28 Pages   **$14.00**

No. 234
J. Fred Muggs
(Copyright by J. Fred Muggs
Enterprises)
Illus.: Schmidt, Edwin
Author: Shapiro, Irwin
1955   28 Pages   **$16.00**

No. 235
Tom And Jerry's Party
(Copyright by Loew's
Incorporated)
Illus.: Eisenberg, Harvey
Author: Fletcher, Steffi
1955   28 Pages   **$7.00**

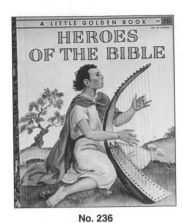

No. 236
Heroes Of The Bible
Illus.: Dixon, Rachel Taft
Author: Watson, Jane Werner
1955   28 Pages $11.00

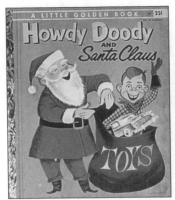

No. 237
Howdy Doody And Santa Claus
(Copyright by Kagran Corporation)
Illus.: Seiden, Art
Author: Kean, Edward
1955   28 Pages $27.00

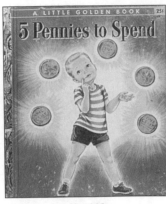

No. 238
5 Pennies To Spend
Illus.: Malvern, Corinne
Author: Young, Miriam
1955   28 Pages $16.00

No. 239
Bedtime Stories
Illus.: Tenggren, Gustaf
Authors: Misc.
1942   28 Pages $7.00

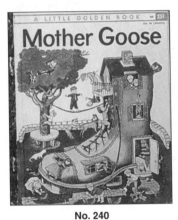

No. 240
Mother Goose
Illus.: Elliott, Gertrude
Author: Mother Goose
1942   28 Pages $12.00

No. 241
Night Before Christmas, The
Illus.: Wilkin, Eloise
Author: Watson, Jane Werner
1955   28 Pages $25.00

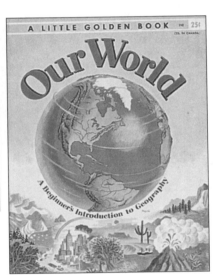

No. 242
Our World
Illus.: Sayeles, William
Authors: Reed, Mary; Oswald, Edith
1955   28 Pages $7.00

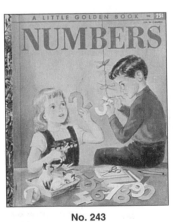

No. 243
Numbers
Illus.: La Mont, Violet
Author: Crampton, Gertrude
1955   28 Pages $6.00

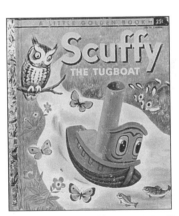

No. 244
Scuffy The Tugboat
Illus.: Gergely, Tibor
Author: Crampton, Gertrude
1955   28 Pages $6.00

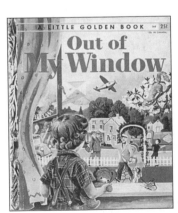

No. 245
Out Of My Window
Illus.: Jackson, Polly
Author: Low, Alice
1955   24 Pages $15.00

No. 246
Rin Tin Tin And Rusty
(Copyright by Screen Gems, Inc.)
Illus.: Crawford, Mel
Author: Hill, Monica
1955   28 Pages $16.00

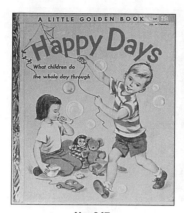

No. 247

Happy Days
Illus.: Dart, Eleanor
Author: Frank, Janet
1955   24 Pages   **$10.00**

No. 248

Shy Little Kitten, The
Illus.: Tenggren, Gustaf
Author: Schurr, Cathleen
1956   24 Pages   **$7.00**

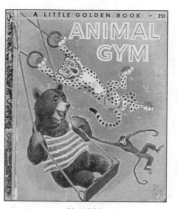

No. 249

Animal Gym
Illus.: Gergely, Tibor
Author: Hoffman, Beth Greiner
1956   24 Pages   **$14.00**

No. 250

My Snuggly Bunny
Illus.: Wilkin, Eloise
Author: Scarry, Patsy
1956   24 Pages   **$25.00**

No. 251

Cars
Illus.: Dugan, William J.
Author: Jackson, Kathryn
1956   24 Pages   **$8.00**

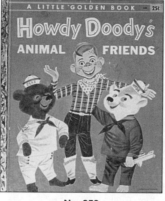

No. 252

Howdy Doody's Animal Friends
(Copyright by Kagran Corporation)
Illus.: Seiden, Art
Author: Daly, Kathleen N.
1956   24 Pages   **$25.00**

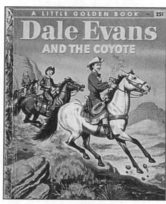

No. 253

Dale Evans And The Coyote
(Copyright by Dale Evans Enterprises)
Illus.: Dreany, E. Joseph
Author: Wyatt, Gladys
1956   24 Pages   **$20.00**

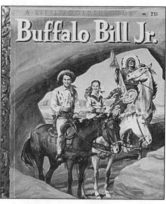

No. 254

Buffalo Bill, Jr.
Illus.: Greene, Hamilton
Author: Wyatt, Gladys
1956   24 Pages   **$20.00**

No. 255

Lassie Shows The Way
Illus.: Ames, Lee
Author: Hill, Monica
1956   24 Pages   **$14.00**

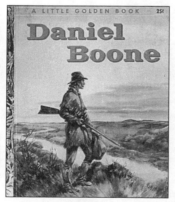

No. 256

Daniel Boone
Illus.: Story, Miriam
Author: Shapiro, Irwin
1956   24 Pages   **$10.00**

No. 257

Counting Rhymes
Illus.: Malvern, Corinne
1947   24 Pages   **$7.00**

No. 258

Heidi
Illus.: Malvern, Corinne
Author: Spyri, Johanna
1954   24 Pages   **$8.00**

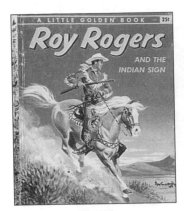

No. 259
Roy Rogers And The Indian Sign
Illus.: Crawford, Mel
Author: Wyatt, Gladys
1956   24 Pages   **$22.00**

No. 260
Little Golden Book Of Dogs, The
Illus.: Gergely, Tibor
Author: Jones, Nita
1952   24 Pages   **$8.00**

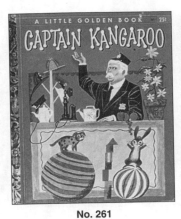

No. 261
Captain Kangaroo
Illus.: Seiden, Art
Author: Daly, Kathleen N.
1956   24 Pages   **$12.00**

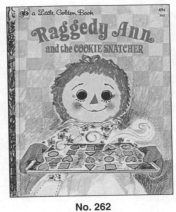

No. 262
Raggedy Ann And The Cookie Snatcher
Illus.: Goldsborough, June
Author: Hazen, Barbara Shook
1972   24 Pages   **$6.00**

No. 263
**Lone Ranger, The
(Copyright by The Lone Ranger, Inc.)**
Illus.: Dreany, E. Joseph
Author: Fletcher, Steffi
1956   24 Pages   **$22.00**

No. 264
Just For Fun
Illus.: Scarry, Richard
Author: Scarry, Patricia
1960   24 Pages   **$6.00**

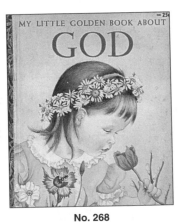

No. 265
Pal And Peter
Illus.: Gottlieb, William P.
Author: Gottlieb, William P.
1956   24 Pages   **$10.00**

No. 268
My Little Golden Book About God
Illus.: Wilkin, Eloise
Author: Watson, Jane Werner
1956   24 Pages   **$8.00**

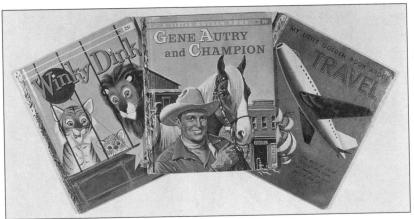

No. 266
**Winky Dink
(Copyright by Marvel Screen Enterprises, Inc.)**
Illus.: Scarry, Richard
Author: Mcgovern, Ann
1956   24 Pages   **$20.00**

No. 267
**Gene Autry And Champion
(Copyright by Gene Autry)**
Illus.: Bolle, Frank
Author: Hill, Monica
1956   24 Pages   **$22.00**

No. 269
Travel
Illus.: Gergely, Tibor
Author: Daly, Kathleen N.
1956   24 Pages   **$7.00**

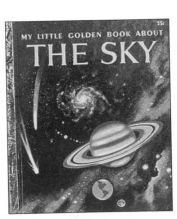

No. 270
Sky, The
Illus.: Gergely, Tibor
Author: Wyler, Rose
1956   24 Pages   **$7.00**

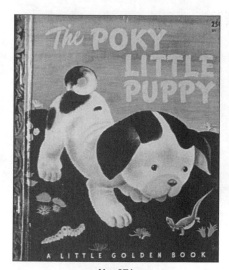

No. 271
Poky Little Puppy, The
Illus.: Tenggren, Gustaf
Author: Lowrey, Janet Sebring
1942   24 Pages   **$7.00**

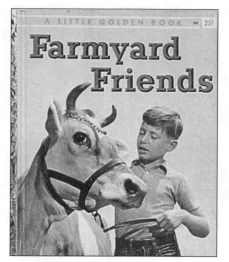

No. 272
Farmyard Friends
Illus.: Gottlieb, William P.
Author: Gottlieb, William P.
1956   24 Pages   **$7.00**

No. 273
**Romper Room Do Bees, A
Book of Manners**
Illus.: Dart, Eleanor
Author: Claster, Nancy
1956   24 Pages   **$8.00**

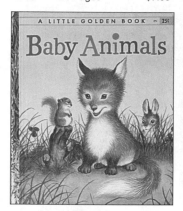

No. 274
Baby Animals
Illus.: Williams, Garth
Author: Williams, Garth
1957   24 Pages   **$7.00**

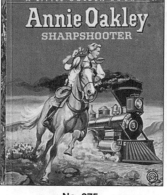

No. 275
**Annie Oakley Sharpshooter
(Copyright by Annie Oakley
Enterprises, Inc.)**
Illus.: Dreany, E. Joseph
Author: Verral, Charles Spain
1956   24 Pages   **$20.00**

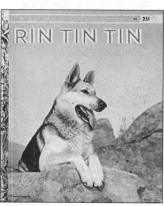

No. 276
**Rin Tin Tin And The Lost Indian
(Copyright by Screen Gems, Inc.)**
Illus.: Greene, Hamilton
Author: Hill, Monica
1956   24 Pages   **$17.00**

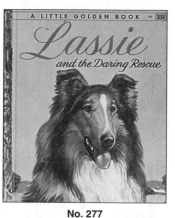

No. 277
**Lassie And The Daring Rescue
(Copyright by Lassie
Programs, Inc.)**
Illus.: Dreany, E. Joseph
Author: Verral, Charles Spain
1956   24 Pages   **$15.00**

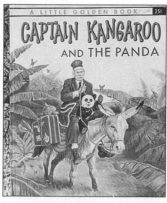

No. 278
**Captain Kangaroo And The Panda
(Copyright by Keeshan-Miller
Enterprises, Inc.)**
Illus.: Schmidt, Edwin
Author: Daly, Kathleen N.
1951   24 Pages   **$12.00**

No. 279
My Baby Brother
Illus.: Wilkin, Eloise
Author: Scarry, Patricia
1956   24 Pages   **$24.00**

No. 280
**Little Golden Paper Dolls, The
(Uncut)**
Illus.: Miloche, Hilda; Kane, Wilma
Authors: Miloche, Hilda; Kane, Wilma
1951   24 Pages   **$125.00**

No. 281
Jack And The Beanstalk
Illus.: Tenggren, Gustaf
Author: English Folk Tale
1953   24 Pages   **$8.00**

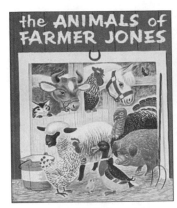

No. 282
Animals Of Farmer Jones, The
Illus.: Scarry, Richard
Author: Gale, Leah
1953   24 Pages   **$8.00**

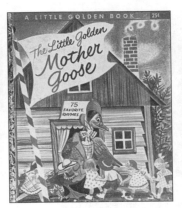

No. 283
Little Golden Mother Goose, The
Illus.: Rojankovsky, Feodor
1957   24 Pages   **$7.00**

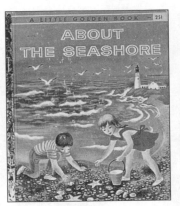

No. 284
Seashore, About The
Illus.: Gergely, Tibor
Author: Daly, Kathleen N.
1957   24 Pages   **$7.00**

No. 285
How To Tell Time
(Early Editions have Gruen on clock face)
Illus.: Dart, Eleanor
Author: Watson, Jane Werner
1957   24 Pages   **$20.00**

No. 286
Fury
(Copyright by Vision Productions, Inc.)
Illus.: Crawford, Mel
Author: Irwin, Kathleen
1957   24 Pages   **$15.00**

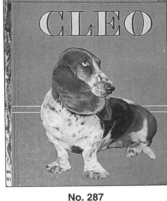

No. 287
Cleo
(From "The Peoples Choice")
Illus.: Graybill, Edward B.
Author: Shapiro, Irwin
1957   24 Pages   **$12.00**

No. 288
Three Little Kittens
Illus.: Masha
1942   24 Pages   **$6.00**

No. 285
How To Tell Time
Illus.: Dart, Eleanor
Author: Watson, Jane Werner
1957   24 Pages   **$11.00**

No. 285
How To Tell Time
(Soft Cover)
Illus.: Dart, Eleanor
Author: Watson, Jane Werner
1957   24 Pages   **$5.00**

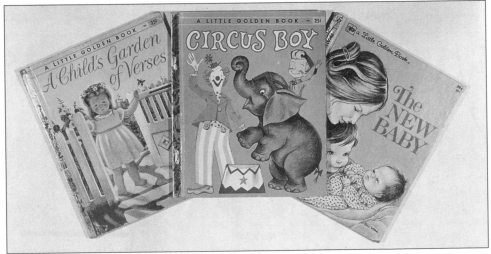

No. 289
Child's Garden Of Verses, A
Illus.: Wilkin, Eloise
Author: Stevenson, Robert Louis
1957   24 Pages   **$8.00**

No. 290
Circus Boy
Illus.: Anglund, Joan Walsh
Author: Shapiro, Irwin
1957   24 Pages   **$25.00**

No. 291
New Baby, The
(New illustrations and text)
Illus.: Wilkin, Eloise
Authors: Shane, Ruth and Harold
1975   24 Pages   **$8.00**

No. 291
New Baby, The
Illus.: Wilkin, Eloise
Authors: Shane, Ruth and Harold
1948   24 Pages   **$14.00**

No. 292
Our Puppy
Illus.: Rojankovsky, Feodor
Author: Nast, Ruth Elsa
1948   24 Pages   **$7.00**

No. 293
Wonders Of Nature
Illus.: Wilkin, Eloise
Author: Watson, Jane Werner
1957   24 Pages   **$12.00**

No. 294
Brave Eagle
(Copyright by Frontiers, Inc.)
Illus.: Vanderlaan, Si
Author: Verral, Charles Spain
1957   24 Pages   **$16.00**

No. 295
Doctor Dan, The Bandage Man
(With Band-Aids)
Illus.: Malvern, Corinne
Author: Gaspard, Helen
1950   24 Pages   **$90.00**

No. 296
Little Red Hen, The
Illus.: Miller, J.P.
Author: Folk Tale
1954   24 Pages   **$7.00**

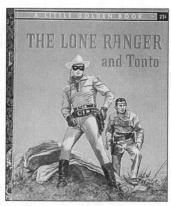

No. 297
Lone Ranger and Tonto, The
(Copyright by The Lone Ranger, Inc.)
Illus.: Schmidt, Edwin
Author: Verral, Charles Spain
1957   24 Pages   **$20.00**

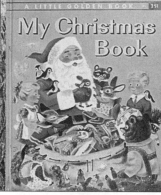

No. 298
My Christmas Book
Illus.: Beckett, Sheilah
Author: Traditional
1957   24 Pages   **$17.00**

No. 295
Doctor Dan, The Bandage Man
(Without Band-Aids)
Illus.: Malvern, Corinne
Author: Gaspard, Helen
1950   24 Pages   **$13.00**

No. 299
Broken Arrow
(Copyright by TCF-Television
Productions, Inc.)
Illus.: Crawford, Mel
Author: Verral, Charles Spain
1957   24 Pages   **$16.00**

No. 300
My Kitten
Illus.: Wilkin, Eloise
Author: Scarry, Patsy
1954   24 Pages   **$8.00**

No. 301
Five Little Firemen
Illus.: Gergely, Tibor
Author: Brown, Margaret Wise
1948   24 Pages   **$11.00**

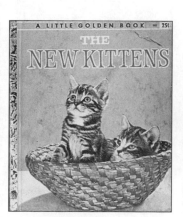

No. 302
New Kittens, The
Illus.: Gottlieb, William P.
Author: Gottlieb, William P.
1957   24 Pages   **$9.00**

No. 303
Baby's Mother Goose
Illus.: Battaglia, Aurelius
Author: Folk Tale
1948   24 Pages   **$8.00**

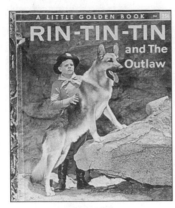

No. 304

**Rin-Tin-Tin and The Outlaw
(Copyright by Screen Gems, Inc.)**

Illus.: Crawford, Mel

Author: Verral, Charles Spain

1957   24 Pages   **$18.00**

No. 305

White Bunny And His Magic Nose, The

Illus.: Rojankovsky, Feodor

Author: Duplaix, Lily

1957   24 Pages   **$12.00**

No. 306

Red Little Golden Book Of Fairy Tales, The

Illus.: Dugan, William J.

Authors: Bros. Grimm; Anderson, H.C.

1958   24 Pages   **$12.00**

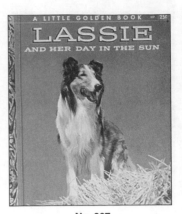

No. 307

**Lassie And Her Day In The Sun
(Copyright by Lassie Programs, Inc.)**

Illus.: Crawford, Mel

Author: Verral, Charles Spain

1958   24 Pages   **$8.00**

No. 308

Jack's Adventure

Illus.: Miller, J.P.

Author: Hurd, Edith Thacher

1958   24 Pages   **$9.00**

No. 309

Three Bedtime Stories

Illus.: Williams, Garth

Author: Fairy Tales

1958   24 Pages   **$8.00**

No. 310

**Lone Ranger And The Talking Pony, The
(Copyright by The Lone Ranger, Inc.)**

Illus.: Bolle, Frank

Author: Brown, Emily

1958   **24 Pages**   **$20.00**

No. 311

**Tom And Jerry Meet Little Quack
(Copyright by Loew's Incorporated)**

Illus.: Eisenberg, Harvey; Maclaughlin, Don

Author: MGM

1953   24 Pages   **$7.00**

No. 312

**Bugs Bunny
(Copyright by Warner Bros. Cartoons, Inc.)**

Illus.: Warner Bros.

Author: Warner Bros.

1949   24 Pages   **$8.00**

No. 313

Peter Rabbit

Illus.: Saviozzi, Adriana Mazza

Author: Potter, Beatrix

1958   24 Pages   **$7.00**

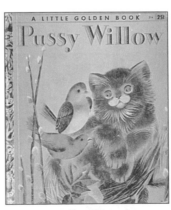

No. 314

Pussy Willow

Illus.: Weisgard, Leonard

Author: Brown, Margaret Wise

1951   24 Pages   **$10.00**

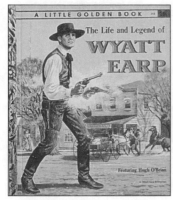

No. 315
Life And Legend Of Wyatt Earp, The
(Copyright by Wyatt Earp
Enterprises, Inc.)
Illus.: Crawford, Mel
Author: Hill, Monica
1958   24 Pages   **$18.00**

No. 316*
Monster At The End Of This Book, The
(Copyright by Children's Television Workshop)
Illus.: Smollin, Michael J.
Author: Stone, Jon
1971   24 Pages   **$5.00**

No. 317
More Mother Goose Rhymes
Illus.: Rojankovsky, Feodor
Author: Mother Goose
1958   24 Pages   **$6.00**

No. 318
Cheyenne
(Copyright by Warner Bros. Pictures, Inc.)
Illus.: Schmidt, Al
Author: Verral, Charles Spain
1958   24 Pages   **$20.00**

No. 316
Barker The Puppy
(Never Printed)
24 Pages

No. 315*
Sesame Street 'The Together Book'
Illus.: Bradfield, Roger
Author: Dwight, Revena
1971   24 Pages   **$4.00**

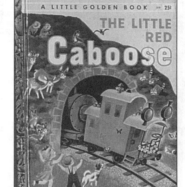

No. 319
Little Red Caboose, The
Illus.: Gergely, Tibor
Author: Potter, Marion
1953   24 Pages   **$8.00**

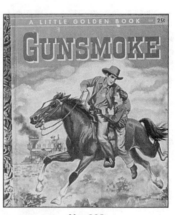

No. 320
Gunsmoke
(Copyright by Columbia Broadcasting, Inc.)
Illus.: Dreany, E. Joseph
Author: Reit, Seymour
1958   24 Pages   **$20.00**

No. 321*
Bert's Hall Of Great Inventions
(Copyright by Children's Television Workshop)
Illus.: Bradfield, Roger
Author: Dwight, Revina
1972   24 Pages   **$4.00**

No. 321
Day At The Zoo
(Never Printed)

No. 322
Four Little Kittens
Illus.: Saviozzi, Adriana Mazza
Author: Daly, Kathleen N.
1957   24 Pages   **$6.00**

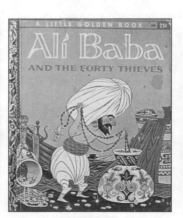

No. 323
Ali Baba And The Forty Thieves
Illus.: Hess, Lowell
Author: The Arabian Nights
1958   24 Pages   **$12.00**

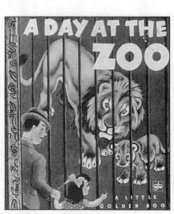

No. 324
Day At The Zoo, A
Illus.: Gergely, Tibor
Author: Conger, Marion
1950   24 Pages   **$8.00**

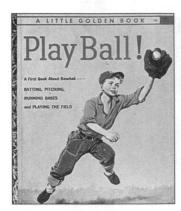

No. 325

Play Ball
Illus.: McCann, Gerald
Author: Verral, Charles Spain
1958   24 Pages   **$10.00**

No. 326

Wagon Train
(Copyright by Revue Productions, Inc.)
Illus.: Bolle, Frank
Author: Broun, Emily
1958   24 Pages   **$17.00**

No. 327

Good-bye, Tonsils
Illus.: Vaughn, Frank
Author: Cuy, Anne Welsh
1966   24 Pages   **$6.00**

No. 328

Tales Of Wells Fargo
(Copyright by Revue Productions, Inc.)
Illus.: Leone, John
Author: Lazarus, Leon
1958   24 Pages   **$18.00**

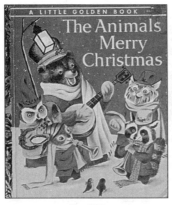

No. 329

Animals Merry Christmas, The
Illus.: Scarry, Richard
Author: Jackson, Kathryn
1958   24 Pages   **$16.00**

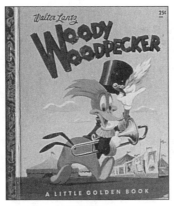

No. 330

Woody Woodpecker
(Copyright by Walter Lantz Productions, Inc.)
Illus.: Thompson, Riley
Author: Bedford, Annie North
1952   24 Pages   **$6.00**

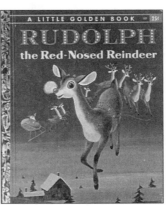

No. 331

Rudolph The Red-Nosed Reindeer
Illus.: Scarry, Richard
Author: Hazen, Barbara
1958   24 Pages   **$7.00**

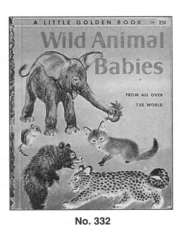

No. 332

Wild Animal Babies
Illus.: Rojankovsky, Feodor
Author: Daly, Kathleen N.
1958   24 Pages   **$6.00**

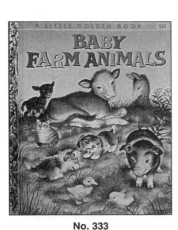

No. 333

Baby Farm Animals
Illus.: Williams, Garth
Author: Williams, Garth
1958   24 Pages   **$6.00**

No. 334

Animal Orchestra
Illus.: Gergely, Tibor
Author: Orleans, Ilo
1958   24 Pages   **$8.00**

No. 335

Big Brown Bear, The
Illus.: Tenggren, Gustaf
Author: Duplaix, George
1947   24 Pages   **$8.00**

No. 336

Fury Takes The Jump
(Copyright by Television Programs of America)
Illus.: Crawford, Mel
Author: Reit, Seymour
1958   24 Pages   **$15.00**

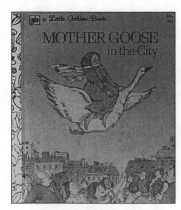

No. 336*

Mother Goose In The City

Illus.: Leder, Dora

1974   24 Pages   **$4.00**

No. 337

Numbers

Illus.: La Mont, Violet

Authors: Reed, Mary; Oswald, Edith

1955   24 Pages   **$5.00**

No. 338

Deep Blue Sea, The

Illus.: Gergely, Tibor

Author: Parker, Bertha Morris

1958   24 Pages   **$6.00**

No. 339

Boats

Illus.: Combes, Lenora and Herbert

Author: Lachman, Ruth Mabee

1951   24 Pages   **$6.00**

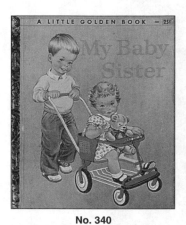

No. 340

My Baby Sister

Illus.: Koester, Sharon

Author: Scarry, Patsy

1958   24 Pages   **$18.00**

No. 341

Captain Kangaroo's Surprise Party

Illus.: Schmidt, Edwin

Author: Lindsay, Barbara

1958   24 Pages   **$12.00**

No. 342

Exploring Space

Illus.: Gergely, Tibor

Author: Wyler, Rose

1958   24 Pages   **$7.00**

No. 343

Lassie And The Lost Explorer

(Copyright by Lassie Programs, Inc.)

Illus.: Bolle, Frank

Author: Lazarus, Leon

1958   24 Pages   **$10.00**

No. 344

Happy Golden ABC, The

Illus.: Allen, Joan

1972   24 Pages   **$4.00**

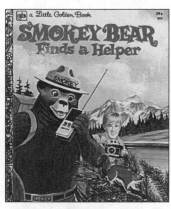

No. 345

Smokey The Bear Finds A Helper

Illus.: Andersen, Al

Author: Daly, Eileen

1972   24 Pages   **$7.00**

No. 346

Nurse Nancy

(Band-Aids pasted to title page)

Illus.: Malvern, Corinne

Author: Jackson, Kathryn

1952   24 Pages   **$100.00**

No. 347

Leave It To Beaver

(Copyright by Gomalco, Productions, Inc.)

Illus.: Crawford, Mel

Author: Alson, Lawrence

1959   24 Pages   **$25.00**

No. 348

Nursery Songs

Illus.: Saviozzi, Adriana Mazza

Author: Gale, Leah

1959   24 Pages   **$6.00**

No. 349

Animal Alphabet

Illus.: Werber, Adele

Author: Hazen, Barbara Shook

1958   24 Pages   **$10.00**

No. 350

Forest Hotel

Illus.: Benvenuti

Author: Davis, Barbara Steincrohn

1972   24 Pages   **$5.00**

No. 351

Tiger's Adventure

Illus.: Gottlieb, William P.

Author: Gottlieb, William P.

1954   24 Pages   **$6.00**

No. 352

We Help Mommy

Illus.: Wilkin, Eloise

Author: Cushman, Jean

1959   24 Pages   **$9.00**

No. 353

Tom Thumb

Illus.: Dugan, William J.

Author: Memling, Carl

1958   24 Pages   **$8.00**

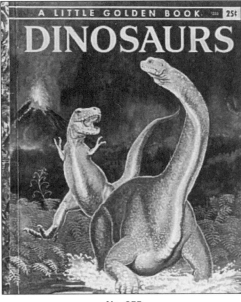

No. 355

Dinosaurs

Illus.: Rutherford, William De

Author: Watson, Jane Werner

1959   24 Pages   **$6.00**

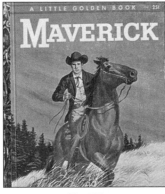

No. 354

Maverick

(Copyright by Warner Bros. Pictures, Inc.)

Illus.: Leone, John

Author: Memling, Carl

1959   24 Pages   **$18.00**

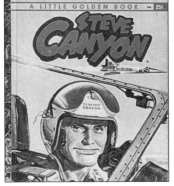

No. 356

Steve Canyon

(Copyright by Field Enterprises, Inc.)

Illus.: Caniff, Milton

Author: Caniff, Milton

1959   24 Pages   **$18.00**

No. 357

Helicopters

Illus.: Crawford, Mel

Author: Memling, Carl

1959   24 Pages   **$8.00**

No. 358

Baby's First Book

Illus.: Williams, Garth

Author: Williams, Garth

1959   24 Pages   **$7.00**

No. 359

Puss In Boots

Illus.: Miller, J.P.

Author: Jackson, Kathryn

1959   24 Pages   **$6.00**

No. 360

Party In Shariland

(Copyright by California National Productions)

Illus.: Henderson, Doris

Authors: Mcgovern, Ann & Marion

1958   24 Pages   **$17.00**

No. 361

Counting Rhymes

Illus.: Kane, Sharon

1960   24 Pages   **$6.00**

No. 362

Pussycat Tiger, The

Illus.: Obligado, Lilian

Author: Bacon, Joan Chase

1972   24 Pages   **$6.00**

No. 362

Tarzan

(Never Printed)

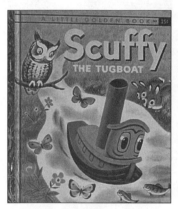

No. 363

Scuffy The Tugboat

Illus.: Gergely, Tibor

Author: Crampton, Certrude

1946   24 Pages   **$5.00**

No. 364

Bedtime Stories

Illus.: Tenggren, Gustaf

Author: Misc. Authors

1942   24 Pages   **$5.00**

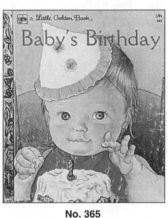

No. 365

Baby's Birthday

Illus.: Wilkin, Eloise

Author: Mowers, Patricia

1972   24 Pages   **$10.00**

No. 366

Cars And Trucks

Illus.: Scarry, Richard

1959   24 Pages   **$6.00**

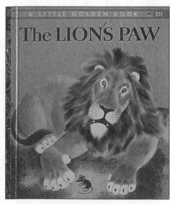

No. 367

Lion's Paw, The

Illus.: Tenggren, Gustaf

Author: Watson, Jane Werner

1959   24 Pages   **$12.00**

No. 368

Baby's First Christmas

Illus.: Wilkin, Eloise

Author: Wilkin, Esther

1959   24 Pages   **$12.00**

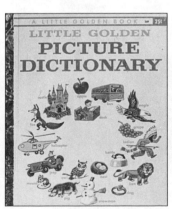

No. 369

Little Golden Picture Dictionary

Illus.: Gergely, Tibor

Author: Hulick, Nancy

1959   24 Pages   **$5.00**

No. 370

New Puppy, The

Illus.: Obligado, Lilian

Author: Daly, Kathleen

1959   24 Pages   **$7.00**

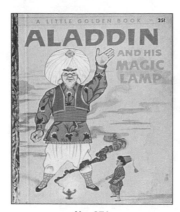

No. 371

Aladdin And His Magic Lamp

Illus.: Hess, Lowell

Author: Daly, Kathleen

1959   24 Pages   **$13.00**

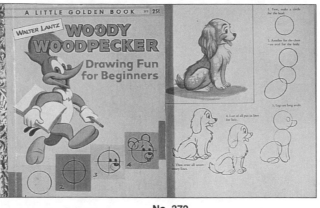

No. 372

Woody Woodpecker, Drawing Fun For Beginners
(Copyright by Walter Lantz Productions, Inc.)

Illus.: Eisenberg, Harvey; Mccary, Norman

Author: Buettner, Carl

1959   24 Pages   **$20.00**

No. 373

Airplanes

Illus.: Combes, Herbert and Lenora

Author: Lachman, Ruth Mabee

1953   24 Pages   **$6.00**

No. 374

Blue Book Of Fairy Tales, The

Illus.: Laite, Gordon

1959   24 Pages   **$13.00**

No. 375

Chipmunks' Merry Christmas, The

Illus.: Scarry, Richard

Author: Corwyn, David

1959   24 Pages   **$9.00**

No. 376

Huckleberry Hound Builds A House
(Copyright by H-B Enterprises, Inc.)

Illus.: Eisenberg, Harvey; White, Al

Author: Mcgovern, Ann

1959   24 Pages   **$18.00**

No. 377

Naughty Bunny

Illus.: Scarry, Richard

Author: Scarry, Richard

1959   24 Pages   **$25.00**

No. 378

Ruff And Reddy
(Copyright by Hanna-Barbera Productions)

Illus.: Eisenburg, Harvey; White, Al

Author: Mcgovern, Ann

1959   24 Pages   **$8.00**

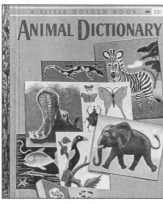

No. 379

Animal Dictionary

Illus.: Rojankovsky, Feodor

Author: Watson, Jane Werner

1960   24 Pages   **$6.00**

No. 380

Birds Of All Kinds

Illus.: Ferguson, Walter

Author: Ferguson, Walter

1959   24 Pages   **$6.00**

No. 381

Three Little Kittens

Illus.: Masha

1942   24 Pages   **$5.00**

No. 382

Fire Engines
Illus.: Tibor
1959   24 Pages   **$6.00**

No. 383

Baby Listens
Illus.: Wilkin, Eloise
Author: Wilkin, Esther
1960   24 Pages   **$12.00**

No. 384

Happy Birthday
Illus.: Worcester, Retta
Author: Nast, Elsa Ruth
1960   24 Pages   **$14.00**

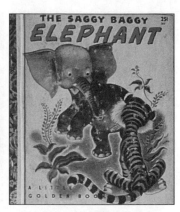

No. 385

Saggy Baggy Elephant, The
Illus.: Tenggren, Gustaf
Authors: Jackson, Kathryn and Byron
1947   24 Pages   **$5.00**

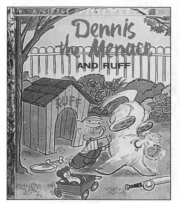

No. 386

**Dennis The Menace And Ruff
(Copyright by Hall Syndicate, Inc.)**
Illus.: Pratt, Hawley
Author: Memling, Carl
1959   24 Pages   **$12.00**

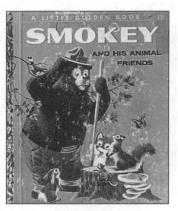

No. 387

Smokey And His Animal Friends
Illus.: Crawford, Mel
Author: Verral, Charles Spain
1960   24 Pages   **$15.00**

No. 388

Our Flag
Illus.: Cook, Steven
Author: Memling, Carl
1960   24 Pages   **$6.00**

No. 389

Cowboy ABC
Illus.: Smath, Jerry
Author: Saxon, Gladys R.
1960   24 Pages   **$12.00**

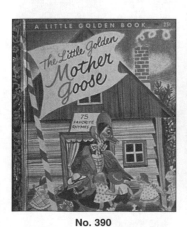

No. 390

Little Golden Mother Goose, The
Illus.: Rojankovsky, Feodor
1957   24 Pages   **$5.00**

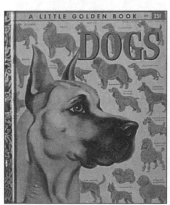

No. 391

Dogs
Illus.: Gergely, Tibor
Author: Jones, Nita
1952   24 Pages   **$5.00**

No. 392

Little Golden Book Of Hymns, The
Illus.: Malvern, Corinne
Author: Werner, Elsa Jane
1947   24 Pages   **$5.00**

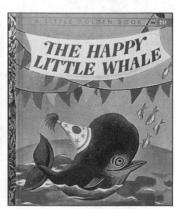

No. 393

Happy Little Whale, The
Illus.: Gergely, Tibor
Author: Watson, Jane Werner
1960   24 Pages   **$10.00**

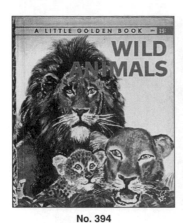

No. 394

Wild Animals

Illus.: Rojankovsky, Feodor

1961   24 Pages   **$6.00**

No. 395

Yogi Bear

(Copyright by Hanna-Barbera Productions)

Illus.: Kawaguchi, M.

Author: Hyatt, S. Quentin

1960   24 Pages   **$18.00**

No. 396

Animal Quiz

Illus.: Crawford, Mel

Author: Hulick, Nancy Fielding

1960   24 Pages   **$6.00**

No. 397

Bear In The Boat, The

Illus.: Vogel, Ilse-Margaret

Author: Vogel, Ilse-Margaret

1972   24 Pages   **$5.00**

No. 398

Quick Draw Mcgraw

(Copyright by H-B Enterprises, Inc.)

Illus.: Pratt, Hawley

Author: Memling, Carl

1960   24 Pages   **$18.00**

No. 399

Doctor Dan At The Circus

(Band-Aids pasted to title page)

Illus.: Sampson, Katherine

Author: Wilkins, Pauline

1960   24 Pages   **$100.00**

No. 400

Old MacDonald Had A Farm

Illus.: Kennel, Moritz

1960   24 Pages   **$5.00**

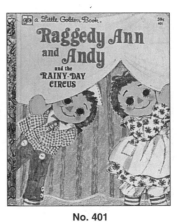

No. 401

Raggedy Ann And Andy And The Rainy Day Circus

Illus.: Goldsborough, June

Author: Hazen, Barbara Shook

1973   24 Pages   **$5.00**

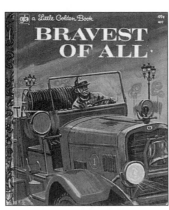

No. 402

Bravest Of All

Illus.: Andersen, Al

Author: Pogue, Katie Emery

1973   24 Pages   **$7.00**

No. 403

Huckleberry Hounds And The Christmas Sleigh

(Copyright by Hanna-Barbera Productions)

Illus.: Satterfield, Charles

Author: Cherr, Pat

1960   24 Pages   **$18.00**

No. 404

Baby Looks

Illus.: Wilkin, Eloise

Author: Wilkin, Eloise

1960   24 Pages   **$17.00**

No. 405

Four Puppies

Illus.: Obligado, Lilian

Authors: Heathers, Anne

1960   24 Pages   **$6.00**

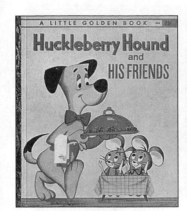

No. 406
Huckleberry Hound And His Friends
(Copyright by H-B Enterprises, Inc.)
Illus.: De Nunez, Ben; Totten, Bob
Author: Cherr, Pat
1960   24 Pages   **$18.00**

No. 407
A Day On The Farm
Illus.: Jiller, J.P.
Author: McGovern, Ann
1960   24 Pages   **$6.00**

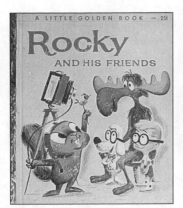

No. 408
Rocky And His Friends
(Copyright by P.A.T. Ward Pro-ductions, Inc.)
Illus.: De Nunez, Ben; White, Al
Author: Soskin, Lillian Gardner
1960   24 Pages   **$20.00**

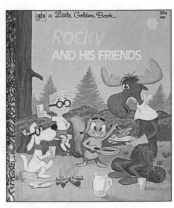

No. 408
Rocky And His Friends
(2nd Cover)
Illus.: De Nunez, Ben; White, Al
Author: Soskin, Lillian Gardner
1960   24 Pages   **$13.00**

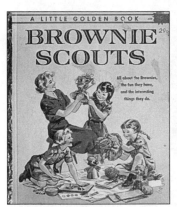

No. 409
Brownie Scouts
Illus.: Rumely, Louise
Author: Persin, Blanche Chenery
1961   24 Pages   **$15.00**

No. 410
New Pony, The
Illus.: Wilson, Dagmar
Author: Wilson, Dagmar
1961   24 Pages   **$10.00**

No. 411
Sly Little Bear
Illus.: Pfloog, Jan
Author: Jackson, Kathryn
1960   24 Pages   **$8.00**

No. 412
Dennis The Menace A Quiet Afternoon
(Copyright by Hall Syndicate, Inc.)
Illus.: Holley, Lee
Author: Memling, Carl
1960   24 Pages   **$10.00**

No. 413
Chicken Little
Illus.: Scarry, Richard
Author: Benstead, Vivienne
1960   24 Pages   **$6.00**

No. 414
Little Cottontail
Illus.: Obligado, Lilian
Author: Memling, Carl
1960   24 Pages   **$6.00**

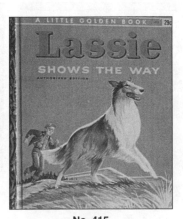

No. 415
Lassie Shows The Way
Illus.: Ames, Lee
Author: Hill, Monica
1956   24 Pages   **$6.00**

No. 416
Wacky Witch
Illus.: Alvarado, Peter; Spector, A.J; Totten
Author: Lewis, Jean
1973   24 Pages   **$10.00**

No. 417
Loopy De Loop Goes West
Illus.: Santos, George
Author: Hitte, Kathryn
1960   24 Pages   **$18.00**

No. 418
My Dolly And Me
Illus.: Wilkin, Eloise
Author: Scarry, Patsy
1960   24 Pages   **$40.00**

No. 419
Rupert The Rhinoceros
Illus.: Gergely, Tibor
Author: Memling, Carl
1960   24 Pages   **$9.00**

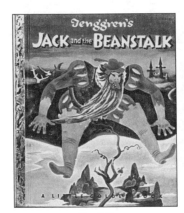

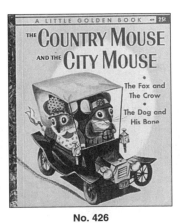

No. 420
Jack And The Beanstalk
Illus.: Tenggren, Gustaf
Author: English Folk Tale
1953   24 Pages   **$5.00**

No. 421
Captain Kangaroo And The Panda
Illus.: Schmidt, Edwin
Author: Daly, Kathleen N.
1957   24 Pages   **$7.00**

No. 422
Baby's Mother Goose
Illus.: Battaglia, Aurelius
Author: Folk Tale
1948   24 Pages   **$5.00**

No. 423
Smokey Bear And The Campers
Illus.: Crawford, Mel
Author: Hyatt, S. Quentin
1961   24 Pages   **$10.00**

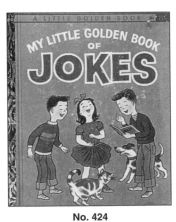

No. 424
My Little Golden Book Of Jokes
Illus.: Gergely, Tibor
Author: George
1961   24 Pages   **$6.00**

No. 425
I'm An Indian Today
Illus.: Dugan, William J.
Author: Hitte, Kathryn
1961   24 Pages   **$8.00**

No. 426
County Mouse And The City Mouse, The
Illus.: Scarry, Richard
Authors: Scarry, Pat; Aesop Tales
1961   24 Pages   **$7.00**

No. 427
Captain Kangaroo And The Beaver (Copyright by Robert Keeshan Associates, Inc.)
Illus.: Nonnast, Marie
Author: Memling, Carl
1961   24 Pages   **$8.00**

No. 428
Home For A Bunny
Illus.: Williams, Garth
Author: Brown, Margaret Wise
1961   24 Pages   **$8.00**

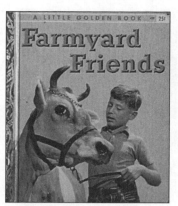

No. 429
Farmyard Friends
Illus.: Gottlieb, William P.
Author: Gottlieb, William P.
1956   24 Pages   **$5.00**

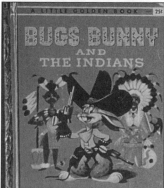

No. 430
Bugs Bunny And The Indians
(Copyright by Warner Bros.
Cartoons, Inc.)
Illus.: Kelsey, Richard.; Mckimson, Tom
Author: Bedford, Annie North
1951   24 Pages   **$8.00**

No. 431
National Velvet
(Copyright by Warner Bros., Inc.)
Illus.: Crawford, Mel
Author: Hitte, Kathryn
1961   24 Pages   **$12.00**

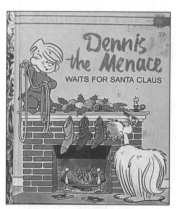

No. 432
Dennis The Menace Waits For
Santa Claus
(Copyright by Hanna-Barbera
Productions)
Illus.: Wisman, Al
Author: Memling, Carl
1961   24 Pages   **$17.00**

No. 433
Yogi Bear-A Christmas Visit
(Copyright by Hanna-Barbera
Productions)
Illus.: Mattinson, Sylvia and Burne
Author: Hyatt, S. Quentin
1961   24 Pages   **$18.00**

No. 434
My First Counting Book
Illus.: Williams, Garth
Author: Moore, Lilian
1957   24 Pages   **$4.00**

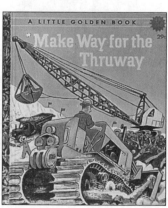

No. 435
When You Were A Baby
Illus.: Malvern, Corinne
Author: Eng, Rita
1949   24 Pages   **$6.00**

No. 436
Color Kittens, The
Illus.: Provensen, Alice and Martin
Author: Brown, Margaret Wise
1949   24 Pages   **$10.00**

No. 437
Gingerbread Man, The
Illus.: Scarry, Richard
Author: Nolte, Nancy
1961   24 Pages   **$6.00**

No. 438
Little Red Hen, The
Illus.: Hauge, Carl and Mary
Author: Begley, Evelyn M.
1973   24 Pages   **$6.00**

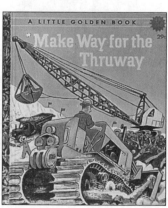

No. 439
Make Way For The Thruway
Illus.: Gergely, Tibor
Author: Emerson, Caroline
1961   24 Pages   **$10.00**

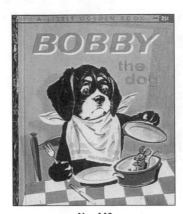

No. 440

Bobby The Dog

Illus.: Probst, Pierre

Author: Probst, Pierre

1961   24 Pages   **$12.00**

No. 441

Bunny's Magic Tricks

Illus.: Martin, Judy and Barry

Authors: D'amato, Janet and Alex

1962   24 Pages   **$12.00**

No. 442

Cindy Bear

(Copyright by Hanna-Barbera Productions)

Illus.: Eisenberg, Harvey

Author: Klinordlinger, Jean

1961   24 Pages   **$18.00**

No. 443

Puff The Blue Kitten

Illus.: Probst, Pierre

Author: Probst, Pierre

1961   24 Pages   **$16.00**

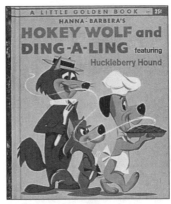

No. 444

Hokey Wolf And Ding-A-Ling

(Copyright by Hanna-Barbera Productions)

Illus.: Van Lamsweerde, Frans

Author: Hyatt, S. Quentin

1961   24 Pages   **$18.00**

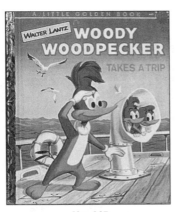

No. 445

Woody Woodpecker Takes A Trip

(Copyright by Walter Lantz Productions, Inc.)

Illus.: De Nunez, Ben; White, Al

Author: Mcgovern, Ann

1961   24 Pages   **$7.00**

No. 446

Bozo The Clown

(Copyright by Capitol Records, Inc.)

Illus.: Satterfield, Charles

Authors: Buettner, Carl

1961   24 Pages   **$10.00**

No. 447

Good Night, Little Bear

Illus.: Scarry, Richard

Author: Scarry, Patsy

1961   24 Pages   **$10.00**

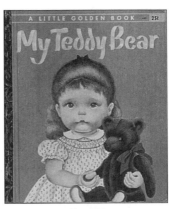

No. 448

My Teddy Bear

Illus.: Wilkin, Eloise

Author: Scarry, Patricia

1953   24 Pages   **$12.00**

No. 449

Yakky Doodle And Chopper

(Copyright by Hanna-Barbera Productions)

Illus.: White, Al

Author: Cherr, Pat

1962   24 Pages   **$20.00**

No. 450

Flintstones, The

(Copyright by Hanna-Barbera Productions)

Illus.: Crawford, Mel

Author: Crawford, Mel

1961   24 Pages   **$20.00**

No. 451

Ten Little Animals

Illus.: Rojankovsky, Feodor

Author: Memling, Carl

1961   24 Pages   **$6.00**

No. 452

Busy Timmy
Illus.: Wilkin, Eloise
Authors: Jackson, Kathryn and Byron
1948   24 Pages   **$12.00**

No. 453

Top Cat
(Copyright by Hanna-Barbera Productions)
Illus.: Pratt, Hawley
Author: Memling, Carl
1962   24 Pages   **$20.00**

No. 454

Pixi and Dixi and Mr. Jinx
(Copyright by Hanna-Barbera Productions)
Illus.: Mattinson, Sylvia and Burne
Author: Buettner, Carl
1961   24 Pages   **$35.00**

No. 455

Machines
Illus.: Dugan, William J.
Author: Dugan, William J.
1961   24 Pages   **$6.00**

No. 456

Golden Egg Book, The
Illus.: Obligado, Lilian
Author: Brown, Margaret Wise
1962   24 Pages   **$7.00**

No. 457

Littlest Raccoon, The
Illus.: Humbert, Claude
Author: Parish, Peggy
1961   24 Pages   **$7.00**

No. 458

Huckleberry Hound Safety Signs
(Copyright by Hanna-Barbera Productions)
Illus.: White, Al
Author: Mcgovern, Ann
1961   24 Pages   **$18.00**

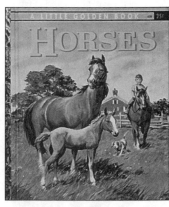

No. 459

Horses
Illus.: Greene, Hamilton
Author: Perrin, Blanche Chenery
1962   24 Pages   **$6.00**

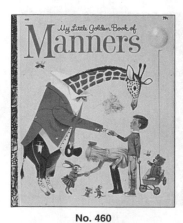

No. 460

My Little Golden Book Of Manners
Illus.: Scarry, Richard
Author: Parish, Peggy
1962   24 Pages   **$6.00**

No. 461

Pick Up Sticks
Illus.: Pfloog, Piet
Author: Wilkins, Pauline
1962   24 Pages   **$10.00**

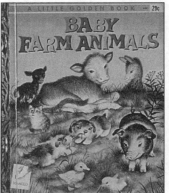

No. 464

Baby Farm Animals
Illus.: Williams, Garth
Author: Williams, Garth
1962   24 Pages   **$6.00**

No. 466

Baby Dear
Illus.: Wilkin, Eloise
Author: Wilkin, Esther
1962   24 Pages   **$16.00**

No. 462
Bullwinkle
(Copyright by P.A.T. Ward
Productions, Inc.)
Illus.: Pratt, Hawley
Author: Corwyn, David
1962   24 Pages   **$18.00**

No. 463
Wait-For-Me-Kitten
Illus.: Obligado, Lilian
Author: Scarry, Patsy
1962   24 Pages   **$8.00**

No. 465
My Little Golden Animal Book
Illus.: Kennel, Moritz
Author: Macpherson, Elizabeth
1962   24 Pages   **$7.00**

No. 467
Where Is The Poky Little Puppy
Illus.: Tenggren, Gustaf
Author: Lowrey, Janet Sebring
1962   24 Pages   **$8.00**

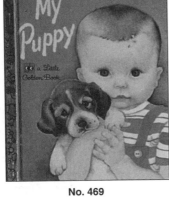

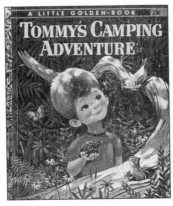

No. 468
We Help Daddy
Illus.: Wilkin, Eloise
Author: Stein, Mini
1962   24 Pages   **$10.00**

No. 469
My Puppy
Illus.: Wilkin, Eloise
Author: Scarry, Patsy
1955   24 Pages   **$8.00**

No. 470
Heidi
Illus.: Malvern, Corinne
Author: Spyri, Johanna
1954   24 Pages   **$5.00**

No. 471
Tommy's Camping Adventure
Illus.: Crawford, Mel
Author: Saxon, Gladys
1962   24 Pages   **$10.00**

No. 472
Little Golden Mother Goose, The
Illus.: Rojankovsky, Feodor
1957   24 Pages   **$5.00**

No. 473
Nurse Nancy
(Band-Aids pasted to title page)
Illus.: Malvern, Corinne
Author: Jackson, Kathryn
1958   24 Pages   **$100.00**

No. 474
Touché Turtle
(Copyright by Hanna-Barbera
Productions)
Illus.: White, Al; McGary, Norm; Lorencz
Author: Memling, Carl
1962   24 Pages   **$20.00**

No. 475
Bugs Bunny
Illus.: Warner Bros.
Author: Warner Bros.
1949   24 Pages   **$5.00**

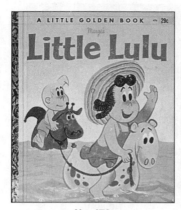

No. 476

Little Lulu
(Copyright by Marjorie
Henderson Buell)
Illus.: Kimbrell, Woody; White, Al
Author: Weiner, Gina Ingoglia
1962   24 Pages   **$15.00**

No. 477

Ruff And Reddy
(Copyright by Hanna-Barbera
Productions)
Illus.: Eisenburg, Harvey; White, Al
Author: Mcgovern, Ann
1959   24 Pages   **$10.00**

No. 478

Christmas ABC, The
Illus.: Wilkin, Eloise
Author: Johnson, Florence
1962   24 Pages   **$25.00**

No. 479

Rusty Goes To School
Illus.: Probst, Pierre
Author: Weingarden, Ann
1962   24 Pages   **$12.00**

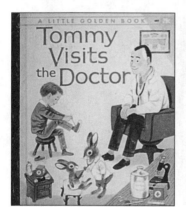

No. 480

Tommy Visits The Doctor
Illus.: Scarry, Richard
Author: Seligmann, Joan
1969   24 Pages   **$6.00**

No. 481

Smokey The Bear
Illus.: Scarry, Richard
Author: Werner, Jane
1955   24 Pages   **$10.00**

No. 482

Big Little Book, The
Illus.: Kennel, Moritz
Author: Smith, Hall
1962   24 Pages   **$7.00**

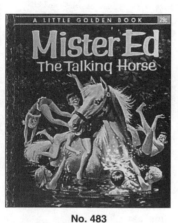

No. 483

Mister Ed, The Talking Horse
(Copyright by The Mister Ed
Company)
Illus.: Crawford, Mel
Author: Hazen, Barbara Shook
1962   24 Pages   **$20.00**

No. 484

Play Street
Illus.: Esley, Joan
Author: Wilkin, Esther
1962   24 Pages   **$17.00**

No. 485

Bozo Finds A Friend
Illus.: Pratt, Hawley
Author: Golberg, Tom
1962   24 Pages   **$10.00**

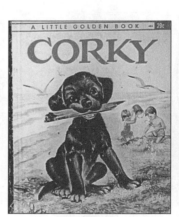

No. 486

Corky
Illus.: Wilde, Irma
Author: Scarry, Patricia
1962   24 Pages   **$12.00**

No. 487

Golden Goose, The
Illus.: Tenggren, Gustaf
Author: Bros. Grimm
1954   24 Pages   **$6.00**

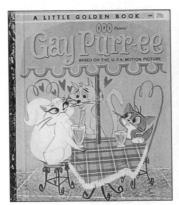

No. 488

Gay Purr-ee
(Copyright by U.P.A. Pictures, Inc.)
Illus.: Pratt, Hawley
Author: Memling, Carl
1962   24 Pages   **$22.00**

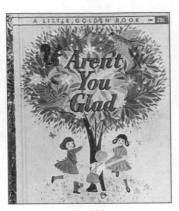

No. 489

Aren't You Glad
Illus.: Kurtz, Eliane
Author: Zolotow, Charlotte
1962   24 Pages   **$6.00**

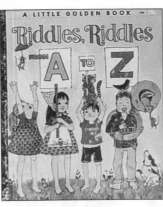

No. 490

Riddles, Riddles From A To Z
Illus.: Schart, Trina
Author: Memling, Carl
1962   24 Pages   **$6.00**

No. 491

Hansel And Gretel
Illus.: Wilkin, Eloise
Author: Bros. Grimm
1954   24 Pages   **$4.00**

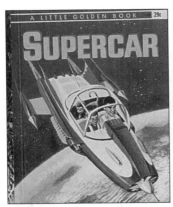

No. 492

Supercar
(Copyright by Independent Television Corp., I)
Illus.: Crawford, Mel
Author: Sherman, George
1962   24 Pages   **$25.00**

No. 493

Child's Garden Of Verses, A (2nd Cover)
Illus.: Wilkin, Eloise
Author: Stevenson, Robert Louis
1957   24 Pages   **$15.00**

No. 493

Child's Garden of Verses, A (3rd Cover changed back to original)
Illus.: Wilkin, Eloise
Author: Stevenson, Robert Louis
1957   24 Pages   **$7.00**

No. 494

Shy Little Kitten, The
Illus.: Tenggren, Gustaf
Author: Schurr, Kathleen
1946   24 Pages   **$5.00**

No. 495

I Have A Secret
Illus.: Giordano, Joseph
Author: Memling, Carl
1962   24 Pages   **$8.00**

No. 496

Colors Are Nice
Illus.: Shortall, Leonard
Author: Holl, Adelaide
1962   24 Pages   **$6.00**

No. 497

Dick Tracy
(Copyright by Chicago Tribune-New York Times)
Illus.: Pratt, Hawley
Author: Memling, Carl
1962   24 Pages   **$22.00**

No. 498

Rumpelstiltskin And The Princess And The Pea
Illus.: Dugan, William J.
Authors: Bros. Grimm; Anderson, H.C.
1962   24 Pages   **$8.00**

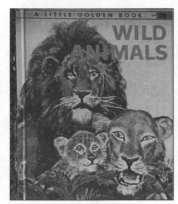

No. 499

Wild Animals
Illus.: Rojankovsky, Feodor
1961   24 Pages   **$5.00**

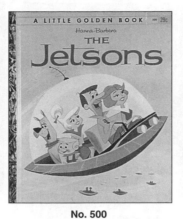

No. 500

Jetsons, The
(Copyright by Hanna-Barbera Productions)
Illus.: Pratt, Hawley
Author: Memling, Carl
1962   24 Pages   **$25.00**

No. 500*

Buck Rogers And The Children Of Hopetown
Illus.: Schaffenberger, Kurt
Author: Dwight, Revena
1971   24 Pages   **$4.00**

No. 501

Boats
Illus.: Combes, Lenora & Herbert
Author: Lachman, Ruth Mabee
1951   24 Pages   **$4.00**

No. 501*

Black Hole, The
(Copyright by Walt Disney Productions)
Illus.: Walt Disney Studios
Author: Walt Disney Studios
1979   24 Pages   **$4.00**

No. 502

Wally Gator
(Copyright by Hanna-Barbera Productions)
Illus.: Pratt, Hawley; Lorencz, Bill
Author: Goldberg, Tom
1963   24 Pages   **$18.00**

No. 503

Corky's Hiccups
Illus.: O'sullivan, Tom
Author: Stack, Nicolete Meredith
1973   24 Pages   **$6.00**

No. 504

Seven Little Postmen
Illus.: Gergely, Tibor
Author: Brown, Margaret Wise
1952   24 Pages   **$6.00**

No. 505

Peter Rabbit
Illus.: Saviozzi, Adriana Mazza
Author: Potter, Beatrix
1958   24 Pages   **$6.00**

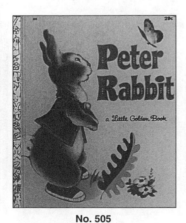

No. 505

Peter Rabbit
(2nd Cover)
Illus.: Saviozzi, Adriana Mazza
Author: Potter, Beatrix
1958   24 Pages   **$5.00**

No. 505

Peter Rabbit
(3rd Cover)
Illus.: Saviozzi, Adriana Mazza
Author: Potter, Beatrix
1970   24 Pages   **$5.00**

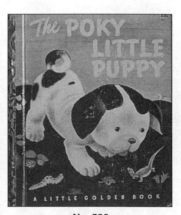

No. 506

Poky Little Puppy, The
Illus.: Tenggren, Gustaf
Author: Lowrey, Janet Sebring
1942   24 Pages   **$5.00**

No. 507

Who Needs A Cat
Illus.: Johnson, Audean
Author: Cassidy, Clara
1963   24 Pages   **$7.00**

No. 508

**Lippy The Lion And Hardy Har Har
(Copyright by Hanna-Barbera
Productions)**
Illus.: Pratt, Hawley
Author: Weiner, Gina Ingoglia
1963   24 Pages   **$18.00**

No. 509

What Am I?
Illus.: De Witt, Cornelius
Author: Ruth, Leon
1949   24 Pages   **$6.00**

No. 511

Visit To The Children's Zoo, A
Illus.: Crawford, Mel
Author: Hazen, Barbara Shook
1963   24 Pages   **$6.00**

No. 510

Large And Growly Bear, The
Illus.: Crawford, Mel
Author: Hazen, Barbara Shook
1961   24 Pages   **$7.00**

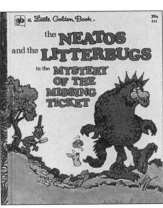

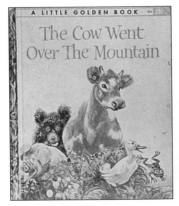

No. 512

Chipmunk's ABC
Illus.: Scarry, Richard
Author: Miller, Roberta
1963   24 Pages   **$6.00**

No. 514

Thumbelina
Illus.: Tenggren, Gustaf
Author: Anderson, Hans Christian
1953   24 Pages   **$6.00**

No. 515

Neatos And The Litterbugs, The
Illus.: Bracke, Charles
Author: Smaridge, Norah
1973   24 Pages   **$6.00**

No. 516

Cow Went Over The Mountain, The
Illus.: Rojankovsky, Feodor
Author: Krinsley, Jeanette
1963   24 Pages   **$6.00**

No. 513

My Baby Sister
(Never Printed)

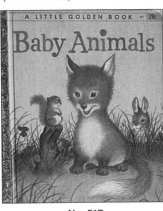

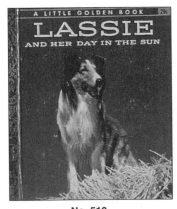

No. 517

Baby Animals
Illus.: Williams, Garth
Author: Williams, Garth
1957   24 Pages   **$5.00**

No. 518

Lassie And Her Day In The Sun
Illus.: Crawford, Mel
Author: Verral, Charles Spain
1958   24 Pages   **$6.00**

No. 519

Little Red Hen, The
Illus.: Miller, J.P.
Author: Folk Tale
1954   24 Pages   **$5.00**

No. 519

**Little Red Hen, The
(2nd Cover)**
Illus.: Miller, J.P.
Author: Folk Tale
1954   24 Pages   **$7.00**

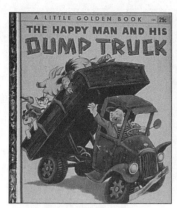

No. 520

Happy Man And His Dumptruck, The

Illus.: Gergely, Tibor

Author: Miryam

1950   24 Pages   **$7.00**

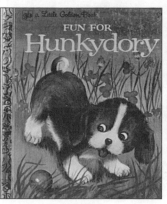

No. 521

Fun For Hunkydory

Illus.: D'avegnon, Sue

Author: Justus, May

1963   24 Pages   **$7.00**

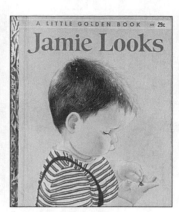

No. 522

Jamie Looks

Illus.: Wilkin, Eloise

Author: Holl, Adelaide

1963   24 Pages   **$18.00**

No. 523

Bow Wow! Meow!, A First Book Of Sounds

Illus.: Shart, Trina

Author: Bellah, Melanie

1963   24 Pages   **$6.00**

No. 524

Chicken Little

Illus.: Goldsborough, June

Author: Nathan, Stella Williams

1973   24 Pages   **$4.00**

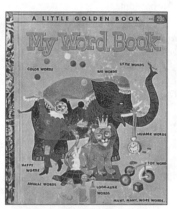

No. 525

My Word Book

Illus.: Humbert, Claude

Author: Miller, Roberta

1963   24 Pages   **$6.00**

No. 526

Twelve Days Of Christmas, The

Illus.: De Luna, Tony

1963   24 Pages   **$8.00**

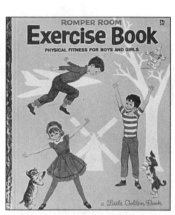

No. 527

Romper Room Exercise Book, The

Illus.: Leone, Sergio

Author: Claster, Nancy

1964   24 Pages   **$8.00**

No. 528

My Kitten

Illus.: Wilkin, Eloise

Author: Scarry, Patsy

1953   24 Pages   **$7.00**

No. 529

Nursery Rhymes

Illus.: Malvern, Corinne

1947   24 Pages   **$4.00**

No. 530

Four Little Kittens

Illus.: Saviozzi, Adriana Mazza

Author: Daly, Kathleen N.

1957   24 pages   **$5.00**

No. 531

Pebbles Flintstone
(Copyright by Hanna-Barbera Productions)

Illus.: Crawford, Mel

Author: Lewis, Jean

1963   24 Pages   **$20.00**

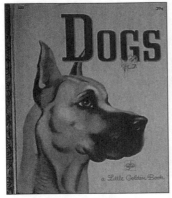

No. 532

Dogs
Illus.: Gergely, Tibor
Author: Jones, Nita
1952   24 Pages   **$5.00**

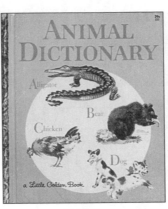

No. 533

Animal Dictionary
Illus.: Rojankovsky, Feodor
Author: Watson, Jane Werner
1960   24 Pages   **$5.00**

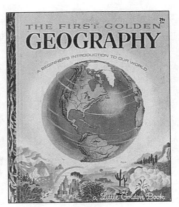

No. 534

First Golden Geography, The
Illus.: Sayeles, William
Author: Watson, Jane Werner
1955   24 Pages   **$5.00**

No. 535

Dennis The Menace And Ruff
(Never Printed)

No. 536

Little Boy And The Giant, The
Illus.: R.O. Fry
Author: Harrison, David L.
1973   24 Pages   **$6.00**

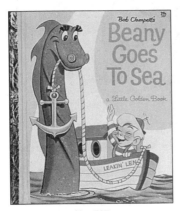

No. 537

Beany Goes To Sea
(Copyright by Robert E. (Bob) Smith)
Illus.: Pratt, Hawley; Lorencz, Bill
Author: Hill, Monica
1963   24 Pages   **$22.00**

No. 538

Bedtime Stories
Illus.: Tenggren, Gustaf
Author: Misc.
1942   24 Pages   **$4.00**

No. 538

Bedtime Stories
(2nd Cover, This Number)
Illus.: Tenggren, Gustaf
Authors: Misc.
1942   24 Pages   **$4.00**

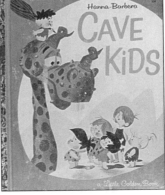

No. 539

Cave Kids
(Copyright by Hanna-Barbera Productions)
Illus.: Crawford, Mel
Author: Carrick, Bruce R.
1963   24 Pages   **$25.00**

No. 540

Bamm-Bamm
(Copyright by Hanna-Barbera Productions)
Illus.: Pratt, Hawley
Author: Lewis, Jean
1963   24 Pages   **$22.00**

No. 541

New Baby, The
Illus.: Wilkin, Eloise
Authors: Shane, Ruth and Harold
1948   24 Pages   **$7.00**

No. 542

Hey There It's Yogi Bear
(Copyright by Hanna-Barbera Productions)
Illus.: Pratt, Hawley
Author: Memling, Carl
1964   24 Pages   **$18.00**

No. 543

ABC Rhymes
Illus.: Rodegast, Roland; Clarke
Author: Memling, Carl
1964   24 Pages   **$6.00**

No. 543

ABC Rhymes
(2nd Cover)

Illus.: Rodegast, Roland; Clarke

Author: Memling, Carl

1964   24 Pages   **$4.00**

No. 544

Three Little Pigs, The

Illus.: R.O. Fry

Author: Ross, Elizabeth

1973   24 Pages   **$5.00**

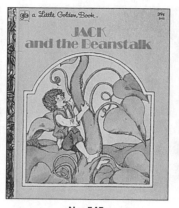

No. 545

Jack And The Beanstalk

Illus.: Leder, Dora

Author: Nathan, Stella Williams

1973   24 Pages   **$5.00**

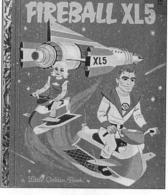

No. 546

Fireball XL5
(Copyright by Independent Television Corp., I)

Illus.: Pratt, Hawley

Author: Hazen, Barbara Shook

1964   24 Pages   **$27.00**

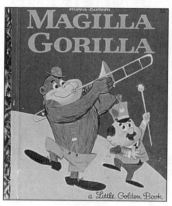

No. 547

Magilla Gorilla
(Copyright by Hanna-Barbera Productions)

Illus.: Pratt, Hawley

Author: Carrick, Bruce R.

1964   24 Pages   **$18.00**

No. 548

Little Engine That Could, The
(Copyright by Platt and Munk Co., Inc.)

Illus.: Hauman, George & Doris

Author: Piper, Wally

1954   24 Pages   **$10.00**

No. 549

Tarzan
(Copyright by Edgar Rice Burroughs, Inc.)

Illus.: Crawford, Mel

Author: Weiner, Gina Ingoglia

1964   24 Pages   **$20.00**

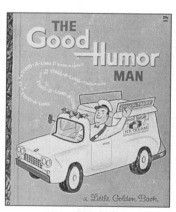

No. 550

Good Humor Man, The

Illus.: Gergely, Tibor

Author: Daly, Kathleen N.

1964   24 Pages   **$75.00**

No. 551

Lively Little Rabbit, The

Illus.: Tenggren, Gustaf

Author: Ariane

1943   24 Pages   **$4.00**

No. 552

We Like Kindergarten

Illus.: Wilkin, Eloise

Author: Cassidy, Clara

1965   24 Pages   **$6.00**

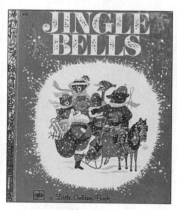

No. 553

Jingle Bells

Illus.: Miller, J.P.

Author: Daly, Kathleen N.

1964   24 Pages   **$6.00**

No. 553

Jingle Bells
(2nd Cover)

Illus.: Miller, J.P.

Author: Daly, Kathleen N.

1964   24 Pages   **$5.00**

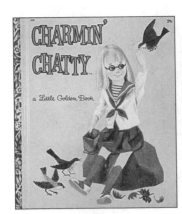

No. 554

Charmin' Chatty
(Copyright by Mattel, Inc.)
Illus.: Wilson, Dagmar
Author: Hazen, Barbara Shook
1964   24 Pages $20.00

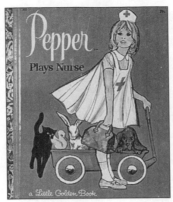

No. 555

Pepper Plays Nurse
(Copyright by Ideal Toy Corporation)
Illus.: Fernie, John
Author: Weiner, Gina Ingoglia
1964   24 Pages $18.00

No. 556

Peter Potamus
(Copyright by Hanna-Barbera Productions)
Illus.: Pratt, Hawley
Author: Memling, Carl
1964   24 Pages $18.00

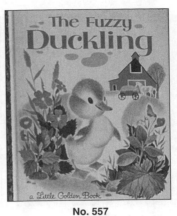

No. 557

Fuzzy Duckling, The
Illus.: Provensen, Alice & Martin
Author: Werner, Jane
1949   24 Pages $4.00

No. 558

Hop, Little Kangaroo
Illus.: Rojankovsky, Feodor
Author: Scarry, Patricia
1965   24 Pages $5.00

No. 559

Betsy McCall
(Copyright by McCall Corporation)
Illus.: Hofmann, Ginnie
Author: Robinson, Selma
1965   24 Pages $75.00

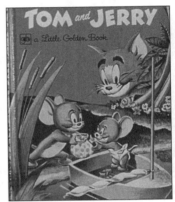

No. 560

Animal Friends
Illus.: Williams, Garth
Author: Werner, Jane
1953   24 Pages $4.00

No. 561

Tom And Jerry
Illus.: Eisenberg, Harvey; Maclaughlin, Don
Author: MGM
1951   24 Pages $6.00

No. 562

Good Little, Bad Little Girl
Illus.: Wilkin, Eloise
Author: Wilkin, Esther
1965   24 Pages $22.00

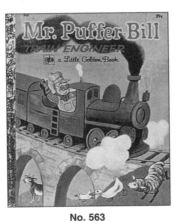

No. 563

Mr. Puffer Bill Train Engineer
Illus.: Gergely, Tibor
Author: Arland, Leonard
1965   24 Pages $6.00

No. 564

New Brother, New Sister
Illus.: Esley, Joan
Author: Fiedler, Jean
1966   24 Pages $15.00

No. 565

Dragon In A Wagon, A
Illus.: Gilbert, John Martin
Author: Rainwater, Jeanette
1966   24 Pages $5.00

No. 566

Cars

Illus.: Totten, Bob

Author: Dugan, William

1973   24 Pages   **$4.00**

No. 567

Play With Me

Illus.: Wilkin, Eloise

Author: Wilkin, Esther

1967   24 Pages   **$12.00**

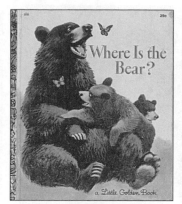

No. 568

Where Is The Bear?

Illus.: Crawford, Mel

Author: Hubka, Betty

1967   24 Pages   **$6.00**

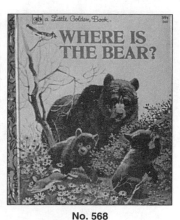

No. 568

Where Is The Bear?

(2nd Cover)

Illus.: Crawford, Mel

Author: Hubka, Betty

1967   24 Pages   **$6.00**

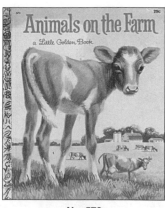

No. 569

Little Mommy

Illus.: Kane, Sharon

Author: Kane, Sharon

1967   24 Pages   **$40.00**

No. 570

Things In My House

Illus.: Kaufman, Joe

Author: Kaufman, Joe

1968   24 Pages   **$5.00**

No. 571

My Little Dinosaur

Illus.: Vogel, Ilse-Margaret

Author: Vogel, Ilse-Margaret

1971   24 Pages   **$6.00**

No. 572

Lassie And The Big Cleanup Day

Illus.: Schaar, Bob

Author: Graham, Kennon

1971   24 Pages   **$6.00**

No. 573

Animals On The Farm

Illus.: Pfloog, Jan

Author: Pfloog, Jan

1968   24 Pages   **$4.00**

No. 574

So Big

Illus.: Wilkin, Eloise

Author: Wilkin, Eloise

1968   24 Pages   **$12.00**

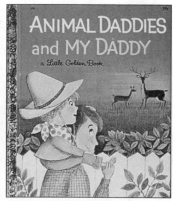

No. 575

Who Comes To Your House?

Illus.: O'sullivan, Tom

Author: Hillert, Margaret

1973   24 Pages   **$5.00**

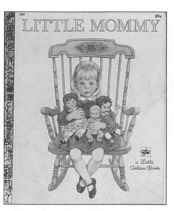

No. 576

Animal Daddies And My Daddy

Illus.: Vogel, Ilse-Margaret

Author: Hazen, Barbara Shook

1968   24 Pages   **$5.00**

No. 577

Hush, Hush, It's Sleepytime

Illus.: Crawford, Mel

Author: Parish, Peggy

1968   24 Pages   **$6.00**

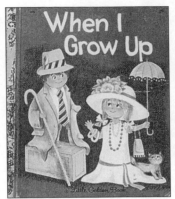

No. 578

When I Grow Up

Illus.: Vogel, Ilse-Margaret

Author: Vogel, Ilse-Margaret

1968   24 Pages   **$5.00**

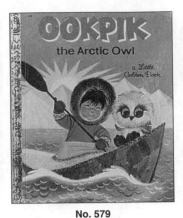

No. 579

Ookpik, The Arctic Owl
(Copyright H.M. the Queen in Right of Canada)

Illus.: Edwards, Beverly

Author: Hazen, Barbara Shook

1968   24 Pages   **$18.00**

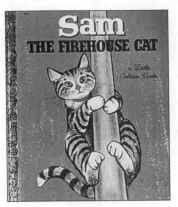

No. 580

Sam The Firehouse Cat

Illus.: Parsons, Virginia

Author: Parsons, Virginia

1968   24 Pages   **$7.00**

No. 581

ChittyChitty BangBang
(Copyright by Glidrose Productions Ltd.)

Illus.: Laite, Gordon

Author: Lewis, Jean

1968   24 Pages   **$10.00**

No. 582

Wonderful School, The

Illus.: Hoffman, Hilde

Author: Justus, May

1969   24 Pages   **$7.00**

No. 583

Little Book, The

Illus.: Wilkin, Eloise

Author: Horvath, Sherl

1969   24 Pages   **$8.00**

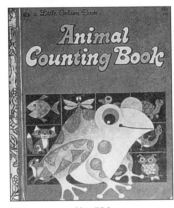

No. 584

Animal Counting Book

Illus.: Kennel, Moritz

Author: Old Nursery Poem

1969   24 Pages   **$4.00**

No. 585

Raggedy Ann And Fido
(Copyright The Bob-Merrill Company, Inc.)

Illus.: Boonshaft, Rochelle

Author: Hazen, Barbara

1969   24 Pages   **$5.00**

No. 586

Rags

Illus.: Miller, J.P.

Author: Scarry, Patsy

1970   24 Pages   **$6.00**

No. 587

Charlie

Illus.: Obligado, Lilian

Author: Downs, Diane Fox

1970   24 Pages   **$6.00**

No. 588

Boy With A Drum, The

Illus.: Wilkin, Eloise

Author: Harrison, David L.

1969   24 Pages   **$12.00**

No. 589

Eloise Wilkin's Mother Goose

Illus.: Wilkin, Eloise

Author: Wilkin, Eloise

1961　24 Pages　**$5.00**

No. 590

Tiny, Tawny Kitten, The

Illus.: Pfloog, Jan

Author: Hazen, Barbara

1969　24 Pages　**$5.00**

No. 591

Old Mother Hubbard

Illus.: Battaglia, Aurelius

Author: Battaglia, Aurelius

1970　24 Page　**$5.00**

No. 592

Friendly Book, The

Illus.: Williams, Garth

Author: Brown, Margaret Wise

1954　24 Pages　**$4.00**

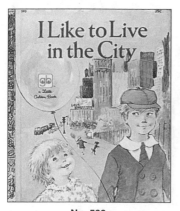

No. 593

I Like To Live In The City

Illus.: Obligado, Lilian

Author: Hillart, Margaret

1970　24 Pages　**$5.00**

No. 594

1, 2, 3, Juggle With Me!

Illus.: Vogel, Ilse-Margaret

Author: Vogel, Ilse-Margaret

1970　24 Pages　**$5.00**

(1st)

(2nd)

No. 595

Christmas Carols

Illus.: Malvern, Corinne

Author: Wyckoff, Marjorie

1946　24 Pages　**$5.00**

No. 595

Christmas Carols

(2nd Cover)

Illus.: Malvern, Corinne

Author: Wyckoff, Marjorie

1946　24 Pages　**$4.00**

No. 596

Jenny's New Brother

Illus.: Esley, Joan

Author: Evans, Elaine

1970　24 Pages　**$17.00**

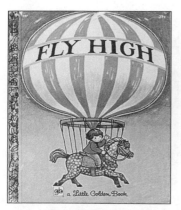

No. 597

Fly High

Illus.: Parsons, Virginia

Author: Parsons, Virginia

1971　24 Pages　**$7.00**

No. 598

Bozo And The Hide 'n' Seek Elephant

Illus.: Hubbard, Allen; Jancar, M

Author: Johnson, William

1968　24 Pages　**$8.00**

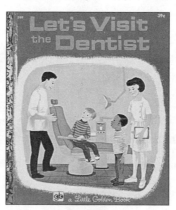

No. 599

Let's Visit The Dentist

Illus.: Wilson, Dagmar

Author: Scarry, Patricia M.

1970　24 Pages　**$5.00**

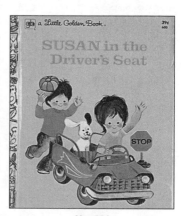

No. 600

Susan In The Driver's Seat

Illus.: Ike, Jane

Author: Gibeault, Kathi

1973　24 Pages　**$15.00**

Little Golden Books—New Numbering

Please note: The book numbers below may not coincide with your book number because the numbers change with each printing of the book. All books listed below have 24 pages.

201-46
Adventures Of Goat
Illus.: Hammond, Lucille
Author: Eugenie
1984   24 Pages   **$5.00**

200-67
All My Chickens
Illus.: Kraus, Robert
Author: Kraus, Robert
1993   24 Pages   **$2.00**

107-73
Alvin's Daydream
Illus.: Prebenna, David
Author: Teitelbaum, Michael
1990   24 Pages   **$3.00**

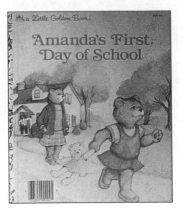

204-56
Amanda's First Day Of School
Illus.: Goodman, Joan Elizabeth
Author: Goodman, Joan Elizabeth
1986   24 Pages   **$5.00**

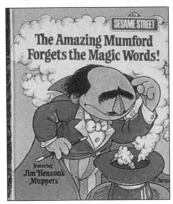

108- 5
Amazing Mumford Forgets The Magic Words!
Illus.: Chartier, Normand
Author: Thackray, Patricia
1979   24 Pages   **$4.00**

98805-00
Anastasia
Illus.: Yee, Josie
Author: James, Kari
1997   24 Pages   **$2.00**

308-44
Animal Quiz Book
Illus.: Kunhardt, Edith T.
Author: Oechsi, Kelly
1983   24 Pages   **$4.00**

202-65
Animals' ABC
(Formerly: Bunnies' ABC)
Illus.: Williams, Garth
1957   24 Pages   **$2.00**

98843
Annabelle's Wish
Illus.: Allan Nowell & Associates
Author: Korman, Susan

98769-01
Another Monster At The End Of This Book
Illus.: Smollin, Michael
Author: Stone, Jon
1996   24 Pages   **$2.00**

305-58
Arthur's Good Manners
Illus.: McCue Karston, Lisa
Author: Calmenson, Stephanie
1987   24 Pages   **$5.00**

304-64
Baby Brown Bear's Big Bellyache
Illus.: Nez, John
Author: Coco, Eugene Bradley
1989   24 Pages   **$6.00**

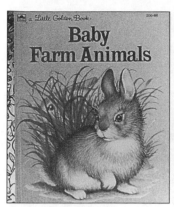

200-66

Baby Farm Animals

Illus.: Williams, Garth

Author: Williams, Garth

1958   24 Pages   **$2.00**

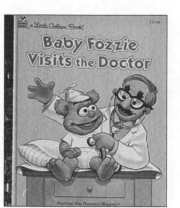

111-89

Baby Fozzie Visits The Doctor

Illus.: Brannon, Tom

Author: Weiss, Ellen

1995   24 Pages   **$2.00**

306-55

Baby Sister

Illus.: Friedman, Joy

Author: Sachs, Dorothea M.

1986   24 Pages   **$4.00**

460-08

Baby's Christmas

Illus.: Wilkin, Eloise

Author: Wilkin, Esther

1959   24 Pages   **$3.00**

98785-01

Baby's Christmas

Illus.: Lanza, Barbara

Author: Muldrow, Diane

1996   24 Pages   **$2.00**

113-01

Baby's Day Out

Illus.: Hughes, John

1994   24 Pages   **$4.00**

107-70

Barbie 'A Picinic Surprise'

Illus.: Ellis, Art and Kim

Author: McGuire, Leslie

1990   24 Pages   **$4.00**

107-71

Barbie 'Soccer Coach'

Illus.: Ruiz, Art; Stevenson, Nancy

Author: Slate, Barbara

1995   24 Pages   **$2.00**

107-86

Barbie 'The Big Splash'

Illus.: Tierney, Tom

Author: Slate, Barbara

1992   24 Pages   **$3.00**

107-94

Barbie 'The Big Splash'
(2nd Cover)

Illus.: Tierney, Tom

Author: Slate, Barbara

1992   24 Pages   **$2.00**

98808-00

Barbie The Special Sleepover

Illus.: S.I. Artists

Author: Hughes, Francine

1997   24 Pages   **$2.00**

98807-01

Barney Catch That Hat!

Illus.: Langley, Bill A.

Author: Bernthal, Mark S.

1997   24 Pages   **$2.00**

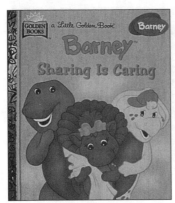

98790
Barney 'Sharing Is Caring'
Illus.: Valentine, June
Author: Bernthal, Mark S.
1996　24 Pages　**$2.00**

98815
Barney The Best Christmas Eve!
Illus.: Baker, Darrell
Author: White, Stephen
1997　24 Pages　**$2.00**

211-68
Batter Up!
Illus.: Friedman, Joy
Author: Gutelle, Andrew
1991　24 Pages　**$3.00**

208-57
Beach Day
Illus.: Wilburn, Kathy
Author: Manushkin, Fran
1988　24 Pages　**$4.00**

306-57
Bears' New Baby, The
Illus.: Goodman, Joan Elizabeth
Author: Goodman, Joan Elizabeth
1988　24 Pages　**$4.00**

208-64
Best Balloon Ride Ever
Illus.: Scarry's, Richard
Author:Scarry's, Richard
1992　24 Pages　**$2.00**

209-46
Best Friends
Illus.: Di Salvoryan, Dyanne
Author: Kenworthy, Cathryn
1983　24 Pages　**$4.00**

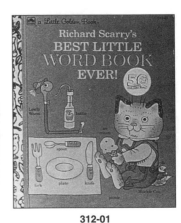

312-01
Best Little Word Book Ever!
Illus.: Scarry, Richard
Author: Scarry, Richard
1992　24 Pages　**$2.00**

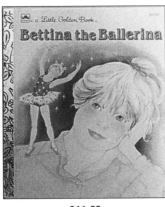

211-69
Bettina The Ballerina
Illus.: Steadman, Barbara
Author: Nelson, Mary Alexander
1991　24 Pages　**$60.00**

204-55
Bialosky's Special Picnic
Illus.: Joyner, Jerry
Author: Mcguire, Leslie
1985　24 Pages　**$4.00**

108-57
Big Bird Brings Spring To Sesame Street
Illus.: Winborn, Marsha
Author: Swindler, Lauren
1985　24 Pages　**$4.00**

98814-01
Big Bird Meets Santa Claus
Illus.: Brannon, Tom
Author: Alexander, Lisa
1997　24 Pages　**$2.00**

98839-01
Big Bird's Ticklish Christmas
Illus.: Ewers, Joe
Author: Albee, Sarah
1997   24 Pages   **$2.00**

108-68
Big Bird Visits Navajo Country
Illus.: Swanson, Maggie
Author: Alexander, Liza
1992   24 Pages   **$2.00**

107-61
Big Bird's Day On The Farm
Illus.: Swanson, Maggie
Author: Rosenbergturow, Cathi
1985   24 Pages   **$4.00**

206-51
Big Elephant, The
Illus.: Rojankovsky, Feodor
Author: Jackson, Kathryn & Byron
1949   24 Pages   **$3.00**

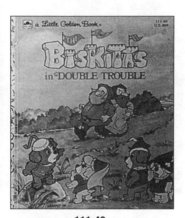

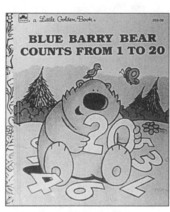

459- 8
Biggest, Most Beautiful Christmas Tree, The
Illus.: Rosenberg, Amye
Author: Rosenberg, Amye
1985   24 Pages   **$4.00**

111-49
Bisketts In Double Trouble, The
Illus.: Kostanza, John
Author: Ingolia, Gina
1984   24 Pages   **$6.00**

203-59
Blue Barry Bear Counts From 1 To 20
Illus.: Bollen, Roger
Author: Sadler, Marilyn
1991   24 Pages   **$2.00**

111-69
Bugs Bunny 'Party Pest'
Illus.: Andersen, Al; McKimson, Thomas J
Author: Johnston, William
1976   24 Pages   **$4.00**

110-60
Bugs Bunny And The Health Hog
Illus.: Baker, Darrell
Author: Slater, Teddy
1986   24 Pages   **$4.00**

110-63
Bugs Bunny And The Pink Flamingoes
Illus.: Costanza, John
Author: Ingoglia, Gina
1987   24 Pages   **$4.00**

111-70
Bugs Bunny Calling!
Illus.: Messerli, Joe
Author: West, Cindy
1988   24 Pages   **$4.00**

110-55
Bugs Bunny Marooned!
Illus.: Messerli, Joe
Author: Korman, Justine
1985   24 Pages   **$4.00**

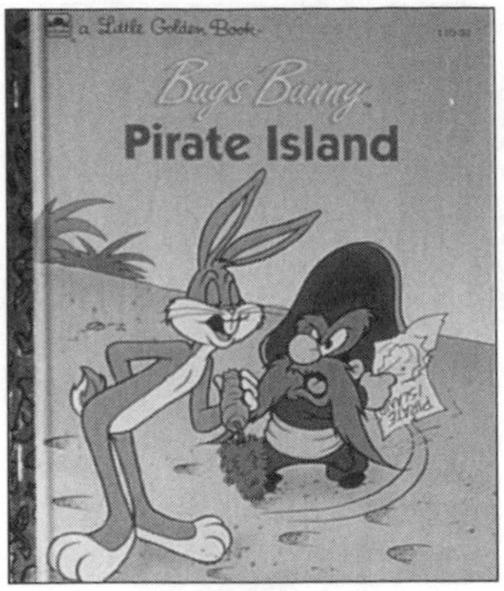

110-52
Bugs Bunny Pirate Island (Formerly: Bugs Bunny Stowaway)
Illus.: Korman, Justine
1991 24 Pages **$3.00**

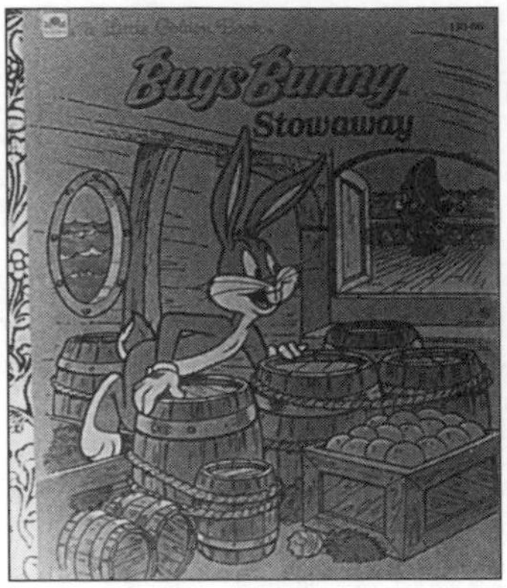

110-66
Bugs Bunny Stowaway
Illus.: Korman, Justine
1991 24 Pages **$3.00**

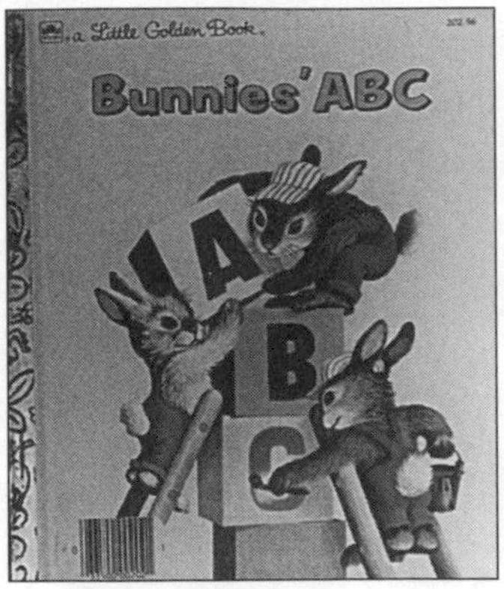

202-56
Bunnies' ABC
Illus.: Williams, Garth
1957 24 Pages **$2.00**

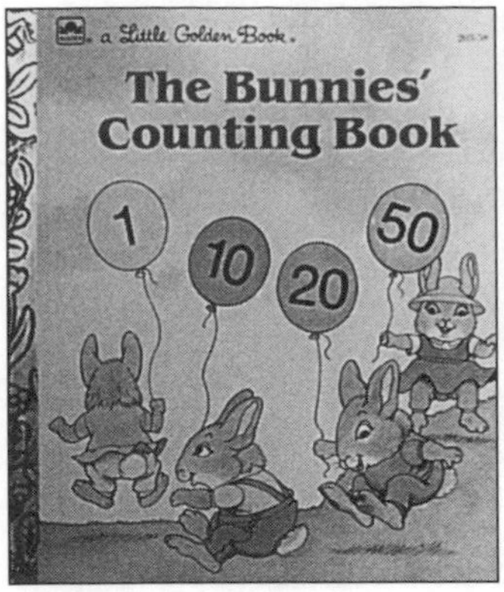

203-58
Bunnies' Counting Book, The
Illus.: Rodger, Elizabeth
Author: Rodger, Elizabeth
1991 24 Pages **$2.00**

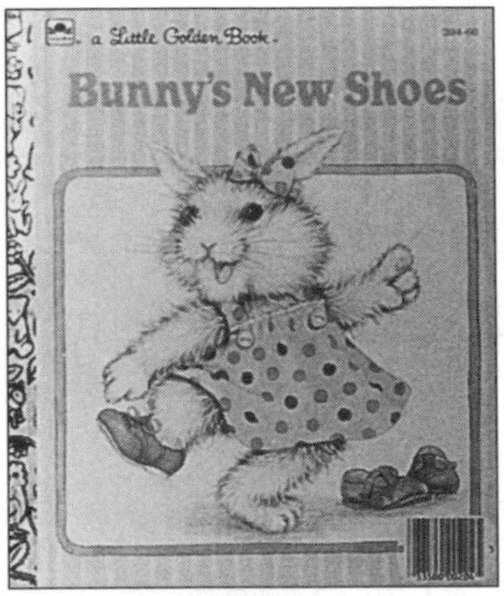

204-60
Bunny's New Shoes
Illus.: Karsten, Lisa McCue
Author: Calmenson, Stephanie
1987 24 Pages **$3.00**

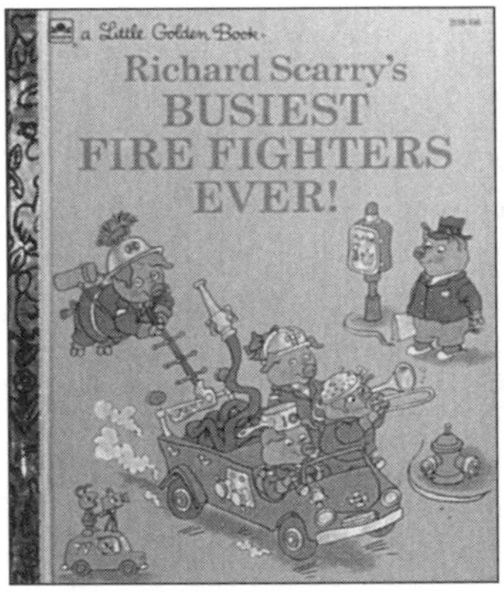

208-66
Busiest Fire Fighters Ever!
Illus.: Scarry, Richard
Author: Scarry, Richard
1993 24 Pages **$2.00**

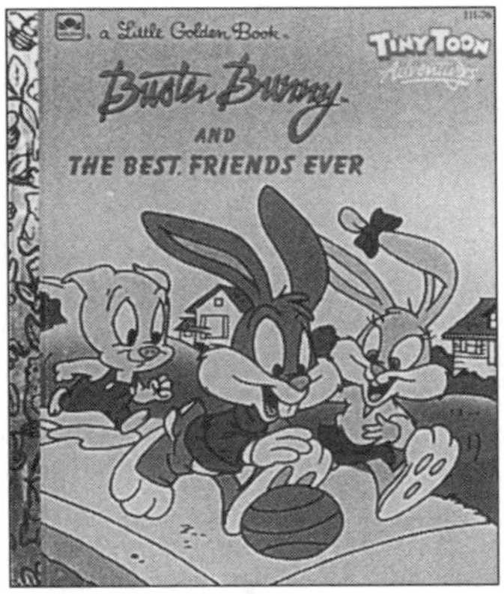

111-76
Buster Bunny And The Best Friends Ever
Illus.: Aber, Linda
1991 24 Pages **$3.00**

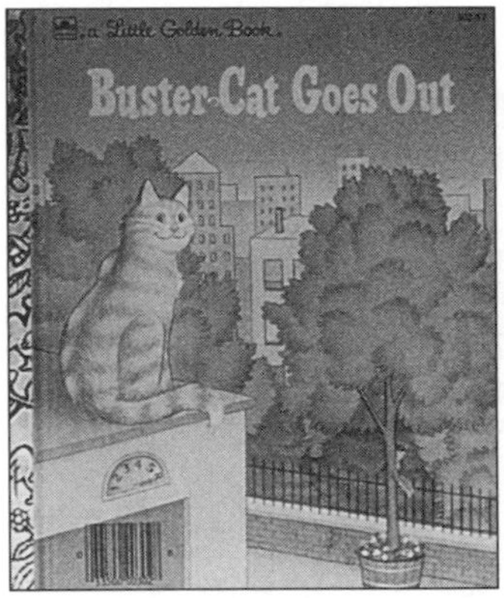

302-57
Buster Cat Goes Out
Illus.: Berlin, Rose Mary
Author: Cole, Joanna
1989 24 Pages **$4.00**

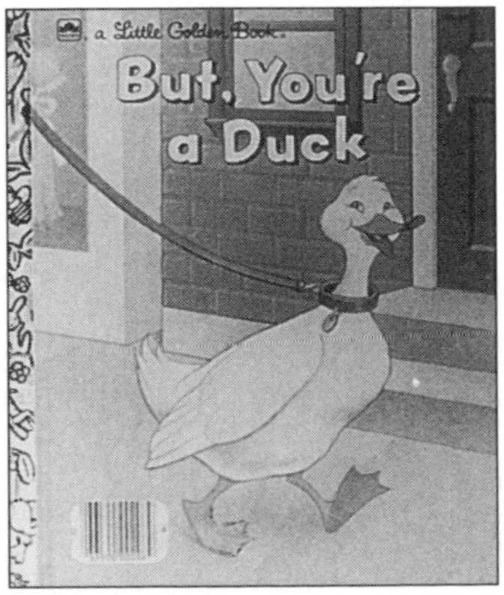

206-58
But, You're A Duck
Illus.: Berlin, Rose Mary
Author: Teitelbaum, Michael
1990 24 Pages **$2.00**

98872
Butterfly Kisses
Illus.: Ewing, Carolyn
Author: Carlisle, Bob & Brooke
1997 24 Pages **$2.00**

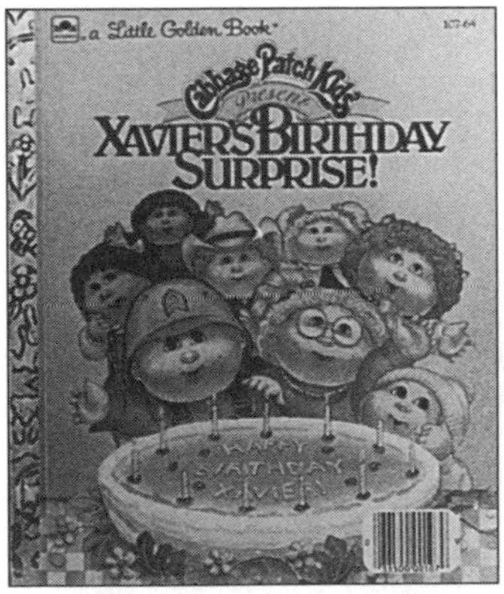

107-64
Cabbage Patch Kids 'Xavier's Birthday Surprise!'
Illus.: Hill, Ari
1987 24 Pages **$5.00**

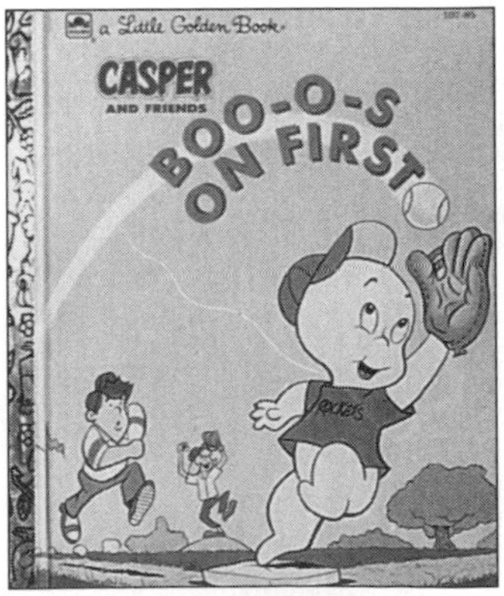

107-85
Casper And Friends 'Boo-o-s On First'
Illus.: Wildman, George
Author: St. Pierre, Stephanie
1992 24 Pages **$2.00**

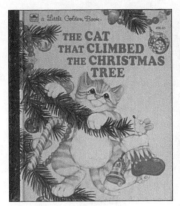

458-03

Cat That Climbed The Christmas Tree, The

Illus.: Santoro, Christopher

Author: Whayne, Susanne Santoro

1992   24 Pages   **$2.00**

309-72

Cats

Illus.: Gay, Patti

Author: French, Laura

1994   24 Pages   **$2.00**

302-44

Charlie

Illus.: Obligado, Lilian

Author: Downs, Diane Fox

1970   24 Pages   **$3.00**

98818-01

Chelli And The Great Sandbox Adventure

Illus.: Shiff, Andrew

Author: Albee, Sarah

1997   24 Pages   **$2.00**

201-56

Cheltenham's Party

Illus.: McQueen, Lucinda

Author: Wahl, Jan

1985   24 Pages   **$4.00**

312-06

Child's Year, A

Illus.: Anglund, Joan Walsh

Author: Anglund, Joan Walsh

1992   24 Pages   **$4.00**

202-44

Chipmunk's ABC

Illus.: Scarry, Richard

Author: Miller, Roberta

1963   24 Pages   **$2.00**

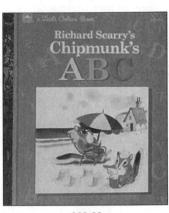

202-63

Chipmunk's ABC

Illus.: Scarry, Richard

Author: Miller, Roberta

1963   24 Pages   **$2.00**

450-13

Christmas Bunny, The

Illus.: Ewing, Carolyn

Author: Rabin, Arnold

1994   24 Pages   **$2.00**

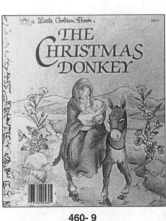

460- 9

Christmas Donkey, The

Illus.: Brooks, Andrea

Author: Taylor, William T.

1984   24 Pages   **$4.00**

456-15

Christmas Story, The

Illus.: Wilkin, Eloise

Author: Werner, Jane

1952   **$2.00**

458- 1

Christmas Tree That Grew, The

Illus.: Wilburn, Kathy

Author: Krasilousky, Phyllis

1987   24 Pages   **$4.00**

202-28
Color Kittens, The
Illus.: Provensen, Alice and Martin
Author: Brown, Margaret Wise
1949   24 Pages   **$3.00**

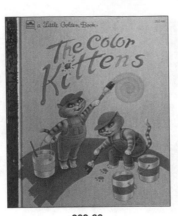

202-66
Color Kittens, The
Illus.: Ember, Kathi
Author: Brown, Margaret Wise
1994   24 Pages   **$2.00**

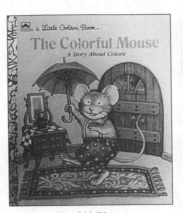

211-71
Colorful Mouse, The
Illus.: Durrell, Julie
Author: Durrell, Julie
1991   24 Pages   **$3.00**

109-52
Cookie Monster And The Cookie Tree
(Jim Henson, name taken off tree)
Illus.: Mathieu, Joe
Author: Korr, David
1977   24 Pages   **$2.00**

203-56
Count All The Way To Sesame Street
Illus.: Brown, Richard
Author: Anastasio, Dina
1985   24 Pages   **$3.00**

304-48
Cow And The Elephant, The
Illus.: Whitilock, R.Z.
Author: Smith, Claude Clayton
1983   24 Pages   **$4.00**

206-57
Curious Little Kitten Around The House, The
Illus.: Swanson, Maggie
Author: Hayward, Linda
1986   24 Pages   **$4.00**

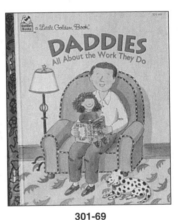

301-69
Daddies All About The Work They Do
Illus.: Meisel, Paul
Author: Lundell, Margo
1996   24 Pages   **$2.00**

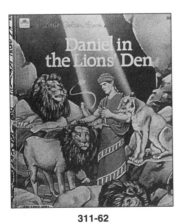

311-62
Daniel In The Lions' Den
Illus.: Lapadula, Tom
Author: Broughton, Pamela
1987   24 Pages   **$4.00**

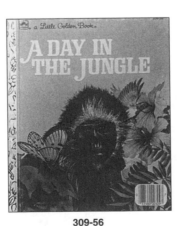

309-56
Day In The Jungle, A
Illus.: Kassian, Olena
Author: Patterson, Pat
1985   24 Pages   **$4.00**

108-59
Day Snuffy Had The Sniffles, The
Illus.: Brannon, Tom
Author: Maifair, Linda Lee
1988   24 Pages   **$4.00**

312-07
Doctor Dan, The Bandage Man
(New Band-Aids)
Illus.: Malvern, Corinne
Author: Gaspard, Helen
1950   24 Pages   **$4.00**

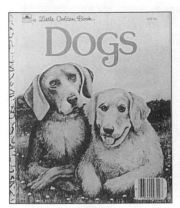

209-53

Dogs

Illus.: Lewis, Jean

Author: Mac Combie, Turi

1983 24 Pages **$4.00**

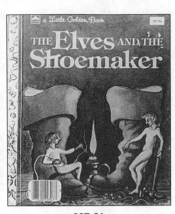

307-61

Elves And The Shoemaker, The (Blue Background)

Illus.: Bloom, Lloyd

Author: Suben, Eric

1983 24 Pages **$2.00**

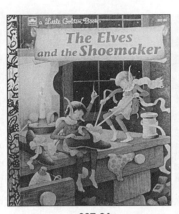

207-64

Elves And The Shoemaker, The

Illus.: Smath, Jerry

Author: Suben, Eric

1992 24 Pages **$3.00**

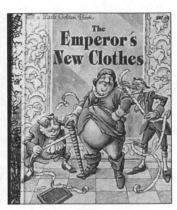

207-66

Emperor's New Clothes, The

Illus.: Walz, Richard

Author: Bonder, Rebecca

1993 24 Pages **$2.00**

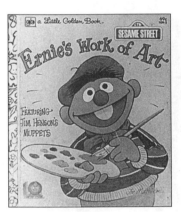

109- 5

Ernie's Work Of Art

Illus.: Mathieu, Joe

Author: Mclenighan, Valjean

1979 24 Pages **$4.00**

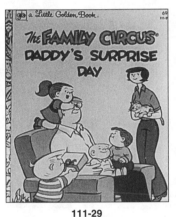

111-29

Family Circus Daddy's Surprise Day, The

Illus.: Keane, Bill

Author: Wiersum, Gale Charlotte

1980 24 Pages **$12.00**

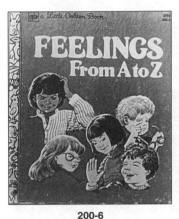

200-6

Feelings From A To Z

Illus.: Ruth, Rod

Author: Visser, Pat

1979 24 Pages **$5.00**

306-58

Fire Engines To The Rescue

Illus.: Courtney Studios

Author: Cambell, Janet

1991 24 Pages **$2.00**

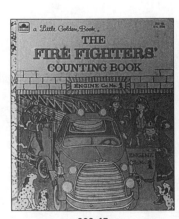

203-45

Fire Fighters' Counting Book, The

Illus.: Stewart, Pat

Author: Curren, Polly

1983 24 Pages **$4.00**

310-57

First Airplane Ride, A (Originally Flying is Fun)

Illus.: Super, Terri

Author: North, Carol

1986 24 Pages **$2.00**

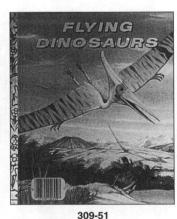

208-65

Floating Bananas

Illus.: Scarry, Richard

Author: Scarry, Richard

1993 24 Pages **$2.00**

309-51

Flying Dinosaurs

Illus.: Santro, Christopher

Author: Lindbolm, Steven

1990 24 Pages **$3.00**

310-53

Flying Is Fun

Illus.: Super, Terri

Author: North, Carol

1986   24 Pages   **$4.00**

108- 4

Four Seasons, The

Illus.: Cooke, Tom

Author: Geiss, Tony

1979   24 Pages   **$4.00**

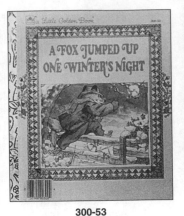

300-53

Fox Jumped Up One Winters Night, A

Illus.: Barbaresi, Nina

Author: Barbaresi, Nina

1985   24 Pages   **$4.00**

111-87

Fozzie's Funnies

Illus.: Brannon, Tom

1993   24 Pages   **$2.00**

209-61

Friendly Bunny, The (Formerly: The Scarebunny)

Illus.: Wilburn, Kathy

Author: Kunhardt, Dorothy

1985   24 Pages   **$4.00**

108-70

From Trash To Treasure

Illus.: Ewers, Joe

Author: Alexander, Liza

1993   24 Pages   **$2.00**

451-11

Frosty The Snowman

Illus.: Super, Terri

Author: Bedford, Annie North

1989   24 Pages   **$3.00**

451-15

Frosty The Snowman

Illus.: Chandler, Jean

Author: Bedford, Annie North

1992   24 Pages   **$2.00**

304-59

Funny Bunny

Illus.: Provensen, Alice and Martin

Author: Learnard, Rachel

1950   24 Pages   **$2.00**

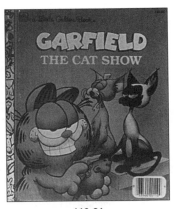

110-61

Garfield 'The Cat Show'

Illus.: Fentz, Mike

Author: Simone, Norma

1990   24 Pages   **$3.00**

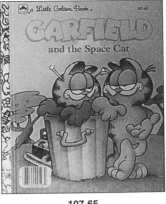

107-65

Garfield And The Space Cat

Illus.: Davis, Jim

Author: McGuire, Leslie

1988   24 Pages   **$3.00**

207- 4

Giant Who Wanted Company, The

Illus.: Hockerman, Dennis

Author: Priestly, Lee

1979   24 Pages   **$4.00**

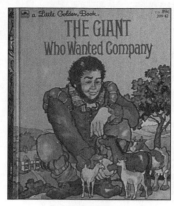

209-42
Giant Who Wanted Company, The
(Blue background)
Illus.: Hockerman, Dennis
Author: Priestly, Lee
1979   24 Pages   **$3.00**

307-69
Golden Egg Book, The
Illus.: Obligado, Lilian
Author: Brown, Margaret Wise
1975   24 Pages   **$2.00**

208-44
Good Night, Aunt Lilly
Illus.: Dawson, Diane
Author: Madagan, Margaret
1983   24 Pages   **$5.00**

204-58
Good Old Days, The
Illus.: Borgo, Deborah
Author: Werner, Dave
1988   24 Pages   **$4.00**

98803-01
Gifts Of Christmas, The
(Precious Moments)
Illus.: Butcher, Sam
Author: Bernthal, Mark S.
1997   24 Pages   **$2.00**

209-57
Good-By Day, The
Illus.: Eugenie
Author: Anderson, Leone Castell
1984   24 Pages   **$4.00**

305-55
Grandma And Grandpa Smith
Illus.: Super, Terri
Author: Kunhardt, Edith
1985   24 Pages   **$4.00**

109-57
Grover Takes Care Of Baby
Illus.: Cooke, Tom
Author: Thompson, Emily
1987   24 Pages   **$4.00**

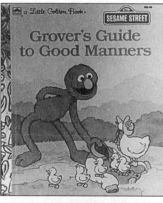

109-66
Grover's Guide To Good Manners
Illus.: Prebenna, David
Author: Allen, Constance
1992   24 Pages   **$2.00**

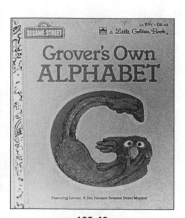

108-46
Grover's Own Alphabet
Illus.: Murdocca, Sal
1978   24 Pages   **$4.00**

98794-01
Growing Up Grouchy
(Sesame Street Muppets)
Illus.: Prebenna, David
Author: Muntean, Michaela
1997   24 Pages   **$2.00**

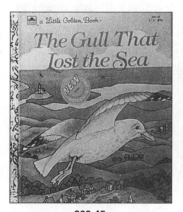

206-45
Gull That Lost The Sea, The
Illus.: McQueen, Lucinda
Author: Claytonsmith, Claude
1984   24 Pages   **$4.00**

313-01
Halloween A B C
Illus.: Meisel, Paul
Author: Albee, Sarah
1993   24 Pages   **$2.00**

207-51

Hansel And Gretel (Blue Background)

Illus.: Wilkin, Eloise

Author: Bros. Grimm

1954   24 Pages   **$2.00**

207-65

Hansel And Gretel (New Cover)

Illus.: Wilkin, Eloise

Author: Bros. Grimm

1954   24 Pages   **$3.00**

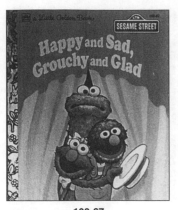

108-67

Happy And Sad, Grouchy And Glad (Sesame Street)

Illus.: Brannon, Tom

Author: Allen, Constance

1992   24 Pages   **$2.00**

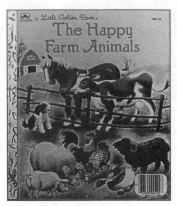

200-54

Happy Farm Animals, The (The Jolly Barnyard)

Illus.: Gergely, Tibor

Author: Bedford, Annie North

1950   24 Pages   **$2.00**

208-64

Hilda Needs Help!

Illus.: Scarry, Richard

Author: Scarry, Richard

1993   24 Pages   **$2.00**

204-43

Hiram's Red Shirt

Illus.: Battaglia, Aurelius

Author: Watts, Mabel

1981   24 Pages   **$5.00**

19917-00

Ho-Ho-Ho Baby Fozzie

Illus.: Attinello, Lauren

Author: Gikow, Louise

1997   24 Pages   **$2.00**

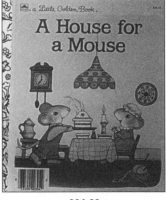

304-63

House For A Mouse, A

Illus.: Miller, John P.

Author: Daly, Kathleen

1990   24 Pages   **$3.00**

308-55

How Does Your Garden Grow?

Illus.: Clark, Brenda; Perma, Debi

Author: Patterson, Pat

1985   24 Pages   **$4.00**

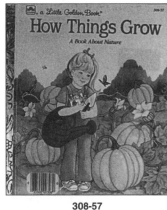

308-57

How Things Grow

Illus.: Allert, Kathy

Author: Buss, Nancy

1986   24 Pages   **$4.00**

301-43

Hush, Hush, It's Sleepytime

Illus.: Pinchevsky, Leonid

Author: Parish, Peggy

1984   24 Pages   **$4.00**

456-10

I Can't Wait Until Christmas

Illus.: Ewers, Joe

Author: Maifair, Linda Lee

1989   24 Pages   **$4.00**

208-59

I Don't Want To Go

Illus.: Rosenberg, Amye

Author: Korman, Justine

1989   24 Pages   **$4.00**

109-47

I Think That It Is Wonderful

Illus.: Delaney, A

Author: Korr, David

1984   24 Pages   **$4.00**

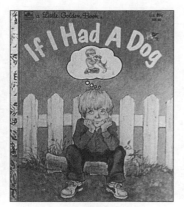

205-40

If I Had A Dog

Illus.: Obligado, Lilian

Author: Obligado, Lillian

1984   24 Pages   **$4.00**

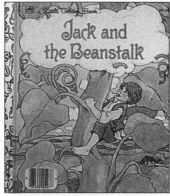

107-49

Inspector Gadget In Africa

Illus.: Gantz, David

Author: Baris, Sandra

1984   24 Pages   **$5.00**

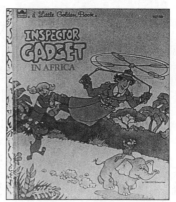

207-54

Jack And The Beanstalk

Illus.: Leder, Dora

Author: Nathan, Stella Williams

1990   24 Pages   **$2.00**

207-67

Jack And The Beanstalk

Illus.: Walz, Richard

Author: Balducci, Rita

1992   24 Pages   **$2.00**

204-39

Jenny's Surprise Summer

Illus.: Eugenie

Author: Eugenie

1981   24 Pages   **$5.00**

458

Jingle Bells

Illus.: Miller, J.P.

Author: Daly, Kathleen N.

1964   24 Pages   **$3.00**

211-61

Just Imagine 'A Book Of Fairy-land Rhymes'

Illus.: Gilchrists, Guy

Author: Gilchrists, Guy

1990   24 Pages   **$3.00**

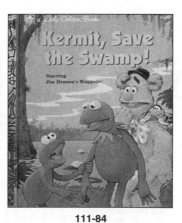

111-84

Kermit, Saves The Swamp!

Illus.: Leigh, Tom

Author: Chevat, Richard

1992   24 Pages   **$2.00**

98810-01

King Midas And The Golden Touch

Illus.: Daily, Renee Quintal

Author: Lundell, Margo

1997   24 Pages   **$2.00**

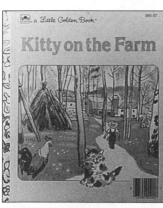

200-57

Kitty On The Farm
(Formerly: A Name For Kitty)

Illus.: Rojankovsky, Feodor

Author: McGinley

1948   24 Pages   **$2.00**

210-63

Kitty's New Doll

Illus.: McQueen, Lucinda

Author: Kunhardt, Dorothy M.

1984   24 Pages   **$4.00**

107-57

Lady Lovely Locks Silkypup Saves The Day

Illus.: Paris, Pat

Author: Brown, Kristin

1987   24 Pages   **$5.00**

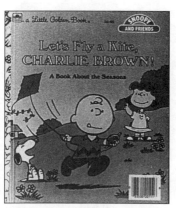

111-62

Let's Fly A Kite, Charlie Brown

Illus.: Schultz, Charles M.

Author: Verr, Harry Coe

1987   24 Pages   **$5.00**

208-58
Let's Go Shopping!
Illus.: Allert, Kathy
Author: Lindbolm, Steven
1988   24 Pages   **$4.00**

98802-01
**Let's Go To The Fire Station
(Mickey And Friends)**
Illus.: DiCicco Digital Arts
Author: Geist, Lucy
1997   24 Pages   **$2.00**

98804-01
**Let's Go To The Vet
(Mickey And Friends)**
Illus.: DiCicco Digital Arts
Author: Lewis, Zoe
1997   24 Pages   **$2.00**

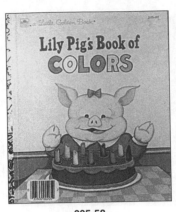

205-58
Lily Pig's Book Of Colors
Illus.: Rosenberg, Amye
Author: Rosenberg, Amye
1987   24 Pages   **$4.00**

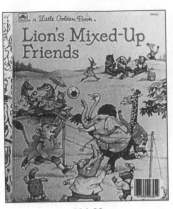

304-62
Lion's Mixed-Up Friends
Illus.: Santoro, Christopher
Author: Hammond, Lucille
1987   24 Pages   **$4.00**

304-60
Little Brown Bear
Illus.: Watson, Wendy
Author: Watson, Wendy
1985   24 Pages   **$4.00**

304-73
Little Cottontail
Illus.: Obligado, Lilian
Author: Memling, Carl
1988   24 Pages   **$4.00**

209-58
**Little Golden Book Of Holidays,
The**
Illus.: Wilburn, Kathy
Author: Lewis, Jean
1985   24 Pages   **$4.00**

211-57
**Little Golden Book Of Hymns,
The**
Illus.: Mitchell, Frances Score
Author: Werner, Elsa, Ebsum, E.D.
1985   24 Pages   **$4.00**

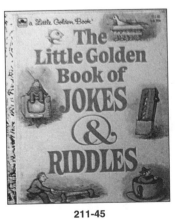

211-45
**Little Golden Book Of Jokes &
Riddles**
Illus.: O'Brien, John
Author: Ebsun, E. D.
1983   24 Pages   **$4.00**

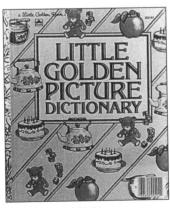

202-51
**Little Golden Picture
Dictionary**
Illus.: De John, Marie
1981   24 Pages   **$4.00**

302-56
Little Lost Kitten
Illus.: Rojankovsky, Feodor
Author: Nina
1951   24 Pages   **$2.00**

211-74
Little Mouse's Book Of Colors
Illus.: Durrell, Julie
Author: Durrell, Julie
1991   24 Pages   **$3.00**

302-51

Little Pussycat

Illus.: Weisgard, Leonard

Author: Brown, Margaret Wise

1979   24 Pages   **$4.00**

307-59

Little Red Riding Hood

Illus.: Winborn, Marsha

Author: Heller, Rebecca

1985   24 Pages   **$4.00**

300-65

Little Red Riding Hood

Illus.: Ewers, Joe

Author: Watts, Mabel

1972   24 Pages   **$3.00**

459-00

Littlest Christmas Elf, The

Illus.: Super, Terri

Author: Buss, Nancy

1987   24 Pages   **$4.00**

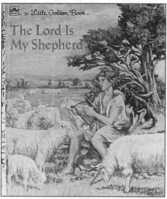

311-60

Lord Is My Shepherd, The 'The Twenty-Third Psalm'

Illus.: Lapadula, Tom

1986   24 Pages   **$4.00**

310-55

Make Way For The Highway (Formerly: Make Way For The Thruway)

Illus.: Gergely, Tibor

Author: Emerson, Caroline

1961   24 Pages   **$4.00**

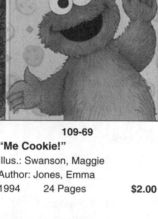

109- 4

Many Faces Of Ernie, The

Illus.: Chartier, Normand

Author: Freudberg, Judy

1979   24 Pages   **$4.00**

109-69

"Me Cookie!"

Illus.: Swanson, Maggie

Author: Jones, Emma

1994   24 Pages   **$2.00**

107-63

Missing Wedding Dress Featuring Barbie, The

Illus.: Westlake, Laura

Author: Krugman, Karen

1986   24 Pages   **$6.00**

98811-01

Mommies All About The Work They Do

Illus.: Meisel, Paul

Author: Lundell, Margo

1997   24 Pages   **$2.00**

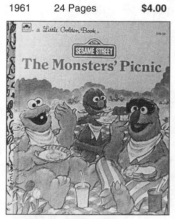

109-59

Monsters' Picnic, The

Illus.: Ewers, Joe

Author: Alexander, Liza

1991   24 Pages   **$2.00**

209-57

Moving Day (Formerly: Goodbye Day)

Illus.: Eugenie

Author: Anderson, Leone Castell

1984   24 Pages   **$4.00**

204-26

Mr. Bear's Birthday

Illus.: Butrik, Lyn Mcclure

Author: Wilcox, Veva

1981   24 Pages   **$4.00**

204-42
Mr. Bell's Fixit Shop
Illus.: Battaglia, Aurelius
Author: Peltzman, Ronne
1981   24 Pages   **$5.00**

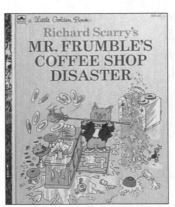

208-67
Mr. Fumble's Coffee Shop Disaster
Illus.: Scarry, Richard
Author: Scarry, Richard
1993   24 Pages   **$2.00**

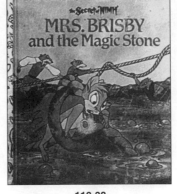

110-38
Mrs. Brisby And The Magic Stone
Illus.: Nicklaus, Carol
Author: Ingoglia, Gina
1982   24 Pages   **$6.00**

111-88
Muppet -Treasure Island
Illus.: Brannon, Tom
Author: Weiss, Ellen
1995   24 Pages   **$2.00**

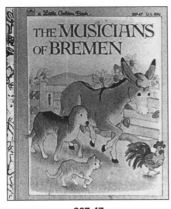

307-47
Musicians Of Bremen, The
Illus.: Schweninger, Ann
Author: Cruise, Ben
1983   24 Pages   **$4.00**

211-58
My Book Of Poems
Illus.: Solly, Gloria
Author: Cruise, Ben
1985   24 Pages   **$4.00**

455
My Christmas Treasury
Illus.: Wiersum, Gale
Author: Emrich, Sylvia
1976   24 Pages   **$4.00**

308-56
My First Book Of Planets
Illus.: Nez, John
Author: Winthrop, Elizabeth
1985   24 Pages   **$4.00**

205-54
My First Book Of Sounds
(Formerly: Bow Wow! Meow!)
Illus.: Schart, Trina
Author: Bellah, Melanie
1963   24 Pages   **$2.00**

203-52
My First Counting Book
(Blue Lettering)
Illus.: Williams, Garth
Author: Moore, Lillian
1957   24 Pages   **$2.00**

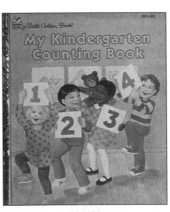

301-68
My Kindergarten Counting Book
Illus.: Mitter, Kathryn
Author: Lundell, Margo
1995   24 Pages   **$2.00**

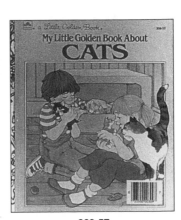

309-57
My Little Golden Book About Cats
Illus.: Leder, Dora
Author: Ryder, Joanne
1988   24 Pages   **$4.00**

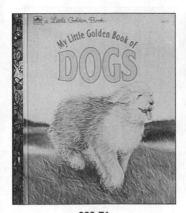

309-71

My Little Golden Book About Dogs

Illus.: Mac Combie, Turi

Author: Lewis, Jean

1983   24 Pages   **$4.00**

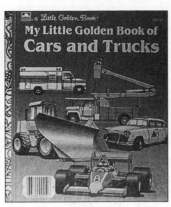

210-57

My Little Golden Book Of Cars And Trucks

Illus.: Courtney, Richard and Trish

Author: Sue, Chari

1990   24 Pages   **$4.00**

211-62

My Little Golden Book Of Fairy Tales

Illus.: Laite, Gordon

1959   24 Pages   **$3.00**

205-57

My Little Golden Book Of Manners

Illus.: Scarry, Richard

Author: Parish, Peggy

1962   24 Pages   **$2.00**

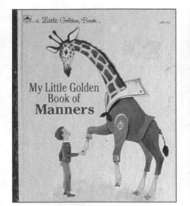

205-64

My Little Golden Book Of Manners

Illus.: Scarry, Richard

Author: Parish, Peggy

1962   24 Pages   **$2.00**

300-69

My Little Golden Mother Goose

Illus.: Brooks, Nan

Author: Cohen, Robin

1994   24 Pages   **$2.00**

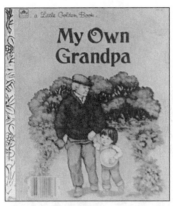

305-53

My Little Golden Word Book

Illus.: Kaufman, Joe

1968   24 Pages   **$2.00**

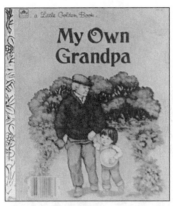

204-56

My Own Grandpa

Illus.: Wilburn, Kathy

Author: Anderson, Leone Castell

1987   24 Pages   **$5.00**

306-68

New Baby, The

(Formerly: Baby Dear)

Illus.: Wilkin, Eloise

Author: Wilkin, Esther

1962   24 Pages   **$3.00**

203-55

New Puppy, The

Illus.: Obligado, Lilian

Author: Daly, Kathleen N.

1969   24 Pages   **$3.00**

450

Night Before Christmas, The

Illus.: Malvern, Corinne

Author: Moore, Clemet C.

1982   25 Pages   **$3.00**

450-10

Night Before Christmas, The

Illus.: Wilburn, Kathy

Author: Moore, Clement C.

1987   24 Pages   **$3.00**

311-64

Noah's Ark

Illus.: La Padula, Tom

Author: Broughton, Pamela

1985   24 Pages   **$4.00**

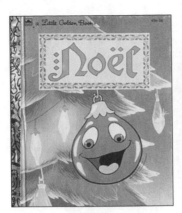

456-16

Noel

Illus.: Langley, Bill A.

Author: Muller, Romeo

1991   24 Pages   **$2.00**

460-15

Nutcracker, The

Illus.: Lanza, Barbara

Author: Balducci, Rita

1991   24 Pages   **$3.00**

304-50

Oh, Little Rabbit!

Illus.: Wilburn, Kathy

Author: Lexau, Joan M.

1989   24 Pages   **$4.00**

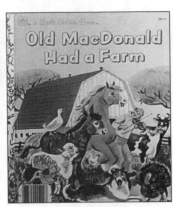

200-55

Old MacDonald Had A Farm

Illus.: Hauge, Carl and Mary

Authors: Hauge, Carl and Mary

1975   24 Pages   **$3.00**

98806-01

Old MacDonald Had A Farm

Illus.: Ember, Kathi

1997   24 Pages   **$2.00**

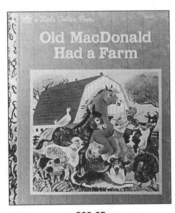

200-65

**Old Mac Donald Had A Farm
(Second Cover)**

Illus.: Hauge, Carl and Mary

Authors: Haug, Carl and Mary

1975   24 Pages   **$3.00**

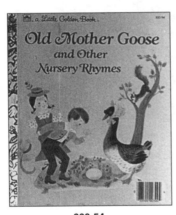

300-54

**Old Mother Goose And Other
Nursery Rhymes**

Illus.: Provensen, Alice and Martin

1988   24 Pages   **$3.00**

208-42

One Of The Family

Illus.: Sanderson, Ruth

Author: Archer, Peggy

1983   24 Pages   **$4.00**

109-67

Oscar's New Neighbor

Illus.: Attinello, Lauren

Author: Margulies, Teddy Slater

1992   24 Pages   **$2.00**

300-41

Owl And The Pussy Cat, The

Illus.: Sanderson, Ruth

Author: Lear, Edward

1982   24 Pages   **$4.00**

300-57

Pied Piper, The

Illus.: Walz, Richard

Author: Benjamin, Alan

1991   24 Pages   **$2.00**

312-04

Pierrot's ABC Garden

Illus.: Lobel, Anita

Author: Lobel, Anita

1992   24 Pages   **$2.00**

111-60

**Pink Panther And Sons Fun At
The Picnic**

Illus.: Gantz, David

Author: Baris, Sandra

1985   24 Pages   **$5.00**

98812-01
Please And Thank You
Illus.: Smath, Jerry
Author: Hazen, Barbara Shook
1997   24 Pages   **$2.00**

312-05
Pocketful Of Nonsense
Illus.: Marshall, James
Author: Marshall, James
1992   24 Pages   **$2.00**

98781-01
The Poky Little Puppy Comes To Sesame Street
Illus.: Brannon, Tom
Author: Dickson, Anna H.
1997   24 Pages   **$2.00**

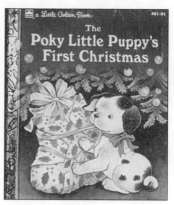

461-01
Poky Little Puppy's First Christmas, The
Illus.: Chandler, Jean
Author: Korman, Justine
1993   24 Pages   **$2.00**

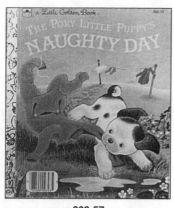

203-57
Poky Little Puppy's Naughty Day, The
Illus.: Chandler, Jean
Author: Chandler, Jean
1985   24 Pages   **$4.00**

302-55
Polly's Pet
Illus.: Rosenberg, Amye
Author: Hammond, Lucille
1984   24 Pages   **$4.00**

111-61
Pound Puppies 'Problem Puppies'
Illus.: Bouman, Carol
Authors: Korman, Justine; Codor, Dick
1986   24 Pages   **$4.00**

110-59
Pound Puppies In Pick Of The Litter
Illus.: Bouman, Carol; Cododr, Dick
Author: Slater, Teddy
1985   24 Pages   **$4.00**

301-10
Prayers For Children
Illus.: Wilkin, Eloise
1952   24 Pages   **$2.00**

301-93
Prayers For Children (Purple Background)
Illus.: Wilkin, Eloise
1952   24 Pages   **$2.00**

107-84
Precious Moments 'Put On A Happy Face'
Illus.: Butcher, Samuel J.
Author: Wiersma, Debbie
1992   24 Pages   **$2.00**

207-68
Princess And The Pea, The
Illus.: Brooks, Nan
Author: Lundell, Margo
1994   24 Pages   **$2.00**

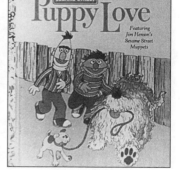

109-46
Puppy Love
Illus.: Nicklaus, Carol
Author: Sunshine, Madeline
1983   24 Pages   **$4.00**

304-52

**Puppy On The Farm
(Duffy On The Farm)**
Illus.: McCue, Lisa
Author: Elson, Marilyn, Elson
1984   24 Pages   **$4.00**

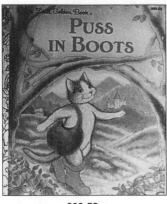

300-58

Puss In Boots
Illus.: McQueen, Lucinda
Authors: Perrault, Charles; Suben, Eric
1990   24 Pages   **$2.00**

98809-01

Pussy Willow
Illus.: Bosson, Jo-Ellen C.
Author: Muldow, Diane
1997   24 Pages   **$2.00**

107-72

Quints 'The Cleanup'
Illus.: Di Ciccio, Sue
Author: McGuire, Leslie
1990   24 Pages   **$3.00**

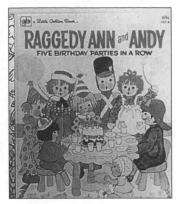

107-4

Raggedy Ann And Andy, 'Five Birthday Parties In A Row'
Illus.: McClain, Mary S.
Author: Daly, Eileen
1979   24 Pages   **$5.00**

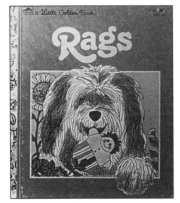

303-44

**Rags
(Brown Background)**
Illus.: Miller, John P.
Author: Scarry, Patricia
1970   24 Pages   **$3.00**

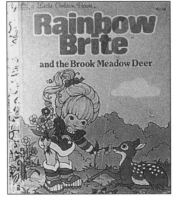

107-48

Rainbow Brite And The Brook Meadow Deer
Illus.: Wilson, Roy
Author: Leslie, Sarah
1984   24 Pages   **$5.00**

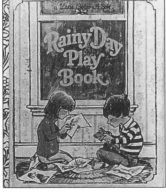

206-35

Rainy Day Play Book
Illus.: Ohlsson, Ib
Author: Young, Susan
1981   24 Pages   **$4.00**

207-57

Rapunzel
Illus.: Beckett, Sheilah
Author: Mayer, Marianna
1991   24 Pages   **$2.00**

109-71

Ready, Set, Go! A Counting Book
Illus.: Cooke, Tom
Author: Jones, Emma
1995   24 Pages   **$2.00**

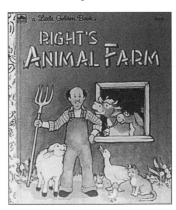

200-9

Right's Animal Farm
Illus.: Goodman, Joan Elizabeth
Author: Goodman, Joan Elizabeth
1983   24 Pages   **$4.00**

110-57

Road Runner 'Mid-Mesa Marathon,' The
Illus.: Costanza, John
Author: Slater, Teddy
1985   24 Pages   **$4.00**

110-58

Robotman And His Friends At School
Illus.: Kostanza, John
Author: Korman, Justine
1985   24 Pages   **$4.00**

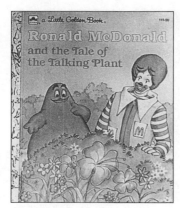

111-50

Ronald McDonald And The Tale Of The Talking Plant

Illus.: Kostanza, John

Author: Albano, John

1984   24 Pages   **$15.00**

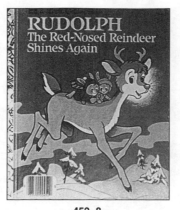

452- 8

Rudolph The Red-Nosed Reindeer Shines Again

Illus.: Baker, Darrell

Author: May, Robert L.

1982   24 Pages   **$4.00**

300-56

Rumpelstiltskin

(Red Golden Book of Fairy Tale)

Illus.: Dugan, William J.

Author: Bros. Grimm

1958   24 Pages   **$3.00**

209-59

Scarebunny, The

Illus.: Wilburn, Kathy

Author: Kunhardt, Dorothy

1985   24 Pages   **$4.00**

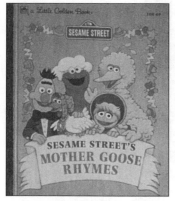

108-69

Sesame Street 'Mother Goose Rhymes'

Illus.: Swanson, Maggie

Author: Allen, Constance

1993   24 Pages   **$2.00**

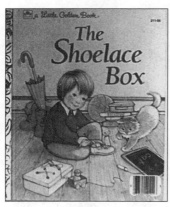

211-56

Shoelace Box, The

Illus.: Wilburn, Kathy

Author: Winthrop, Elizabeth

1984   24 Pages   **$4.00**

204-59

Silly Sisters, The

Illus.: McQueen, Lucinda

Author: Werner, Dave

1989   24 Pages   **$4.00**

98856-00

Sing With Me My Name Is Ernie

Illus.: Swanson, Maggie

Author: Rabe, Tish

1997   24 Pages   **$2.00**

301-41

Sleepy Book, The

(The Golden Sleepy Book)

Illus.: Williams, Garth

Author: Brown, Margaret Wise

1948   24 Pages   **$3.00**

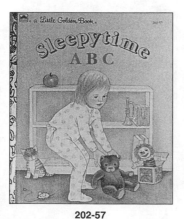

202-57

Sleepytime A B C

Illus.: Chandler, Jean

Author: Campbell, Janet

1991   24 Pages   **$2.00**

208-55

Snoring Monster, The

Illus.: Walz, Richard

Author: Harrison, David L.

1985   24 Pages   **$5.00**

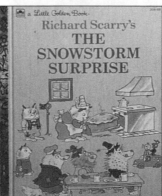

208-69

Snowstorm Surprise

Illus.: Scarry, Richard

Author: Scarry, Richard

1994   24 Pages   **$2.00**

204-54

Store-Bought Doll, The

Illus.: Sanderson, Ruth

Author: Meyer, Lois

1983   24 Pages   **$4.00**

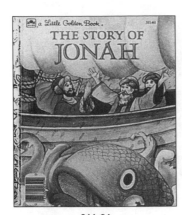

311-61

Story Of Jonah, The

Illus.: Collier, Roberta

Author: Broughton, Pamela

1986   24 Pages   **$4.00**

206-56

Summer Vacation

Illus.: Allert, Kathy

Author: Kunhardt, Edith

1986   24 Pages   **$4.00**

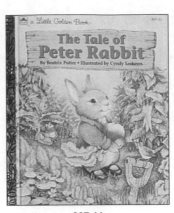

307-11

Tale Of Peter Rabbit, The

Illus.: Szekeres, Cindy

Author: Potter, Beatrix

1993   24 Pages   **$2.00**

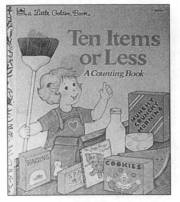

203-54

Ten Items Or Less

Illus.: Super, Terri

Author: Calmerson, Stephanie

1985   24 Pages   **$4.00**

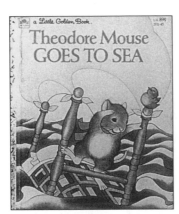

201-45

Theodore Mouse Goes To Sea

Illus.: McQueen, Lucinda

Author: Muntean, Michaela

1983   24 Pages   **$4.00**

204-57

Theodore Mouse Up In The Air

Illus.: McQueen, Lucinda

Author: Muntean, Michaela

1986   24 Pages   **$4.00**

209-64

There Are Tyrannosaurs Trying On Pants In My Bedroom

Illus.: Heartney, Jim

Author: Heartney, Jim

1991   24 Pages   **$6.00**

209- 9

Things I Like
(Originally The Friendly Book)

Illus.: Williams, Garth

Author: Brown, Margaret Wise

1982   24 Pages   **$3.00**

312-02

This Is My Family

Illus.: Mayer, Gina and Mercer

Author: Mayer, Gina and Mercer

1992   24 Pages   **$2.00**

300-66

Thumbelina

Illus.: Tenggren, Gustaf

Author: Anderson, Hans Christian

1981   24 Pages   **$4.00**

300-68

Thumbelina

Illus.: Palmer, Jan

Author: Anderson, Hans Christian

1994   24 Pages   **$2.00**

308-51

Tickety-Tock, What Time Is It?

Illus.: Durrell, Julie

Author: Durrell, Julie

1990   24 Pages   **$2.00**

98837-01

Tickle Me My Name Is Elmo

Illus.: Swanson, Maggie

Author: Allen, Constance

1997   24 Pages   **$2.00**

301-55

Time For Bed

Illus.: Goodman, Joan Elizabeth

Author: Goodman, Joan Elizabeth

1989   24 Pages   **$4.00**

209-60

Timothy Tiger's Terrible Tooth-ache

Illus.: McCue Karsten, Lisa

Author: Wahl, Jan

1988   24 Pages   **$4.00**

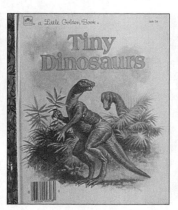

308-58

Tiny Dinosaurs

Illus.: Gino, D'achille

Author: Lindblom, Steven

1988   24 Pages   **$4.00**

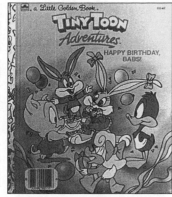

111-67

Tiny Toon Adventures 'Happy Birthday Babs'

Illus.: Costanza, John

Author: Aber, Linda

1990   24 Pages   **$2.00**

111-68

Tiny Toon Adventures 'Lost In The Funhouse'

Illus.: Costanza, John

Author: Harris, Jack

1990   24 Pages   **$2.0**

111-72

Tiny Toon Adventures 'The Adventures Of Buster Hood'

Illus.: Costanza, John

Author: Korman, Justine

1991   24 Pages   **$2.00**

457-42

Tom And Jerry's Merry Christmas

Illus.: Eisenberg, Harvey; Arm-strong, Samuel

Author: Archer, Peter

1954   24 Pages   **$3.00**

207-56

Tortoise And The Hare, The

Illus.: Nez, John

Author: Lundell, Margo

1987   24 Pages   **$4.00**

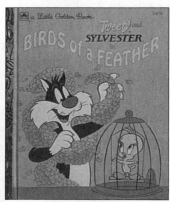

110-78

Tweety And Sylvester In 'Birds Of A Feather'

Illus.: Messerli, Joe

Author: Lewis, Jean

1992   24 Pages   **$2.00**

110-82

Tweety Global Patrol

Illus.: Messerli, Joseph

Author: Lewis, Jean

1993   24 Pages   **$2.00**

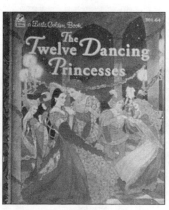

310-64

Twelve Dancing Princesses, The

Illus.: Marvin, Fred

Author: Muldrow, Diane

1995   24 Pages   **$2.00**

454-42

Twelve Days Of Christmas, The

Illus.: Eagle, Mike

1983   24 Pages   **$5.00**

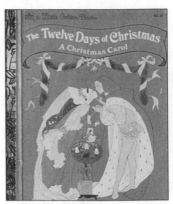

451-16
Twelve Days Of Christmas, The
Illus.: Beckett, Sheilah
1992   24 Pages   **$2.00**

207-72
Ugly Duckling, The
Illus.: McCue, Lisa
Author: Andersen, Hans Christian
1995   24 Pages   **$2.00**

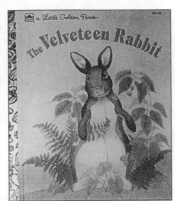

307-68
Velveteen Rabbit, The
Illus.: Sutton, Judith
Author: Williams, Margery
1992   24 Pages   **$2.00**

98795-01
Very Best Easter Bunny, The
Author: Braybrooks, Ann
1997   24 Pages   **$2.00**

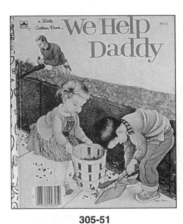

204-25
Very Best Home For Me!, The
(Formerly: Animal Friends)
Illus.: Williams, Garth
Author: Watson, Jane Werner
1953   24 Pages   **$3.00**

206-52
Very Best Home For Me!, The
Illus.: Williams, Garth
Author: Watson, Jane Werner
1953   24 Pages   **$3.00**

107-90
Very Busy Barbie
(1st edition missing text on 11th page)
Illus.: Mortimer, Winslow
Author: Slate, Barbara
1993   24 Pages   **$2.00**

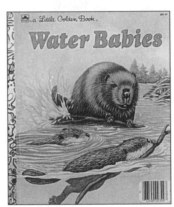

309-59
Water Babies
Illus.: Bonforte, Lisa
Author: Ingoglia, Gina
1990   24 Pages   **$2.00**

305-51
We Help Daddy
(Pipe taken out of pictures)
Illus.: Wilkin, Eloise
Author: Stein, Mini
1962   24 Pages   **$2.00**

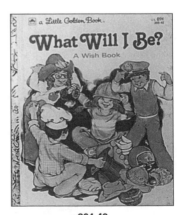

204-42
What Will I Be?
Illus.: Conner, Eulala
Author: Cowles, Kathleen Krull
1979   24 Pages   **$4.00**

206-61
What's Next Elephant?
(Formerly: The Big Elephant)
Illus.: Rojankovsky, Feodor
Author: Jackson, Kathryn and Byron
1949   24 Pages   **$3.00**

108-58
What's Up In The Attic?
Illus.: Cooke, Tom
Author: Alexander, Liza
1987   24 Pages   **$4.00**

311-71
When Bunny Grows Up
(Formerly: The Bunny Book)
Illus.: Scarry, Richard
Author: Scarry, Patsy
1955   24 Pages   **$2.00**

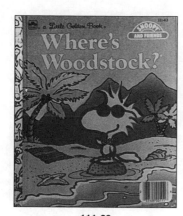

111-63

Where's Woodstock?

Illus.: Schultz, Charles M.; Ellis, Art and Kim

Author: Lundell, Margo

1988   24 Pages   **$3.00**

98770-01

Which Witch Is Which?

Illus.: Brannon, Tom

Author: Muntean, Machaela

1996   24 Pages   **$2.00**

313-03

Whispering Rabbit, The (From The Sleepy Book)

Illus.: Szekeres, Cindy

Author: Brown, Margaret Wise

1992   24 Pages   **$2.00**

Willie Found a Wallet

205-56

Willie Found A Wallet

Illus.: Obligado, Lilian

Author: Markham, Mary Beth

1984   24 Pages   **$4.00**

Disney—By Book Number

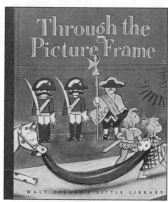

D1

Through The Picture Frame

Illus.: Walt Disney Studios

Author: Edmonds, Robert

1944   24 Pages   **$45.00**

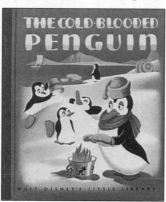

D2

Cold Blooded Penguin, The

Illus.: Walt Disney Studios

Author: Edmonds, Robert

1944   24 Pages   **$40.00**

D3

Dumbo

Illus.: Walt Disney Studios

Author: Walt Disney Studios

1947   42 Pages   **$45.00**

D4

Snow White And The Seven Dwarfs

Illus.: O'Brien, Ken

Author: Bros. Grimm

1948   42 Pages   **$18.00**

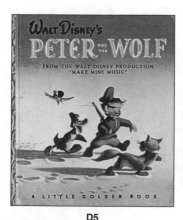

D5

Peter And The Wolf

Illus.: Kelsey, Richard

Authors: Bros. Grimm; Serge; Prokofieff Musi

1947   42 Pages   **$16.00**

D6

Uncle Remus

Illus.: Grant, Bob; Palmer, Marion

Author: Harris, Joel

1947   42 Pages   **$18.00**

D7

Bambi

Illus.: Grant, Bob

Author: Salten, Felix

1948   42 Pages   **$18.00**

D8

Pinocchio

Illus.: Grant, Campbell

Author: Walt Disney Studios

1948   42 Pages   **$18.00**

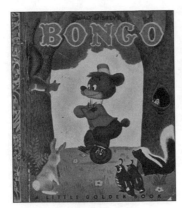

D9

Bongo

Illus.: Grant, Campbell

Author: Lewis, Sinclair

1948   42 Pages   **$18.00**

D10

Three Little Pigs

Illus.: Banta, Milton; Dempster, Al

Author: Walt Disney Studios

1948   42 Pages   **$18.00**

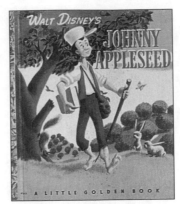

D11

Johnny Appleseed

Illus.: Parmalee, Ted

Author: Walt Disney Studios

1949   42 Pages   **$18.00**

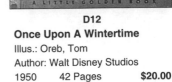

D12

Once Upon A Wintertime

Illus.: Oreb, Tom

Author: Walt Disney Studios

1950   42 Pages   **$20.00**

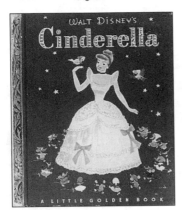

D13

Cinderella

Illus.: Grant, Campbell

Author: Walt Disney Studios

1950   28 Pages   **$16.00**

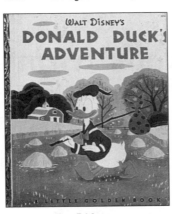

D14

Donald Duck's Adventure

Illus.: Grant, Campbell

Author: Bedford, Annie North

1950   28 Pages   **$16.00**

D15

Mickey Mouse's Picnic

Illus.: Walt Disney Studios

Author: Werner, Jane

1950   28 Pages   **$16.00**

D15

**Mickey Mouse's Picnic
(Blue Background)**

Illus.: Walt Disney Studios

Author: Werner, Jane

1950   24 Pages   **$4.00**

D16

Santa's Toy Shop

Illus.: Dempster, Al

Author: Walt Disney Studios

1950   28 Pages   **$16.00**

D16

Santa's Toy Shop

Illus.: Dempster, Al

Author: Walt Disney Studios

1950   24 Pages   **$4.00**

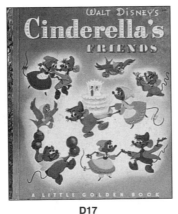

D17

Cinderella's Friends

Illus.: Dempster, Al

Author: Werner, Jane

1950   28 Pages   **$16.00**

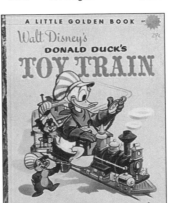

D18

Donald Duck's Toy Train

Illus.: Kelsey, Richard; Justice, Bill

Author: Werner, Jane

1950   28 Pages   **$16.00**

D19

**Alice In Wonderland Meets The
White Rabbit**

Illus.: Dempster, Al

Author: Werner, Jane

1951   28 Pages   **$16.00**

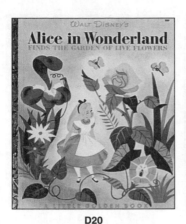

D20

Alice In Wonderland Finds The Garden Of Live Flowers

Illus.: Grant, Cambell

Author: Werner, Jane

1951   28 Pages   **$16.00**

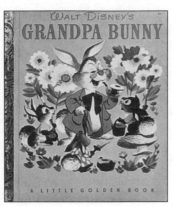

D21

Grandpa Bunny

Illus.: Walt Disney Studios

Author: Werner, Jane

1951   28 Pages   **$25.00**

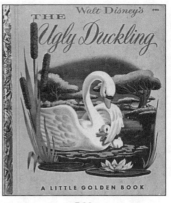

D22

Ugly Duckling, The

Illus.: Maclaughlin, Don

Author: Bedford, Annie North

1952   28 Pages   **$18.00**

D23

Mad Hatter's Tea Party, The

Illus.: Kelsey, Richard; Griffith, Don

Author: Werner, Jane

1952   28 Pages   **$16.00**

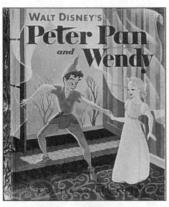

D24

Peter Pan And Wendy

Illus.: Earle, Eyvind

Author: Bedford, Annie North

1952   28 Pages   **$16.00**

D25

Peter Pan And The Pirates

Illus.: Moore, Bob

Author: Barrie, Sir James

1952   28 Pages   **$16.00**

D26

Peter Pan And The Indians

Illus.: Mack, Brice; Kinney, Dick

Author: Bedford, Annie North

1952   28 Pages   **$16.00**

D27

Donald Duck And Santa Claus

Illus.: Dempster, Al

Author: Bedford, Annie North

1952   28 Pages   **$16.00**

D27

Donald Duck And Santa Claus (Yellow Background)

Illus.: Dempster, Al

Author: Bedford, Annie North

1952   24 Pages   **$5.00**

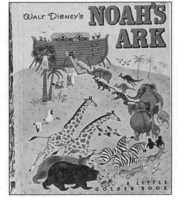

D28

Noah's Ark

Illus.: Grant, Campbell

Author: Bedford, Annie North

1952   28 Pages   **$16.00**

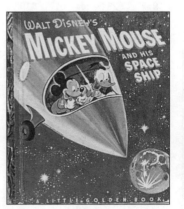

D29

Mickey Mouse And His Space Ship

Illus.: Banta, Milton; Ushler, John

Author: Werner, Jane

1952   28 Pages   **$16.00**

D30

Pluto Pup Goes To Sea

Illus.: Gracey, Yale

Author: Bedford, Annie North

1952   28 Pages   **$16.00**

D31
Hiawatha
Illus.: Walt Disney Studios
Author: Walt Disney Studios
1953   28 Pages   **$16.00**

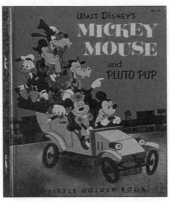

D32
Mickey Mouse And Pluto Pup
Illus.: Grant, Campbell
Author: Beecher, Elizabeth
1953   28 Pages   **$12.00**

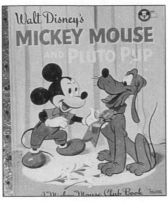

D32
Mickey Mouse And Pluto Pup (2nd Cover)
Illus.: Grant, Campbell
Author: Beecher, Elizabeth
1953   24 Pages   **$15.00**

D33
Mickey Mouse Goes Christmas Shopping
Illus.: Moore, Bob; Atencio, Xavier
Author: Bedford, Annie North
1953   28 Pages   **$15.00**

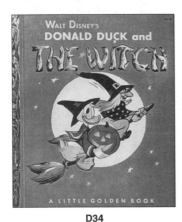

D34
Donald Duck And The Witch
Illus.: Kelsey, Richard
Author: Bedford, Annie North
1953   28 Pages   **$20.00**

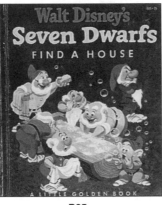

D35
Seven Dwarfs Find A House, The
Illus.: Svendsen, Julius
Author: Bedford, Annie North
1952   28 Pages   **$15.00**

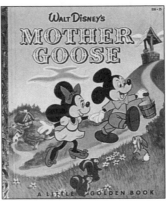

D36
Mother Goose
Illus.: Dempster, Al
Author: Walt Disney Studios
1952   28 Pages   **$30.00**

D37
Ben And Me
Illus.: Grant, Campbell
Author: Lawson, Robert
1954   28 Pages   **$16.00**

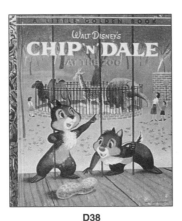

D38
Chip 'n Dale At The Zoo
Illus.: Bosche, Bill
Author: Bedford, Annie North
1954   28 Pages   **$16.00**

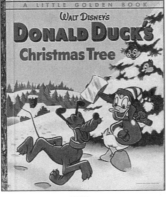

D39
Donald Duck's Christmas Tree
Illus.: Moore, Bob
Author: Bedford, Annie North
1954   28 Pages   **$16.00**

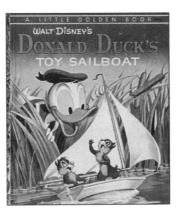

D40
Donald Duck's Toy Sailboat
Illus.: Armstrong, Samuel
Author: Bedford, Annie North
1954   28 Pages   **$16.00**

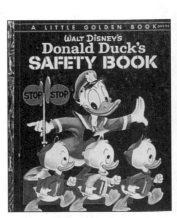

D41
Donald Duck's Safety Book
Illus.: Gonzales, Manuel; Wheeler, George
Author: Bedford, Annie North
1954   28 Pages   **$20.00**

D42

Lady

Illus.: Greene, Ward

Author: Armstrong, Samuel

1954   28 Pages   **$16.00**

D43

Disneyland On The Air

Illus.: Armstrong, Samuel

Author: Bedford, Annie North

1955   28 Pages   **$15.00**

D44

Donald Duck In Disneyland

Illus.: Walt Disney Studios

Author: Bedford, Annie North

1954   28 Pages   **$16.00**

D45

Davy Crockett 'King Of The Wild Frontier'

Illus.: Crawford, Mel

Author: Shapiro, Irwin

1955   28 Pages   **$15.00**

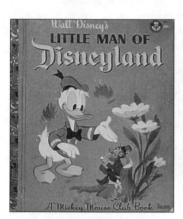

D46

Little Man Of Disneyland

Illus.: Kelsey, Richard

Author: Bedford, Annie North

1955   28 Pages   **$16.00**

D47

Davy Crockett's Keelboat Race

Illus.: Shapiro, Irwin

1955   24 Pages   **$18.00**

D48

Robin Hood

Illus.: Walt Disney Studios

Author: Bedford, Annie North

1955   24 Pages   **$16.00**

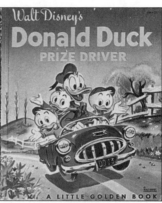

D49

Donald Duck Prize Driver

Illus.: Boyle, Neil

Author: Bedford, Annie North

1956   24 Pages   **$18.00**

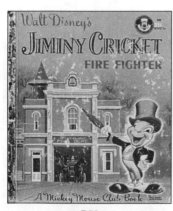

D50

Jiminy Cricket Fire Fighter

Illus.: Armstrong, Samuel

Author: Bedford, Annie North

1956   24 Pages   **$18.00**

D51

Mother Goose

Illus.: Dempster, Al

1952   24 Pages   **$15.00**

D52

Goofy, Movie Star

Illus.: Armstrong, Samuel

Author: Bedford, Annie North

1956   24 Pages   **$18.00**

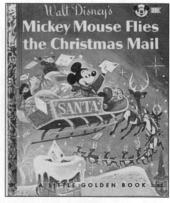

D53

Mickey Mouse Flies The Christmas Mail

Illus.: Svendsen, Julius; Boyle, Neill

Author: Bedford, Annie North

1956   24 Pages   **$16.00**

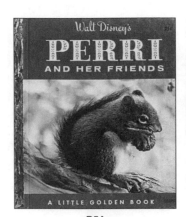

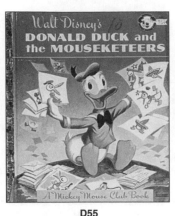

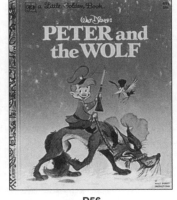

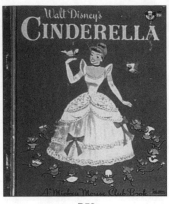

D54

Perri And Her Friends

Illus.: Walt Disney Studios

Authors: Salten, Felix; Bedford, Annie North

1956   24 Pages   **$16.00**

D55

Donald Duck And The Mouseketeers

Illus.: Armstrong, Samuel

Author: Bedford, Annie North

1956   24 Pages   **$16.00**

D56

Peter And The Wolf

Illus.: Kelsey, Richard

Author: Prokofieffl, Serge

1946   24 Pages   **$9.00**

D59

Cinderella

Illus.: Grant, Campbell

Author: Walt Disney Studios

1950   24 Pages   **$10.00**

D60

No Book Published

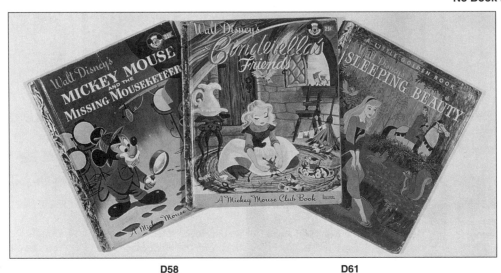

D57

Mickey Mouse And The Missing Mouseketeers

Illus.: Svendsen, Julius; Totten, Bob

Author: Bedford, Annie North

1956   24 Pages   **$12.00**

D58

Cinderella's Friends

Illus.: Dempster, Al

Author: Werner, Jane

1950   24 Pages   **$10.00**

D61

Sleeping Beauty

Illus.: Svendsen, Julius; Armitage, Frank

Author: Bedford, Annie North

1957   24 Pages   **$13.00**

D58

Mickey Mouse Club Stamp Book (Never Printed)

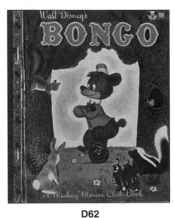

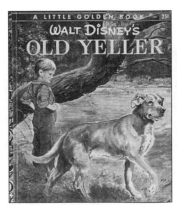

D62

Bongo

Illus.: Grant, Campbell

Author: Lewis, Sinclair

1948   24 Pages   **$10.00**

D63

Scamp

Illus.: Rinaldi, Joe; Mcgary, Norm

Author: Bedford, Annie North

1957   24 Pages   **$12.00**

D64

Paul Revere

Illus.: Luhrs, Paul

Author: Shapiro, Irwin

1957   24 Pages   **$12.00**

D65

Old Yeller

Illus.: Schmidt, Edwin; Daly, E.J.

Author: Shapiro, Irwin

1957   24 Pages   **$13.00**

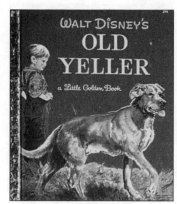

D65

Old Yeller
(Blue Background)
Illus.: Schmidt, Edwin; Daly, E.J.
Author: Shapiro, Irwin
1957   24 Pages   **$6.00**

D66

Snow White
Illus.: O'Brien, Ken; Dempster, Al
Author: Bros. Grimm
1948   24 Pages   **$8.00**

D67

Seven Dwarfs Find A House,
The
Illus.: Svendsen, Julius
Author: Bedford, Annie North
1948   24 Pages   **$9.00**

D68

Zorro
Illus.: Steel, John
Author: Verral, Charles Spain
1958   24 Pages   **$16.00**

D68

Zorro
(Yellow Background)
Illus.: Steel, John
Author: Verral, Charles Spain
1958   24 Pages   **$10.00**

D69

Never Printed

D72

Peter Pan And Wendy
Illus.: Earle, Eyvind
Author: Bedford, Annie North
1952   24 Pages   **$8.00**

D73

Peter Pan And The Pirates
Illus.: Moore, Bob
Author: Walt Disney Studios
1952   24 Pages   **$8.00**

D74

Peter Pan And The Indians
Illus.: Mack, Brice; Kinney, Dick
Author: Bedford, Annie
1952   24 Pages   **$8.00**

D70

Scamp's Adventure
Illus.: Rinaldi, Joe; Boyle, Neil
Author: Bedford, Annie North
1958   24 Pages   **$12.00**

D71

Sleeping Beauty & The Fairies
Illus.: Svendsen, Julius; Strobe,
Dorothy
Author: Bedford, Annie North
1958   24 Pages   **$12.00**

D76

Mickey Mouse And Pluto Pup
Illus.: Grant, Campbell
Author: Beecher, Elizabeth
1953   24 Pages   **$8.00**

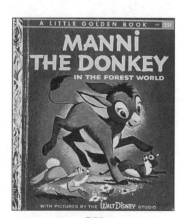

D75

Manni The Donkey
Illus.: Walt Disney Studios
Author: Salten, Felix
1959   24 Pages   **$12.00**

D77

Zorro And The Secret Plan

Illus.: Greene, Hamilton

Author: Verral, Charles Spain

1958   24 Pages   **$14.00**

D78

Three Little Pigs

Illus.: Banta, Milton; Dempster, Al

Author: Walt Disney Studios

1953   24 Pages   **$11.00**

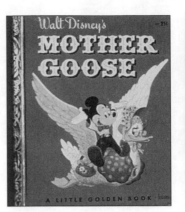

D79

Mother Goose

Illus.: Dempster, Al

Author: Walt Disney Studios

1952   24 Pages   **$8.00**

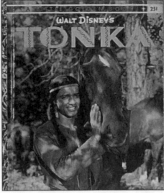

D80

Tonka

Illus.: Walt Disney Studios

Author: Beecher, Elizabeth

1959   24 Pages   **$14.00**

D81

Darby O'Gill

Illus.: Gantz, David

Author: Bedford, Annie North

1959   24 Pages   **$16.00**

D82

Shaggy Dog, The

Illus.: Anderson, Rus

Author: Verral, Charles Spain

1959   24 Pages   **$15.00**

D83

Goliath II

Illus.: Peet, Bill

Author: Peet, Bill

1959   24 Pages   **$15.00**

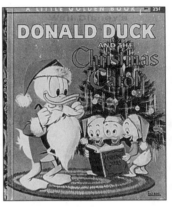

D84

Donald Duck And The Christmas Carol

Illus.: McGary, Norman

Author: Bedford, Annie

1960   24 Pages   **$40.00**

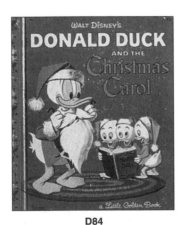

D84

Donald Duck And The Christmas Carol (Green Background)

Illus.: McGary, Norman

Author: Bedford, Annie

1960   24 Pages   **$25.00**

D85

Uncle Remus

Illus.: Harris, Joel Chandler

Author: Palmer, Marion

1947   24 Pages   **$8.00**

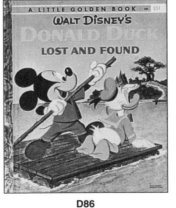

D86

Donald Duck, Lost And Found

Illus.: Grant, Bob; Totten, Bob

Author: Buettner, Carl

1960   24 Pages   **$15.00**

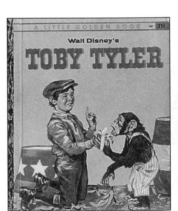

D87

Toby Tyler

Illus.: McKim, Sam

Author: Memling, Carl

1960   24 Pages   **$13.00**

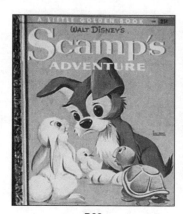

D88
Scamp's Adventure
Illus.: Rinaldi, Joe
Author: Bedford, Annie North
1958   24 Pages   **$10.00**

D89
Lucky Puppy, The
(Window Panes)
Illus.: Hubbard, Allen; Bester, Don
Author: Watson, Jane Werner
1960   24 Pages   **$12.00**

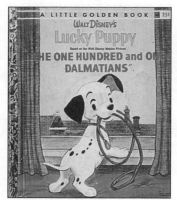

D89
Lucky Puppy, The
(No Window Panes)
Illus.: Hubbard, Allen; Bester, Don
Author: Watson, Jane Werner
1960   24 Pages   **$12.00**

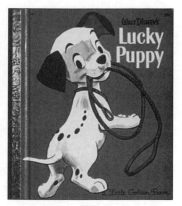

D89
Lucky Puppy, The
(Green Background)
Illus.: Hubbard, Allen; Bester, Don
Author: Watson, Jane Werner
1960   24 Pages   **$8.00**

D90
Bambi
Illus.: Grant, Bob
Author: Salten, Felix
1948   24 Pages   **$8.00**

D90
Bambi
(No trees on cover)
Illus.: Grant, Bob
Author: Salten, Felix
1948   24 Pages   **$3.00**

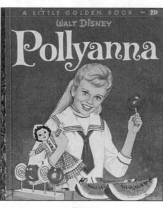

D91
Pollyanna
Illus.: Hedstrom, Karen
Author: Beecher, Elizabeth
1960   24 Pages   **$20.00**

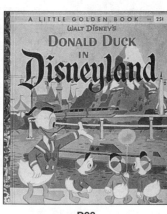

D92
Donald Duck In Disneyland
Illus.: Campbell, Grant
Author: Bedford, Annie North
1960   24 Pages   **$12.00**

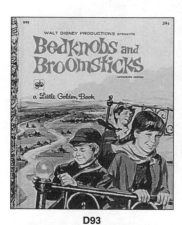

D93
Bedknobs And Broomsticks
Illus.: Walt Disney Studios
Author: Walt Disney Studios
1971   24 Pages   **$8.00**

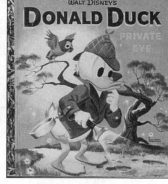

D94
Donald Duck Private Eye
Illus.: White, Al
Author: Buettner, Carl
1961   24 Pages   **$16.00**

D95
Swiss Family Robinson
Illus.: Granger, Paul
Author: Lewis, Jean
1961   24 Pages   **$14.00**

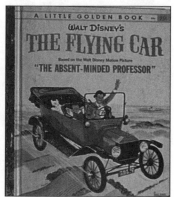

D96
Flying Car, The
Illus.: Irvin, Fred
Author: Verral, Charles Spain
1961   24 Pages   **$15.00**

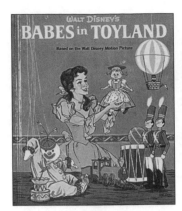

D97

**Babes In Toyland
(Blue Background)**

Illus.: Marshall, Earl and Carol

Author: Hazen, Barbara Shook

1961   24 Pages   **$12.00**

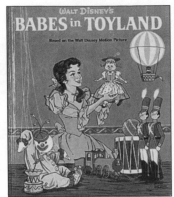

D97

**Babes In Toyland
(Green Background)**

Illus.: Marshall, Earl and Carol

Author: Hazen, Barbara Shook

1961   24 Pages   **$12.00**

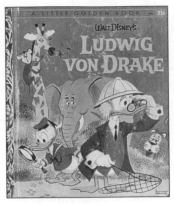

D98

Ludwig Von Drake

Illus.: Pratt, Hawley

Author: Ingoglia, Gina; Sherman,
George

1961   24 Pages   **$15.00**

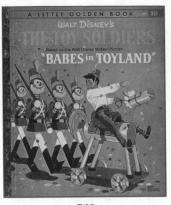

D99

Toy Soldiers, The

Illus.: Thompson, Robert

Author: Hazen, Barbara Shook

1961   24 Pages   **$12.00**

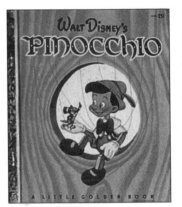

D100

Pinocchio

Illus.: Grant, Campbell

Author: Walt Disney Studios

1948   24 Pages   **$8.00**

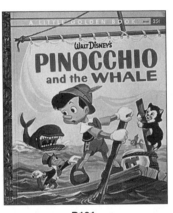

D101

Pinocchio And The Whale

Illus.: White, Al

Author: Ingoglia, Gina

1961   24 Pages   **$20.00**

D102

Big Red

Illus.: Crawford, Mel

Author: Daly, Kathleen N.

1962   24 Pages   **$12.00**

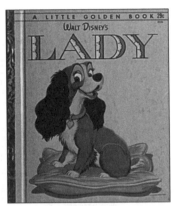

D103

Lady

Illus.: Greene, Ward

Author: Armstrong, Samuel

1954   24 Pages   **$7.00**

D104

Savage Sam

Illus.: Greene, Hamilton

Author: Memling, Carl

1963   24 Pages   **$10.00**

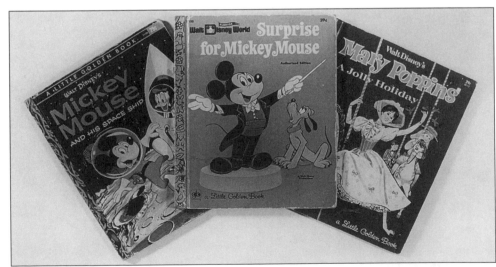

D108

**Mickey Mouse And His Space
Ship**

Illus.: Banta, Milton; Ushler, John

Author: Werner, Jane

1963   24 Pages   **$10.00**

D105

Surprise For Mickey Mouse

Illus.: Walt Disney Studios

Author: Walt Disney Studios

1971   24 Pages   **$5.00**

D112

Mary Poppins, A Jolly Holiday

Illus.: Edwards, Beverly; Jason, Leon

Author: Bedford, Annie North

1964   24 Pages   **$10.00**

D106

Sword In The Stone, The

Illus.: White, Al

Author: Mcgary, Norm

1963   24 Pages   **$12.00**

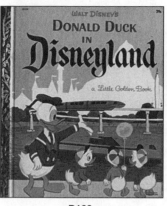

D109

Donald Duck In Disneyland

Illus.: Grant, Campbell

Author: Bedford, Annie North

1954   24 Pages   **$8.00**

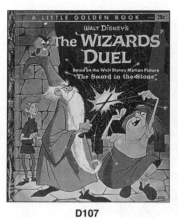

D107

Wizards' Duel, The

Illus.: White, Al

Author: Memling, Carl

1963   24 Pages   **$15.00**

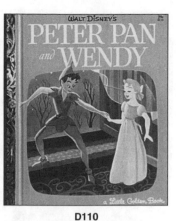

D110

Peter Pan And Wendy

Illus.: Earle, Eyvind

Author: Bedford, Annie North

1952   24 Pages   **$7.00**

D111

Bunny Book

Illus.: Kelsey, Richard; Justice, Bill

Author: Werner, Jane

1951   24 Pages   **$12.00**

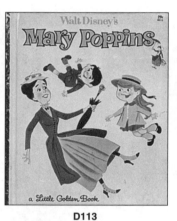

D113

Mary Poppins

Illus.: White, Al

Author: Bedford, Annie North

1964   24 Pages   **$12.00**

D114

Cinderella

Illus.: Grant, Campbell

Author: Walt Disney Studios

1950   24 Pages   **$10.00**

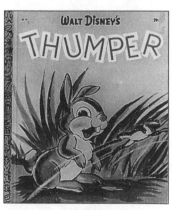

D115

Cinderella's Friends

Illus.: Dempster, Al

Author: Werner, Jane

1950   24 Pages   **$7.00**

D116

Winnie-The-Pooh And The Honey Tree

Illus.: Totten, Bob

Author: Milne, A.A.

1965   24 Pages   **$7.00**

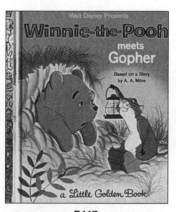

D117

Winnie-The-Pooh Meets Gopher

Illus.: Desantis, George

Author: Milne, A.A.

1972   24 Pages   **$6.00**

D118

Ugly Dachshund, The

Illus.: Crawford, Mel

Author: Memling, Carl

1966   24 Pages   **$15.00**

D119

Thumper

Illus.: Walt Disney Studios

Author: Walt Disney Studios

1942   24 Pages   **$10.00**

D120
Jungle Book, The
Illus.: Crawford, Mel
Author: Bedford, Annie North
1967   24 Pages   **$8.00**

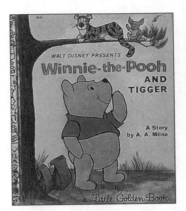

D121
Winnie-The-Pooh And Tigger
Illus.: Walt Disney Studios
Author: Milne, A.A.
1968   24 Pages   **$5.00**

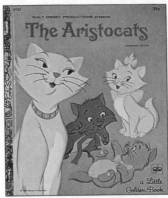

D122
Aristocats, The
Illus.: Walt Disney Studios
Author: Walt Disney Studios
1970   24 Pages   **$12.00**

D123
Disneyland Parade
Illus.: Walt Disney Studios
1971   24 Pages   **$8.00**

D124
Pluto And The Adventure Of The Golden Sceptor
Illus.: Walt Disney Studios
1972   24 Pages   **$6.00**

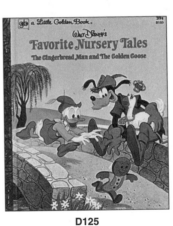

D125
Favorite Nursery Rhymes
Illus.: Walt Disney Studios
1973   24 Pages   **$5.00**

D126
Robin Hood
Illus.: Walt Disney Studios
1973   24 Pages   **$8.00**

D127
Donald Duck And The Witch Next Door
Illus.: Walt Disney Studios
1974   24 Pages   **$6.00**

D128
Robin Hood And The Daring Mouse
Illus.: Walt Disney Studios
1974   24 Pages   **$10.00**

D129
Mickey Mouse And The Great Lot Plot
Illus.: Walt Disney Studios
1974   24 Pages   **$5.00**

D130
Love Bug, The
Illus.: Walt Disney Studios
1974   24 Pages   **$10.00**

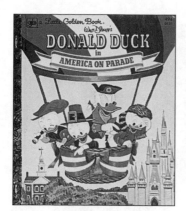

D131
Donald Duck, America On Parade
Illus.: Walt Disney Studios
1975   24 Pages   **$8.00**

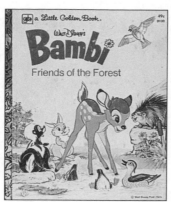

D132
Bambi - Friends Of The Forest
Illus.: Walt Disney Studios
1975   24 Pages   **$5.00**

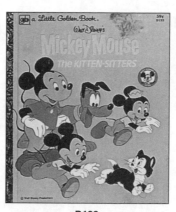

D133
Mickey Mouse, The Kitten Sitters
Illus.: Walt Disney Studios
1976   24 Pages   **$5.00**

D134
Mickey Mouse And The Best-Neighbor Contest
Illus.: Walt Disney Studios
1977   24 Pages   **$5.00**

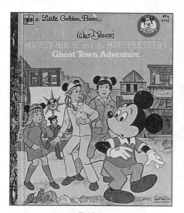

D135
Mickey Mouse And The Mouseketeers Ghost Town Adventure
Illus.: Walt Disney Studios
1977   24 Pages   **$5.00**

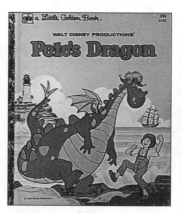

D136
Rescuers, The
Illus.: Walt Disney Studios
1977   24 Pages   **$7.00**

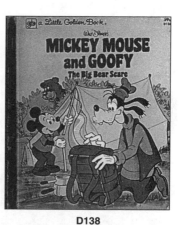

D137
Pete's Dragon
Illus.: Walt Disney Studios
1977   24 Pages   **$7.00**

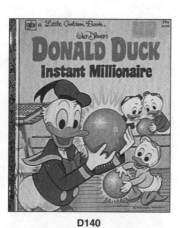

D138
Mickey Mouse and Goofy, The Big Bear Scare
Illus.: Walt Disney Studios
1978   24 Pages   **$5.00**

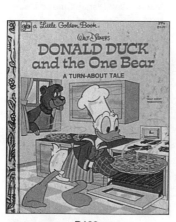

D139
Donald Duck And The One Bear
Illus.: Walt Disney Studios
1978   24 Pages   **$5.00**

D140
Donald Duck 'Instant Millionaire'
Illus.: Walt Disney Studios
Author: Walt Disney Studios
1978   24 Pages   **$7.00**

Disney—New Numbering

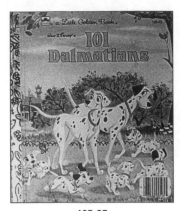

105-65
101 Dalmatians
Illus.: Walt Disney Studios
Author: Walt Disney Studios
1985   24 Pages   **$4.00**

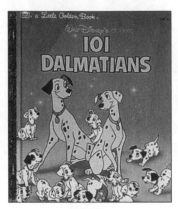

105-81
101 Dalmatians
Illus.: Langley, Bill; Dias, Ron
Author: Korman, Justine
1991   24 Pages   **$2.00**

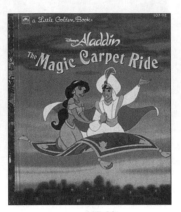

107-88
Aladdin
Illus.: Baker, Darrell
Author: Kreider, Karen
1992   24 Pages   **$3.00**

107-92
Aladdin, 'The Magic Carpet Ride'
Illus.: Thompkins, Kenny; Eggleston, Gary
Author: Margulies, Teddy Slater
1993   24 Pages   **$3.00**

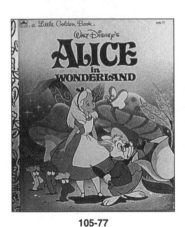

105-77
Alice In Wonderland
Illus.: Mateu, Franc
Author: Slater, Teddy
1991   24 Pages   **$3.00**

105-67
Aristocats, The
(New Cover)
Illus.: Walt Disney Studios
Author: Walt Disney Studios
1970   24 Pages   **$4.00**

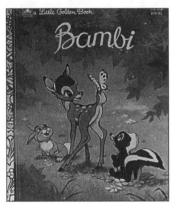

106-41
Bambi
(New Edition)
Illus.: Dias, Ron
Authors: Walt Disney Studios; Salten, Felix
1984   24 Pages   **$4.00**

101-62
Bambi - Friends Of The Forest
Illus.: Walt Disney Studios
Author: Walt Disney Studios
1975   24 Pages   **$5.00**

104-65
Beauty And The Beast
Illus.: Dias, Ron; Gonzalez, Ric
Author: Slater, Teddy
1991   24 Pages   **$3.00**

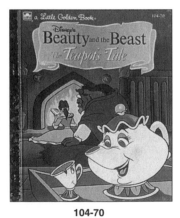

104-70
Beauty And The Beast, 'The Teapot's Tale'
Illus.: Emslie, Peter; Hunt, Darren
Author: Korman, Justine
1993   24 Pages   **$2.00**

105-54
Black Cauldron Taran Finds A Friend, The
Illus.: Walt Disney Studios
Author: Walt Disney Studios
1985   24 Pages   **$5.00**

105-78
Chip 'n Dale Rescue Rangers 'The Big Cheese Caper'
Illus.: Baker, Darrell
Author: Kovacs, Deborah
1991   24 Pages   **$3.00**

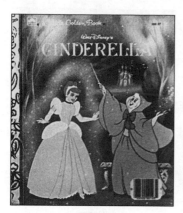

103-57

Cinderella

Illus.: Dias, Ron

Author: Walt Disney Studios

1986   24 Pages $4.00

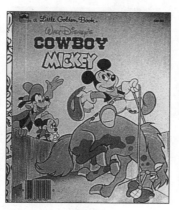

100-63

Cowboy Mickey

Illus.: Guelle

Author: West, Cindy

1990   24 Pages $3.00

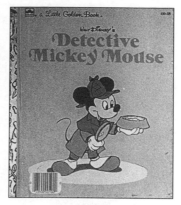

102-67

Darkwing Duck, 'The Silly Canine Caper'

Illus.: Williams, Don

Author: Korman, Justine

1992   24 Pages $3.00

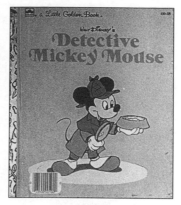

100-58

Detective Mickey Mouse

Illus.: Walt Disney Studios

Author: Walt Disney Studios

1985   24 Pages $5.00

102-56

Donald Duck, Some Ducks Have All The Luck

Illus.: Walt Disney Studios

Author: Walt Disney Studios

1987   24 Pages $5.00

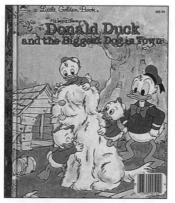

102-55

Donald Duck And The Biggest Dog In Town

Illus.: Walt Disney Studios

Author: Walt Disney Studios

1986   24 Pages $6.00

102-55

Donald Duck And The Big Dog

Illus.: Walt Disney Studios

Author: Walt Disney Studios

1986   24 Pages $5.00

460-13

Donald Duck's Christmas Tree

Illus.: Walt Disney Studios

Author: Walt Disney Studios

1991   24 Pages $2.00

102-59

Donald Duck's Toy Sailboat (New Cover)

Illus.: Walt Disney Studios

Author: Bedford, Annie North

1990   24 Pages $2.00

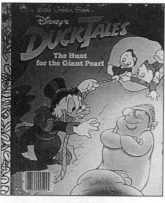

102-58

Duck Tales 'The Hunt For The Giant Pearl'

Illus.: Walt Disney Studios

Author: Walt Disney Studios

1987   24 Pages $4.00

102-57

Duck Tales 'The Secret City Under The Sea'

Illus.: Langley, Bill; Guenther, Annie

Author: Newman, Paul S.

1988   24 Pages $4.00

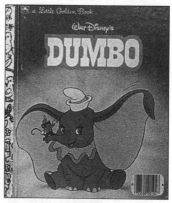

104-59

Dumbo

Illus.: Dias, Ron; Guenther, Annie

Author: Walt Disney Studios

1988   24 Pages $4.00

98737-01

Grand And Wonderful Day, The
Winnie-The-Pooh

Illus.: Baker, Darrell

Author: Packard, Mary

1996   24 Pages $2.00

107-35

Hunchback Of Notre Dame, The

Illus.: Williams, Don

Author: Korman, Justine

1996   24 Pages $2.00

107-36

Hunchback Of Notre Dame, The
'Quasimodo's New Friend'

Illus.: Michaels, Serge; Gutierrez, Edward

Author: Korman, Justine

1996   24 Pages $2.00

104-45

Jungle Book, The

Illus.: Walt Disney Studios

Author: Walt Disney Studios

1967   24 Pages $3.00

105-55

Lady And The Tramp
(Cover Variation)

Illus.: Walt Disney Studios

Author: Walt Disney Studios

1954   24 Pages $3.00

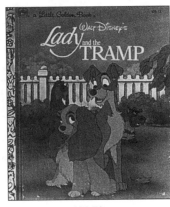

105-72

Lady And The Tramp

Illus.: Dias, Ron; Langley, Bill

Author: Slater, Teddy

1991   24 Pages $2.00

107-93

Lion King, The

Illus.: Williams, Don; Russell, H. R.

Author: Korman, Justine

1994   24 Pages $3.00

107-97

Lion King, The, 'No Worries'

Illus.: Williams, Don; Russell, H. R.

Author: Korman, Justine

1995   24 Pages $3.00

107-52

Lion King, The, 'The Cave Mon-
ster'

Illus.: Williams, Don

Author: Korman, Justine

1996   24 Pages $3.00

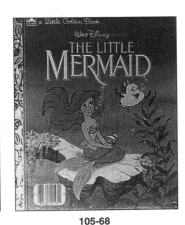

105-68

Little Mermaid, The

Illus.: Dias, Ron

Author: Teitelbaum, Michael

1989   24 Pages $7.00

105-68

Little Mermaid, The 'Ariel's
Underwater Adventure'

Illus.: Dias, Ron

Author: Teitelbaum, Michael

1989   24 Pages $4.00

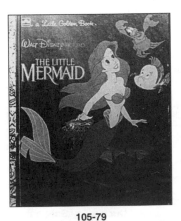

105-79

Little Mermaid, The
(Pictures From Movie)

Illus.: Teitelbaum, Michael

1991   24 Pages $4.00

105-85

**Little Mermaid, The
(Whole Story)**

Illus.: Di Ciccio, Sue

Author: Teitelbaum, Michael

1992   24 Pages   **$3.00**

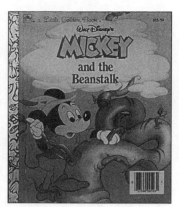

103-59

Mickey And The Beanstalk

Illus.: Ross, Sharon

Author: Anastasio, Dina

1988   24 Pages   **$4.00**

100-61

**Mickey Mouse, 'Those Were
The Days'**

Illus.: Mones

Author: Carey, Mary

1988   24 Pages   **$4.00**

100-60

**Mickey Mouse Heads For The Sky
(1st Edition)**

Illus.: Walt Disney Studios

Author: Walt Disney Studios

1987   24 Pages   **$4.00**

100-68

**Mickey Mouse Heads For The Sky
(Airplane Hanger in Background)**

Illus.: Walt Disney Studios

Author: Walt Disney Studios

1987   24 Pages   **$3.00**

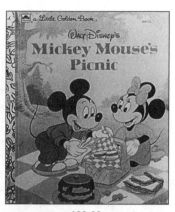

100-62

Mickey Mouse's Picnic

Illus.: Walt Disney Studios

Author: Werner, Jane

1950   24 Pages   **$3.00**

459-9

Mickey's Christmas Carol

Illus.: Dias, Ron

Author: Walt Disney Studios

1983   24 Pages   **$5.00**

100-65

Minnie's Slumber Party

Author: West, Cindy

1990   24 Pages   **$3.00**

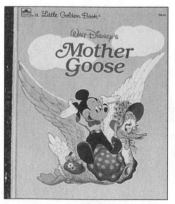

106-61

Mother Goose

Illus.: Walt Disney Studios

Author: Dempster, Al

1952   24 Pages   **$2.00**

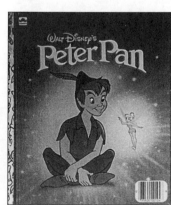

104-60

Peter Pan

Illus.: Dias, Ron

Author: Coco, Eugene Bradley

1989   24 Pages   **$4.00**

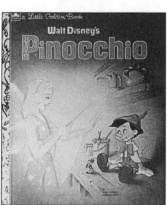

104-52

**Pinocchio
(New Cover)**

Illus.: Walt Disney Studios

Author: Walt Disney Studios

1948   24 Pages   **$2.00**

104-61

**Pinocchio
(New Art)**

Illus.: Dias, Ron

Author: Coco, Eugene Bradley

1990   24 Pages   **$3.00**

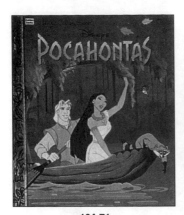

104-71

Pocahontas

Illus.: Williams, Don

Author: Korman, Justin

1995   24 Pages   **$2.00**

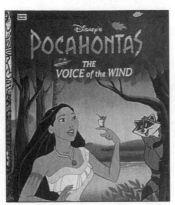

104-72

Pocahontas, 'The Voice Of The Wind'

Illus.: Emslie, Peter; Williams, Don

Author: Korman, Justine

1995   24 Pages   **$2.00**

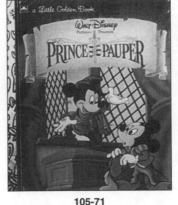

105-71

Prince And The Pauper, The

Illus.: Schroeder, Russel; Williams, Don

Author: Manushkin, Fran

1990   24 Pages   **$4.00**

105-70

Rescuers Down Under, The

Illus.: Mateu, Franc

Author: Teitelbaum, Michael

1990   24 Pages   **$4.00**

105-69

**Rescuers, The
(New Cover)**

Illus.: Walt Disney Studios

Author: Walt Disney Studios

1977   24 Pages   **$3.00**

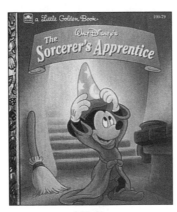

103-56

Return To Oz, 'Dorothy Saves The Emerald City'

Illus.: Walt Disney Studios

Author: Walt Disney Studios

1985   24 Pages   **$9.00**

105-56

Return To Oz, 'Escape From The Witch's Castle'

Illus.: Walt Disney Studios

Author: Walt Disney Studios

1985   24 Pages   **$9.00**

104-56

Sleeping Beauty

Illus.: Dias, Ron

Author: Walt Disney Studios

1986   24 Pages   **$5.00**

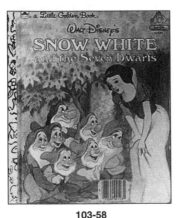

103-58

Snow White And The Seven Dwarfs

Illus.: Dias, Ron

Author: Walt Disney Studios

1984   24 Pages   **$5.00**

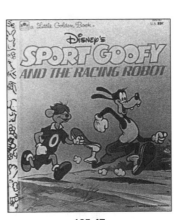

100-79

Sorcerer's Apprentice, The

Illus.: Emslie, Peter

Author: Ferguson, Don

1994   24 Pages   **$3.00**

105-47

Sport Goofy And The Racing Robot

Illus.: Walt Disney Studios

Author: Walt Disney Studios

1984   24 Pages   **$8.00**

104-62

Tale Spin 'Ghost Ship'

Illus.: Di Ciccio, Sue

Author: Helfer, Andrew

1991   24 Pages   **$3.00**

106-59

Three Little Pigs

Illus.: Walt Disney Studios

Authors: Dempster, Al; Banta, Milt

1953   24 Pages   **$2.00**

103-44

Toad Flies High

Illus.: Walt Disney Studios

Author: Grahame, Kenneth

1982   24 Pages   **$5.00**

105-66

Uncle Remus

(Cover Variation)

Illus.: Walt Disney Studios

Author: Walt Disney Studios

1947   24 Pages   **$2.00**

100-77

Where's Fifi?

(Minnie 'n Me)

Illus.: Vaccaro Associates, Inc.

Author: Calder, Lyn

1992   24 Pages   **$2.00**

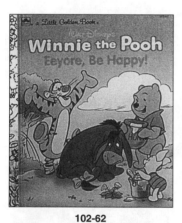

102-62

Winnie The Pooh 'Eeyore, Be Happy!'

Illus.: Walt Disney Studios

Author: Ferguson, Don

1991   24 Pages   **$3.00**

101-26

Winnie-The-Pooh 'A Day To Remember'

Illus.: Walt Disney Studios

Author: Walt Disney Studios

1980   24 Pages   **$10.00**

101-54

Winnie-The-Pooh And The Honey Patch

Illus.: Walt Disney Studios

Author: Walt Disney Studios

1980   24 Pages   **$5.00**

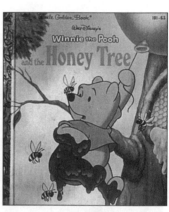

101-63

Winnie The Pooh And The Honey Tree

Illus.: Hicks, Russell

Author: Packard, Mary

1994   24 Pages   **$2.00**

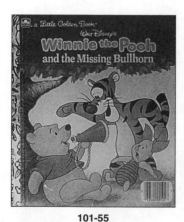

101-55

Winnie The Pooh And The Missing Bullhorn

Illus.: Schroeder, Russel; Williams, Don

Author: Teitelbaum, Michael

1990   24 Pages   **$3.00**

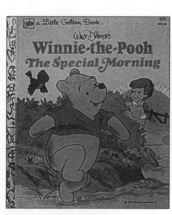

101-25

Winnie-The-Pooh 'The Special Morning'

Illus.: Walt Disney Studios

Author: Walt Disney Studios

1980   24 Pages   **$8.00**

98267-01

Winnie-The-Pooh And The Honey Tree

(New Book)

Illus.: Hicks, Russell

Author: Packard, Mary

1996   24 Pages   **$2.00**

New Disney Titles

98765-01
Eeyore, You're The Best
Illus.: Kurtz, John
Author: Braybrooks, Ann
1996　　24 Pages　　**$0.00**

98828-01
Enchanted Christmas, The
(Beauty And The Beast)
Illus.: Nowell, Alan
Author; Muldrow, Diane
1997　　24 Pages　　**$2.00**

98800-01
Hercules
Illus.: Emslie, Peter & Williams, Don
Author: Korman, Justine
1997　　24 Pages　　**$2.00**

98801-01
Hercules A Race To The Rescue
Illus.: Cardona Studio
Author: Bazaldua, Barbara
1997　　24 Pages　　**$2.00**

98798-01
Pooh And The Dragon
Illus.: Baker, Darrell
Author: Braybrooks, Ann
1997　　24 Pages　　**$2.00**

98841-00
Pooh's Grand Adventure 'The
Search For Christopher Robin'
Author: Kormas, Justine Rigol
1997　　24 Pages　　**$2.00**

98797-01
Quasimodo The Hero
Illus.: Williams, Don
Author: Bazaldua, Barbara
1997　　24 Pages　　**$2.00**

Activity Books

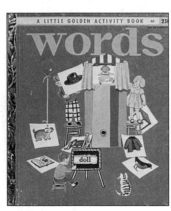

A1
Words
(Wheel Book)
Illus.: Elliott, Gertrude
Author: Chambers, Selma Lola
1955　　20 Pages　　**$18.00**

A2
Circus Time
(Wheel Book)
Illus.: Gergely, Tibor
Author: Conger, Marion
1955　　20 Pages　　**$18.00**

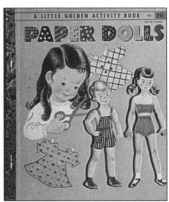

A3
Paper Dolls
Illus.: Miloche, Hilda; Kane, Wilma
Authors: Miloche, Hilda; Kane, Wilma
1951　　20 Pages　　**$100.00**

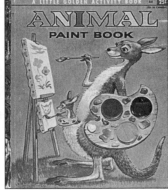

A4
Animal Paint Book
(3 Paints In Cover)
Illus.: Helwig, Hans
Author: Helweg, Hans
1955　　20 Pages　　**$45.00**

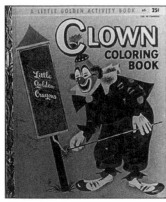

A5
Clown Coloring Book
Illus.: Seiden, Art
1955　　20 Pages　　**$75.00**

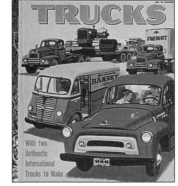

A6
Trucks (2 Paper Model Trucks)
Illus.: Quigley, Ray
Author: Jackson, Kathryn
1955　　24 Pages　　**$100.00**

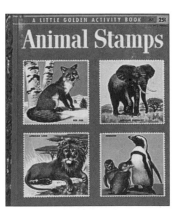

A7
Animal Stamps
Illus.: Irving, James Gordon; Dugan,
William
Author: Daly, Kathleen
1955　　24 Pages　　**$30.00**

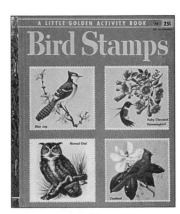

A8
Bird Stamps
Illus.: Irving, James Gordon
Author: Daly, Kathleen
1955　　24 Pages　　**$30.00**

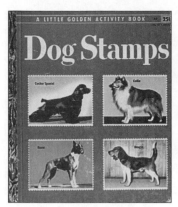

A9

Dog Stamps

Illus.: Megargee, Edwin

Author: Mcgovern, Ann

1955   24 Pages   **$30.00**

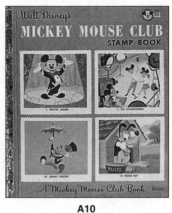

A10

Mickey Mouse Club Stamp Book

Illus.: Svendsen, Julius

Author: Daly, Kathleen

1956   24 Pages   **$40.00**

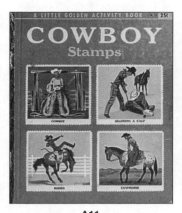

A11

Cowboy Stamps

Illus.: Scarry, Richard

Author: Shimek, John Lyle

1957   24 Pages   **$35.00**

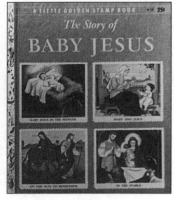

A12

Story of Baby Jesus, The

Illus.: Wilkin, Eloise

1957   24 Pages   **$100.00**

A13

Indian Stamps

Illus.: Schmidt, Edwin

Author: Huberman, Edward

1957   24 Pages   **$30.00**

A14

Ginger Paper Doll

Illus.: Saviozzi, Adriana Mazza

Author: Daly, Kathleen

1957   24 Pages   **$75.00**

A15

Trim The Christmas Tree

Illus.: Henderson, Doris and Marion

Author: Nast, Elsa Ruth

1957   24 Pages   **$45.00**

A16

Count To Ten (Wheel Book)

Illus.: Krush, Bob

Author: Moore, Lilian

1957   24 Pages   **$18.00**

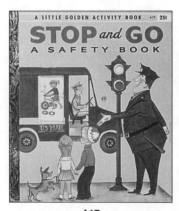

A17

Stop And Go (Wheel Book)

Illus.: Anglund, Joan Walsh

Author: Higgins, Loyta

1957   24 Pages   **$40.00**

A18

ABC Around The House (Wheel Book)

Illus.: La Mont, Violet

1957   24 Pages   **$18.00**

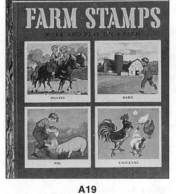

A19

Farm Stamps

Illus.: Saviozzi, Adriana Mazza

Author: Jackson, Kathryn

1957   24 Pages   **$30.00**

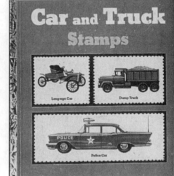

A20

Car And Truck Stamps

Illus.: Dreany, E. Joseph

Author: Daly, Kathleen

1957   24 Pages   **$30.00**

A21
Let's Save Money
(Wheel Book)
Illus.: La Mont, Violet
Author: Higgins, Loyta
1958   24 Pages   **$18.00**

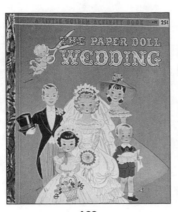

A22
Paper Doll Wedding
Illus.: Miloche, Hilda; Kane, Wilma
Authors: Miloche, Hilda; Kane, Wilma
1958   24 Pages   **$125.00**
A23
Never Printed

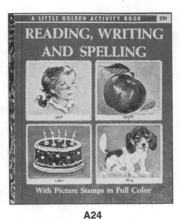

A24
Reading, Writing And Spelling Stamps
Illus.: Obligado, Lilian; La Mont, Violet
Author: Kaufman, Carol
1959   24 Pages   **$30.00**

A25
Insect Stamps
Illus.: Zallenger, Jean
Author: Martin, Richard A.
1958   24 Pages   **$30.00**

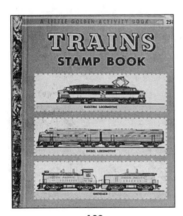

A26
Trains Stamp Book
Illus.: Dreany, E. Joseph
Author: Daly, Kathleen N.
1958   24 Pages   **$30.00**

A27
Firemen And Fire Engine Stamps
Illus.: Scarry, Richard
Author: Goldsmith, Jane
1959   24 Pages   **$40.00**

A28
Colors
(Wheel Book)
Illus.: Scarry, Richard
Author: Daly, Kathleen N.
1959   24 Pages   **$18.00**

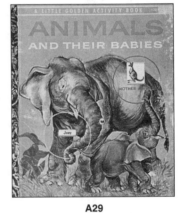

A29
Animals And Their Babies
(Wheel Book)
Illus.: Obligado, Lilian
Author: Hazen, Barbara
1959   24 Pages   **$18.00**

A30
Words
(Wheel Book)
Illus.: Elliott, Gertrude
Author: Chambers, Selma Lola
1955   24 Pages   **$18.00**

A31
Mike And Melissa
(Paper Dolls)
Illus.: Saviozzi, Adriana Mazza
Author: Watson, Jane
1959   24 Pages   **$125.00**

A32
Ginger Paper Doll
Illus.: Saviozzi, Adriana Mazza
Author: Daly, Kathleen
1957   24 Pages   **$80.00**

A33
Sleeping Beauty
(Paper Dolls)
Illus.: Svendsen, Julius; Armitage, Frank
Author: Walt Disney Studios
1959   24 Pages   **$150.00**

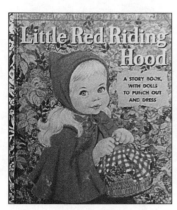

A34
Red Riding Hood
(Paper Dolls)
Illus.: Koester, Sharon
1959   24 Pages   **$150.00**
A35
Never Printed

A36
Cinderella
(Paper Dolls)
Illus.: Laite, Gordon
1960   24 Pages   **$150.00**
A37
Three Kittens (Animated Book)
(Never Printed)

A39
My Little Golden Calendar
Illus.: Scarry, Richard
1961   24 Pages   **$75.00**
A38
Sparky The Fireman (Animated Book)
(Never Printed)

A40
Never Printed

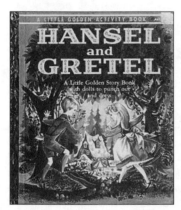

A41
Hansel & Gretel
(Paper Dolls)
Illus.: Martin, Judy and Barry
Author: Bros. Grimm
1961   24 Pages   **$150.00**
A42
Never Printed

A43
Count To Ten
(Wheel Book)
Illus.: Krush, Beth
Author: Moore, Lillian
1957   24 Pages   **$18.00**

A44
ABC Around The House
(Wheel Book)
Illus.: La Monte, Violet
Author: Daly, Kathleen
1957   24 Pages   **$18.00**

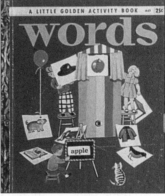

A45
Words
(Wheel Book)
Illus.: Elliott, Gertrude
Author: Chambers, Selma Lola
1955   24 Pages   **$18.00**
A46
Never Printed

A47
Paper Dolls
Illus.: Miloche, Hilda; Kane, Wilma
Authors: Miloche, Hilde; Kane, Wilma
1951   24 Pages   **$100.00**

A48
Gordon's Jet Flight
(Paper Model Jet)
Illus.: Crawford, Mel
Author: Glasson, Naomi J.
1961   24 Pages   **$100.00**

A49
Snow White And Rose Red
(Paper Doll) (Never Printed)
Laite, Gordon
24 Pages

A50
Trim The Christmas Tree
(Paper Christmas Decoration)
Illus.: Henderson, Doris and Marion
Author: Nast, Elsa Ruth
1957   24 Pages   **$30.00**

119

A51
Never Printed

A52
Tammy
(Paper Doll)
Illus.: Salva, Ada
Author: Daly, Kathleen N.
1963   24 Pages $60.00

Ding Dong School Books

On Nov. 24, 1952, *Ding Dong School* appeared on NBC Television. Hosted by Dr. Frances Horwich, the show was taken off the air in 1956 for lack of sponsors and because of its limited appeal. One of Miss Frances' characters which appeared occasionally on the show was a puppet named Lucky Rabbit. Lucky later appeared in his own book under numbers 221 and Din 7, which was later done as a Little Golden Book, *Lucky Rabbit*.

Rand McNally originally published the series, A Ding Dong School Book, around July 1953. These books were produced in the same format as Little Golden Books, with the exception of a silver foil spine. All of the titles produced by Rand McNally contained 28 pages. Books were numbered 200 to 225, with printing run listed on the last page at the bottom left.

Miss Frances was very upset with the quality of TV shows being produced for children, and in 1959 she was finally able to get *Ding Dong School* reproduced. The show ran for another 130 episodes before being taken off the air forever.

During the show's new release (1959–1960), Golden Press published A Ding Dong School Book. The numbers ran from DIN 1 to DIN 8 and contained 24 pages. First printings will have the "A" on the last page, bottom right.

No. 200
Your Friend, The Policeman
Illus.: Nebbe, William
Author: Horwich, Dr. Frances R.
1953   24 Pages $8.00

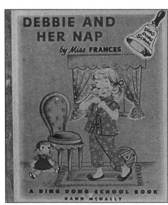

No. 201
Debbie And Her Nap
Illus.: Wehr, Adele
Author: Horwich, Dr. Frances R.
1953   24 Pages $10.00

No. 202
Suitcase With A Surprise, A
Illus.: Tellingen, Ruth Van
Author: Horwich, Dr. Frances R.
1953   24 Pages $8.00

No. 203
Big Coal Truck, The
Illus.: Nebbe, William
Author: Horwich, Dr. Frances R.
1953   24 Pages $8.00

No. 204

I Decided
Illus.: Opitz, Marge
Author: Horwich, Dr. Frances R.
1953　　24 Pages　　**$8.00**

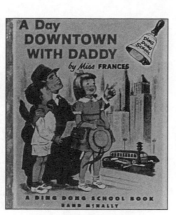

No. 205

Day Downtown With Daddy, A
Illus.: Pickett, Helen
Author: Horwich, Dr. Frances R.
1953　　24 Pages　　**$8.00**

No. 206

Dressing Up
Illus.: Evans, Katherine
Author: Horwich, Dr. Frances R.
1953　　24 Pages　　**$8.00**

No. 207

Daddy's Birthday Cakes
Illus.: Tellingen, Ruth Van
Author: Horwich, Dr. Frances R.
1953　　24 Pages　　**$8.00**

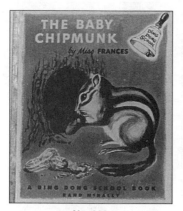

No. 208

Baby Chipmunk, The
Illus.: Nebbe, William
Author: Horwich, Dr. Frances R.
1953　　24 Pages　　**$8.00**

No. 209

Peek In
Illus.: Evans, Katherine
Author: Horwich, Dr. Frances R.
1954　　24 Pages　　**$8.00**

No. 210

Growing Things
Illus.: Tellingen, Ruth Van
Author: Horwich, Dr. Frances R.
1954　　24 Pages　　**$8.00**

No. 211

My Goldfish
Illus.: McLean, Mina Grow
Author: Horwich, Dr. Frances R.
1954　　24 Pages　　**$8.00**

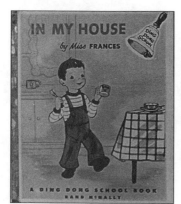

No. 212

In My House
Illus.: Friend, Esther
Author: Horwich, Dr. Frances R.
1954　　24 Pages　　**$8.00**

No. 213

Dolls Of Other Lands
Illus.: Flory, Jane
Author: Horwich, Dr. Frances R.
1954　　24 Pages　　**$10.00**

No. 214

My Big Brother
Illus.: McLean, Mina Grow
Author: Horwich, Dr. Frances R.
1954　　24 Pages　　**$8.00**

No. 215

Robin Family, The
Illus.: Ozone, Lucy
Author: Horwich, Dr. Frances R.
1954　　24 Pages　　**$8.00**

No. 216
Grandmother Is Coming
Illus.: Tellingen, Ruth Van
Author: Horwich, Dr. Frances R.
1954   24 Pages   **$8.00**

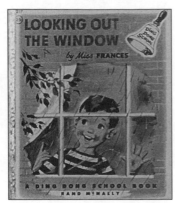

No. 217
Looking Out The Window
Illus.: Shortall, Leonard
Author: Horwich, Dr. Frances R.
1954   24 Pages   **$8.00**

No. 218
Our Baby
Illus.: Pointer, Priscilla
Author: Horwich, Dr. Frances R.
1955   24 Pages   **$18.00**

No. 219
Jingle Bell Jack
Illus.: Evans, Katherine
Author: Horwich, Dr. Frances R.
1955   24 Pages   **$10.00**

No. 220
Mr. Myer's Cow
Illus.: Nebbe, William
Author: Horwich, Dr. Frances R.
1955   24 Pages   **$8.00**

No. 221
Lucky Rabbit
Illus.: Bendel, Ruth
Author: Horwich, Dr. Frances R.
1955   24 Pages   **$10.00**

No. 222
Magic Wagon, The
Illus.: Webbe, Elizabeth
Author: Horwich, Dr. Frances R.
1955   24 Pages   **$8.00**

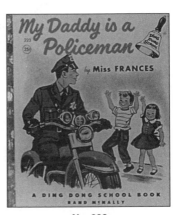

No. 223
My Daddy Is A Policeman
Illus.: Pickett, Helen
Author: Horwich, Dr. Frances R.
1956   24 Pages   **$8.00**

No. 224
Here Comes The Band
Illus.: Timmins, William
Author: Horwich, Dr. Frances R.
1956   24 Pages   **$8.00**

No. 225
We Love Grandpa
Illus.: Grider, Dorothy
Author: Horwich, Dr. Frances R.
1956   24 Pages   **$8.00**

Ding Dong School Books by Golden Press:

These books were published in the Little Golden Book format. The authors, illustrators, and copyrights of these books are the same as the Rand McNally editions.

Printing of these books appears to have been late 1959 or early 1960.

No. DIN1
Jingle Bell Jack
Illus.: Evans, Katherine
Author: Horwich, Dr. Frances R.
1955   24 Pages   **$10.00**

DIN2
Mr. Meyer's Cow
Illus.: Nebbe, William
Author: Horwich, Dr. Frances R.
1955   24 Pages   **$10.00**

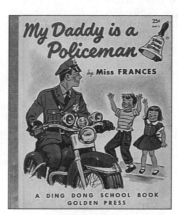

No. DIN3
My Daddy Is A Policeman
Illus.: Prickett, Helen
Author: Horwich, Dr. Frances R.
1956   24 Pages   **$12.00**

No. DIN4
We Love Grandpa
Illus.: Grider, Dorothy
Author: Horwich, Dr. Frances R.
1956   24 Pages   **$10.00**

No. DIN5
Here Comes The Band
Illus.: Timmins, William
Author: Horwich, Dr. Frances R.
1956   24 Pages   **$10.00**

DIN6
Magic Wagon, The
Illus.: Webbe, Elizabeth
Author: Horwich, Dr. Frances R.
1955   24 Pages   **$10.00**

No. DIN7
Lucky Rabbit
Illus.: Bendel, Ruth
Author: Horwich, Dr. Frances R.
1955   24 Pages   **$10.00**

No. DIN8
Our Baby
Illus.: Pointer, Priscilla
Author: Horwich, Dr. Frances R.
1955   24 Pages   **$20.00**

My First Golden Learning Library

My First Golden Learning Library was sixteen volumes of more than 1,500 full-color illustrations. Each book was identical in size to a Little Golden Book, with the foil spines being different solid colors. The books were written by Jane Werner Watson, with the consulting help of Berth Morris Parker, author of *The Gold Book Encyclopedia*, and the illustrations were done by William Dugan. Each book contained 24 pages, and they were released around August 1965. The books were sold in a boxed carrying case and may have been sold individually. (Value: Boxed Set $70.00-$90.00.)

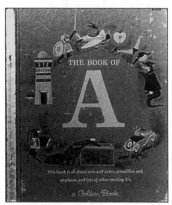

No. 615
Book Of A, The
Illus.: Dugan, William J.
Author: Watson, Jane Werner
1965   24 Pages   **$4.00**

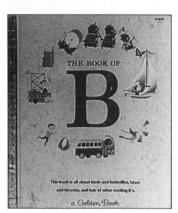

No. 616
Book Of B, The
Illus.: Dugan, William
Author: Watson, Jane Werner
1965   24 Pages   **$4.00**

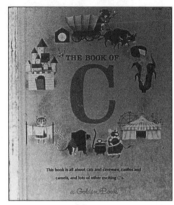

No. 617
Book Of C, The
Illus.: Dugan, William
Author: Watson, Jane Werner
1965   24 Pages   **$4.00**

No. 618
Book Of D E, The
Illus.: Dugan, William
Author: Watson, Jane Werner
1965   24 Pages   **$4.00**

No. 619
Book Of F, The
Illus.: Dugan, William
Author: Watson, Jane Werner
1965   24 Pages   **$4.00**

No. 620
Book Of G H, The
Illus.: Dugan, William
Author: Watson, Jane Werner
1965   24 Pages   **$4.00**

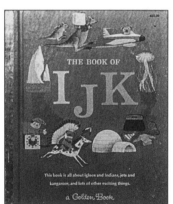

No. 621
Book Of I J K, The
Illus.: Dugan, William
Author: Watson, Jane Werner
1965   24 Pages   **$4.00**

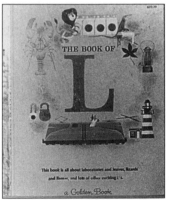

No. 622
Book Of L, The
Illus.: Dugan, William
Author: Watson, Jane Werner
1965   24 Pages   **$4.00**

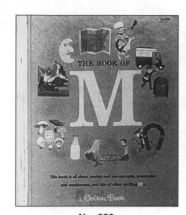

No. 623
Book Of M, The
Illus.: Dugan, William
Author: Watson, Jane Werner
1965   24 Pages   **$4.00**

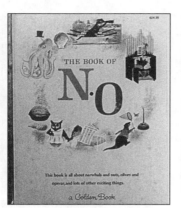

No. 624
Book Of N O, The
Illus.: Dugan, William
Author: Watson, Jane Werner
1965   24 Pages   **$4.00**

No. 625
Book Of P Q, The
Illus.: Dugan, William
Author: Watson, Jane Werner
1965   24 Pages   **$4.00**

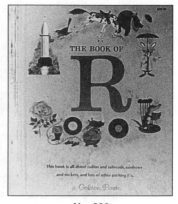

No. 626
Book Of R, The
Illus.: Dugan, William
Author: Watson, Jane Werner
1965   24 Pages   **$4.00**

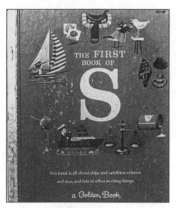

No. 628
First Book Of S, The
Illus.: Dugan, Willlam
Author: Watson, Jane Werner
1965   24 Pages   **$4.00**

No. 628
Second Book Of S, The
Illus.: Dugan, William
Author: Watson, Jane Werner
1965   24 Pages   **$4.00**

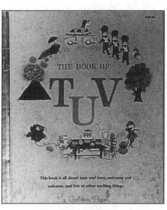

No. 629
Book Of T U V, The
Illus.: Dugan, William
Author: Watson, Jane Werner
1965   24 Pages   **$4.00**

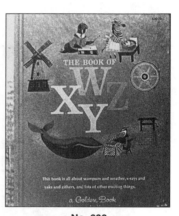

No. 630
Book Of W X Y Z, The
Illus.: Dugan, William
Author: Watson, Jane Werner
1965   24 Pages   **$4.00**

Giant Little Golden Books

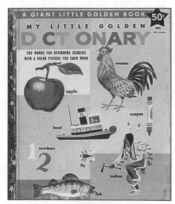

No. 5001
My Little Golden Dictionary
Illus.: Scarry, Richard
Authors: Reed, Mary; Oswald, Edith
1957   56 Pages   **$15.00**

No. 5002
Five Bedtime Stories
Illus.: Tenggren, Gustaf
1957   56 Pages   **$15.00**

No. 5003
My Christmas Treasury
Illus.: Hess, Lowell
1957   72 Pages   **$20.00**

No. 5003
My Christmas Treasury
Illus.: Hess, Lowell
1957   56 Pages   **$12.00**

No. 5004
Walt Disney's Favorite Stories
Illus.: Walt Disney Studios
Author: Walt Disney Studios
1957   56 Pages   **$25.00**

No. 5005
Donald Duck Treasury
Illus.: Walt Disney Studios
Author: Walt Disney Studios
1957   56 Pages   **$25.00**

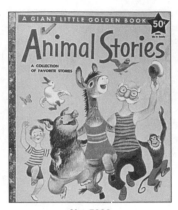

No. 5006
Animal Stories
Illus.: Gergely, Tibor
Authors: Miryam; Hoffman, Beth;
Duplaix, George
1957   56 Pages   **$16.00**

No. 5007
Mother Goose
Illus.: La Mont, Violet
Author: Folk Tales
1958   56 Pages   **$16.00**

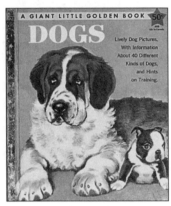

No. 5008
Dogs
Illus.: Gergely, Tibor
Author: Daly, Kathleen N.
1957   56 Pages   **$16.00**

No. 5009
Nursery Tales
Illus.: Scarry, Richard
1958   72 Pages   **$16.00**

No. 5010
Wild Animals
Illus.: Suschitzky, W.
1958   72 Pages   **$16.00**

No. 5011
Birds
Illus.: Wilkin, Eloise
Author: Watson, Jane Werner
1958   56 Pages   **$16.00**

No. 5012
Adventures Of Lassie, The
Illus.: Crawford; Dreany, E. Joseph;
Ames, Lee
Authors: Verral, Charles Spain; Hill,
Monica
1958   56 Pages   **$25.00**

No. 5013
Kittens
Illus.: Masha; Tenggren, Gustaf;
Wilkin, Eloise
Authors: Schurr, Cathleen; Scarry,
Patricia
1958   56 Pages   **$16.00**

No. 5014
Walt Disney's Storytime Book
Illus.: Walt Disney Studios
Author: Walt Disney Studios
1958   56 Pages   **$27.00**

No. 5015
Off To School
Illus.: Malvern, Corrine; La Mont,
Violet
Author: Jackson, Kathleen
1658   56 Pages   **$16.00**

No. 5016
Mother Goose Rhymes
Illus.: Rojankovsky, Feodor
1958   56 Pages   **$16.00**

No. 5017
Plants And Animals
Illus.: Chaiko, Ted
Author: Watson, Jane Werner
1958   56 Pages   **$16.00**

No. 5018
Train Stories
Illus.: Gergely, Tibor; Seiden, Art
Authors: Potter, Mariam; Crampton; Brown
1958   56 Pages   **$16.00**

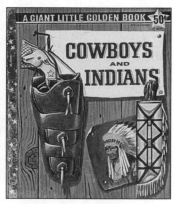

No. 5019
Cowboys And Indians
Illus.: Scarry, Richard
Author: Lindquist, Willis
1958   72 Pages   **$20.00**

No. 5020
Fairy Tales
Illus.: Hess, Lowell
Author: Anderson, Hans; H.C. White
1958   72 Pages   **$18.00**

No. 5021
Captain Kangaroo
Illus.: Seiden, Art; Schmidt, Edwin
Author: Daly, Kathleen N.; Lindsay, Barb
1959   56 Pages   **$20.00**

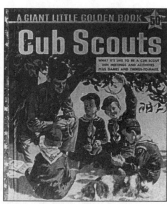

No. 5022
Cub Scouts
Illus.: Crawford, Mel
Author: Brian, Bruce
1959   56 Pages   **$25.00**

No. 5024
Quiz Fun
Illus.: Gergely, Tibor
Authors: Elmo, Horace; Hullick, Nancy Fielding
1959   56 Pages   **$16.00**

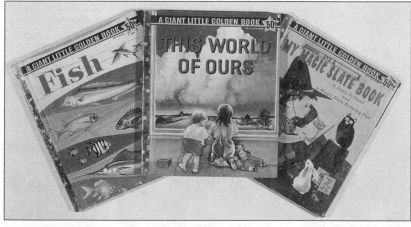

No. 5023
Fish
Illus.: Jean Zallinger
Author: Herbert S. Zimm
1959   56 Pages   **$16.00**

No. 5026
This World Of Ours
Illus.: Wilkin, Eloise
Author: Watson, Jane Werner
1959   56 Pages   **$25.00**

No. 5025
My Magic Slate Book
Illus.: Dugan, William
Author: Memling, Carl
1959   22 Pages   **$30.00**

No. 5027
My Pets
Illus.: Wilkin, Eloise
Author: Scarry, Patsy
1959   56 Pages   **$30.00**

5028
Silly Will
(Cut-Out Book) (Never Printed)

Eager Reader Series

These books were identical to Little Golden Books, but with a solid gold spine. Each book had large type and easy words for beginning readers. A boxed set of eight titles sold for $3.95 when they were released around July 1975. The books also sold individually with a 39-cent cover price starting around 1974.

No. 800
New Home For Snow Ball, A
Illus.: Pyk, Jan
Author: Bowden, Joan
1974   24 Pages $5.00

No. 801
Pet In The Jar, The
Illus.: Stang, Judy
Author: Stang, Judy
1974   24 Pages $5.00

No. 802
Hat For The Queen, A
Illus.: Giacomini, Olindo
Author: Bacon, Joan Chase
1974   24 Pages $5.00

No. 803
Boo And The Flying Flews
Illus.: Leake, Donald
Author: Bacon, Joan Chase
1974   24 Pages $5.00

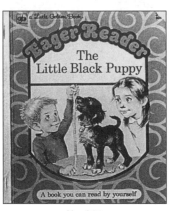

No. 804
Little Black Puppy, The
Illus.: Obligado, Lilian
Author: Zolotow, Charlotte
1974   24 Pages $5.00

No. 805
Who Took The Top Hat Trick?
Illus.: Cummins, Jim
Author: Bowden, Joan
1974   24 Pages $5.00

No. 806
Cat Who Stamped His Feet
Illus.: O'sullivan, Tom
Author: Wright, Betty Ren
1974   24 Pages $5.00

No. 807
Elephant On Wheels
Illus.: Scott, Jerry
Author: Thacher, Alida McKay
1974   24 Pages $5.00

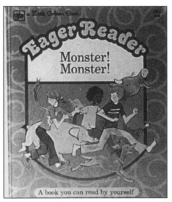

No. 808
Monster! Monster!
Illus.: Fry, Rosalind
Author: Harrison, David L.
1974   24 Pages $5.00

No. 809
Bear's Surprise Party
Illus.: Scott, Jerry
Author: Bowden, Joan
1974   24 Pages $5.00

Little Golden Book Land Series

In 1989, a series of eight Little Golden Books were supposed to be released with *Tootle*, *Poky*, *Shy Little Kitten*, *Saggy Baggy Elephant*, *Baby Brown Bear*, *Scuffy The Tugboat*, and *The Tawny Scrawny Lion*. Each character's story was to take place in the magical Little Golden Book Land. Two characters did not appear in their scheduled Little Golden Books, Scuffy and Baby Brown Bear, but they did appear in larger-sized editions.

Two different back covers were printed for these Lit-tle Golden Books, and both are marked as first editions. The first original back cover has a full-color picture of the Little Golden Book gang taking a ride through the mountains on Tootle. The second back cover is the standard yellow one used on all Little Golden Books of the period.

Value: Mountain back cover $5.00; regular back cover $2.00

No. GBL370
Welcome To Little Golden Book Land
Illus.: Mateu
Author: West, Cindy
1989　24 Pages　**$5.00**

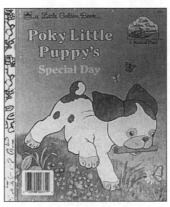

No. GBL371
Poky Little Puppy's Special Day
Illus.: Jones, Keenan
Author: West, Cindy
1989　24 Pages　**$5.00**

No. GBL372
Shy Little Kitten's Secret Place
Illus.: Jones, Keenan
Author: Lawrence, Jim
1989　24 Pages　**$5.00**

No. GBL373
Saggy Baggy Elephant No Place For Me
Illus.: Walz, Richard
Author: Ingoglia, Gina
1989　24 Pages　**$5.00**

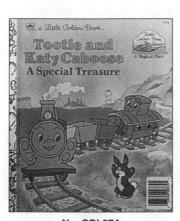

No. GBL374
Tootle And Katy Caboose 'A Special Treasure'
Illus.: Mones, Isidre
Author: Ingoglia, Gina
1989　24 Pages　**$5.00**

No. GBL377
Tawny Scrawny Lion 'Saves The Day'
Illus.: Ellis, Art & Kim
Author: Teitelbaum, Michael
1989　24 Pages　**$5.00**

Back cover for Little Golden Book Land books

Newer Books in the Little Golden Book Family

The following series of book titles are listed for informational purposes only. None of these books are listed in this guide's master indexes. Since most of these books are still found regularly at garage sales and flea markets for as low as 25 cents, the values given are really higher than what you normally would pay.

Big Little Golden Books (1986-1988)

Value: $2.00-$3.00

10250	Bugs Bunny and the Health Hog
10252	Grab-Bag Party, The
10253	House that Enough, The
10254	Little Raccoon Takes Charge
10255	Little Raccoon's Nighttime Adventure
10256	Little Sister
10257	Old Friends, New Friends
10258	Pandas Take a Vacation, The
10259	Peter Pan in Tinker Bell and the Pirates
10260	Secret Life of Walter Kitty, The
10261	Sleep-Over Visit, The
10262	Bialosky and the Big Parade Mystery
10263	Jumping Jacky
10264	King Mitch Had an Itch
10265	Best Nickname, The
10266	Perfect Picnic, The
10267	Red Jacket Mix-Up, The
10268	Right House for Rabbit, The
10269	Ordinary Amos and the Amazing Fish
10270	Puppy Nobody Wanted, The (Pound Puppies)
10271	Animals in the Woods
10272	Dinosaurs
10273	How Come You're So Shy?
10274	Let's Go Fishing!
10275	Big Little Golden Book of Knock-Knocks, The
10276	Big Little Golden Book of Funny Poems
10277	Lady Lovely Locks 'Silkypup's Butterfly Adventure'
10278	Duck Tales: The Road to Riches
10279	Big Little Book of Planets, The
10280	Snoopy, The Worlds Greatest Arthur
10281	It's How You Play the Game (Snoopy)
10282	Garfield the Fussy Cat
10283	Dinosaur Discoveries
10284	No Stage Fright For Me!
10285	Be Kind to Animals!
10290	Animals Merry Christmas, The
10291	My Christmas Tree

Little Little Golden Books

Value: .25¢-$1.00 each
(1988-present)
Packaged two on a card.
Value per card: $1.00

1	Poky Little Puppy, The
2'	Fire Engines
3	Little Red Hen, The
4	Saggy Baggy Elephant, The
5	Scuffy the Tugboat
6	Theodore Mouse Goes to Sea
7	Curious Little Kitten Around the House
8	Tootle
9	Fuzzy Duckling, The
10	Sleepy Book, The
11	We Help Mommy
12	Baby Farm Animals
13	Animals of Farmer Jones, The
14	We Help Daddy
15	Four Little Kittens
16	Three Little Pigs, The
17	Very Best Home For Me, The
18	Little Red Riding Hood
19	Four Puppies
20	Tawny Scrawny Lion
21	Walt Disney's Pinocchio
22	Three Bears, The
23	Walt Disney's Snow White and the Seven Dwarfs
24	Jack and the Beanstalk
25	I Can Dress Myself
26	Big Bird's Busy Day
27	We Like Kindergarten
28	My First Book of Sounds
29	Walt Disney's Peter Pan
30	Walt Disney's Dumbo
31	Welcome to Little Golden Book Land
32	Poky Little Puppy's Special Day
33	Walt Disney's Mickey's Christmas Carol
34	Walt Disney's Santa's Toyshop
35	Baby's Christmas
36	Christmas Story, The
37	Rudolph the Red-Nosed Reindeer
38	Littlest Christmas Elf, The
39	Baby Animals
40	Bunnies' ABC
41	Walt Disney's Bambi
42	Walt Disney's Alice in Wonderland
44	Walt Disney's Cinderella
45	Nutcracker, The
46	Christmas Pageant
47	Colorful Mouse, The
48	Blue Barry Bear Counts From 1 to 20

First Little Golden Books

(1981-present)
Value: $.50-$1.50

Alice's First Word
Animal Fair
Animal Homes
Baby Animals on the Farm
Baby's First Book
Baby Mickey Plays Follow-the-Leader
Baby Mickey's Book of Shapes
Baby Mickey's Book of Sounds
Bambi & the Butterfly
Barney's Sand Castle

Beauty and the Beast 'The Tale of Chip the Teapot'
Big Birds Busy Day
Busy Timmy
Chip 'n Dale Book Of Seasons
Christmas Pageant, The
Count's Poems, The (Sesame Street)
Count to Ten (Sesame Street)
Country Mouse and the City Mouse
Curious Little Kittens First Christmas, The
Day In The Park, A
Dog Goes To Nursery School
Dumbo's Book of Colors!
Five Little Bunnies
Friendly Beast, The
Fuzzy Duckling
Gingerbread Man, The
Good Morning, Muffin Mouse
Good Night Magellan (Eureeka's Castle)
Happy Easter Mother Duck
Happy Man and His Dump Truck, The
Henry and Theresa's Race
I Can Dress Myself (Sesame Street)
I Like to Help My Mommy
I'll Share With You
I Can Fly
I Love You More
It's Bedtime
It's Christmas
Jack Prelutsky's Sweet and Silly Muppet Poems
Jungle Book, The (Mowgli and the Jungle Animals)
Katie the Kitten
Let's Go All Around The Neighborhood
Let's Play Peek-a-Boo
Little Calf That Couldn't Moo, The
Little Duck and the New Baby
Little Duck's Moving Day
Little Quack and Baby Ducky
Little Red Hen, The
Little Squirt 'The Fire Engine'
Martha's House
Max Helps Out
Meet My Buddy
Muffin Mouse On The Go
My Alphabet
My Book Of Words
My First Book of Animal Sounds

My Book of the Seasons
My Little Book of Poems
My Little Book of Prayers
My Little Book of Words
My Little Mother Goose
My Alphabet
Med's Number Book
Over In The Meadow
Panda Bear's Paint Box
Panda Bear's Secret
Perfect Lunch, The (Eureeka's Castle)
Pinky's First Spring Day
Pinocchio
Poky Little Puppy's Wonderful Winter Day, The
Polite Elephant
Richard Scarry's Christmas Mice
Richard Scarry's Gingerbread Man
Saggy Baggy Elephant's Birthday
Shake a Leg (Sesame Street)
Simon Visits the Doctor
Simon Visits the Doctor
Sleepy Story, A
Stable in Bethlehem
Stevie's Tricycle
Sweet and Silly Muppet Poems
Sweetie Book of ABC, The (Tiny Toons)
Three Bears, The
Three Billy Goat Gruffs
Three Little Kittens, The
Three Little Pigs, The
To Grandmother's House We Go
Truck That Drove All Night, The
Tweety Trap!, The
Tommy's New Bed
Very Best Picnic, The
Visit From Grandma and Grandpa, A
Wait Disney's Bambi & the Butterfly
What Am I?
What Kind of Truck?
Wheels on the Bus, The
When Dog Grows Up!
When Dog Was Little
Where's Goldie
Who Says That?
Winnie-the-Pooh and the Pebble Hunt
Yes I Love You

Promotional and Special Little Golden Books

Burger King

Value: $3.00

Sometime in the late 1980s, Burger King gave away *The Train To Timbuctoo* during its TRAK-PAK CLASSIC TRAIN BOOKS promotion. Three other stories, *The Circus Train*, *Roundabout Train*, and *My Little Book Of Trains*, all previous Tell-A-Tales, were also given away.

Chick-fil-A

Meal bag value: $4.00-$8.00

Books value: $3.00-$4.00

Chick-fil-A, a fast-food chain specializing in the original, boneless breast of chicken sandwich, gave eight Little Golden Book titles away in its children's meal in 1995. The meal was served in a LGB character's decorated bag with puzzles and games. Of the 620 family owned stores in the chain, most are located in the Southeast and Midwest.

The back cover has the chain's logo and lists the following books: *Poky Little Puppy*, *Tawny Scrawny Lion*, *Saggy Baggy Elephant*, *Sailor Dog*, *Little Red Caboose*, *Velveteen Rabbit*, *Little Red Riding Hood*, and the *Elves and the Shoemaker*.

Hardee's

Value: Box with book $14.00

Book only $ 3.00

Hardee's gave away a Little Little Golden Book with its children's meal in the late 1980s and early 1990s. Each meal box was printed with characters from the book that was enclosed. There were three series of four books each.

Series One

Poky Little Puppy, The

Little Red Riding Hood (Illustrated by Watts)

Little Red Hen, The

Three Little Pigs, The

Series Two

Three Little Kittens

Little Red Caboose,

The Three Bears, The

Old MacDonald Had A Farm

Series Three (Pound Puppies & Pound Purries)

Pick Of The Litter

Puppy Nobody Wanted, The

Problem Puppies

Kitten Companions

Kimbies

Value: $3.00-$5.00

KIMBIES disposable diapers were packaged with soft-cover Little Golden Books around 1976. The books' covers and insides were identical, except for a black and white photo of a box of KIMBIES diapers in either the left or right bottom corners. The back covers had full-page ads for KIMBIES. No numbers or prices were noted on the covers.

The following are some of the titles given away. There may have been others.

The Lively Little Rabbit

The Poky Little Puppy

The Shy Little Kitten

The Saggy Baggy Elephant

The Little Red Caboose

Scuffy the Tugboat

Tootle

Wienerschnitzel Hot Dogs

Value: $3.00

Wienerschnitzel hot-dog shops gave out regular hard-cover Little Golden Books, with its logo in the bottom left corner, sometime around 1987–1988. I know of only the following two titles, but there may have been more:

The Poky Little Puppy's Naughty Day

When You Were A Baby

Crispy Critters® Special Edition Little Golden Books

Value: Crispy's Bedtime Book: $15.00

Others: $3.00-$5.00

These books were packaged on the backs of the cereal's box. The two titles were *Crispy In The Birthday Band* and *Crispy In No Place Like Home*. A third title, *Crispy's Bedtime Book*, was also available, but only through the mail. The stories used character animal shapes found in the cereal. Each book was published in 1987 and contained 36 pages. The books were all written by Justine Korman, illustrated by Dave Yaegle, and painted by Mike Favata.

Cleo Storybook Greetings

Value: $3.00

Three Little Golden Book titles were printed in this series of four holiday stories. They were manufactured and distributed by Cleo, Inc., a Gibson Greeting Company, in 1991. These softcover Little Golden Books came with an envelope to be mailed like a Christmas card. Measuring 6 inches by 7-3/4 inches, these books were a little smaller then a Little Golden Book, with the same 24 pages. They originally sold for around $2.00.

Titles:

Mickey's Christmas Carol

Frosty The Snowman (illustrated By Terri Super)

Rudolph The Red-Nosed Reindeer

Non-LGB Title

The Night Before Christmas

Author: Moore, Clement

Illus.: Szekeres, Cyndy

A Little Golden Book Special Edition

Value: $8.00

Six titles were done in 1985 with dust jackets. These books, measuring 7 inches by 8-1/4 inches, were a little larger than the normal Little Golden Book. These titles were also released as normal Little Golden Books with copyrights of 1985.

11630 Cheltenham's Party

11631 A Fox Jumped Up One Winter's Day

11632 Little Brown Bear

11633 Little Red Riding Hood Marsha Winborn illustrated edition.

11634 My Book Of Poems

11635 The Scarebunny

Soft-cover Little Golden Books

Value: $2.00

I'm not giving much time to soft-cover editions because there is no way of telling how many titles have been printed over the years. They have been in print since the 1950s and were sold through the same outlets as their hard-cover counterparts, with many also being sold through elementary school book clubs.

Special Bound-in-Cloth Little Golden Books

Value: same as regular LGB

In 1948, seven Little Golden Book titles were released in special cloth-bound editions. Each book has the familiar golden wheat spine design of the 1930s. Along the opposite sides in a 1/4" white border are the words, "special bound in cloth." These words are repeated around the border. The regular Little Golden Book covers, front, and back, were reproduced on these books. The books were the same width as a regular LGB and a 1/4" taller.

Known titles are:

Fix It, Please

Animal Babies

Shy Little Kitten

Saggy Baggy Elephant

Taxi That Hurried

New House In The Forest

Noises And Mr. Flibberty-Jib

Follett Duro-Tuff Editions

Value: Same or a little less than a regular LGB

These editions were produced in a solid color cloth cover with two-color artwork around 1950. The books are the same size as regular Little Golden Books, but with very dull cover art. Follett Duro-Tuff bindings were supposed to be washable and vermin proof.

Goldencraft Editions

Value: Same as regular LGB

These books were bound in a cloth fabric for heavy handling in schools and libraries. There have been different cover style variations since they were first produced in the early 1950s. All hard-cover edition were 1/4" taller than regular Little Golden Books.

The first covers had a solid-colored background with a basket-weave pattern. The cover art consisted of a 4-1/4" x 5-1/2" full-color picture. This picture is different from the regular Little Golden Books' cover art on every copy I've seen.

The next style change came around 1955—a solid background with a continuing leaf pattern design. The LGB cover pictures were the same as the first style, but this time the pictures were done in only three colors, with more of a line drawn effect, and placed more to the upper right portion the cover.

Cover style changed again in the late 1950s, when the leaf pattern was changed to a solid dot and asterisk pattern. The three-color art was not centered on the cover.

Sometime in the early 1960s, the covers were changed to a copy of the original LGB cover. The artwork filled all of the cover except for a 1/4" colored border that matched the spine and back of the book.

Some soft-cover editions were also done by Goldencraft. These were stiff cardboard covers with a fabric spine. The covers had the weave pattern with a full-color cover picture.

Products Marketed Using Licensed Little Golden Book Characters

Aladdin plastic lunchbox 1989

Value: $10.00
   Little Golden Book Land

Applause Inc.

Miniature plastic figures with soft cover Little Golden Book

   1991-present
Value: $5.00 Each
   Poky Little Puppy and book
   Saggy Baggy Elephant and book
   Scuffy The Tugboat and book
   Tawny Scrawny Lion and book
   Curious Little Kitten and book
   Tootle and book
   Babs and Lost in the Funhouse Book
   Buster Bunny and Lost in the Funhouse Book
   Porky Pig and Just Like Magic Book
   Bugs Bunny and Just Like Magic Book
   Minnie Mouse and Mickey Mouse's Picnic Book
   Mickey Mouse and Mickey Mouse's Picnic Book
   Patch and 101 Dalmatians Book
   Belle and Beauty and the Beast Book

Plastic bookmark 1992

Value: $4.00 each
   Poky Little Puppy
   Shy Little Kitten
   Tootle

Stuffed animals 6 inches 1991

Value: $8.00
   Poky Little Puppy
   Tawny Scrawny Lion

Collegeville costumes in the 1970s

Value: $25.00 each
   904 Shy Little Kitten
   902 Saggy Baggy Elephant

   907 Lively Little Rabbit
   914 Little Bear
   905 Tawny Scrawny Lion
      Poky Little Puppy

Beach products 1987-1992

Values: $1.00-$10.00
   Plates, invitations, napkins, tablecloths, and wrapping paper

Dolly Toy Co., The 1972

Wall plaques

Value: $25.00 Each
   349 Poky Little Puppy
   350 Shy Little Kitten
   351 Tawny Scrawny Lion

Nursery lamp and shade

Value: $35.00 Each
   Shy Little Kitten
   Poky Little Puppy

Enesco Corporation 1989

Giftbags

Value: $2.00-$4.00
   225274   Little Golden Book Land medium
   225266   Little Golden Book Land mid-size
   225258   Little Golden Book Land large

Bookends (wooden)

Value: $25.00
   408360   Tootle the Train and Katy Caboose

Baby's sipper cup

Value: $8.00
   860417   Little Golden Book Land

Child's cup and toothbrush

Value: $8.00
  860409 Little Golden Book Land

Ceramic nightlights

Value: $25.00 Each
  415138 Saggy Baggy Elephant
  408999 Scuffy The Tugboat

Ceramic musical figurine

Value: $25.00
  415154 Scuffy the Tugboat

Picnic basket tin with coloring book

Value: $15.00
  569518 Little Golden Book Land

Ceramic figures

Value: $10.00 each
  409022 Poky Little Puppy sitting
  409022 Poky Little Puppy lying
  409022 Shy Little Kitten sitting
  409022 Shy Little Kitten standing

Ceramic train set

  409014 Tootle The Train (musical) $25.00
  410365 Tawny Scrawny Lion $10.00
  410357 Baby Brown Bear $10.00
  410373 Poky Little Puppy $10.00
  410349 Katy Caboose $15.00

Bank

Value: $15.00
  414662 Tootle the Train

Melamine child's dinner set (six piece)

Value: $25.00
  860396   Little Golden Book Land (plate, bowl, mug, bib, spoon, and fork, and Welcome To Little Golden Book Land book)

English candy tins 1950s

Value: $50.00
  Three Little Kittens

Gund Mfg. Co. 1970s

Puppets

Value: $5.00
  Saggy Baggy Elephant

Stuffed animals

Value: $15.00 each
  Tawny Scrawny Lion
  Poky Little Puppy

Handkerchief 1950s

Value: $10.00 each
  Saggy Baggy Elephant   Gustaf Tenggren
  Lively Little Rabbit   Gustaf Tenggren
  Poky Little Puppy   Gustaf Tenggren

Old Mother Hubbard	Alice and Martin Provensen
Cat And The Fiddle	Alice and Martin Provensen

Hard plastic toys by Larami Corp. 1978

1950-5	Tootle Wind-Up Train-Set	$40.00
1900-0	Poky Little Puppy Wind-Up Rocker	$15.00
1900-0	Saggy Baggy Elephant Wind-Up Rocker	$15.00

Ideal Toy Company Talking Toys 1955

Value: With box $200.00 each
Value: Without box $100.00 Each
  4302 Scuffy The Tugboat
  4303 Tootle The Train
  4304 Poky Little Puppy
  4305 Saggy Baggy Elephant

Kleenex 1954

Value: $20.00

Yellow wrapper advertising *Little Lulu And Her Magic Tricks*. Wrapper went around three boxes of Kleenex. The wrapper also had instructions for making Mr. Scarecrow.

Miscellaneous

Plastic cup (yellow) 1982

Value: $8.00 each
  Saggy Baggy Elephant
  Tawny Scrawny Lion
  The Curious Little Kitten
  Poky Little Puppy

Sheets and pillow case 1970s

  From the World of Little Golden Books
  Sheets $20.00
  Pillowcase $10.00

Miscellaneous giveaways

  A Billion Golden Memories 1987
  Medallion $10.00
  Book mark (metal) $15.00
  Lucite cube paperweight (soft-cover miniature *Poky Little Puppy* book inside) $25.00

50th Anniversary 1992

Mug (Share The Golden Moments 50 Year Golden Books blue with gold lettering coffee cup) $10.00

Play Pal Plastics Inc. in 1972

Plastic bank and nightlight
The same figures were produced in both formats by removing the bottom plug out of the bank and inserting in the light base.
Value: $12.00 each
Poky Little Puppy
Shy Little Kitten

Playskool 1989

Stuffed animals

Value: $30.00 each
263/264 Poky Little Puppy
266/264 Tawny Scrawny Lion
267/264 Saggy Baggy Elephant
268/264 Shy Little Kitten
Not as many of the kitten were produced

Plastic figures

Value: $7.00
272/271 Poky Little Puppy
273/271 Tawny Scrawny Lion
274/271 Saggy Baggy Elephant
275/271 Shy Little Kitten
276/271 Baby Brown Bear
277/271 Little Red Hen

Playskool Plastic Figures

Rosewall Inc. 1989

Little Golden Book land growth chart
and character set $20.00
Little Golden Book land peel
and place stickers $25.00
Wallpaper rolls $25.00
Wallpaper border rolls $20.00
Wallpaper Book, An Adventure In
Little Golden Book Land $50.00

Simon & Schuster 1951

Forty-two pieces of stationery consisting of twelve single and six double sheets, twelve postcards, and envelopes. Each piece is decorated with characters from *The Poky Little Puppy, The Saggy Baggy Elephant, Tootle, The Lively Little Rabbit, The Golden Sleepy Book, I Can Fly, Color Kittens, Little Black Sambo, Big Brown Bear,* and *The Fuzzy Duckling.* Box originally sold for 50 cents.
350 My Little Golden Writing Paper
(rabbit and dog on box cover) $75.00
351 My Little Golden Writing Paper (little boy lying down writing on box cover) $70.00

Stevan-Silbro jewelry pins 1950s

Value: $20.00 each
Lively Little Rabbit
Poky Little Puppy
Saggy Baggy Elephant
Scuffy The Tugboat
Shy Little Kitten
Tootle

Story Time pajamas and book by The Wormser Co. 1988

Produced in both pajamas and nightshirts.
Value: $17.00 each
Poky Little Puppy
Tootle

Worcester Toy Co. 1970s

Value: $35.00
7034 Saggy Baggy Elephant plastic tea set

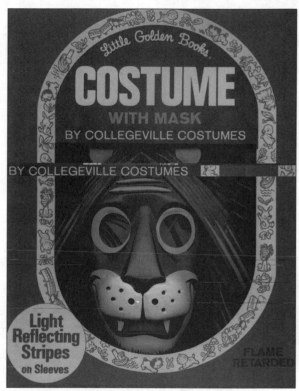

A Little Golden Books Collegeville Custome.

Little Golden Books on Records and Little Golden Books with Records

A Little Golden Record (1948)

Value 10.00-15.00

After two years of preparation, Little Golden Records were released in the fall of 1948. They were produced by Simon & Schuster and printed by Western Printing and Lithographing Company. The music was by Mitch Miller. The yellow plastic records were 78 RPM.

5 The Poky Little Puppy/The Naughty Duck
6 Circus Time (Big Top)/Circus Time (Sideshows)

7 The Funny Little Mouse (not a Little Golden Book story)
8 Wynken, Blynken and Nod (not a Little Golden Book story)

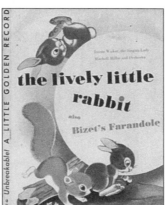

1 Scuffy the Tugboat/Good Morning
2 The Lively Little Rabbit/Bizet's Farandole

3 The Shy Little Kitten/Humoresque
4 Tootle/Norwegian Dance

9 Little Peewee/Turkish March
10 The Golden Egg/Country Dance

11 The Big Brown Bear/Merry Music
12 Out of the Window/The Busy Elevator

Little Golden Record (1950)

Value 7.00-15.00

These records were produced by Simon & Schuster and printed by Western Printing and Lithographing Company. The music was by Mitch Miller. The yellow plastic records were 78 RPM.

R40 The Little Golden Sleepy Record/Close Your Eyes/Sleeping Child

R41 The White Bunny and His Magic Nose/Bunny Hop
R42 The Saggy Baggy Elephant/Elephant Walk

R43 The Seven Sneezes/My Toothbrush Song

R45 Little Fat Policeman/The Safety Song

R46 Brave Cowboy Bill

R51 Doctor Dan, the Bandage Man/Billy Boy

R52 Timmy Is a Big Boy Now/The Three Bears
R53 Poor Mr. Flibberty-Jib/The Noise Song

R54 Happy Man and His Dump Truck/Haydn's The Happy Man's Dance

R55 Scuffy the Tugboat/My Bonnie Lies over the Ocean

Golden Books and Records Sets (1956)

Value: $15.00-$20.00

These records were produced by Western and Simon & Schuster. The book and record came in a cardboard envelope a little larger than a Little Golden Book. The book was a regular Little Golden Book. The record had a picture of the book on the label.

C-329 The Night Before Christmas $12.00
C-330 Hansel and Gretel $12.00
C-331 Heidi $12.00

C-332 The Saggy Baggy Elephant $12.00
C-333 Roy Rogers and Cowboy Toby $20.00

C-334 Walt Disney's Little Man of Disneyland $15.00
C-428 Poky Little Puppy
C-429 Seven Dwarfs Find a Home
C-430 The Three Bears
C-431 Little Red Riding Hood
C-432 Jack and the Beanstalk
C-433 Bambi

Golden Story Book and Record Album (1960s)

Value $25.00

12" 33-1/3 long-playing record.
Six soft cover Little Golden Books. Came in a 12-1/2" x 12-1/2" boxed set.

GST-1
1. The Three Bears
2. Thumbelina
3. Smokey the Bear
4. Hansel and Gretel
5. Wizard of Oz
6. Peter Rabbit

GST-2
1. Little Red Riding Hood
2. Old MacDonald Had a Farm
3. Bozo
4. Heidi
5. Peter and the Wolf
6. Puss in Boots

GST-3
1. Jack and the Beanstalk
2. Gingerbread Man
3. Snow White and Rose Red
4. Saggy Baggy Elephant
5. Little Red Caboose
6. A Country Mouse and a City Mouse

GST-4
1. Rumpelstiltskin
2. Scuffy the Tug Boat
3. Musicians of Bremen
4. Poky Little Puppy
5. Chicken Little
6. Little Boy with a Big Horn

GST-8
1. How Lovely is Christmas
2. Jingle Bells
4. Rudolph the Red Nosed Reindeer
5. 12 Days of Christmas
6. Frosty the Snowman

READ and HEAR (1060s)

Value $4.00-$6.00 unless noted.

Produced by Golden Records. Soft-cover record fit in front cover; 45 RPM.

151 Hansel and Gretel
152 Heidi
153 Saggy Baggy Elephant
154 Poky Little Puppy

155 The Three Little Bears
156 Little Red Riding Hood

157 Three Bedtime Stories
158 Baby's Mother Goose

159 Little Red Caboose

160 How To Tell Time

161 Nursery Songs
162 Chicken Little

166 Little Red Hen
167 Numbers
168 The Night Before Christmas
169 Bozo Finds a Friend

163 Jack and the Beanstalk

164 The Gingerbread Man
165 Rumpelstiltskin and The Princess and the Pea

170 Smokey the Bear $10.00
171 Happy Birthday Party $15.00

172 Cinderella $45.00
173 Peter Rabbit
174 A Country Mouse and A City Mouse/The Fox and the Crow/The Dog and His Bone

179 Frosty the Snowman
181 Scuffy the Tugboat
182 Old MacDonald Had a Farm
183 Little Boy with the Big Horn

175 Puss in Boots
176 Snow White-Rose Red (read by Danny Kaye)

177 Musicians of Bremen (read by Danny Kaye)
178 Rudolph the Red-nosed Reindeer

184 Thumbelina
185 Peter and the Wolf
186 Jingle Bells
207 The Twelve Days of Christmas

208 Tootle
212 Bozo
213 The Three Little Kittens
214 The Seven Little Postmen
216 The Little Engine that Could
217 The White Bunny and His Magic Nose
218 The Animals of Farmer Jones
219 The Happy Man and His Dump Truck

220 The Big Brown Bear
221 Three Billy Goats Gruff

238 Chitty-Chitty Bang-Bang

239 Circus Time

232 A Visit to the Children's Zoo
233 ABC Rhymes

234 Riddles, Riddles from A to Z
235 A Day on the Farm

240 The Taxi that Hurried
241 Five Little Firemen

236 A Child's Garden of Verses
237 Counting Rhymes

242 The Shy Little Kitten
243 The Lively Little Rabbit

244 When I Grow Up
245 Ali Baba
246 The Little Fat Policeman
247 The Tawny Scrawny Lion
248 The Wonderful School
249 Ukelele And Her New Doll $10.00
250 Mister Dog $8.00
251 Naughty Bunny $15.00
252 Happy Days
253 Tigers Adventure
254 The Boy With The Drum
255 Little Indian
256 The Fuzzy Duckling
259 The Pussycat Tiger
260 Bravest of All $15.00
261 Wacky Witch
262 Corky's Hickups
263 Who Comes To Your House
264 Susan in the Driver's Seat

A Disneyland Record (1970s)

Value $5.00-$8.00

A Little Golden Book and Record. Soft-cover book with record in back cover; 33-1/3 RPM.

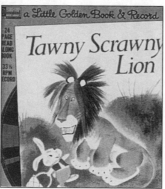

201 The Saggy Baggy Elephant
202 Tawny Scrawny Lion

203 The Poky Little Puppy
204 Rumpelstiltskin

205 Scuffy The Tugboat
206 Thumbelina

207 Little Boy With a Big Horn
208 Puss in Boots

209 Chicken Little
210 The Large and Growly Bear

211 Tootle
212 The Color Kittens

213 The Happy Man and His Dump Truck
214 The Taxi That Hurried
215 Smokey the Bear

216 The Little Engine That Could

217 The Pussycat Tiger

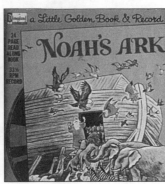

218 David and Goliath
219 Noah's Ark
220 The Lively Little Rabbit

221 Circus Time
222 Seven Little Postmen

223 There's No Such Thing as a Dragon (never done as a hard cover
    Little Golden Book)
224 The Little Fat Policeman
252 Rudolph the Red-Nose Reindeer

253 Frosty the Snowman

254 The Twelve Days of Christmas
255 Jingle Bells

Peter Pan Book and Record (1977)

Value $4.00-$6.00

Soft cover with record in back cover; 45 RPM.

1990 The Road Runner, A Very Scary Lesson
1999 Lassie and Her Day in the Sun

Bing Crosby Sings Mother Goose

Golden Record R364
Copyright 1957
Cover price 25 cents
Mint value $15.00

The photograph on this record jacket has Bing Crosby reading *Ali Baba and the Forty Thieves*. The cover on the Little Golden Book that he is reading was never used. Crosby had also done another Golden Record, Bing Crosby's Ali Baba. It is the cover of the record jacket I believe was used to make the mock-up book he is reading. The Little Golden Book was done in 1958 and had nothing to do with the record.

Foreign Little Golden Books

Argentina (Spanish)

UN LIBRITO DE ORO

Distributed by Liberia Hachette S.A. and printed by Pablo Paoppi e Hijos, both of Buenos Aires, Argentina. I have found no edition markings, but some editions do contain date of printing.

Australia

Published by Golden Press PTY. Ltd., Sydney.

The first books were printed by Geo. Gibbons Ltd., Leicester, England. These books had spines identical to the American gold- paper spines of the 1940s.

The second spines were black with coppery-golden leaves and flowers. These were printed by Colourtone Pty. Ltd, Australia. Spines are either a gold paper similar to early American Little Golden Books, with black and gold flaked look or black with gold leaves on spine.

If the spines are black with silvery leaves and flowers, they were printed in Singapore by the Toppan Printing Company, Ltd.

Titles with an * were only published as a Little Golden Book in Australia.

1   Prayers For Children
2   Animals Of Farmer Jones, The
3   Lively Little Rabbit, The
4   Tootle
5   Hansel And Gretel
6   Shy Little Kitten, The

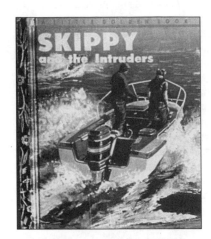

*395   Skippy And The Intruder

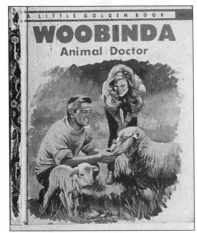

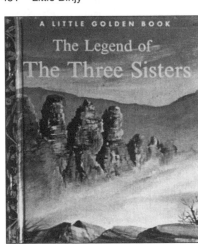

*452   Legend Of Three Sisters, The

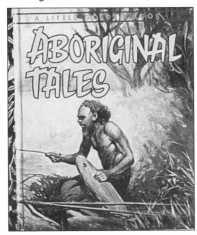

*453   Aboriginal Tales

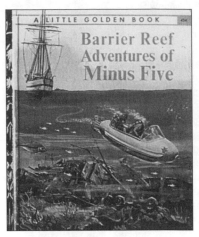

*A1   New Bike, The

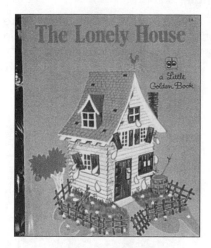

*A2   Lonely House, The

*A3   Mr. Merriweather's Zoo

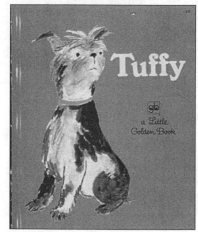

*A4   Tuffy
D1   Johnny Appleseed
D2   Peter And The Wolf
D3   Cinderella
D4   Three Little Pigs, The
D5   Donald Duck's Adventure
D6   Mickey Mouse's Picnic
D7   Santa's Toy Shop
D8   Cinderella's Friends
D9   Alice In Wonderland Meets The White Rabbit

D10   Alice In Wonderland Finds The Garden Of Live Flowers
D11   Mad Hatter's Tea Party, The
D12   Grandpa Bunny
D13   Donald Duck's Toy Train
D14   Snow White And The Seven Dwarfs
D15   Noah's Ark
D16   Mickey Mouse And His Space Ship
D17   Pluto Pup Goes To Sea
D18   Donald Duck And Santa Claus
D19   Peter Pan And Wendy
D20   Peter Pan And The Pirates
D21   Peter Pan And The Indians
D22   Seven Dwarfs Find A House, The
D23   Mother Goose
D24   Hiawatha
D25   Mickey Mouse And Pluto Pup
D26   Ugly Duckling, The
D27   Mickey Mouse Goes Christmas Shopping
D28   Chip 'n Dale At The Zoo
D29   Pinocchio
D30   Donald Duck's Toy Sailboat
D31   Donald Duck's Christmas Tree
D32   Donald Duck's Safety Book
D33   Lady
D34   Davy Crockett 'King Of The Wild Frontier'
D35   Donald Duck In Disneyland
D36   Davy Crockett's Keelboat Race
D37   Jiminy Cricket Fire Fighter
D38   Robin Hook
D39   Donald Duck Prize Driver
D40   Goofy Movie Star
D41   Disneyland On The Air
D42   Little Man Of Disneyland
D43   Mickey Mouse & The Missing Mouseketeers
D44   Mickey Mouse Flies The Christmas Mail
D45   Donald Duck & The Mouseketeers
D46   Perri & Her Friends
D47   Sleeping Beauty
D48   Scamp The Adventure Of A Little Puppy
D49   Zorro
D50   Scamp's Adventure
D51   Old Yeller
D52   Zorro And The Secret Plan
D53   Bambi
D54   Sleeping Beauty & The Fairies
D55   Shaggy Dog
D56   Goliath
D57   Mannie The Donkey In The Forest World
D58   Donald Duck Lost & Found
D59   Darby O'Gill
D60   Tonka
D61   Dumbo
D62   Lucky Puppy, The
D63   Toby Tyler
D64   Pollyanna
D65   Bongo
D66   Swiss Family Robinson
D68   Donald Duck And The Private Eye

D69   Babes In Toyland
D70   Toy Soldier, The
D71   Pinocchio And The Whale
D72   Big Red
D74   Savage Sam
D75   Sword In The Stone, The
D76   Wizard's Duel, The
D77   Mary Poppins A Jolly Holiday
D78   Mary Poppins
D79   Cinderella's Friends
D80   Mad Hatter's Tea Party
D81   Chip 'n Dale At The Zoo
D82   Donald Duck Prize Driver
D83   Three Little Pigs
D85   Winnie The Pooh & The Honey Tree
D86   Winnie The Pooh Meets Gopher
D87   Mickey Mouse & His Space Ship
D88   Peter Pan & The Indians
D89   Uncle Remus
D90   Mother Goose
D91   Ugly Dachshund
D92   Thumper
D93   Mickey Mouse & The Mouseketeers
D94   Hiawatha
D95   Donald Duck And The Mouseketeers
D96   Ugly Duckling, The
D97   Mickey Mouse And Pluto Pup
D98   Bunny Book
D99   Peter And The Wolf
D100   Disneyland On The Air
D101   Jungle Book, The
D102   Little Man Of Disneyland
D103   Paul Revere
D104   Donald Duck And The Witch
D105   Donald Duck In Disneyland
D106   Dumbo
D107   Perri And Her Friends
D108   Jiminy Cricket Fire Fighter
D109   Donald Duck's Toy Sailboat
D110   Winnie The Pooh And Tigger

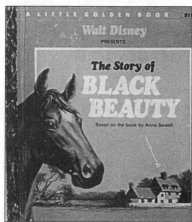

*D111   Story Of Black Beauty
*D112   How The Camel Got His Hump
*D113   Acting Out The ABC
*D114   Seven Dwarfs And Their Diamond Mine
*D115   Goldilocks And The Three Bears
*D116   Mickey Mouse Brave Little Tailor

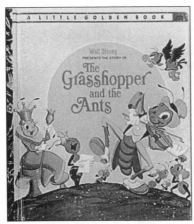

*D117   Grasshopper And The Ants, The
*D118   Story Of Rapunzel
*D119   Bremen Town Musicians
D120   Aristocats, The
D121   Disneyland Parade

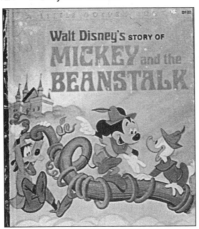

*D122   Mickey Mouse And The Beanstalk
*D123   Wizard Of Oz, The
D124   Surprise For Mickey Mouse
D126   Pluto & The Adventure Of The Gold-
        en Scepter
*D127   More Jungle Book
*D128   It's A Small World
*D129   Little House, The
*D131   Susie The Little Blue Coupe
*D132   Lampert The Sheepish Lion

*D133   Thumper's Race

*D135   Emperor's New Clothes
D136   Story Of The Ugly Duckling
D143   Robin Hood
D144   Robin Hood & The Daring Mouse
*LLP322 Story Of Heidi, The

*LLP350 Pecos Bill
*LLP364 Johnny Fedora And Alice Bluebonnet

Croatia

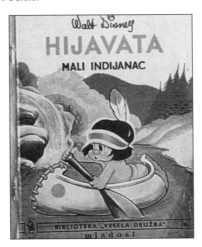

Denmark

FREMADS GULDBOGER

Copyrighted by Forlaget Fremad, Copenhagen, Denmark.

England

1950s Little Golden Books were distributed throughout Great Britain by Frederick Muller Limited, London.

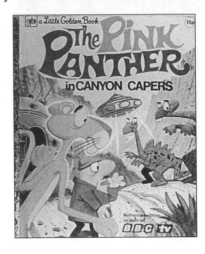

Books were printed in the Netherlands or Singapore and distributed by World Distributors (Manchester) Limited in the 1970s. These editions contained only 16 pages. The only non-American titles I know of were No. 19, The Road Runner 'Tumbleweed Trouble,' and No. 25, The Pink Panther in Canyon Caper. Today the books are printed and published by Western Publishing Company, Inc., in the United States.

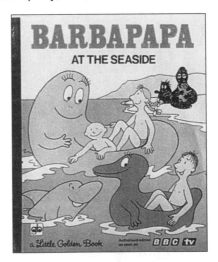

In the 1960s, the Happy Time Series was produced by Golden Pleasure Books, Ltd. London. Each book was a softcover with 24 pages. All of the more than 65 titles were previously done as Little Golden Books.

Soft cover, 24-page Little Golden Books were done in the 1970s called A Golden TV Book. One title from this series was *Tom and Jerry 'Kangaroo Wrangle'*.

Finland

TAMMEN KULTAISET KIRJAT

In the 1980s, these books were published by Arvi A. Karisto Oy, kirjapaino, Hameenlinna. The spines were similar to the American 1950s' spines in design, but with brown outlined flowers and animals on the gold.

France

UN PETIT LIVRE D'OR

Originally published by Cocorico and printed by M. Dechaux, both of Paris. Later Deux d'Or became the publisher with printing by Cite-Press-Paris. With both of these publishers, the spines remained a solid gold foil. Titles did appear in this series that were not printed in an American edition

LES ALBUMS ROSES

This series contained Little Golden Book stories along with others and were printed by Imprimeries d Bobigny or Gilbert-Clarey. Spines were of a yellow ribbon material.

UN PETIT LIVRE D'ARGENT

These soft-cover editions were the American "Little Silver Books." Printings were done by the same publishers as the UN PETIT LIVRE D'OR series. More than 120 titles were printed, but the titles did not have the same numbering as the previous series.

Germany

EIN GOLDENES KINDERBUCH

Holland

EEN GOUDEN BOEKJE

Distributed by Annie M.G. Schmidt and Han G. Hoekstra, Holland. Spines are gold with a black design similar to a half star. Later spines had a solid silvery-gold.

Israel

The books had a gold foil spine and were published by Steimatsky's Agency Ltd., Tel-Aviv, Israel. Books are hinged on the right side.

Mexico

UN PEQUEN LIBRO DE ORO

Published by: Editorial Novaro, Mexico, S.A.

Editorial Novaro had offices in Mexico City, Mexico; Barcelona, Spain; Bogota, Columbia; Lima, Peru; and Santiago, Chili.

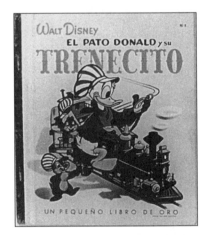

Some editions published by Editorial Novaro will tell you how many copies were printed along with the day, month, and year of printing. This information will be found on either the copyright page or the last page. Soft cover editions have been printed since the 1960s.

Norway

TIDENS GULL BOKE

Some of the later printing was done by Tiden Norsk Forlag of Finland. Spines were a golden ribbon with brownish leaves.

Philippines

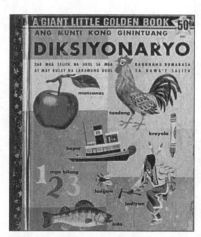

This special edition of My Little Golden Dictionary lists hundreds of familiar words in both English and the Philippino language of Tagalog.

Sweden

FIB:S GYLLENE BOK

Published by Folket i Bilds Forlag, Stockholm

Dating Little Golden Books by Spine Design

1942-47 Solid blue spine—blue-bound books had dust jacket

1947-49 Gold paper spine—pattern of leaves, flowers, and animals

1949-69 Antique gold spine—various patterns of leaves, flowers, and plants

1955-59 Christmas spine—Christmas design used on Christmas stories

1954-56 Mickey Mouse Club spine—only used on Mickey Mouse Club Edition, red spine with portraits

1969-present gold spine—design of chickens, crickets, and elephants

Back Cover Designs Through the Years

One can date Little Golden Books by the design on the back cover. Use the following pages as a guide—the date given should give you the date of issue of your book within about six months, plus or minus.

Last title listed is #12   *1942-1943*

Last title listed is #16	*1943-1945*
Last title listed is #19	*1945-1946*
Last title listed is #20	*1946-1947*
Last title listed is #27	*1947-1948*
Last title listed is #34	*1948*
Last title listed is #D6	*1948*
Last title listed is #D8	*1948*
Last title listed is #53/#D10	*1948-1949*
Last title listed is #59	*1949*
Last title listed is #64	*1949*
Last title listed is #78	*1949-1950*
Last title listed is #D11	*1950*
Last title listed is #D12	*1950*

Last title listed is #97	*1950*
Last title listed is #99	*1950-1951*
Last title listed is #114	*1951*
Last title listed is #119	*1951-1952*
Last title listed is #143	*1952*
Last title listed is #D23	*1952*
Last title listed is #D30	*1952-1953*
Last title listed is #D31	*1953*
Last title listed is #D32	*1953-1954*
Last title listed is #D38	*1954*
Last title listed is #D44	*1954-1955*
Last title listed is #D45	*1955*
Last title listed is #A6	*1955-1956*
Last title listed is #D9	*1956*

*300,000,000 Message
1954-1955*

1954-1955

1957-1958

1958

1959

1959

1959-1960

1959-1960

1959-1960

1960

1960-1961

1960-1962

1960-1962

1960-1962

1960-1962

1960-1962

1960-1962

1961

156

1961-1962

1962

1962

1962

1962

1963

1963

1963

1963

1963

1963

1963

1963

1963

1964-1970

1970-1971

1970-1973

1973-1976

1976-1983

1972

1983

1986-1996

1996-Present

Last title listed is #D48   ©1955
Last title listed is #D52   ©1955-1956
Last title listed is #D58   ©1955-1956

Index of Little Golden Books

If the Little Golden Book title you are looking for has a dash (-) in the number, go to the new numbering Little Golden Book section and locate the book by title (alphabetically). I don't have information on all dash numbers so you may own one that is not listed. The new numbering dash section only covers dash books that were not printind in the original series or have a cover or title variation.

166

A Brief History of Rand McNally

In 1856, William Rand, a young printer from Boston, arrived in Chicago and opened his own print shop. While Rand was starting up his company, another young man was getting ready to leave his homeland in search of his fortune in the United States. Andrew McNally, having finished his seven years as a printer's apprentice, was preparing to leave the county of Armagh in Ireland.

McNally arrived in Chicago and, while looking for work, came upon Rand's business. In just a few years the two men were able to purchase the Chicago Tribune's job printing shop and formed Rand McNally & Company. While looking for new ventures, they started printing passenger tickets, timetables, and guides for railroads. Later they started printing the Railroad Guide, which was a route map for a single railroad.

By the early 1900s the automobile started allowing people to move outside of their neighborhoods and see the country. To help people in their travels, the company started producing road maps. In 1907, Andrew McNally II and his wife drove from Chicago to New York, taking pictures of every turn they made on their trip. This was later published as the Chicago-to-New York-Auto Guide.

As more and more roads crossed the country, Rand McNally, not the government, created the numbering of highways. The first road map to list major roads with numbers was for the state of Illinois. Road maps of the forty-eight states were available by 1922. The Rand McNally Road Atlas that is in print today was first printed in 1924.

The company had been printing children's books since around 1913. In 1949 the company acquired the W. B. Conkey Company and started printing books on a much larger scale. With the success of Little Golden Books having been proven, the company released the first four titles of its own 6-5/8" x 8-3/4" books, A Rand McNally Elf Book, around September 1947. Later titles were not released until around the summer or fall of 1948.

The primary construction difference between the Elf Books and Golden Books are that the Elf books are not a flush-cut book. This means that a Little Golden Book is put together and then the sides are trimmed, making the pages flush to the cover. With most Elf Books (some were done flush-cut between 1954 and 1957) the cover is made separately from the book. The front and back cover are all one piece, which is glued to the cover cardboard. The pages are stitched together and are then glued to the cover by the first and last page. With this method, the cover extends past the pages by about 1/4". Because the covers on Elf Books did not hold up to use as well as Little Golden Books did, they are a lot harder to find in nice condition.

From 1947 until around 1954 the books were called a Rand McNally Book/Elf Book and had a picture of an elf in a 3/4" x 7/8" box in the upper left corner; in 1954 the picture of the elf grew to 1/2" x 1-1/4". In 1955 the books were called A Rand McNally Elf Book. Tip-Top Elf Books, which were first printed around 1959, have a little elf standing on a globe. Start-Right Elf Books were started around 1966. These have an elf sitting down reading a book in the upper left corner and "Rand McNally Publisher" appears at the bottom of the cover. Rand McNally also printed Ding Dong School Books between July 1953 and June 1956 before they were done as Golden Books.

When trying to date a Rand McNally Elf Book prior to February 1963, look on the last page. You will see a number preceded by CS. The first number preceding the dash stands for the month, while the next number is the year of printing. For example, CS6-54 means the book was printed in June 1954, and CS12-52 stands for December 1952. There is no way of telling for sure if a book is first edition on most books after February 1963.

You will also see two numbers on the last page separated by a dash (-). These two numbers denote the recommended reading age for that particular book. The first number is the recommended beginning age while the second is the ending age, divided by 10. For example, a book with "50-90" would be for children 5 to 9 years of age.

Elf books were originally printed with 36 pages, but books below number 600 could have had 28, 30, or 32 pages. Books numbered higher than 3000 typically had 20 pages, although some had 28.

Quite a few of the books were printed in different numbered series over the years. The first series ran from 425 to as high as 620, but some numbers had no titles before the 8300 period. The second series was from 3800 to around 8460. The fourth series was the Tip-Top Elf Book series which originally went from 1001 to 1038, before it was changed to 8600 and continued to around 8743. The fifth series, the Start-Right Elf Book, began with 8500.

Rand McNally sold its low-end children's line to MacMillan Publishing in 1986. Checkerboard Press was formed and became a subsidiary from 1986 to 1990. In 1990 Checkerboard Press became a private company. The name of the company comes from the very popular Rand McNally Reads Mother Goose, first printed in 1916. This book has a checkerboard background on the front cover.

No. 424

Mother Goose

Illus.: Friend, Esther

1947   **$15.00**

No. 424

Mother Goose
(2nd Cover)

Illus.: Friend, Esther

1947   **$7.00**

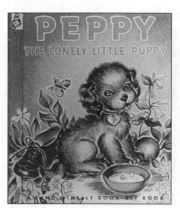

No. 425

Peppy, The Lonely Little Puppy

Illus.: Blake, Vivienne Leah

Author: Friedman, Frieda

1947   **$15.00**

No. 426

Twilight Tales

Illus.: Bryant, Dean

Author: Potter, Miriam Clark

1947   **$15.00**

No. 427

Wonderful Train Ride, The

Illus.: Mastri, Fiore and Jackie

Author: Weir, R. C.

1947   **$15.00**

No. 427

Wonderful Train Ride, The
(2nd Cover)

Illus.: Mastri, Fiore and Jackie

Author: Weir, R. C.

1947   **$7.00**

No. 428

Title Unknown

No. 429

Teddy Bear Of Bumpkin Hollow

Illus.: Bryant, Dean

Author: Boucher, Sharon

1948   **$25.00**

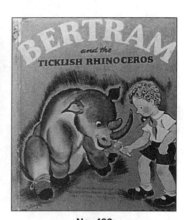

No. 430

Bertram And The Ticklish
Rhinoceros

Illus.: Thompson Van Tellingen,
Ruth

Author: Gilbert, Paul

1948   **$25.00**

No. 431

My Truck Book

Illus.: Grider, Dorothy

Author: Reichert, E. C.

1948   **$15.00**

No. 432

Day On The Farm, A

Illus.: Grider, Dorothy

Author: Evers, Alf

1948   **$15.00**

No. 432

Day On The Farm, A
(2nd Cover)

Illus.: Grider, Dorothy

Author: Evers, Alf

1948   **$7.00**

No. 433

Wonderful Plane Ride, The

Illus.: Mastri, Fiore and Jackie

1947   **$15.00**

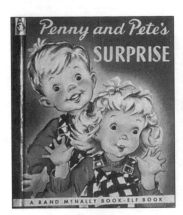

No. 434
Penny And Pete's Surprise
Illus.: McKinley, Clare
1949 $15.00

No. 435
Forest Babies
Illus.: Webbe, Elizabeth
1949 $15.00

No. 436
Kerry, The Fire-Engine Dog
Illus.: Grider, Dorothy
Authors: Lewis, Frank; Corchia, Alfred J.
1949 $15.00

No. 437
Cowboy Eddie
Illus.: Grider, Dorothy
Author: Glasscock, Joyce
1950 $12.00

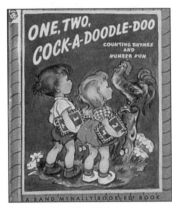

No. 438
One, Two, Cock-A-Doodle-Doo
Illus.: Wosmek, Frances
Author: Pease, Josephine Van Dolzen
1950 $12.00

No. 439
Johnny And The Birds
Illus.: Webbe, Elizabeth
Author: Munn, Ian
1950 $12.00

No. 440
Little Kittens' Nursery Rhymes, The
Illus.: Frees, Harry Whittier
1941 $12.00

No. 441
Smart Little Mouse, The
Illus.: Phillips, Katherine L.
Author: Sherwan, Earl
1950 $12.00

No. 442
Hiawatha
Illus.: Wilde, Irma
Author: Gridley, Marion E.
1950 $12.00

No. 443
Three Little Bunnies
Illus.: Rooks, Dale and Sally
Author: Dixon, Ruth
1950 $12.00

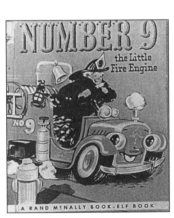

No. 444
Number 9 The Little Fire Engine
Illus.: Corwin, Eleanor
Author: Wadsworth, Wallace
1950 $12.00

No. 445
Three Bears Visit Goldilocks, The
Illus.: McKinley, Clare
1951 $12.00

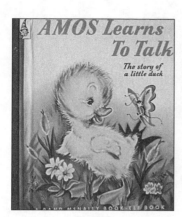

No. 446

Amos Learns To Talk: The Story Of A Little Duck

Illus.: McKinley, Clare

1950 **$12.00**

No. 447

Three Little Puppies

Illus.: Rooks, Dale and Sally

Author: Dixon, Ruth

1951 **$12.00**

No. 448

Farm For Andy, A

Illus.: Gayer, M

1951 **$12.00**

No. 449

Mr. Punnymoon's Train

Illus.: Phillips, Katherine L.

Author: Hadsell, Alice

1951 **$12.00**

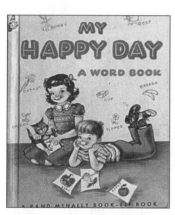

No. 450

My Happy Day: A Word Book

Illus.: Bruce, Suzanne

Author: Shaw, Thelma

1963 **$10.00**

No. 451

Alice In Wonderland

Illus.: Holland, Janice

Author: Carroll, Lewis

1951 **$18.00**

No. 452

Chester: The Little Pony

Illus.: McKinley, Clare

Author: Gunder, Eman

1951 **$10.00**

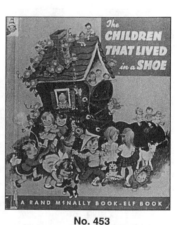

No. 453

Children That Lived In A Shoe, The

Illus.: Webbe, Elizabeth

Author: Pease, Josephine Van Dolzen

1951 **$10.00**

No. 454

Wild Animals

Illus.: Vlasaty, J.L.

Author: Ratzesberger, Anna

1951 **$10.00**

No. 455

Little Friends: Kittens, Puppies, Bunnies

Illus.: Gaddis, Rie

Author: Dixon, Ruth

1951 **$10.00**

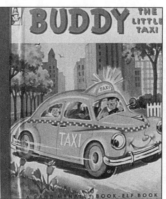

No. 456

Buddy, The Little Taxi

Illus.: Corwin, Elizabeth

1951 **$10.00**

No. 457

Our Auto Trip

Illus.: Grider, Dorothy

Author: Edsall, Marian

1952 **$10.00**

173

No. 458

Little Mailman Of Bayberry Lane, The

Illus.: Webbe, Elizabeth

Author: Munn, Ian

1952 **$18.00**

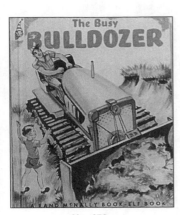

No. 459

Busy Bulldozer, The

Illus.: Grider, Dorothy

Author: Browning, James

1951 **$7.00**

No. 460

To The Store We Go

Illus.: Walker, O

1952 **$7.00**

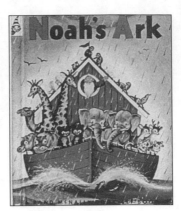

No. 461

Noah's Ark

Illus.: Webbe, Elizabeth

Author: Briggs, Dorothy Bell

1952 **$6.00**

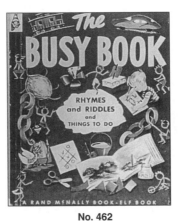

No. 462

Busy Book, The

(Rhymes & Riddles & Things To Do)

Illus.: Szepelak, Helen

Authors: Bartlett, Floy; Pease, Josephine

1952 **$6.00**

No. 463

Aesop's Fables

Illus.: Leaf, Anne Sellers

1952 **$8.00**

No. 464

Old Woman And Her Pig, The

Illus.: Friend, Esther

Author: Wadsworth, Wallace

1952 **$6.00**

No. 465

Lucinda, The Little Donkey

Illus.: Wilde, George

Author: Wilde, Irma

1952 **$6.00**

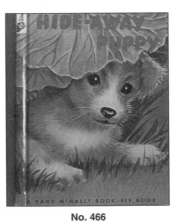

No. 466

Hide-Away Puppy

Illus.: Dottie

Author: Broderick, Jessica Potter

1952 **$6.00**

No. 467

Farm Animals

Illus.: Gayer, M

Author: Hunter, Virginia

1952 **$6.00**

No. 468

Popcorn Party

Illus.: Szepelak, Helen

Authors: Boyles, Trudy; Macmartin, Louise

1952 **$6.00**

No. 469

Goat That Went To School, The

Illus.: Tamburine, Jean

Author: Francis, Sally R.

1952 **$6.00**

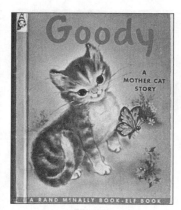

No. 470
Goody: A Mother Cat Story
Illus.: Leaf, Anne Sellers
Author: Bertail, Inez
1957 $6.00

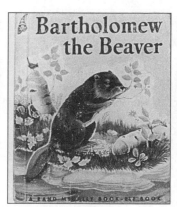

No. 471
Bartholomew The Beaver
Illus.: Pierce, Alice
Author: Dixon, Ruth
1952 $6.00

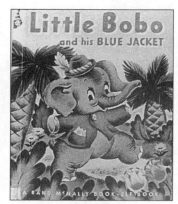

No. 472
Little Bobo And His Blue Jacket
Illus.: Brice, Tony
Author: Evers, Alf
1953 $8.00

No. 473
Space Ship To The Moon
Illus.: Bilder, A.K.
Author: Reichert, E.C.
1952 $16.00

No. 474
Superliner United States, The: World's Fastest Liner
Illus.: Bilder, A.K.
1953 $16.00

No. 475
Mr. Bear's House
Illus.: McKinley, Clare
Author: Rothe, Fenella
1953 $8.00

No. 476
Squiffy The Skunk
Illus.: Neff, George; Brett, Grace Neff
Author: Brett, Grace Neff
1953 $7.00

No. 477
Scalawag The Monkey
Illus.: Gaddis, Rie
Author: Dixon, Ruth
1953 $7.00

No. 478
Funland Party
Illus.: Szepelak, Helen
Author: Devine, Louise Lawrence
1953 $6.00

No. 479
Outdoor Fun
Illus.: Tamburine, Jean
Authors: Shaw, Thelma and Ralph
1953 $6.00

No. 480
Find The Way Home
Illus.: Wilson, Beth
Author: Broderick, Jessica Potter
1953 $6.00

No. 482
Happy Holidays
Illus.: Bruce, Suzanne
Author: Reichert, E.C.
1953 $6.00

No. 481
Title Unknown

No. 483

Little Lost Angel
Illus.: Scott, Janet Laura
Author: Heath, Janet Field
1953   **$10.00**

No. 484

Stories Of The Christ Child
Illus.: Corwin, Eleanor
Author: Jones, Mary Alice
1953   **$6.00**

No. 485

Choo-Choo, The Little Switch Engine
Illus.: Chase, Mary Jane
Author: Wadsworth, Wallace
1954   **$7.00**

No. 486

Pets
Illus.: Webbe, Elizabeth
1954   **$6.00**

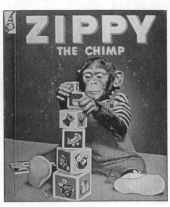

No. 487

Zippy The Chimp
Illus.: Mitchell, Benn
Author: Ecuyer, Lee
1953   **$8.00**

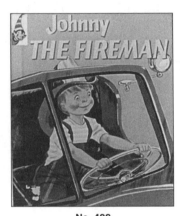

No. 488

Johnny The Fireman
Illus.: Wood, Ruth
Author: Sprinkle, Rebecca K.
1954   **$7.00**

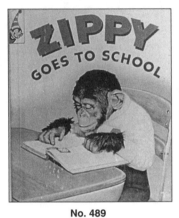

No. 489

Zippy Goes To School
Illus.: Westelin, Albert G.; Ecuyer, Lee
Author: Ecuyer, Lee
1954   **$8.00**

No. 490

Parakeet Peter
Illus.: Grider, Dorothy
Author: Sprinkle, Rebecca K.
1954   **$6.00**

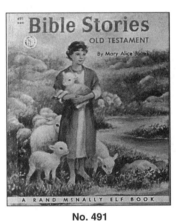

No. 491

Bible Stories: Old Testament
Illus.: Webbe, Elizabeth
Author: Jones, Mary Alice
1954   **$6.00**

No. 492

Title Unknown

No. 493

Campbell Kids At Home, The
Illus.: Schlining Studios, G
Author: Lack, Alma S.
1954   **$22.00**

No. 494

Campbell Kids Have A Party, The
Illus.: Schlining Studios, G.
1954   **$22.00**

No. 495

Sparky The Fire Dog
Illus.: Chase, Mary Jane
Author: Browning, James
1954   **$12.00**

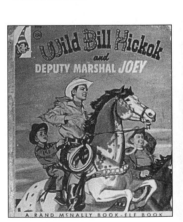

No. 496

Wild Bill Hickok And Deputy Marshal Joey
Illus.: Timmins, William
1954   **$20.00**

No. 497

Sailing On A Very Fine Day

Illus.: Myers, Lou

Author: Ives, Burl

1954 **$7.00**

No. 498

Five Busy Bears, The

Illus.: Tamburine, Jean

1955 **$6.00**

No. 499

Bedtime Stories

Illus.: Clyne, Barbara

Author: Watts, Mabel

1955 **$6.00**

No. 500

Sergeant Preston And Yukon King

Illus.: Nebbe, William

Author: Comfort, Mildred H.

1955 **$18.00**

No. 501

Playtime Poodles

Illus.: Westelin, Albert; Schmidling, Jack

Author: Wing, Helen

1955 **$7.00**

No. 502

Prayers And Graces For A Small Child

Illus.: Webbe, Elizabeth

Author: Webbe, Elizabeth

1955 **$5.00**

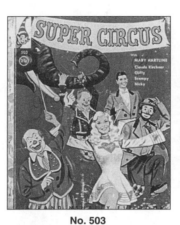

No. 503

Super Circus

Illus.: Timmins, William

Author: Wing, Helen

1955 **$16.00**

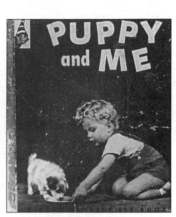

No. 504

Puppy And Me

Illus.: Bannister, Constance

Author: Ratzesberger, Anna

1955 **$6.00**

No. 505

Daniel The Cocker Spaniel

Illus.: Grider, Dorothy

Author: Watts, Mabel

1955 **$7.00**

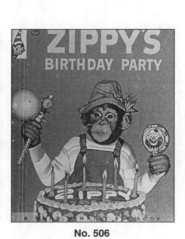

No. 506

Zippy's Birthday Party

Illus.: Photographs

1955 **$7.00**

No. 507

Puss-In-Boots

Illus.: Myers, Bernice and Lou

1955 **$6.00**

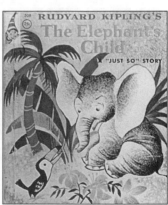

No. 508

Elephant's Child, The: A Kipling "Just So" Story

Illus.: Weihs, Erika

1955 **$7.00**

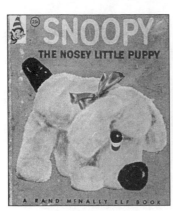

No. 509
Snoopy, The Nosey Little Puppy
Illus.: Nebbe, William
Author: Lieberthal, Jules M.
1955 $7.00

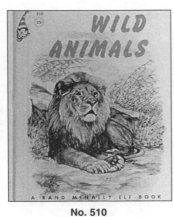

No. 510
Wild Animals
Illus.: Vlasaty, J.L.
Author: Ratzesberger, Anna
1951 $6.00

No. 511
Mr. Bear's House
Illus.: McKinley, Clare
Author: Rothe, Fenella
1953 $6.00

No. 512
One, Two, Cock-A-Doodle-Doo
Illus.: Wosmek, Frances
Author: Pease, Josephine Van Dolzen
1950 $6.00

No. 513
Puss-In-Boots
Illus.: Myers, Bernice and Lou
1955 $6.00

No. 514
Farm Animals
Illus.: Photographs
Author: Hunter, Virginia
1956 $5.00

No. 515
Title Unknown

No. 516
Title Unknown

No. 517
Title Unknown

No. 518
Title Unknown

No. 519
Title Unknown

No. 520
Title Unknown

No. 521
Title Unknown

No. 522
Title Unknown

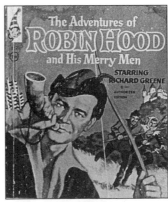

No. 523
Davy Crockett: American Hero
Illus.: Timmins, William
1955 $8.00

No. 524
Title Unknown

No. 525
Title Unknown

No. 526
Title Unknown

No. 527
Title Unknown

No. 528
Title Unknown

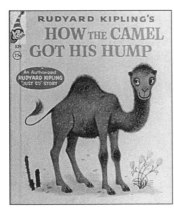

No. 529
**How The Camel Got His Hump:
A Kipling "Just So" Story**
Illus.: Weihs, Erika
Author: Kipling, Rudyard
1955 $7.00

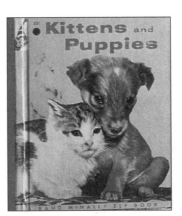

No. 530
Fussbunny
Illus.: Evers, Helen and Alf
Authors: Evers, Helen and Alf
1955 $6.00

No. 531
Kittens And Puppies
Illus.: Photographs
1955 $6.00

No. 532
**Adventures Of Robin Hood
And His Merry Men**
Starring Richard Green
Illus.: Timmins, William
Author: Grant, Bruce
1955 $16.00

No. 533
Davy's Little Horse
Illus.: Dennis, Wesley
Author: Devine, Louise Lawrence
1956   **$6.00**

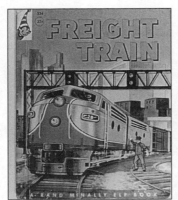

No. 534
Freight Train
Illus.: Pollard, G
1956   **$6.00**

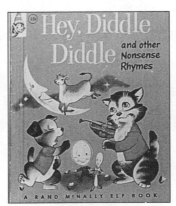

No. 535
Hey, Diddle, Diddle And Other Nonsense Rhymes
Illus.: Botts, Davi
1956   **$6.00**

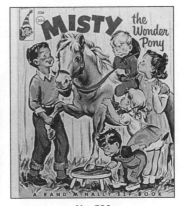

No. 536
Misty The Wonder Pony
Illus.: McKinley, Clare
1956   **$6.00**

No. 537
Muggsy, The Make-Believe Puppy
Illus.: Webbe, Elizabeth
1956   **$7.00**

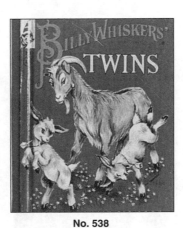

No. 538
Billy Whiskers' Twins
Illus.: Tamburine, Jean
1956   **$6.00**

No. 539
Farm Babies
Illus.: Photographs
Author: Hunter, Virginia
1956   **$6.00**

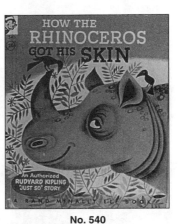

No. 540
How The Rhinoceros Got His Skin: A Kipling "Just So" Story
Illus.: Weihs, Erika
Author: Kipling, Rudyard
1956   **$7.00**

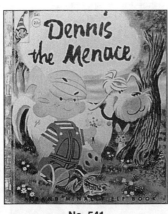

No. 541
Dennis The Menace
Illus.: Paplo, Bob
Author: Toole, Fred
1956   **$10.00**

No. 542
Plump Pig
Illus.: Evers, Helen and Alf
Authors: Evers, Helen and Alf
1956   **$7.00**

No. 543
Ten Commandments For Children, The
Illus.: Bonfils, Robert
Author: Jones, Mary Alice
1956   **$6.00**

No. 544
Little Lost Kitten: Story Of Williamsburg
Illus.: Lee, Manning De V
Author: Comfort, Mildred
1956   **$7.00**

No. 545
Goody: A Mother Cat Story
Illus.: Leaf, Anne Sellers
Author: Bertail, Inez
1957   **$6.00**

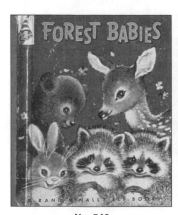

No. 546

Forest Babies

Illus.: Webbe, Elizabeth

1956 **$6.00**

No. 547

Crybaby Calf

Illus.: Evers, Helen and Alf

Authors: Evers, Helen and Alf

1954 **$6.00**

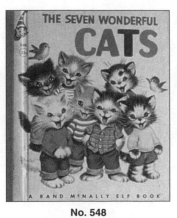

No. 548

Seven Wonderful Cats, The

Illus.: Nebbe, William

1956 **$6.00**

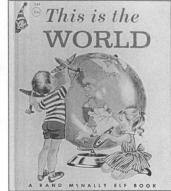

No. 549

This Is The World

Illus.: Wood, Ruth

Author: Pease, Josephine

1957 **$5.00**

No. 550

Nonsense ABCs

Illus.: Lear, Edward

1956 **$6.00**

No. 551

Cinderella

Illus.: Endred, Helen; Neebe, William

Author: Bates, Katherine Lee

1956 **$7.00**

No. 552

Pillowtime Tales

Illus.: Tamburine, Jean

Author: De Groot, Marion K.

1956 **$6.00**

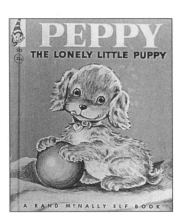

No. 553

Peppy, The Lonely Little Puppy

Illus.: Blake, Vivienne Leah

Author: Friedman, Frieda

1957 **$6.00**

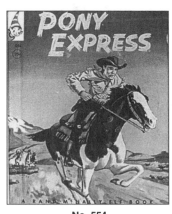

No. 554

Pony Express

Illus.: Timmins, William

Author: Grant, Bruce

1956 **$6.00**

No. 555

**Little Boy Blue And Other
Nursery Rhymes**

Illus.: Leaf, Anne Sellers

1956 **$6.00**

No. 556

**Little Miss Muffet And Other
Nursery Rhymes**

Illus.: Chase, Mary Jane

1956 **$6.00**

No. 557

Mr. Punnymoon's Train

Illus.: Phillips, Katherine L.

Author: Hadsell, Alice

1951 **$8.00**

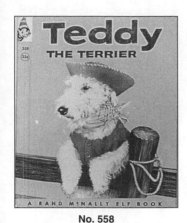

No. 558

Teddy The Terrier

Illus.: Latimer, Constance; Love, Mary

Author: Hunter, Virginia

1956 **$8.00**

No. 559

Mr. Wizard's Junior Science Show

Illus.: Bonfils, Robert

Author: Thayer, Ruth Hubley

1957 **$8.00**

No. 560

Growing Up

Illus.: Webbe, Elizabeth

Author: Fritz, Webbe

1956 **$5.00**

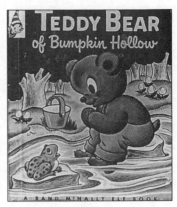

No. 561

Teddy Bear Of Bumpkin Hollow

Illus.: Bryant, Dean

Author: Boucher, Sharon

1948 **$8.00**

No. 562

Surprise!

Illus.: Ozone, Lucy

Author: Ozone, Lucy

1956 **$5.00**

No. 563

Our Animal Friends

Illus.: Photographs

Author: Hunter, Virginia

1956 **$5.00**

No. 564

Little Ballerina

Illus.: Grider, Dorothy

Author: Grider, Dorothy

1958 **$6.00**

No. 565

Hiawatha

Illus.: Wilde, Irma

Author: Gridley, Marion E.

1950 **$6.00**

No. 566

Four Little Kittens

Illus.: Frees, Harry Whittier

Author: Dixon, Ruth

1957 **$5.00**

No. 567

Busy Bulldozer, The

Illus.: Grider, Dorothy

Author: Browning, James

1952 **$5.00**

No. 568

Santa's Rocket Sleigh

Illus.: Webbe, Elizabeth

Author: Storch, Florence

1957 **$10.00**

No. 569

Sergeant Preston And Rex

Illus.: Nebbe, William

1956 **$16.00**

No. 570

Wild Bill Hickok And The Indians

Illus.: Timmins, William

Author: Stone, Ethel B.

1956 **$18.00**

No. 571

Wynken, Blynken And Nod And Other Nursery Rhymes

Illus.: McKinley, Clare

1956 **$6.00**

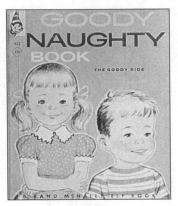

No. 572

Goody Naughty Book

Illus.: Prickett, Helen

Author: Watts, Mabel

1956 **$6.00**

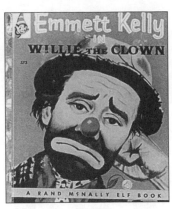

No. 573

Emmett Kelly In Willie The Clown

Illus.: Timmins, William

Author: Wing, Helen

1957 **$18.00**

No. 574

Bunny Tales

Illus.: Endred, Helen; Nebbe, William

Author: Burroes, Peggy

1956 **$7.00**

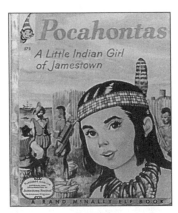

No. 575

Pocahontas, A Little Indian Girl Of Jamestown

Illus.: Lee, Manning De V

Author: Cavanah, Frances

1957 **$7.00**

No. 576

Amos Learns To Talk: The Story Of A Little Duck

Illus.: McKinley, Clare

Author: Bradbury, Bianca

1958 **$6.00**

No. 576

Cowboys

(Never Printed)

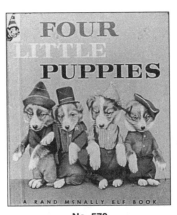

No. 577

Enchanted Egg, The

Illus.: Webbe, Elizabeth

Author: Burrows, Peggy

1956 **$7.00**

No. 578

Four Little Puppies

Illus.: Frees, Harry Whittier

Author: Dixon, Ruth

1957 **$6.00**

No. 579

Kerry, The Fire-Engine Dog

Illus.: Grider, Dorothy

Authors: Lewis, Frank; Corchia, Alfred J.

1949 **$8.00**

No. 580

Little Lost Angel

Illus.: Scott, Janet Laura

Author: Heath, Janet Field

1953 **$7.00**

No. 581

Chester, The Little Pony

Illus.: McKinley, Clare

Author: Gunder, Eman

1951 **$6.00**

No. 582

Slowpoke, The Lazy Little Puppy

Illus.: Nebbe, William

Author: Lieberthal

1957 **$6.00**

No. 583

Three Billy Goats Gruff, The

Illus.: Neebe, William

Authors: O'Grady, Alice; Throop, Frances

1957 **$6.00**

No. 584

Copy-Kitten

Illus.: Evers, Helen and Alf

1954 **$6.00**

No. 585
Number 9 The Little Fire Engine
Illus.: Corwin, Eleanor
Author: Wadsworth, Wallace
1950 $6.00

No. 586
Day On The Farm, A
Illus.: Grider, Dorothy
Author: Evers, Alf
1948 $6.00

No. 587
Hide-Away Puppy
Illus.: Dottie
Author: Broderick, Jessica Potter
1952 $6.00

No. 588
Moving Day
Illus.: Grider, Dorothy
Author: Conmfort, Mildred
1958 $6.00

No. 589
Three Little Bunnies
Illus.: Rooks, Dale and Sally
Author: Dixon, Ruth
1950 $6.00

No. 590
Little Mailman Of Bayberry Lane, The
Illus.: Webbe, Elizabeth
Author: Munn, Ian
1952 $7.00

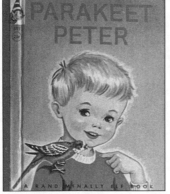

No. 591
Parakeet Peter
Illus.: Grider, Dorothy
Author: Sprinkle, Rebecca K.
1954 $6.00

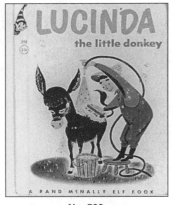

No. 592
Lucinda, The Little Donkey
Illus.: Wilde, George
Author: Wilde, Irma
1952 $6.00

No. 593
Little Friends: Kittens, Puppies, Bunnies
Illus.: Gaddis, Rie
Author: Dixon, Ruth
1951 $6.00

No. 594
Goat That Went To School, The
Illus.: Tamburine, Jean
Author: Francis, Sally R.
1952 $6.00

No. 595
Bedtime Stories
Illus.: Clyne, Barbara
Author: Watts, Mabel
1955 $6.00

No. 596
Farm For Andy, A
Illus.: Gayer, M
1951 $6.00

No. 597
Bartholomew The Beaver
Illus.: Pierce, Alice
Author: Dixon, Ruth
1952 $6.00

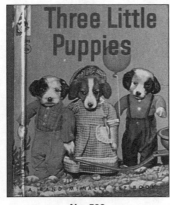

No. 598
Three Little Puppies
Illus.: Rooks, Dale and Sally
Author: Dixon, Ruth
1951 $6.00

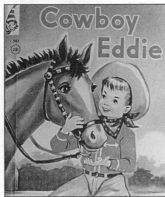

No. 599
Cowboy Eddie
Illus.: Grider, Dorothy
Author: Glasscock, Joyce
1950 $6.00

No. 1001
Jack And Jill
Illus.: Leaf, Anne Sellers
1958 $5.00

No. 1002
Dennis The Menace Camps Out
Illus.: Ketchum, Hank
1958 $9.00

No. 1003
Little Ballerina
Illus.: Grider, Dorothy
Author: Grider, Dorothy
1958 **$5.00**

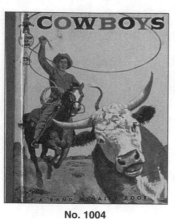

No. 1004
Cowboys
Illus.: Timmins, William
1958 **$5.00**

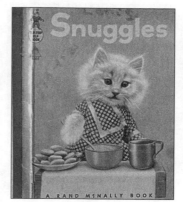

No. 1005
Snuggles
Illus.: Frees, Harry Whittier
Author: Dixon, Ruth
1958 **$5.00**

No. 1006
What Happened To George?
Illus.: Opitz, Marge
Author: Engebretson, Betty
1958 **$6.00**

No. 1007
Old Mother Hubbard
Illus.: Leaf, Anne Sellers
1958 **$5.00**

No. 1008
Johnny And The Birds
Illus.: Webbe, Elizabeth
Author: Munn, Ian
1950 **$5.00**

No. 1009
Title Unknown

No. 1010
Title Unknown

No. 1011
Title Unknown

No. 1012
Title Unknown

No. 1013
Title Unknown

No. 1014
Kitten Twins, The
Illus.: Webbe, Elizabeth
Author: Wing, Helen
1960 **$5.00**

No. 1015
Title Unknown

No. 1016
Title Unknown

No. 1017
Title Unknown

No. 1018
Title Unknown

No. 1019
Aesop's Fables
Illus.: Leaf, Ann Sellers
1958 **$4.00**

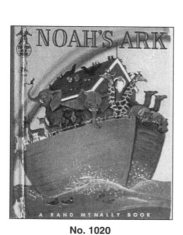

No. 1020
Noah's Ark
Illus.: Webbe, Elizabeth
Author: Briggs, Dorothy Bell
1952 **$5.00**

No. 1021
Moonymouse
Illus.: Evers, Helen & Alf
1958 **$5.00**

No. 1022
Yip And Yap
Illus.: Frees, Harry Whittier
Author: Dixon, Ruth
1958 **$5.00**

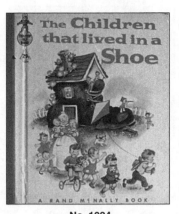

No. 1023
Penny And Pete's Surprise
Illus.: McKinley, Clare
1949   **$4.00**

No. 1024
Children That Lived In A Shoe, The
Illus.: Webbe, Elizabeth
Author: Pease, Josephine Van Dolzen
1951   **$5.00**

No. 1025
Pets
Illus.: Webbe, Elizabeth
Author: Ratzesberger, Anna
1954   **$3.00**

No. 1026
Little Bobo And His Blue Jacket
Illus.: Brice, Tony
Author: Evers, Alf
1953   **$6.00**

No. 1027
Title Unknown

No. 1028
Mother Goose
Illus.: Friend, Esther
1947   **$5.00**

No. 1029
Title Unknown

No. 1030
Title Unknown

No. 1031
Title Unknown

No. 1032
ABC Book
Illus.: Bryant, Dean
1958   **$4.00**

No. 1033
Title Unknown

No. 1034
Choo-Choo, The Little Switch Engine
Illus.: Chase, Mary Jane
Author: Wadsworth, Wallace
1954   **$5.00**

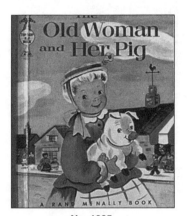

No. 1035
Old Woman And Her Pig, The
Illus.: Friend, Esther
Author: Wadsworth, Wallace
1952   **$4.00**

No. 1036
So Long
Illus.: Evers, Helen & Alf
1958   **$5.00**

No. 1037
Little Red Riding Hood
Illus.: Leaf, Anne Sellers
1958   **$5.00**

No. 1038
Busy Book, The
(Rhymes & Riddles & Things To Do)
Illus.: Szepelak, Helen
Authors: Bartlett, Floy; Pease, Josephine
1952   **$5.00**

No. 1039
Smart Little Mouse, The
Illus.: Phillips, Katherine L.
Author: Sherwan, Earl
1950   **$5.00**

No. 8300
Mother Goose
Illus.: Friend, Esther
1947   **$5.00**

No. 8300
Mother Goose
(2nd Cover)
Illus.: Friend, Esther
1947   **$5.00**

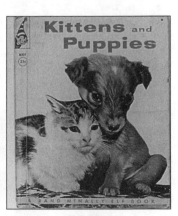

No. 8301
Kittens And Puppies
Illus.: Photographs
1955   **$5.00**

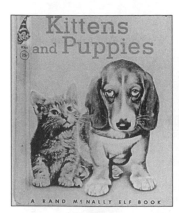

No. 8301
Kittens And Puppies
(2nd Cover)
Illus.: Photographs
1955 **$5.00**

No. 8302
Little Miss Muffet And Other Nursery Rhymes
Illus.: Chase, Mary Jane
1956 **$5.00**

No. 8302
Little Miss Muffet And Other Nursery Rhymes
(2nd Cover)
Illus.: Chase, Mary Jane
1956 **$5.00**

No. 8303
Popcorn Party
Illus.: Szepelak, Helen
Authors: Boyles, Trudy; Macmartin, Louise
1952 **$5.00**

No. 8303
Popcorn Party
(2nd Cover)
Illus.: Szepelak, Helen
Authors: Boyles, Trudy; Macmartin, Louise
1952 **$5.00**

No. 8304
Hey, Diddle, Diddle And Other Nonsense Rhymes
Illus.: Botts, Davi
1956 **$5.00**

No. 8305
Peppy, The Lonely Little Puppy
Illus.: Blake, Vivienne Leah
Author: Friedman, Frieda
1957 **$5.00**

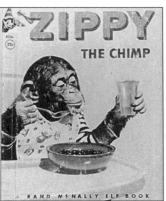

No. 8306
Zippy The Chimp
Illus.: Mitchell, Benn
Author: Ecuyer, Lee
1953 **$5.00**

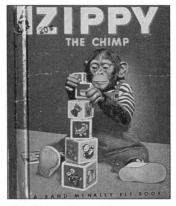

No. 8306
Zippy The Chimp
(2nd Cover)
Illus.: Mitchell, Benn
Author: Ecuyer, Lee
1953 **$5.00**

No. 8307
Hiawatha
Illus.: Wilde, Irma
Author: Gridley, Marion E.
1950 **$5.00**

No. 8308
Teddy The Terrier
Illus.: Latimer, Constance; Love, Mary
Author: Hunter, Virginia
1956 **$5.00**

No. 8309
Plump Pig
Illus.: Evers, Helen and Alf
Authors: Evers, Helen and Alf
1956 **$5.00**

No. 8310
Goody: A Mother Cat Story
Illus.: Leaf, Anne Sellers
Author: Bertail, Inez
1957 **$5.00**

No. 8311

Little Kittens' Nursery Rhymes, The

Illus.: Frees, Harry Whittier

1941 **$5.00**

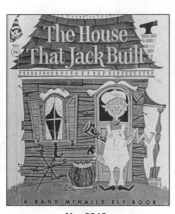

No. 8312

House That Jack Built, The

Illus.: Leaf, Anne Sellers

1959 **$5.00**

No. 8313

Three Bears, The

Illus.: Webbe, Elizabeth

1959 **$5.00**

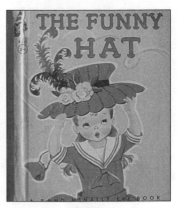

No. 8314

Funny Hat, The

Illus.: Grider, Dorothy

Author: Barrows, Marjorie

1959 **$5.00**

No. 8315

Elves And The Shoemaker, The

Illus.: Lee, Manning De V

1959 **$5.00**

No. 8316

Helpful Henrietta

Illus.: Caraway, James

Author: Watts, Mabel

1959 **$5.00**

No. 8317

Mommy Cat And Her Kittens

Illus.: Rockwell, Eve

Author: Devine, Louise Lawrence

1959 **$5.00**

No. 8318

Rumpelstiltskin

Illus.: Webbe, Elizabeth

1959 **$5.00**

No. 8319

Fraidy Cat

Illus.: Tamburine, Jean

Author: Barrows, Marjorie

1959 **$5.00**

No. 8320

Sleeping Beauty

Illus.: Webbe, Elizabeth

1959 **$5.00**

No. 8321

Tubby Turtle

Illus.: Adler, Helen

Author: Wing, Helen

1959 **$5.00**

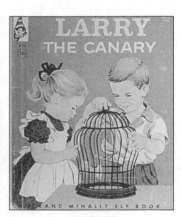

No. 8322

Larry The Canary

Illus.: Koester, Sharon

Author: Wilkie, Ellen

1959 **$5.00**

No. 8323

Tom Thumb

Illus.: Wallace, Lucille

1959 **$5.00**

No. 8324

Timothy Tiger

Illus.: Wilde, Irma

1959 **$5.00**

No. 8325

Trucks

Illus.: Wilde, George

Author: Reichert, E.C.

1959 **$5.00**

No. 326

Scamper

Illus.: Tamburine, Jean

1959 **$5.00**

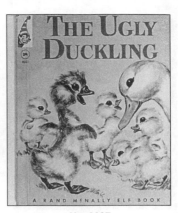

No. 8327

Ugly Duckling, The

Illus.: Opitz, Marge

1959 **$5.00**

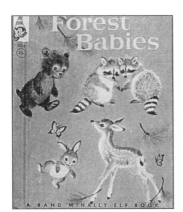

No. 8328

Forest Babies

Illus.: Webbe, Elizabeth

1956 **$5.00**

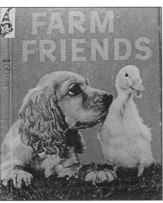

No. 8329

Farm Friends

Illus.: Photographs

Author: Hunter, Virginia

1956 **$5.00**

No. 8330

Playtime Poodles

Illus.: Westelin, Albert; Schmidling, Jack

Author: Wing, Helen

1955 **$5.00**

No. 8331

Daniel The Cocker Spaniel

Illus.: Grider, Dorothy

Author: Watts, Mabel

1955 **$5.00**

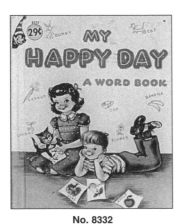

No. 8332

My Happy Day: A Word Book

Illus.: Bruce, Suzanne

Author: Shaw, Thelma

1963 **$5.00**

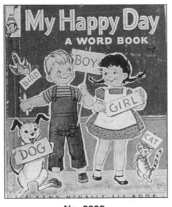

No. 8332

My Happy Day: A Word Book (2nd Cover)

Illus.: Bruce, Suzanne

Author: Shaw, Thelma

1963 **$5.00**

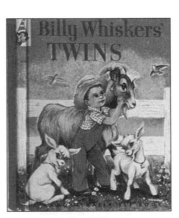

No. 8333

Billy Whiskers' Twins

Illus.: Tamburine, Jean

1956 **$5.00**

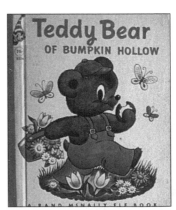

No. 8334

Teddy Bear Of Bumpkin Hollow

Illus.: Bryant, Dean

Author: Boucher, Sharon

1948 **$5.00**

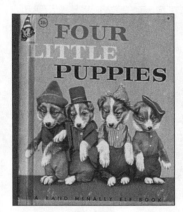

No. 8335

Four Little Puppies

Illus.: Frees, Harry Whittier

Author: Dixon, Ruth

1957 $5.00

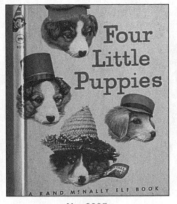

No. 8335

Four Little Puppies
(2nd Cover)

Illus.: Frees, Harry Whittier

Author: Dixon, Ruth

1957 $5.00

No. 8336

Four Little Kittens

Illus.: Frees, Harry Whittier

Author: Dixon, Ruth

1957 $5.00

No. 8337

Farm Animals

Illus.: Photographs

Author: Hunter, Virginia

1956 $5.00

No. 8338

Pillowtime Tales

Illus.: Tamburine, Jean

Author: De Groot, Marion K.

1956 $5.00

No. 8339

Our Auto Trip

Illus.: Grider, Dorothy

Author: Edsall, Marian

1952 $5.00

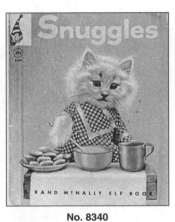

No. 8340

Snuggles

Illus.: Photographs

1958 $5.00

No. 8341

Cowboys

Illus.: Timmins, William

1958 $5.00

No. 8342

So Long

Illus.: Evers, Helen and Alf

1958 $5.00

No. 8343

Happy Holidays

Illus.: Bruce, Suzanne

Author: Reichert, E.C.

1953 $5.00

No.8344

Pony Express

Illus.: Timmins, William

Author: Grant, Bruce

1956 $5.00

No. 8345

Animal ABC Book

Illus.: Kane, Herbert

1964 $5.00

No. 8346

Sleepy-Time Rhymes

Illus.: Szepelak, Helen

Author: Smith, Goldie Capers

1964 $5.00

No. 8347

Little Horseman

Illus.: Grider, Dorothy

1961 **$5.00**

No. 8348

Wild Animals

Illus.: Vlasaty, J.L.

Author: Ratzesberger, Anna

1951 **$5.00**

**Wild Animals
(2nd Cover)**

$4.00

No. 349

Mr. Bear's House

Illus.: McKinley, Clare

Author: Rothe, Fenella

1953 **$5.00**

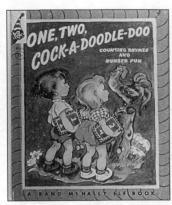

No. 8350

One, Two, Cock-A-Doodle-Doo

Illus.: Wosmek, Frances

Author: Pease, Josephine Van Dolzen

1950 **$5.00**

No. 8351

Buddy, The Little Taxi

Illus.: Corwin, Elizabeth

1951 **$5.00**

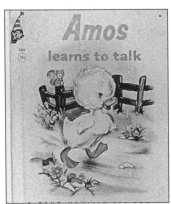

No. 8352

**Amos Learns To Talk: The
Story Of A Little Duck**

Illus.: McKinley, Clare

Author: Bradbury, Bianca

1950 **$5.00**

No. 8352

**Amos Learns To Talk: The
Story Of A Little Duck
(2nd Cover)**

Illus.: McKinley, Clare

Author: Bradbury, Bianca

1950 **$5.00**

No. 8353

Kerry, The Fire-Engine Dog

Illus.: Grider, Dorothy

Authors: Lewis, Frank; Corchia, Alfred J.

1949 **$6.00**

No. 8354

Chester, The Little Pony

Illus.: McKinley, Clare

Author: Gunder, Eman

1951 **$5.00**

**Chester, The Little Pony
(2nd Cover)**

$4.00

No. 8355

Bedtime Stories

Illus.: Clyne, Barbara

Author: Watts, Mabel

1955 **$5.00**

No. 8356

Puss-In-Boots

Illus.: Myers, Bernice and Lou

1955 **$5.00**

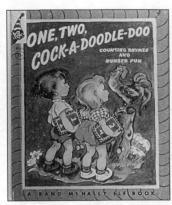

No. 8357

Hide-Away Puppy

Illus.: Dottie

Author: Broderick, Jessica Potter

1952 **$5.00**

No. 8358
Farm For Andy, A
Illus.: Gayer, M
1951   **$5.00**

No. 8359
Title Unknown

No. 8360
Day On The Farm, A
Illus.: Grider, Dorothy
Author: Evers, Alf
1948   **$5.00**

No. 8361
Little Mailman Of Bayberry Lane, The
Illus.: Webbe, Elizabeth
Author: Munn, Ian
1952   **$8.00**

No. 8362
Lucinda, The Little Donkey
Illus.: Wilde, George
Author: Wilde, Irma
1952   **$5.00**

Lucinda, The Little Donkey (2nd Cover)
                                        $4.00

No. 8363
Three Little Puppies
Illus.: Rooks, Dale and Sally
Author: Dixon, Ruth
1951   **$5.00**

No. 8364
ABC Book
Illus.: Bryant, Dean
1958   **$5.00**

No. 8365
Hansel And Gretel
Illus.: Smith, Kay Lovelace
1960   **$4.00**

No. 8366
Little Boy Blue And Other Nursery Rhymes
Illus.: Leaf, Anne Sellers
1956   **$5.00**

No. 8367
Wynken, Blynken And Nod And Other Nursery Rhymes
Illus.: McKinley, Clare
1956   **$5.00**

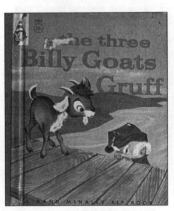

No. 8368
Three Billy Goats Gruff, The
Illus.: Nebbe, William
Authors: O'Grady, Alice; Throop, Frances
1957   **$5.00**

No. 8369
Number 9 The Little Fire Engine
Illus.: Corwin, Eleanor
Author: Wadsworth, Wallace
1950   **$5.00**

No. 8370
Copy-Kitten
Illus.: Evers, Helen and Alf
1957   **$5.00**

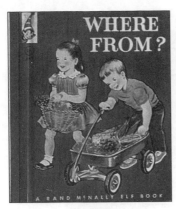

No. 8371

Where From?

Illus.: Smith, Eunice Young
Author: Smith, Eunice Young
1961   **$5.00**

No. 8372

Jack And The Beanstalk

Illus.: Leaf, Anne Sellers
1961   **$4.00**

No. 8373

Angel Child

Illus.: Doane, Pelagie
Author: Teal, Val
1946   **$4.00**

No. 8374

Parakeet Peter

Illus.: Grider, Dorothy
Author: Sprinkle, Rebecca K.
1954   **$4.00**

No. 8375

Busy Bulldozer, The

Illus.: Grider, Dorothy
Author: Browning, James
1951   **$4.00**

No. 8376

Little Lost Angel

Illus.: Scott, Janet Laura
Author: Heath, Janet Field
1953   **$5.00**

No. 8377

Johnny And The Birds

Illus.: Webbe, Elizabeth
Author: Munn, Ian
1950   **$4.00**

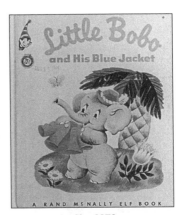

No. 8378

Little Bobo And His Blue Jacket

Illus.: Brice, Tony
Author: Evers, Alf
1953   **$5.00**

No. 8379

Old Woman And Her Pig, The

Illus.: Friend, Esther
Author: Wadsworth, Wallace
1952   **$4.00**

No. 8380

Yip And Yap

Illus.: Frees, Harry Whittier
Author: Dixon, Ruth
1958   **$4.00**

No. 8381

Squirrel Twins, The

Illus.: Webbe, Elizabeth
Author: Wing, Helen
1961   **$4.00**

No. 8382

My Flower Book

Illus.: Webbe, Elizabeth
Author: Landis, Dorothy Thompson
1961   **$4.00**

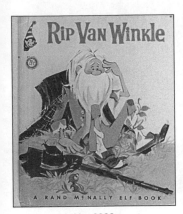

No. 8383

Rip Van Winkle

Illus.: Leaf, Anne Sellers
Author: Briggs, Dorothy Bell
1961 $4.00

No. 8384

Surprise!

Illus.: Ozone, Lucy
Author: Ozone, Lucy
1956 $4.00

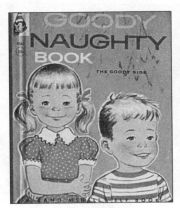

No. 8385

Goody Naughty Book

Illus.: Prickett, Helen
Author: Watts, Mabel
1956 $4.00

No. 8386

Goat That Went To School, The

Illus.: Tamburine, Jean
Author: Francis, Sally R.
1952 $4.00

No. 8387

Davy's Little Horse

Illus.: Dennis, Wesley
Author: Devine, Louise Lawrence
1956 $4.00

No. 8388

Three Little Bunnies

Illus.: Rooks, Dale and Sally
Author: Dixon, Ruth
1950 $4.00

No. 8389

Little Skater

Illus.: Grider, Dorothy
Author: Sherman, Diane
1959 $5.00

No. 8390

Little Ballerina

Illus.: Grider, Dorothy
Author: Grider, Dorothy
1958 $5.00

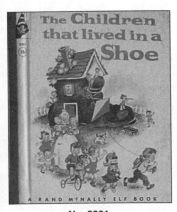

No. 8391

Children That Lived In A Shoe, The

Illus.: Webbe, Elizabeth
Author: Pease, Josephine Van Dolzen
1951 $4.00

No. 8392

Pets

Illus.: Webbe, Elizabeth
1954 $4.00

No. 8393

Storybook For Little Tots

Illus.: Chase, Mary Jane
Author: Hunter, Virginia
1958 $4.00

No. 8394

Choo-Choo, The Little Switch Engine

Illus.: Chase, Mary Jane
Author: Wadsworth, Wallace
1954 $4.00

No. 8395

Jack And Jill

Illus.: Leaf, Anne Sellers

1958 **$5.00**

No. 8396

Penny And Pete's Surprise

Illus.: McKinley, Clare

1949 **$4.00**

No. 8397

Growing Up

Illus.: Webbe, Elizabeth

Author: Fritz, Webbe

1956 **$4.00**

No. 8398

Story Of Our Flag, The

Illus.: Wilde, Irma

1955 **$4.00**

No. 8399

My Counting Book

Illus.: Koester, Sharon

Author: Sherman, Diane

1960 **$4.00**

No. 8400

Moonymouse

Illus.: Evers, Helen and Alf

1958 **$4.00**

No. 8401

Three Bears Visit Goldilocks, The

Illus.: McKinley, Clare

1951 **$4.00**

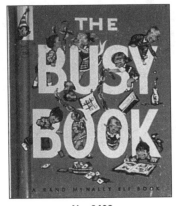

No. 8402

Busy Book, The

(Rhymes And Riddles And Things To Do)

Illus.: Szepelak, Helen

Author: Bartlett, Floy: Pease, Josephine

1952 **$4.00**

No. 8403

Our Animal Friends

Illus.: Photographs

Author: Hunter, Virginia

1956 **$4.00**

No. 8404

Five Busy Bears, The

Illus.: Tamburine, Jean

Author: North, Sterling

1955 **$4.00**

No. 8405

Fussbunny

Illus.: Evers, Helen and Alf

Authors: Evers, Helen and Alf

1955 **$4.00**

No. 8406

Bunny Tales

Illus.: Endred, Helen; Nebbe, William

Author: Burroes, Peggy

1956 **$4.00**

No. 8407

Enchanted Egg, The

Illus.: Webbe, Elizabeth

Author: Burrows, Peggy

1956 **$5.00**

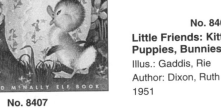

No. 8408

Little Friends: Kittens, Puppies, Bunnies

Illus.: Gaddis, Rie

Author: Dixon, Ruth

1951 **$4.00**

No. 8409

What Happened To George?

Illus.: Opitz, Marge

Author: Engebretson, Betty

1958   **$6.00**

No. 8410

Little Majorette

Illus.: Grider, Dorothy

Author: Grider, Dorothy

1959   **$4.00**

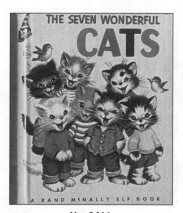

No. 8411

Seven Wonderful Cats, The

Illus.: Nebbe, William

1956   **$4.00**

No. 8412

Johnny The Fireman

Illus.: Wood, Ruth

Author: Sprinkle, Rebecca K.

1954   **$4.00**

No. 8413

Old Mother Hubbard

Illus.: Leaf, Anne Sellers

1958   **$6.00**

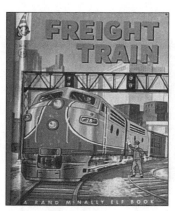

No. 8414

Freight Train

Illus.: Pollard, G

1956   **$4.00**

No. 8415

Mr. Punnymoon's Train

Illus.: Phillips, Katherine L.

Author: Hadsell, Alice

1951   **$4.00**

No. 8416

Little Swimmers

Illus.: Grider, Dorothy

Author: Grider, Dorothy

1960   **$6.00**

No. 8417

Cinderella

Illus.: Endred, Helen; Neebe, William

Author: Bates, Katherine Lee

1956   **$4.00**

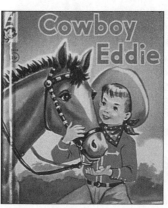

No. 8418

Cowboy Eddie

Illus.: Grider, Dorothy

Author: Glasscock, Joyce

1950   **$5.00**

No. 8419

Little Red Riding-Hood

Illus.: Leaf, Anne Sellers

1958   **$6.00**

No. 8420

Puppy Twins, The

Illus.: Bendel, Ruth

Author: Wing, Helen

1959   **$4.00**

No. 8421
Smart Little Mouse, The
Illus.: Phillips, Katherine L.
Author: Sherwan, Earl
1950   **$4.00**

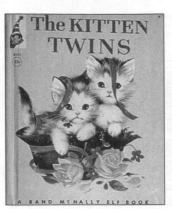

No. 8422
Kitten Twins, The
Illus.: Webbe, Elizabeth
Author: Wing, Helen
1960   **$4.00**

No. 8423
Bartholomew The Beaver
Illus.: Pierce, Alice
Author: Dixon, Ruth
1952   **$4.00**

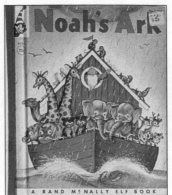

No. 8424
Noah's Ark
Illus.: Webbe, Elizabeth
Author: Briggs, Dorothy Bell
1952   **$4.00**

No. 8425
Present For The Princess, A
Illus.: Webbe, Elizabeth
Author: Paschall, Janie Lowe
1959   **$6.00**

No. 8426
Crybaby Calf
Illus.: Evers, Helen and Alf
1954   **$4.00**

No. 8427
Twilight Tales
Illus.: Bryant, Dean
Author: Potter, Miriam Clark
1947   **$4.00**

No. 8428
Bunny Book, The
Illus.: Cooper, Marjorie
Author: Wing, Helen
1964   **$4.00**

No. 8429
Pony Twins, The
Illus.: Cooper, Marjorie
Author: Wing, Helen
1964   **$4.00**

No. 8430
Three Pigs, The
Illus.: Storytoon Express
1962   **$8.00**

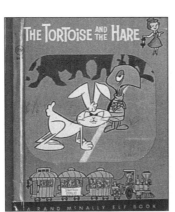

No. 8431
Tortoise And The Hare, The
Illus.: Storytoon Express
1962   **$8.00**

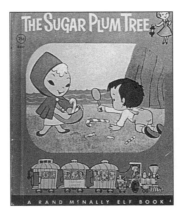

No. 8432
Sugar Plum Tree, The
Illus.: Storytoon Express
1962   **$8.00**

No. 8433
Magic Pot, The
Illus.: Storytoon Express
1962   **$8.00**

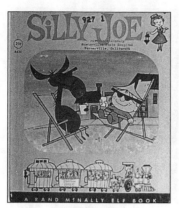

No. 8434

Silly Joe
Illus.: Storytoon Express
Author: Storytoon Express
1962 **$8.00**

No. 8435

Lazy Jack
Illus.: Storytoon Express
Author: Storytoon Express
1962 **$8.00**

No. 8436

Early One Morning
Illus.: Cooper, Marjorie
Author: Graland, Valerie
1963 **$5.00**

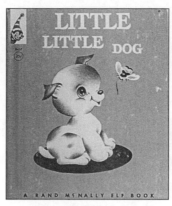

No. 8437

Little Little Dog
Illus.: Adler, Helen
Author: Brailsford, Frances
1963 **$4.00**

No. 8438

Garden Is Good, A
Illus.: Cooper, Marjorie
Author: Chaffin, Lillie D.
1963 **$4.00**

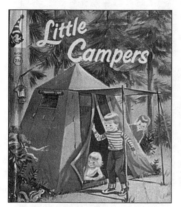

No. 8439

Little Campers
Illus.: Grider, Dorothy
Author: Watts, Mabel
1963 **$4.00**

No. 8440

Aesop's Fables
Illus.: Leaf, Anne Sellers
1952 **$4.00**

No. 8441

Pudgy The Little Bear
Illus.: Tamburine, Jean
Author: Barrows, Marjorie
1964 **$4.00**

No. 8442

Crosspatch
Illus.: Evers, Helen and Alf
Authors: Evers, Helen and Alf
1964 **$4.00**

No. 8443

Title Unknown

No. 8444

Muggins Mouse
Illus.: Leaf, Anne Sellers
Author: Barrows, Marjorie
1964 **$5.00**

No. 8445

Title Unknown

No. 8446

Title Unknown

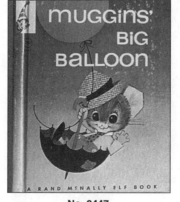

No. 8447

Muggins' Big Balloon
Illus.: Leaf, Anne Sellers
Author: Marjorie Barrows
1964 **$5.00**

No. 8448

Muggins Becomes A Hero
Illus.: Leaf, Anne Sellers
1965 **$5.00**

No. 8449

Title Unknown

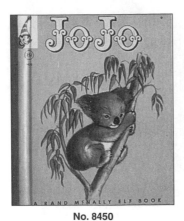

No. 8450

Jo Jo
Illus.: Barrows, Marjorie
Author: Wallace, Ivy L.
1964 **$4.00**

No. 8451

Pokey Bear
Illus.: Evers, Helen and Alf
Authors: Evers, Helen and Alf
1965 **$5.00**

No. 8452

**Pink Lemonade
(And Other Peter Patter
Rhymes)**
Illus.: Grider, Dorothy
Author: Jackson, Leroy F.
1965 **$4.00**

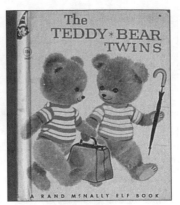

No. 8453

Teddy Bear Twins, The
Illus.: Cooper, Marjorie
Author: Wing, Helen
1965 **$7.00**

No. 8454

Title Unknown

No. 8455

Princess And The Pea
Illus.: Leaf, Anne Sellers
1965 **$5.00**

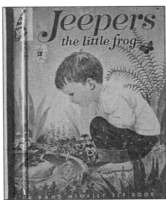

No. 8456

Jeepers, The Little Frog
Illus.: Cooper, Marjorie
Author: Cooper, Marjorie
1965 **$4.00**

No. 8457

Gingerbread Man, The
Illus.: Leaf, Ann Sellers

$4.00

No. 8458

Rocket For A Cow, A
Illus.: Wilde, Irma
Author: Devine, Louise Lawrence
1965 **$6.00**

No. 8459

Animal Stories
Illus.: Grider, Dorothy
Author: Jackson, Leroy F.
1965 **$4.00**

No. 8460

Happy Twins, The
Illus.: Cooper, Marjorie
Author: Wing, Helen
1956 **$4.00**

No. 8461

Title Unknown

No. 8462

Three Little Kittens
Illus.: Cooper, Marjorie
1966 **$4.00**

No. 8550

From Tadpoles To Frogs
$4.00

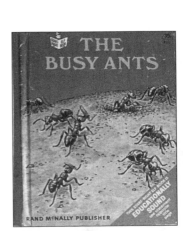

No. 8551

Busy Ants, The
Illus.: Street, T.
1973 **$4.00**

No. 8552
Building A Skyscraper
Illus.: Frame, Paul
Author: Kozak, Louis Lawrence
1973 $4.00

No. 8553
Alphabet Walks
Illus.: Stahlman, Catherine
Author: Petie, Haris
1973 $4.00

No. 8554
Title Unknown

No. 8555
My First Book Of Jesus
                         $4.00

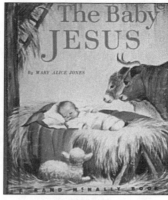

No. 8556
Baby Jesus, The
Illus.: Webbe, Elizabeth
Author: Jones, Mary Alice
1961 $4.00

No. 8557
Prayers For Little Children
Illus.: Bruce, Suzanne
Author: Jones, Mary Alice
1959 $4.00

No. 8558
Look For A Rainbow
Illus.: Cooper, Marjorie
1972 $4.00
No. 8559
Title Unknown

No. 8560
Billy's Treasure
Illus.: Grider, Dorothy
Author: Snow, Dorothea J.
1972 $4.00

No. 8561
Turtles Turn Up On Tuesday
Illus.: Frame, Paul
Author: Shaw, Thelma
1972 $4.00

No. 8562
Time For Everything
Illus.: Kane, Sharon
1972 $4.00

No. 8563
Title Unknown

No. 8564
Title Unknown

No. 8565
Puppies To Love
Illus.: Lougheed, Robert
Author: Wing, Helen
1971 $4.00

No. 8566
Trip In Space, A
Illus.: Fleishman, Seymour
Author: Grant, Bruce
1968 $6.00

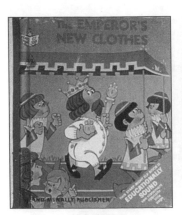

No. 8567
Emperor's New Clothes, The
Illus.: Leaf, Anne Sellers
1968   **$4.00**

No. 8568
Looking In And Other Poems
Illus.: Grider, Dorothy
Author: Aldis, Dorothy
1968   **$4.00**

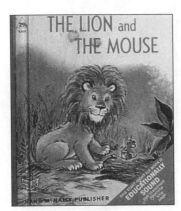

No. 8569
Lion And The Mouse, The
Illus.: Blake, Vivienne Leah
Author: Duff, Emma Lorne
1968   **$4.00**

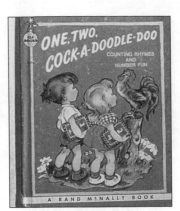

No. 8570
One, Two, Cock-A-Doodle-Doo
Illus.: Wosmek, Frances
Author: Pease, Josephine Van Dolzen
1950   **$4.00**

No. 8571
Let's Grow Things
Illus.: Wilde, Irma
Author: Comfort, Iris Tracy
1967   **$4.00**

No. 8572
Hop-Away Joey
Illus.: Fleishman, Seymour
Author: Broderick, Jessica Potter
1967   **$5.00**

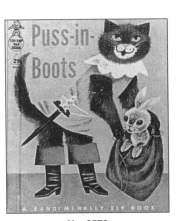

No. 8573
Puss-In-Boots
Illus.: Myers, Bernice and Lou
1955   **$4.00**

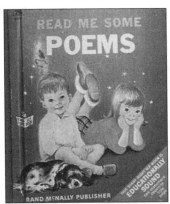

No. 8574
Read Me Some Poems
Illus.: Cooper, Marjorie
1968   **$4.00**

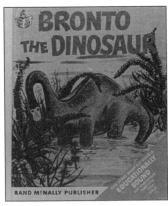

No. 8575
Bronto The Dinosaur
Illus.: Wilde, George
Author: Landis, Dorothy Thompson
1967   **$4.00**

No. 8576
Chatterduck
Illus.: Evers, Helen and Alf
Authors: Evers, Helen and Alf
1967   **$4.00**

No. 8577
Our World Of Color And Sound
Illus.: Cooper, Marjorie
Author: Bartkowski, Renee
1967   **$4.00**

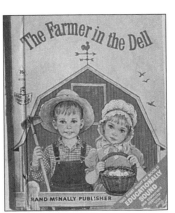

No. 8578
Farmer In The Dell, The
Illus.: Kane, Sharon
1967   **$7.00**

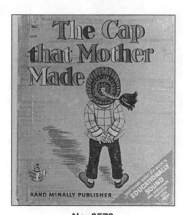

No. 8579
Cap That Mother Made, The
Illus.: Friend, Esther
Authors: O'Grady, Alice; Throop, Frances
1967   **$4.00**

No. 8580
Snow White And Rose Red
Illus.: Cooper, Marjorie
1967   **$4.00**
No. 8581
Title Unknown

No. 8582
Three Little Kittens
Cooper, Marjorie
1966   **$4.00**

No. 8583
Title Unknown

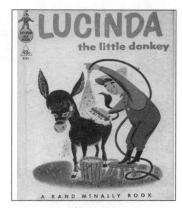

No. 8584
Lucinda, The Little Donkey
Illus.: Wilde, George
Author: Wilde, Irma
1952   **$4.00**
No. 8585
Title Unknown
No. 8586
Day On The Farm, A
Illus.: Evers, Alf
Author: Evers, Alf
1948   **4.00**

No. 8587
Hide-Away Puppy
Illus.: Dotti
Author: Broderick, Jessica Potter
1952   **$4.00**

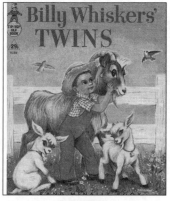

No. 8588
Billy Whiskers' Twins
Illus.: Tamburine, Jean
No. 8589
Title Unknown

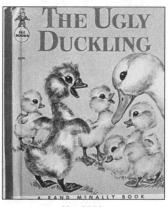

No. 8590
Ugly Duckling, The
Illus.: Opitz, Marge
1959   **$4.00**

No. 8591
Title Unknown

No. 8592
Plump Pig, The
Illus.: Evers, Helen and Alf
Authors: Evers, Helen and Alf
1956   **$4.00**

No. 8593
Goody Naughty Book
Illus.: Prickett, Helen
Author: Watts, Mabel
1956   **$4.00**

No. 8594
Goat That Went To School, The
Illus.: Tamburine, Jean
Author: Francis, Sally R.
1952   **$4.00**

No. 8595
Title Unknown

No. 8596
Title Unknown

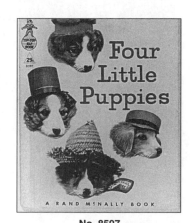

No. 8597
Four Little Puppies
Illus.: Frees, Harry Whittier
Author: Dixon, Ruth
1957   **$3.00**

No. 8598
Peaky Beaky
Illus.: Oechsli, Kelly
1967 **$5.00**

No. 8599
Gingerbread Man, The
Illus.: Leaf, Anne Sellers
1965 **$5.00**

No. 8600
Little Lost Kitten: Story Of Williamsburg
Illus.: Lee, Manning De V
Author: Comfort, Mildred
1956 **$4.00**

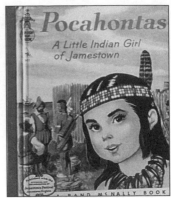

No. 8601
Pocahontas, A Little Indian Girl Of Jamestown
Illus.: Lee, Manning De V
Author: Cavanah, Frances
1957 **$4.00**

No. 8602
Present For The Princess, A
Illus.: Webbe, Elizabeth
Author: Paschall, Janie Lowe
1959 **$5.00**

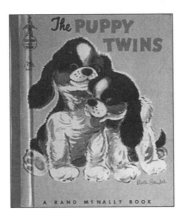

No. 8603
Puppy Twins, The
Illus.: Bendel, Ruth
Author: Wing, Helen
1959 **$4.00**

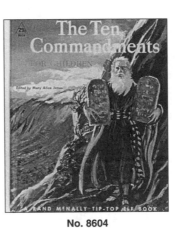

No. 8604
Ten Commandments For Children, The
Illus.: Bonfils, Robert
Author: Jones, Mary Alice
1956 **$4.00**

No. 8604
Ten Commandments For Children, The (2nd Cover)
Illus.: Bonfils, Robert
Author: Jones, Mary Alice
1956 **$4.00**

No. 8605
Little Majorette
Illus.: Grider, Dorothy
Author: Grider, Dorothy
1959 **$4.00**

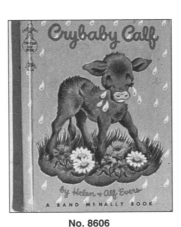

No. 8606
Crybaby Calf
Illus.: Evers, Helen and Alf
1954 **$4.00**

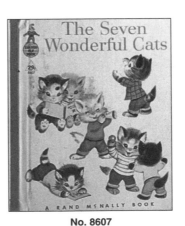

No. 8607
Seven Wonderful Cats, The
Illus.: Nebbe, William
1956 **$4.00**

No. 8608
Twilight Tales
Illus.: Bryant, Dean
Author: Potter, Miriam Clark
1947 **$4.00**

No. 8608

**Twilight Tales
(2nd Cover)**

Illus.: Bryant, Dean

Author: Potter, Miriam Clark

1947 **$4.00**

No. 8609

Prayers And Graces For A Small Child

Illus.: Webbe, Elizabeth

Author: Webbe, Elizabeth

1955 **$4.00**

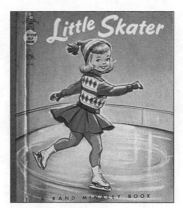

No. 8610

Little Skater

Illus.: Grider, Dorothy

Author: Sherman, Diane

1959 **$4.00**

No. 8611

Johnny The Fireman

Illus.: Wood, Ruth

Author: Sprinkle, Rebecca K.

1954 **$5.00**

No. 8611

**Johnny The Fireman
(2nd Cover)**

Illus.: Wood, Ruth

Author: Sprinkle, Rebecca K.

1954 **$5.00**

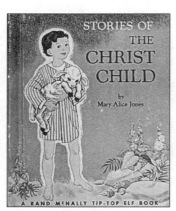

No. 8612

Stories Of The Christ Child

Illus.: Corwin, Eleanor

Author: Jones, Mary Alice

1953 **$4.00**

No. 8612

**Stories Of The Christ Child
(2nd Cover)**

Illus.: Corwin, Eleanor

Author: Jones, Mary Alice

1953 **$4.00**

No. 8613

Bible Stories: Old Testament

Illus.: Webbe, Elizabeth

Author: Jones, Mary Alice

1954 **$4.00**

No. 8614

Little Ballerina

Illus.: Grider, Dorothy

Author: Grider, Dorothy

1958 **$5.00**

No. 8615

Aesop's Fables

Illus.: Leaf, Anne Sellers

1952 **$5.00**

No. 8616

Children That Lived In A Shoe, The

Illus.: Webbe, Elizabeth

Author: Pease, Josephine Van Dolzen

1951 **$4.00**

No. 8617

Pets

Illus.: Webbe, Elizabeth

1954 **$4.00**

No. 8618
Bugle, A Puppy In Old Yorktown
Illus.: Lee, Manning De V
Author: Andrews, Mary
1958   **$4.00**

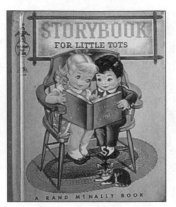

No. 8619
Storybook For Little Tots
Illus.: Chase, Mary Jane
Author: Hunter, Virginia
1958   **$4.00**

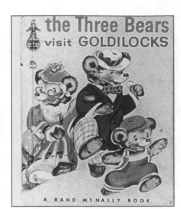

No. 8620
Three Bears Visit Goldilocks, The
Illus.: McKinley, Clare
1951   **$4.00**

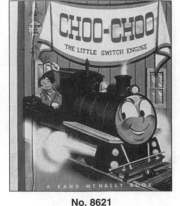

No. 8621
Choo-Choo, The Little Switch Engine
Illus.: Chase, Mary Jane
Author: Wadsworth, Wallace
1954   **$4.00**

No. 8622
So Long
Illus.: Evers, Helen and Alf
1958   **$4.00**

No. 8623
Busy Book, The
(Rhymes & Riddles & Things To Do)
Illus.: Szepelak, Helen
Authors: Bartlett, Floy; Pease, Josephine
1952   **$4.00**

No. 8624
Old Mother Hubbard
Illus.: Leaf, Anne Sellers
1958   **$5.00**

No. 8625
Jack And Jill
Illus.: Leaf, Anne Sellers
1958   **$5.00**

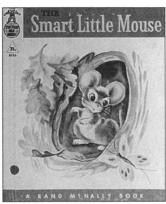

No. 8626
Smart Little Mouse, The
Illus.: Phillips, Katherine L.
Author: Sherwan, Earl
1950   **$4.00**

No. 8627
Penny And Pete's Surprise
Illus.: McKinley, Clare
1949   **$4.00**

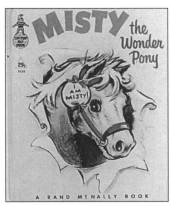

No. 8628
Misty The Wonder Pony
Illus.: McKinley, Clare
1956   **$4.00**

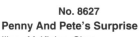

No. 8629
Five Busy Bears, The
Illus.: Tamburine, Jean
Author: North, Sterling
1955   **$4.00**

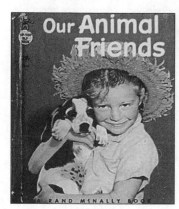

No. 8630
Our Animal Friends
Illus.: Photographs
Author: Hunter, Virginia
1956   **$4.00**

No. 8631
Freight Train
Illus.: Pollard, G
1956   **$4.00**

No. 8632
Mr. Punnymoon's Train
Illus.: Phillips, Katherine L.
Author: Hadsell, Alice
1951   **$5.00**

No. 8632
**Mr. Punnymoon's Train
(2nd Cover)**
Illus.: Phillips, Katherine L.
Author: Hadsell, Alice
1951   **$5.00**

No. 8633
Little Swimmers
Illus.: Grider, Dorothy
Author: Grider, Dorothy
1960   **$4.00**

No. 8634
Growing Up
Illus.: Webbe, Elizabeth
Author: Fritz, Webbe
1956   **$4.00**

No. 8635
Story Of Our Flag, The
Illus.: Wilde, Irma
1955   **$4.00**

No. 8636
My Counting Book
Illus.: Koester, Sharon
Author: Sherman, Diane
1960   **$4.00**

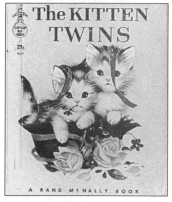

No. 8637
Kitten Twins, The
Illus.: Webbe, Elizabeth
Author: Wing, Helen
1960   **$5.00**

No. 8638
Hansel And Gretel
Illus.: Smith, Kay Lovelace
1960   **$4.00**

No. 8639
Moonymouse
Illus.: Evers, Helen and Alf
1958   **$4.00**

No. 8640
Enchanted Egg, The
Illus.: Webbe, Elizabeth
Author: Burrows, Peggy
1956   **$4.00**

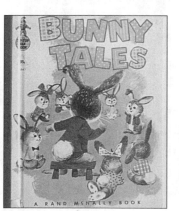

No. 8641
Bunny Tales
Illus.: Endres, Helen; Neebe, William
Author: Burroes, Peggy
1956   **$4.00**

No. 8642
Fuss Bunny
Illus.: Evers, Helen and Alf
Authors: Evers, Helen and Alf
1955   **$4.00**

No. 8643
Bartholomew The Beaver
Illus.: Pierce, Alice
Author: Dixon, Ruth
1952 $4.00

No. 8644
Cinderella
Illus.: Endred, Helen; Neebe, William
Author: Bates, Katherine Lee
1956 $4.00

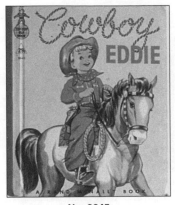

No. 8645
Cowboy Eddie
Illus.: Grider, Dorothy
Author: Glasscock, Joyce
1950 $5.00

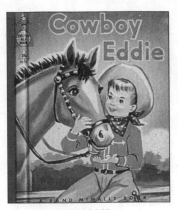

No. 8645
Cowboy Eddie
(2nd Cover)
Illus.: Grider, Dorothy
Author: Glasscock, Joyce
1950 $5.00

No. 8646
Little Red Riding-Hood
Illus.: Leaf, Anne Sellers
1958 $5.00

No. 8647
Mother Goose
Illus.: Friend, Esther
1947 $4.00

No. 8648
Noah's Ark
Illus.: Webbe, Elizabeth
Author: Briggs, Dorothy Bell
1952 $4.00

No. 8649
Little Horseman
Illus.: Grider, Dorothy
1961 $5.00

No. 8650
Squirrel Twins, The
Illus.: Webbe, Elizabeth
Author: Wing, Helen
1961 $4.00

No. 8651
Child's Thought Of God, A
Illus.: Grider, Dorothy
1957 $4.00

No. 8652
I Think About Jesus
Illus.: Friend, Esther
1958 $4.00

No. 8653
ABC Book
Illus.: Bryant, Dean
1958 $4.00

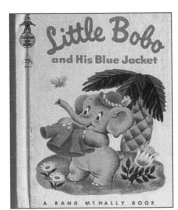

No. 8654
Little Bobo And His Blue Jacket
Illus.: Brice, Tony
Author: Evers, Alf
1953 $4.00

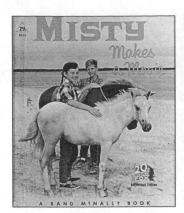

No. 8655

Misty Makes A Movie

Illus.: Photographs

1961   **$4.00**

No. 8656

Early One Morning

Illus.: Cooper, Marjorie

Author: Grayland, Valerie

1963   **$4.00**

No. 8657

Garden Is Good, A

Illus.: Cooper, Marjorie

1963   **$4.00**

No. 8658

Animal ABC Book

Illus.: Kane, Herbert

1964   **$4.00**

No. 8659

Pony Twins, The

Illus.: Cooper, Marjorie

Author: Wing, Helen

1964   **$4.00**

No. 8660

Little Campers

Illus.: Grider, Dorothy

1963   **$4.00**

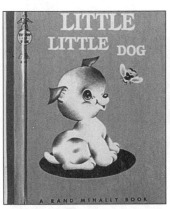

No. 8661

Little Little Dog

Illus.: Adler, Helen

Author: Brailsford, Frances

1963   **$4.00**

No. 8662

Title Unknown

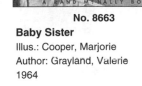

No. 8663

Baby Sister

Illus.: Cooper, Marjorie

Author: Grayland, Valerie

1964   **$4.00**

No. 8664

Sleepy-Time Rhymes

Illus.: Szepelak, Helen

Author: Smith, Goldie Capers

1964   **$4.00**

No. 8665

Little Cub Scout

Illus.: Timmins, William

Author: Watts, Mabel

1964   **$6.00**

No. 8666

Cowboys

Illus.: Timmins, William

1958   **$4.00**

No. 8667

What Happened to George?

     $5.00

No. 8668

Jack And The Beanstalk

Illus.: Leaf, Anne Sellers

1961   **$5.00**

No. 8669
Rumpelstiltskin
Illus.: Webbe, Elizabeth
1959   **$4.00**

No. 8670
Squirrel Twins, The
Illus.: Webbe, Elizabeth
Author: Wing, Helen
1961   **$4.00**

No. 8671
Rip Van Winkle
Illus.: Leaf, Anne Sellers
Author: Briggs, Dorothy Bell
1961   **$4.00**

No. 8672
Timothy Tiger
Illus.: Wilde, Irma
1959   **$4.00**

No. 8673
Muggins Mouse
Illus.: Leaf, Anne Sellers
1964   **$5.00**

No. 8674
Pudgy The Little Bear
Illus.: Tamburine, Jean
Author: Barrows, Marjorie
1964   **$4.00**

No. 8675
Crosspatch
Illus.: Evers, Helen and Alf
Author: Evers, Helen and Alf
1964   **$4.00**

No. 8676
Bunny Twins, The
Illus.: Cooper, Marjorie
Author: Wing, Helen
1964   **$5.00**

No. 8677
Funny Hat, The
Illus.: Grider, Dorothy
Author: Barrows, Marjorie
1959   **$5.00**
No. 8678
Title Unknown

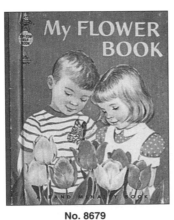

No. 8679
My Flower Book
Illus.: Webbe, Elizabeth
Author: Landis, Dorothy Thompson
1961   **$4.00**

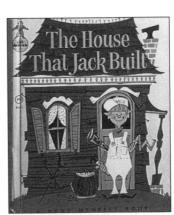

No. 8680
Little Lost Angel
Illus.: Scott, Janet Laura
Author: Heath, Janet Field
1953   **$5.00**

No. 8681
House That Jack Built, The
Illus.: Leaf, Anne Sellers
1959   **$5.00**

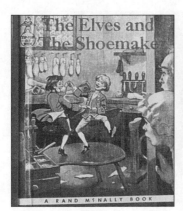

No. 8682

Elves And The Shoemaker, The

Illus.: Lee, Manning De V

1959 $4.00

No. 8683

Sleeping Beauty

Illus.: Webbe, Elizabeth

1959 $4.00

No. 8684

Tom Thumb

Illus.: Wallace, Lucille

1959 $4.00

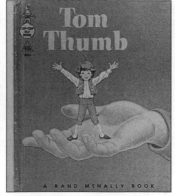

No. 8684

Tom Thumb

(2nd Cover)

Illus.: Wallace, Lucille

1959 $4.00

No. 8685

Larry The Canary

Illus.: Koester, Sharon

Author: Wilkie, Ellen

1959 $4.00

No. 8686

Hiawatha

Illus.: Wilde, Irma

Author: Gridley, Marion E.

1961 $4.00

No. 8687

Trucks

Illus.: Wilde, George

Author: Reichert, E.C.

1959 $4.00

No. 8688

Title Unknown

No. 8689

Copy-Kitten

Illus.: Evers, Helen and Alf

Authors: Evers, Helen and Alf

1957 $4.00

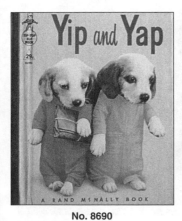

No. 8690

Yip And Yap

Illus.: Frees, Harry Whittier

Author: Dixon, Ruth

1958 $4.00

No. 8691

Title Unknown

No. 8692

Tubby Turtle

Illus.: Adler, Helen

Author: Wing, Helen

1959 $5.00

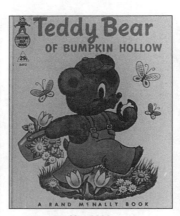

No. 8693

Teddy Bear Of Bumpkin Hollow

Illus.: Bryant, Dean

Author: Boucher, Sharon

1948 $4.00

No. 8694

Title Unknown

No. 8695

Volksy: The Little Yellow Car

Illus.: Chase, Mary Jane

Author: Wing, Helen

1965 $9.00

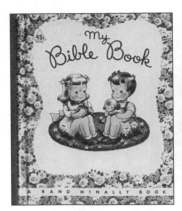

No. 8696
My Bible Book
Illus.: Bryant, Dean
Author: Walker, Janie
1946   **$4.00**

No. 8697
My Prayer Book
                              $4.00

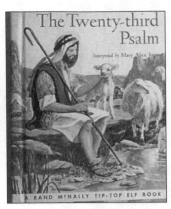

No. 8698
Twenty-Third Psalm, The
Illus.: Lee, Manning De V
1964   **$4.00**

No. 8699
Title Unknown

No. 8700
Muggins Takes Off
Illus.: Leaf, Anne Sellers
Author: Barrows, Marjorie
1964   **$5.00**

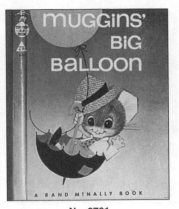

No. 8701
Muggins' Big Balloon
Illus.: Leaf, Anne Sellers
1964   **$5.00**

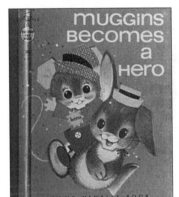

No. 8702
Muggins Becomes A Hero
Illus.: Leaf, Anne Sellers
Author: Barrow, Marjorie
1965   **$5.00**

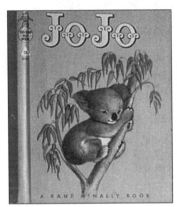

No. 8703
Jo Jo
Illus.: Wallace, Ivy L.
Author: Barrows, Marjorie
1964   **$4.00**

No. 8704
Johnny And The Birds
Illus.: Webbe, Elizabeth
Author: Munn, Ian
1950   **$4.00**

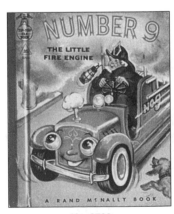

No. 8704
**Johnny And The Birds
(2nd Cover)**
Illus.: Webbe, Elizabeth
Author: Munn, Ian
1950   **$4.00**

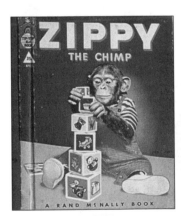

No. 8705
Zippy The Chimp
Illus.: Mitchell, Benn
Author: Ecuyer, Lee
1953   **$4.00**

No. 8706
Three Bears, The
Illus.: Webbe, Elizabeth
1959   **$4.00**

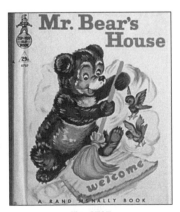

No. 8707
Mr. Bear's House
Illus.: McKinley, Clare
Author: Rothe, Fenella
1953   **$4.00**

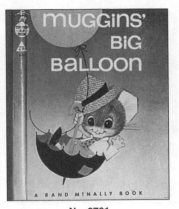

No. 8708
Number 9 The Little Fire Engine
Illus.: Corwin, Eleanor
Author: Wadsworth, Wallace
1950   **$4.00**

No. 8709

**Little Miss Muffet And Other
Nursery Rhymes**

Illus.: Chase, Mary Jane
1956   **$4.00**

No. 8710

Title Unknown

No. 8711

**Little Boy Blue And Other
Nursery Rhymes**

Illus.: Leaf, Anne Sellers
1956   **$5.00**

No. 8711

**Little Boy Blue And Other
Nursery Rhymes
(2nd Cover)**

Illus.: Leaf, Anne Sellers
1956   **$5.00**

No. 8712

Title Unknown

No. 8713

Where From?

Illus.: Smith, Eunice Young
Author: Smith, Eunice Young
1961   **$4.00**

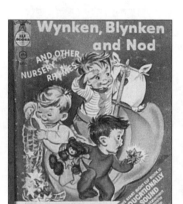

No. 8714

**Wynken, Blynken And Nod And
Other Nursery Rhymes**

Illus.: McKinley, Clare
1956   **$4.00**

No. 8715

Angel Child

Illus.: Doane, Pelagie
Author: Teal, Val
1946   **$4.00**

No. 8716

Scamper

Illus.: Tamburine, Jean
1959   **$4.00**

No. 8717

Title Unknown

No. 8718

Four Little Kittens

Illus.: Frees, Harry Whittier
Author: Barrows, Marjorie
1957   **$4.00**

No. 8719

Title Unknown

No. 8720

Pokey Bear

Illus.: Evers, Helen and Alf
Authors: Evers, Helen and Alf
1965   **$4.00**

No. 8721

Title Unknown

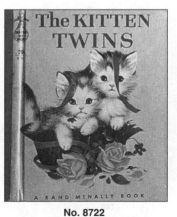

No. 8722

Kitten Twins, The

Illus.: Webbe, Elizabeth
Author: Wing, Helen
1960   **$4.00**

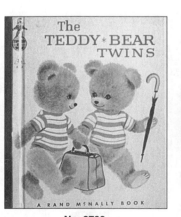

No. 8722

Teddy Bear Twins, The

Illus.: Cooper, Marjorie
Author: Wing, Helen
1965   **$5.00**

No. 8723

Mother Goose

Illus.: Friend, Esther
1947   **$4.00**

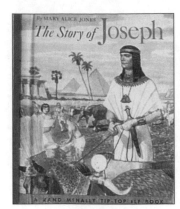

No. 8724
Story Of Joseph, The
Illus.: Lee, Manning De V
1965   **$4.00**

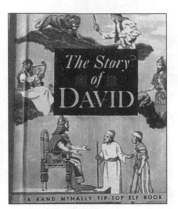

No. 8725
Story Of David, The
Illus.: Lee, Manning De V
1965   **$4.00**

No. 8726
Nancy Plays Nurse
Illus.: Grider, Dorothy
Author: Sherman, Diane
1965   **$4.00**

No. 8727
Princess And The Pea
Illus.: Leaf, Anne Sellers
1965   **$5.00**

No. 8728
Title Unknown

No. 8729
Little Mailman Of Bayberry Lane, The
Illus.: Webbe, Elizabeth
Author: Munn, Ian
1952   **$5.00**

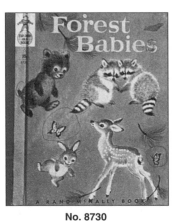

No. 8730
Forest Babies
Illus.: Webbe, Elizabeth
Author: Parrish, Jean J.
1949   **$4.00**

No. 8731
Title Unknown

No. 8732
Busy Bulldozer, The
Illus.: Grider, Dorothy
Author: Browning, James
1952   **$4.00**

No. 8733
Jeepers, The Little Frog
Illus.: Cooper, Marjorie
Author: Cooper, Marjorie
1965   **$4.00**

No. 8734
Title Unknown

No. 8734
Goody: A Mother Cat Story
Illus.: Leaf, Anne Sellers
Author: Bertail, Inez
1957   **$4.00**

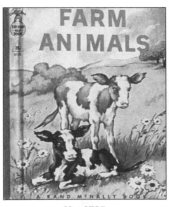

No. 8735
Farm Animals
Illus.: Gayer, Marguerite
Author: Ratzesberger, Anna
1952   **$4.00**

No. 8736
Buddy, The Little Taxi
Illus.: Corwin, Elizabeth
1951   **$5.00**

No. 8737
Little Friends: Kittens, Puppies, Bunnies
Illus.: Gaddis, Rie
Author: Dixon, Ruth
1951   **$4.00**

No. 8738

Title Unknown

No. 8739

Title Unknown

No. 8741

Title Unknown

No. 8742

Title Unknown

No. 8740

Pillowtime Tales
Illus.: Tamburine, Jean
Author: De Groot, Marion K.
1956   **$4.00**

No. 8743

Popcorn Party
Illus.: Szepelak, Helen
Authors: Boyles, Trudy; Macmartin, Louise
1952   **$4.00**

No. 8744

Title Unknown

No. 8746

Title Unknown

No.8747

Title Unknown

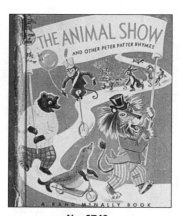

No. 8745

Three Little Puppies
Illus.: Rooks, Dale and Sally
Author: Dixon, Ruth
1951   **$4.00**

No. 8748

Animal Show, The
Illus.: Grider, Dorothy
Author: Jackson, Leroy F.
1965   **$4.00**

Hanna-Barbera Character Series

Devlin
Illus.: Carleton, James F
Author: Daly, Kathleen
1975   **$8.00**

Dynomutt And The Pie In The Sky Caper
Illus.: Wise, Marilou
Author: Brown, Fern G.
1977   **$8.00**

Great Grape Ape At The Circus
Illus.: Wise, Marilou
Author: Lewis, Jean
1976   **$8.00**

Hong Kong Phooey And The Bird Nest Snatchers
Illus.: Ostapczuk, Phil
Author: Lewis, Jean
1976   **$8.00**

Hong Kong Phooey And The Fire Engine Mystery
Illus.: Ostapczuk, Phil
Author: Sherman, Diane
1977   **$8.00**

Hong Kong Phooey And The Fortune Cookie Caper
1975   **$8.00**

Jabberjaw Out West
Illus.: Franzen, Jim
Author: Lewis, Jean
1977   **$8.00**

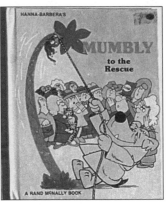

Josie And The Pussycats/The Bag Factory Detour
Illus.: Franzen, Jim
Author: Russell, Solveig Paulson
1976   **$8.00**

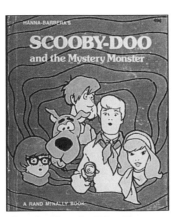

Mumbly To The Rescue
Illus.: Wise, Marilou
Author: Lewis, Jean
1977   **$8.00**

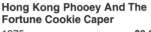

Scooby-Doo And The Case Of The Counterfeit Money
Illus.: Lowe, Richard
Author: Brown, Fern G.
1976   **$8.00**

Scooby-Doo And The Haunted Doghouse
Illus.: Lowe, Richard
Author: Lewis, Jean
1975   **$8.00**

Scooby-Doo And The Headless Horseman
Illus.: Lowe, Richard
Author: Brown, Fern G.
1976   **$8.00**

Scooby-Doo And The Mystery Monster
Illus.: Canaday, Ralph
Author: Lewis, Jean
1975   **$8.00**

Scooby-Doo And The Old Ship Mystery
1977   **8.00**

Speed Buggy And The Secret Message
Illus.: Anderson, Bill and Judie
Author: Warren, Mary Phraner
1976 $8.00

Valley Of The Dinosaurs
Illus.: Kantz, Phil
Author: Daly, Kathleen N.
1975 $8.00

Wheelie And The Chopper Bunch
Illus.: Elmi, Don
Author: Daly, Kathleen N.
1975 $8.00

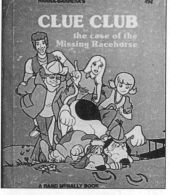

Clue Club The Case Of The Missing Racehorse
Illus.: Franzen, Jim
Author: Brown, Fern G.
1972 $8.00

Index of Rand McNally Elf Books

A Brief History of Wonder Books

Around 1898, two men, Alexander Grosset and George T. Dunlap, with combined capital of $1,350, formed the partnership of Grosset & Dunlap. The company was created to sell and distribute books.

While using the works of authors like Rudyard Kipling, the company moved into the business of rebinding paperbacks with hard covers. This method was used for a few years before the company started producing its own reprints of books. The company's reprints sold for around 50 cents at this time.

1908 saw Grosset & Dunlap publishing its own line of children's books after the purchase of the Chatterton & Peck company, which was already successful with The Rover Boys and The Bobbsey Twins. Around 1910 the company was publishing the adventures of Tom Swift. By the 1920s it was producing popular book series like Zane Grey and the Hardy Boys. With the success of the Hardy Boys, the company gave girls their own sleuth, Nancy Drew, in the 1930s.

A paper shortage during WWII, similar the one during WWI, pushed the selling cost of reprinted books up to around $1.00, but when the war ended, the price went back to 50 cents.

In 1944, the Book-of-the-Month Club, Harper, Little, Brown, Scribners, and Random House purchased Grosset & Dunlap. A year later Bantam Books was formed— the Curtis Company owned 30 percent. Bantam was to eventually become one of the largest paperback publishers.

Wonder Books, Inc. was formed in 1947 with a joint Curtis-Grosset distribution. The first Wonder Books were distributed by Random House, then Grosset & Dunlap, and by the early 1950s, by Wonder Books, Inc. In 1952 Treasure Books was formed. Treasure book were the same size as Wonder Books, but their bindings were in red tape and the books were side stapled like Little Golden Books.

The first Wonder Books measured 7-1/2" x 9-3/4" and contained 46 pages, with 20 in full color. This size was around for only a short while and was changed to the 6-1/2" x 8-1/8" size around 1948.

Of the first fifteen titles, most were carried over to this new size except for the following:

#508 How The Rabbit Fooled The Whale And The
    Elephant And Other Stories
Illus.: Sari

#511 Animal Stories
Illus.: Robinson

#515 How The Baby Hippo Found A Home
Illus.: Ruth Ganneet
Author: Dorothy Thomas

These three numbers were eventually replaced with different titles. Bound in dirt-resistant "Durasheen," Wonder Books became known as the books with the washable covers. Even though their covers were washable, their spines did not hold up very well. With a paper cover that went from front to back, the more the book was opened, the more chances there were of the spine falling off or tearing.

Filmways purchased Grosset & Dunlap in 1974. In turn, Grosset & Dunlap purchased Platt & Munk in 1977. The Putnam Publishing Group purchased Grosset & Dunlap in 1982. Price Stern Sloan now owns the rights to Wonder Books. Because of the frequent changes in ownership through the years, it is difficult to pinpoint accurate historical Wonder Books information.

How To Tell Editions

There are no markings on Wonder Books that will tell you exactly what edition you own, but you should be able to narrow down the time period of publication by using a little deductive reasoning.

I do not give page numbers for first edition Wonder Books because it would get too confusing. With Little Golden Books, when the books were cut to 28 pages, all subsequent printings of 42-page books would have 28 pages. This was not always the case with Wonder Books; you could have 42 and 34-page books being printed during the same period of time.

In the back of the earlier books there is a page with titles in print. You can use this list to approximate the time of a book's printing. For example, you own #557, *Billy And His Steam Roller*, with a copyright of 1951. The last title listed is #742, *Whose Hat Is That*. When you look up #742, you find that it has a copyright of 1960, so your copy of #557 must of been published around 1960. If the last title number had been #560 instead of #742, the book probably would be a first edition. Unfortunately this method of dating Wonder Books cannot guarantee that you have a first edition. Once the company stopped listing the books in print, one is only able to approximate the date of printing by using the cover price. Prices stayed steady for a years at a time, but this method will only give you a period of printing.

Wonder Books, like most Elf Books, had a one-piece wrap around cover. This makes it very difficult to find nice early copies with their spines intact. Some titles, like those by certain illustrators and books based on cartoon and TV characters, will continue to increase in value.

Wonder Books—By Book Number

No. 501

Mother Goose
Illus.: Hirsch, Joseph
1946   **$15.00**

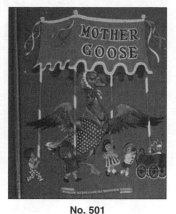

No. 501

Mother Goose
(2nd Cover)
Illus.: Hirsch, Joseph
1946   **$5.00**

No. 502

Cozy Little Farm, The
Illus.: Angela
Author: Bonino, Louise
1946   **$15.00**

No. 503

Three Little Kittens And Other Nursery Tales
Illus.: Dixon, Rachel Taft
Author: Graham, Eleanor
1946   **$15.00**

No. 504

Little Dog Who Forgot How To Bark, The
Illus.: Hopkins, Hildegarde
Author: Bailey, Carolyn S.
1946   **$15.00**

No. 505

Famous Fairy Tales
Illus.: Jules, Mervin
Author: Graham, Eleanor
1946   **$15.00**

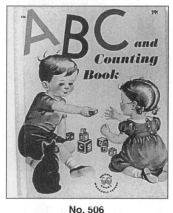

No. 506

ABC And Counting Book
Illus.: Sarkin, Jack
Author: Fraser, Phyllis
1946   **$15.00**

No. 507

Bedtime Stories
(Cinderella & Snow White)
Illus.: Masha
Author: Graham, Eleanor
1946   **$15.00**

No. 508

Why The Bear Has A Short Tail
Illus.: Sari
Author: Williams, Louise B.
1946   **$15.00**

No. 509

Randolph, The Bear Who Said No
Illus.: Walker, Nedda
Author: Nelson, Faith
1946   **$20.00**

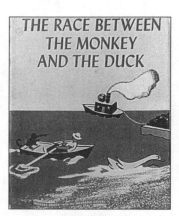

No. 510

Race Between The Monkey And The Duck, The
Illus.: Hurd, Clement
Author: Hurd, Clement
1940   **$18.00**

No. 511

Shy Little Horse, The
Illus.: Robinson
Author: Scott, Therese
1947   **$15.00**

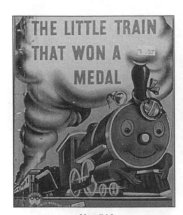

No. 512

Little Train That Won A Medal, The

Illus.: Loeb, Anton

Author: Geis, Darlene

1947 **$15.00**

No. 513

Peter Rabbit And Other Stories

Illus.: Erickson, Phoebe

Author: Potter, Beatrix

1947 **$15.00**

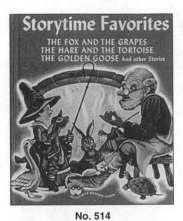

No. 514

Storytime Favorites

Illus.: Leob, Anton

Author: Scott, Theresa Ann

1947 **$15.00**

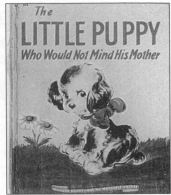

No. 515

Little Puppy Who Would Not Mind His Mother, The

Illus.: Hopkins, Hildegarde

Author: Misc.

1949 **$12.00**

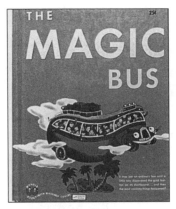

No. 516

Magic Bus, The

Illus.: Gergely, Tibor

Author: Dolbier, Maurice

1948 **$25.00**

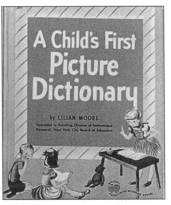

No. 517

Child's First Picture Dictionary, A

Illus.: Weber, Nettie and Clement, Charles

Author: Moore, Lilian

1948 **$10.00**

No. 518

Who Lives On The Farm?

Illus.: Jackson, Pauline

Author: Elting, Mary

1949 **$10.00**

No. 519

Surprise Doll, The

Illus.: Lerch, Steffie

Author: Gipson, Morrell

1949 **$40.00**

No. 520

Make-Believe Parade, The

Illus.: Wilkin, Eloise

Author: Margo, Jan

1949 **$20.00**

No. 521

Monkey See, Monkey Do

Illus.: Moyers, William

Author: Tooze, Ruth

1949 **$12.00**

No. 522

Five Little Finger Playmates

Illus.: Steiner, Charlotte

1949 **$10.00**

No. 523

Mr. Bear Squash-You-All-Flat

Illus.: Angela

Author: Gipson, Morrell

1950 **$75.00**

No. 524

Wheels And Noises

Illus.: Dauber, Elizabeth

Author: Elting, Mary

1950 $8.00

No. 525

Who Does Baby Look Like?

Illus.: Rowand, Phyllis

Author: Rowand, Phyllis

1950 $10.00

No. 526

Too-Little Fire Engine, The

Illus.: Flory, Jane

Author: Flory, Jane

1950 $10.00

No. 527

Kitten's Secret, The

Illus.: Barton, Mary

Author: Gossett, Margaret

1950 $10.00

No. 528

Little Lost Puppy, The

Illus.: Spicer, Jesse

Author: Otto, Margaret G.

1950 $10.00

No. 529

Kittens Who Hid From Their Mother, The

Illus.: Werber, Adele; Laslo, Doris

Author: Woodcock, Louise

1950 $10.00

No. 530

Four Puppies Who Wanted A Home, The

Illus.: Frankel, Simon

Authors: Bryan, Dorothy and Marguerite

1950 $10.00

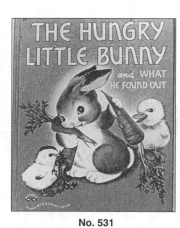

No. 531

Hungry Little Bunny, The

Illus.: Wilde, Irma

Author: Wilde, Irma

1950 $8.00

No. 532

Heidi: Child Of The Mountains

Illus.: Lerch, Steffie

Author: Spyri, Johanna

1950 $8.00

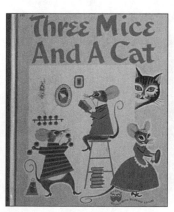

No. 533

Three Mice And A Cat

Illus.: Seiden, Art

Author: Berg, Jean Horton

1950 $18.00

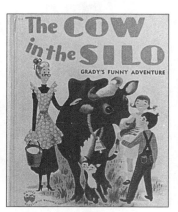

No. 534

Cow In The Silo, The

Illus.: Cunningham, Dellwyn

Author: Goodell, Patricia

1950 $16.00

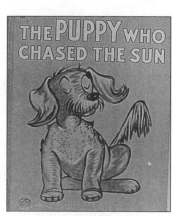

No. 535

Puppy Who Chased The Sun, The

Illus.: Grand, Le

Author: Grand, Le

1950 $10.00

No. 536

Come Visit My Ranch

Illus.: Hawes, Baldwin
Author: Hawes, Baldwin
1950   **$8.00**

No. 536*

Calling All Cowboys

(Never printed)

No. 537

Jolly Jumping Man, The

Illus.: Frankel, Simon
Author: Berg, Jean Horton
1950   **$8.00**

No. 538

Let's Play Indian

Illus.: Chastain, Madye Lee
Author: Chastain, Madye Lee
1950   **$8.00**

No. 539

Noisy Clock Shop, The

Illus.: Seiden, Art
Author: Berg, Jean Horton
1950   **$8.00**

No. 540

It's A Secret

Illus.: Myers, Bernice
Author: Brewster, Benjamin
1950   **$8.00**

No. 541

Baby Elephant, The

Illus.: Burchard, Peter
Author: Brewster, Benjamin
1950   **$8.00**

No. 542

Fraidy Cat Kitten, The

Illus.: Wilde, Irma
Author: Wilde, Irma
1950   **$8.00**

No. 543

Wizard Of Oz, The

Illus.: Sinnickson, Tom
Author: Baum, Frank L.
1951   **$15.00**

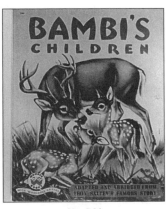

No. 544

Bambi's Children

Illus.: Bartlett, William
Author: Salten, Felix
1951   **$10.00**

No. 545

Copycat Colt, The

Illus.: Steiner, Charlotte
Authors: Steiner, Charlotte; Hoff, Virginia
1951   **$8.00**

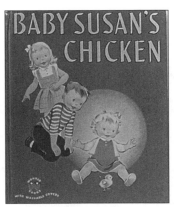

No. 546

Baby Susan's Chicken

Illus.: Cummings, Alison
Author: Berg, Jean Horton
1951   **$8.00**

No. 547

Churkendoose, The

Illus.: Cunningham, Dellwyn
Author: Berenberg, Ben Ross
1946   **$25.00**

No. 548
Baby Bunny, The
Illus.: Stone, Dick
Author: Evers, Alf
1951 $8.00

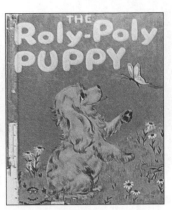

No. 549
Roly-Poly Puppy, The
Illus.: Berthold
Author: Bates, Barbara S.
1950 $8.00

No. 550
Bingity-Bangity School Bus, The
Illus.: Wood, Ruth
Author: Conkling, Fleur
1950 $25.00

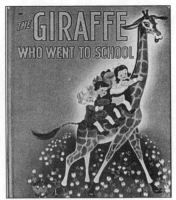

No. 551
Giraffe Who Went To School, The
Illus.: Wilde, Irma
Author: Wilde, Irma
1951 $8.00

No. 552
Five Jolly Brothers, The
Illus.: Slnnickson, Tom
Author: Chaffee, Tish
                      $8.00

No. 553
Boy Who Wanted To Be A Fish, The
Illus.: Le Grand
Author: Le Grand
1951 $8.00

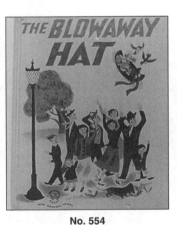

No. 554
Blowaway Hat, The
Illus.: Cunningham, Dellwyn
Author: Adelson, Leone
1946 $8.00

No. 555
Brave Little Steam Shovel, The
Illus.: Myers, Bernice
Author: Bertail, Inez
1951 $8.00

No. 556
Cats Who Stayed For Dinner, The
Illus.: Burchard, Peter
Author: Rowand, Phyllis
1951 $12.00

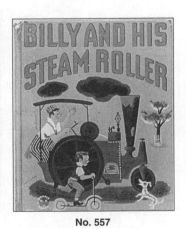

No. 557
Billy And His Steam Roller
Illus.: Myers, Bernice
Author: Bertail, Inez
1951 $8.00

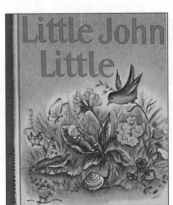

No. 558
Little John Little
Illus.: Steiner, Charlotte
Author: Steiner, Charlotte
1951 $8.00

No. 559
Who Will Play With Me?
Illus.: Dillon, Corinne
Author: Sutton, Margaret
1951 $8.00

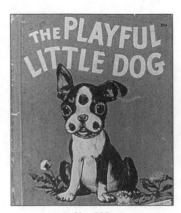

No. 560
Playtime For Nancy
Illus.: Stolgerg, Doris
Author: Hyde, Margaret O.
1951 $8.00

No. 561
Puppy Who Found A Boy, The
Illus.: Wilde, George and Irma
Authors: Wilde, George and Irma
1951 $8.00

No. 562
Playful Little Dog, The
Illus.: Robertson, Maurice
Author: Berg, Jean Horton
1951 $8.00

No. 563
Brave Firemen, The
Illus.: Medvey, Steven
Author: Bradbury, Bianca
1951 $8.00

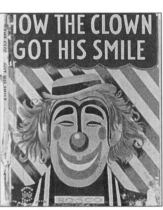

No. 564
Happy Birthday Present, The
Illus.: Scott, Marguerite K.
Author: Bates, Barbara S.
1951 $8.00

No. 565
Are Dogs Better Than Cats?
Illus.: Le Grand
Author: Le Grand
1953 $8.00

No. 566
How The Clown Got His Smile
Illus.: Hull, John
Author: Martin, Marcia
1951 $8.00

No. 567
Goose Who Played The Piano, The
Illus.: Cunningham, Dellwyn
Author: Evers, Alf
1951 $8.00

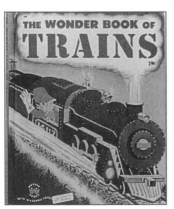
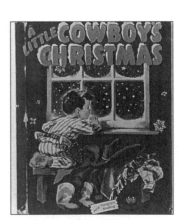

No. 568
Hide-And-Seek Duck, The
Illus.: Wilde, Irma
Author: Wilde, Irma
1952 $8.00

No. 569
Wonder Book Of Trains, The
Illus.: Sinnickson, Tom
Author: Peters, Lisa
1952 $10.00

No. 570
Little Cowboy's Christmas, A
Illus.: Dart, Eleanor
Author: Martin, Marcia
1951 $19.00

No. 571
Little Train That Saved The Day, The
Illus.: Steiner, Charlotte
Author: Steiner, Charlotte
1952 $8.00

No. 572
Snowman's Christmas Present, The
Illus.: Wilde, Irma
Author: Wilde, Irma
1951   **$12.00**

No. 573
Little Car That Wanted A Garage, The
Illus.: Meshekoff, Edward
Author: Woolley, Catherine
1952   **$10.00**

No. 574
Alice In Wonderland
Illus.: Matulay, Laszlo
Author: Martin, Marcia
1951   **$15.00**

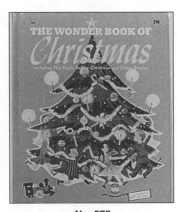

No. 575
Wonder Book Of Christmas, The
Illus.: Myers, Lou
1951   **$10.00**

No. 576
Wonder Book Of Fun, The
Illus.: Cunningham, Dellwyn
Author: Orleans, Ilo
1951   **$8.00**

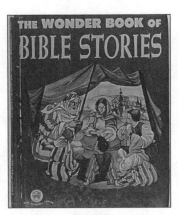

No. 577
Wonder Book Of Bible Stories, The
Illus.: Frost, Bruno
Author: Juergens, Mary
1951   **$8.00**

No. 578
Magic Word, The
Illus.: Dart, Eleanor
Author: Zolotow, Charlotte
1952   **$8.00**

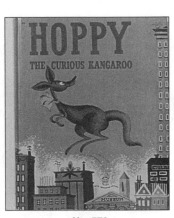

No. 579
Hoppy, The Curious Kangaroo
Illus.: Fraydas, Stan
Author: Fraydas, Stan
1952   **$8.00**

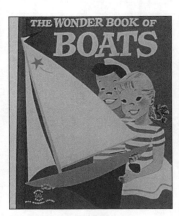

No. 580
Wonder Book Of Boats, The
Illus.: Hurst, Earl Oliver
Author: Hurst, Earl Oliver
1953   **$8.00**

No. 581
Wonderful Tar-Baby, The
Illus.: Cunningham, Dellwyn
Author: Harris, Joel Chandler
1952   **$18.00**

No. 582
Happy Surprise, The
Illus.: Wood, Ruth
Author: Klein, Leonore
1952   **$8.00**

No. 583
Good Morning, Good Night
Illus.: Derwinski, Beatrice
Author: Luther, Frank
1953   **$8.00**

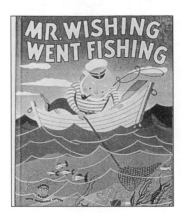

No. 584

Mr. Wishing Went Fishing

Illus.: Wilde, George

Author: Wilde, Irma

1952 **$10.00**

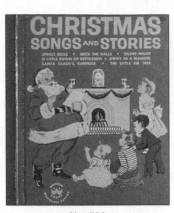

No. 585

Christmas Puppy, The

Illus.: Wilde, Irma

Author: Wilde, Irma

1953 **$15.00**

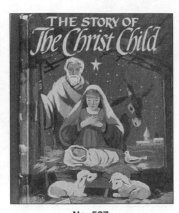

No. 586

Christmas Songs And Stories

Illus.: Scholz, Catherine

Author: Berg, Jean Horton

1953 **$12.00**

No. 587

Story Of The Christ Child, The

Illus.: Lap, Pranas

Author: Edwards, Annette

1953 **$8.00**

No. 588

Raggedy Ann And Marcella's First Day At School

Illus.: Sinnickson, Tom

Author: Gruelle, Johnny

1952 **$22.00**

No. 589

Just Like Mommy, Just Like Daddy

Illus.: Cummings, Alison

Author: Simon, Patty

1952 **$8.00**

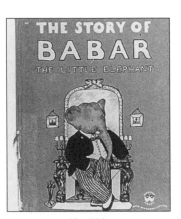

No. 590

Story Of Babar, The

Illus.: Brunhoff, Jean De

Author: Brunhoff, Jean De

1952 **$18.00**

No. 591

Sonny The Bunny

Illus.: Seiden, Art

Author: Martin, Marcia

1952 **$8.00**

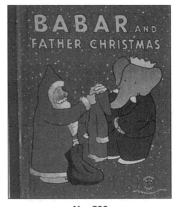

No. 592

Babar And Father Christmas

Illus.: Hass, Merle S.

Author: De Brunoff, Jean

1940 **$20.00**

No. 593

Christmas Is Coming

Illus.: Cummings, Alison

Author: Martin, Marcia

1952 **$10.00**

No. 594

Raggedy Ann's Merriest Christmas

Illus.: Sinnickson, Tom

Author: Gruelee, Johnny

1952 **$22.00**

No. 595

Black Beauty

Illus.: Santos, George

Author: Martin, Marcia

1952 **$8.00**

No. 596

Traveling Twins, The
(With uncut play money)
Illus.: Smalley, Janet
Author: Berg, Jean Horton
1953   **$10.00**

No. 597

Peter Pan
Illus.: Derwinski, Beatrice
Author: Martin, Marcia
1952   **$8.00**

No. 598

Who Likes Dinner?
Illus.: Cunningham, Dellwyn
Author: Beyer, Evelyn
1953   **$8.00**

No. 599

Hans Christian Andersen's
Fairy Tales
Illus.: Caraway, James
Author: Andersen, Hans Christian
1952   **$8.00**

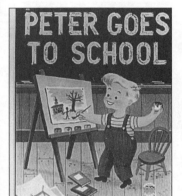

No. 600

Peter Goes To School
Illus.: Doremus, Hal W.
Author: House, Wanda Rogers
1953   **$7.00**

No. 601

Surprise For Mrs. Bunny, A
Illus.: Steiner, Charlotte
Author: Steiner, Charlotte
1953   **$8.00**

No. 602

Babar The King
Illus.: Brunhoff, Jean De
Author: Brunhoff, Jean De
1953   **$18.00**

No. 603

Tom Corbett's Wonder Book Of
Space
Illus.: Vaughn, Frank
Author: Martin, Marcia
1953   **$20.00**

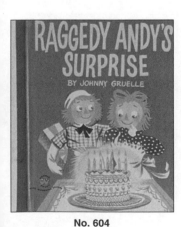

No. 604

Raggedy Andy's Surprise
Illus.: Sinnickson, Tom
Author: Gruelle, Johnny
1953   **$18.00**

No. 605

Guess What?
Illus.: Wood, Ruth
Author: Klein, Leonore
1953   **$7.00**

No. 606

Baby's First Book
Illus.: Schad, Helen G.
Author: Edwards, Annette
1953   **$7.00**

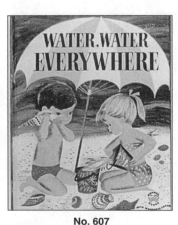

No. 607

Water, Water Everywhere
Illus.: Seiden, Art
Author: Raphael, Ralph B.
1953   **$7.00**

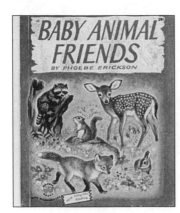

No. 608
Baby Animal Friends
Illus.: Erickson, Phoebe
Author: Erickson, Phoebe
1954   **$7.00**

No. 609
Three Little Pigs And Little Red Riding Hood
Illus.: Peller, Jackie; Tamburine, Jean
1954   **$7.00**

No. 610
My ABC Book
Illus.: Seiden, Art
1953   **$7.00**

No. 611
Peter Rabbit And Reddy Fox
Illus.: Hauge, Carl and Mary
Author: Burgess, Thorton W.
1954   **$8.00**

No. 612
Sleepytime For Everyone
Illus.: Castagnoli, Martha
Author: Castagnoli, Martha
1954   **$7.00**

No. 613
Picnic At The Zoo
Illus.: Myers, Bernice and Lou
Author: Libbey, Ruth Everding
1954   **$7.00**

No. 614
Bunny Hopwell's First Spring
Illus.: Dixon, Rachel Taft
Author: Fritz, Jean
1954   **$7.00**

No. 615
Pinocchio
Illus.: Seiden, Art
Author: Andreas, Evelyn
1954   **$7.00**

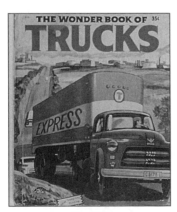
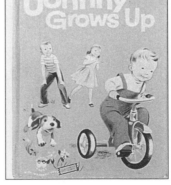

No. 616
Wonder Book Of Trucks, The
Illus.: Schusker, James
Author: Peters, Lisa
1954   **$7.00**

No. 617
Puppy On Parade, The
Illus.: Hoecker, Hazel
Author: Grilley, Virginia
1956   **$7.00**

No. 618
Johnny Grows Up
Illus.: Cummings, Alison
Author: Martin, Marcia
1954   **$7.00**

No. 619
Wonder Book Of Nursery Songs, The
Illus.: Schlesinger, Alice
Author: Cummins, Dorothy Berliner
1954   **$7.00**

No. 620
Surprise Party, The
Illus.: Newell, Crosby
Author: Newell, Crosby
1955   **$7.00**

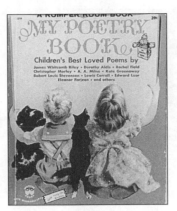

No. 621
My Poetry Book
Illus.: Smith, Flora
Author: Pierce, June
1954   **$7.00**

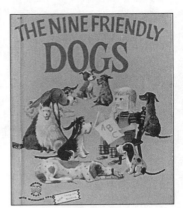

No. 622
Nine Friendly Dogs, The
Illus.: Goldsborough, June
Author: Sutton, Felix
1954   **$7.00**

No. 623
Meet The Bobbsey Twins
Illus.: Dillon, Corinne
Author: Hope, Laura Lee
1954   **$10.00**

No. 624
Raggedy Ann's Tea Party
Illus.: Wilde, George and Irma
Author: Gruelle, Johnny
1954   **$18.00**

No. 625
Littlest Christmas Tree, The
Illus.: Hauge, Carl and Mary
Author: Burgess, Thornton W.
1954   **$15.00**

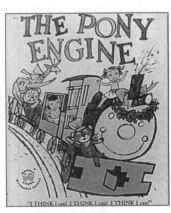

No. 626
Pony Engine, The
Illus.: Prestopino, Gregorio
Author: Garn, Doris
1957   **$7.00**

No. 627
**Wonder Book Of Finger Plays
And Action Rhymes, The**
Illus.: Wood, Ruth
Author: Pierce, June
1955   **$7.00**

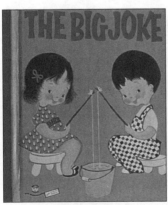

No. 628
Big Joke, The
Illus.: Newell, Crosby
Author: Bonsall, George
1955   **$7.00**

No. 629
What Happened To Piggy?
Illus.: Hauge, Carl and Mary
Author: Potter, Miriam Clark
1955   **$7.00**

No. 630
See How It Grows
Illus.: Smith, Flora
Author: Walters, Marguerite
1954   **$7.00**

No. 631
Helpful Friends, The
Illus.: Bonsall, George; Newell,
Crosby
Authors: Bonsall, George; Newell,
Crosby
1955   **$7.00**

No. 632
It's A Lovely Day
Illus.: Smith, Flora
Author: Walters, Marguerite
1956 $7.00

No. 633
Mrs. Goose's Green Trailer
Illus.: Weisgard, Leonard
Author: Potter, Miriam Clark
1956 $7.00

No. 634
Make-Believe Book, The
Illus.: Newell, Crosby
Author: Newell, Crosby
1959 $7.00

No. 635
Sleeping Beauty
Illus.: Ives, Ruth
Author: Andreas, Evelyn
1956 $7.00

No. 636
Little Duck Said Quack, Quack, Quack, The
Illus.: Kendrick, Alcy
Author: Barnett, Grace and Olive
1955 $7.00

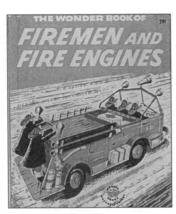

No. 637
Wonder Book Of Firemen And Fire Engines, The
Illus.: Weisner, William
Author: Peters, Lisa
1956 $10.00

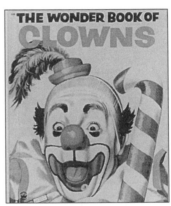

No. 638
Wonder Book Of Clowns, The
Illus.: Schucker, James
Author: Weigle, Oscar
1955 $8.00

No. 639
Lassie Come-Home
Illus.: Drutzu, Anne Marie
Author: Knight, Eric
1956 $8.00

No. 640
Wonder Book Of Cowboys, The
Illus.: Vaughn, Frank
Author: Peters, Lisa
1956 $7.00

No. 641
Little Peter Cottontail
Illus.: Erickson, Phoebe
Author: Burgess, Thornton W.
1956 $7.00

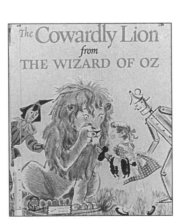

No. 642
Cowardly Lion, The
Illus.: Wood, Ruth
Author: Baum, Frank L.
1956 $22.00

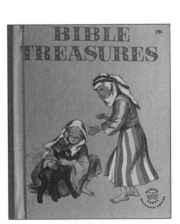

No. 643
Bible Treasures
Illus.: Raw, J. G.
Author: Ryder, Lillian
1961 $7.00

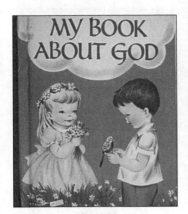

No. 644

My Book About God

Illus.: Varga, Judith

1956 **$7.00**

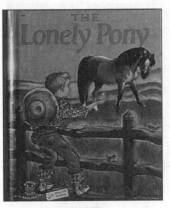

No. 645

Lonely Pony, The

Illus.: Oogjen, Barbara and Thomas
Author: Christopher, John

1956 **$7.00**

No. 646

Who Is My Friend?

Illus.: McLaughlin, Birdice
Author: Corum, Louise

1959 **$7.00**

No. 647

Lord's Prayer, The

Illus.: Brul, Al

1956 **$7.00**

No. 648

10 Rabbits

Illus.: Dixon, Rachel Taft
Author: Potter, Miriam Clark

1957 **$7.00**

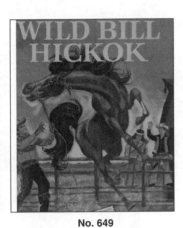

No. 649

Wild Bill Hickok

Illus.: Nielsen, Jon
Author: Sutton, Felix

1956 **$20.00**

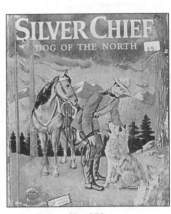

No. 650

Silver Chief

Illus.: Hauge, Carl and Mary
Author: Weigle, Oscar

1956 **$18.00**

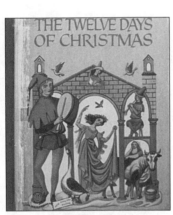

No. 651

Twelve Days Of Christmas, The

Illus.: Mars, W. T.

1956 **$8.00**

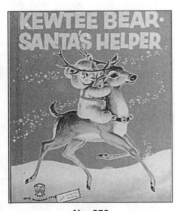

No. 652

Kewtee Bear-Santa's Helper

Illus.: Dixon, Rachel Taft
Authors: Reed, Alan; Stout, Bert;
Quigley, Truman

1956 **$15.00**

No. 653

Most Beautiful Tree In The World, The

Illus.: Weisgard, Leonard
Author: Weisgard, Leonard

1956 **$10.00**

No. 654

Quiet Book, The

Illus.: Kendrick , Alcy
Author: Flynn, Helen M.

1958 **$7.00**

No. 655

Rattle-Rattle Train, The

Illus.: Bobertz, Carl
Author: Geis, Darlene

1957 **$7.00**

No. 656
Rattle-Rattle Dump Truck, The
Illus.: Bobertz, Carl
Author: Geis, Darlene
1958   **$7.00**

No. 657
I Love You
Illus.: Bonsall, George; Newell, Crosby
Authors: Bonsall, George; Newell, Crosby
1956   **$7.00**

No. 658
Title Unknown

No. 659
Snow White And The Seven Dwarfs
Illus.: Seiden, Art
1955   **$7.00**

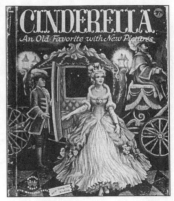

No. 660
Cinderella
Illus.: Ives, Ruth
Author: Andreas, Evelyn
1954   **$7.00**

No. 661
My First Book Of Prayers
Illus.: Ives, Ruth
Author: Juergens, Mary
1953   **$7.00**

No. 662
Mighty Mouse-Santa's Helper
Illus.: Chad
Author: Sutton, Felix
1955   **$20.00**

No. 663
Baby's Day
Illus.: Pointer, Priscilla
Author: Edwards, Annette
1953   **$7.00**

No. 664
Henry In Lollipop Land
Illus.: Anderson, Carl
Author: Anderson, Carl
1953   **$16.00**

No. 665
Felix The Cat
Illus.: Sullivan, Pat
Author: Sullivan, Pat
1953   **$18.00**

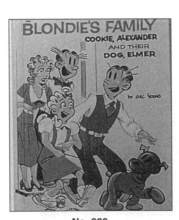

No. 666
Blondie's Family Cookie, Alexander, And Their Dog, Elmer
Illus.: Young, Chic
Author: Young, Chic
1954   **$18.00**

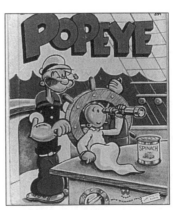

No. 667
Popeye
Illus.: Sagendorf, Bud
Author: Sagendorf, Bud
1955   **$16.00**

No. 668
How Peter Cottontail Got His Name
Illus.: Jackson, Pauline
Author: Burgess, Thornton W.
1957   **$7.00**

No. 669
Who Lives Here?
Illus.: Varga, Judith
Author: Varga, Judith
1958 $7.00

No. 670
Title Unknown

No. 671
Title Unknown

No. 672
Just Like Me
Illus.: Weisgard, Leonard
Author: Weisgard, Leonard
1954 $6.00

No. 673
Let's Take A Ride
Illus.: Dillon, Corrine
Author: Hope, Laura Lee
1954 $6.00

No. 674
Lassie's Long Trip
Illus.: Hoecker, Hazel
Author: Knight, Jere
1957 $8.00

No. 675
Jingle Dingle Book, The
Illus.: Ruhman, Ruth
Author: Jason, Leon
1957 $8.00

No. 676
I Can I Can I Can
Illus.: Schad, Helen G.
Author: Schad, Helen G.
1958 $6.00

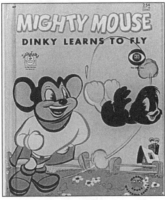

No. 677
Mighty Mouse-Dinky Learns To Fly
Illus.: Chad
Author: Sutton, Felix
1953 $16.00

No. 678
Mighty Mouse And The Scarecrow
Illus.: Chad
Author: Sutton, Felix
1954 $16.00

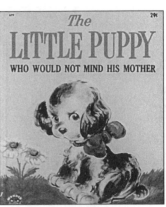

No. 679
Little Puppy Who Would Not Mind His Mother, The
Illus.: Hopkins, Hildegarde
Author: Fyleman, Rose
1949 $6.00

No. 680
Let's Pretend
Illus.: Clarke, Joan
Author: Clarke, Frances
1959 $6.00

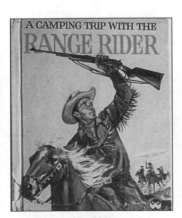

No. 681
Camping Trip With The Range Rider, A
Illus.: Nielsen, Jon
Author: Sutton, Felix
1957 $6.00

No. 682
Wonder Book Of Counting Rhymes, The
Illus.: Parsons, Virginia
Author: Pierce, June
1957 $6.00

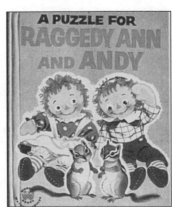

No. 683
Puzzle For Raggedy Ann And Andy, A
Illus.: Dixon, Rachel Taft
Author: Gruelee, Johnny
1957 $16.00

No. 684
Flash Gordon And The Baby Animals
Illus.: Berger, Alex
Author: King Features Syndicate
1956 **$15.00**

No. 685
Henny-Penny
Illus.: Ponter, James
1954 **$6.00**

No. 686
Let's Play Nurse And Doctor
Illus.: Stang, Judy
Author: Stang, Judy
1953 **$6.00**

No. 687
Wonder Book Of Happy Animals, The
Illus.: Jones, Robert
Author: Weigle, Oscar
1957 **$6.00**

No. 688
Dress-Up Parade, The
Illus.: Wilde, George
Author: Wilde, Irma
1953 **$7.00**

No. 689
What Time Is It?
(A Romper Room Book)
Illus.: Zabinski, Joseph
Author: Peter, John
1954 **$6.00**

No. 690
Visit To The Hospital, A
Illus.: Rossi, Ken
Author: Chase, Francine
1958 **$6.00**

No. 691
Let's Go To School
Illus.: Hoecker, Hazel
Author: Edwards, Annette
1954 **$6.00**

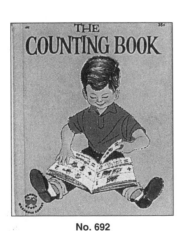

No. 692
Counting Book, The
Illus.: Riley, Bob
Author: Peter, John
1957 **$6.00**

No. 693
Let's Go Shopping
Illus.: Meyerhoff, Nancy
Author: Brooke, Guyon
1958 **$6.00**

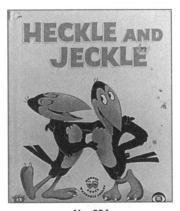

No. 694
Heckle And Jeckle
Illus.: Jason, Leon
Author: Jason, Leon
1957 **$14.00**

No. 695
Gandy Goose
Illus.: Ruhman, Ruth
Author: Jason, Leon
1957 **$18.00**

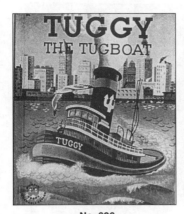

No. 696

Tuggy The Tugboat

Illus.: Hauge, Carl and Mary

Author: Berg, Jean Horton

1958   **$6.00**

No. 697

Popeye Goes On A Picnic

Illus.: Sagendorf, Bud

Author: Newell, Crosby

1958   **$6.00**

No. 698

Crusader Rabbit

Illus.: Krusz, Arthur

Author: Weigle, Oscar

1958   **$20.00**

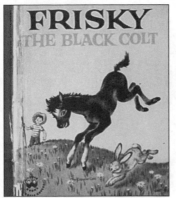

No. 699

Frisky, The Black Colt

Illus.: Steiner, Charlotte

Authors: Steiner, Charlotte; Hoff, Virginia

1951   **$6.00**

No. 700

**Once Upon A Time
(The Cow In The Silo)**

Illus.: Cunningham, Dellwyn

Author: Goudell, Patricia

1950   **$7.00**

No. 701

Can You Guess? (Guess What)

Illus.: Wood, Ruth

Author: Klein, Leonore

1953   **$6.00**

No. 702

Count The Baby Animals

Illus.: Plummer, Virginia

Author: Walters, Marguerite

1958   **$6.00**

No. 703

Tom Terrific With Mighty Manfred The Wonder Dog

Illus.: Bartsch, Arthur

Author: Newell, Crosby

1958   **$16.00**

No. 704

Child's Garden Of Versus, A

Illus.: Wood, Ruth

Author: Stevenson, Robert Louis

1958   **$6.00**

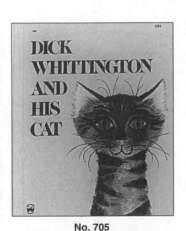

No. 705

Dick Whittington And His Cat

Illus.: Cunningham, Dellwyn

Author: Weigle, Oscar

1958   **$6.00**

No. 706

Aesop's Fables

Illus.: Seiden, Art

1958   **$6.00**

No. 707

Magilla Gorilla And The Super Kite

Illus.: Hanna-Barbera Productions, Inc.

Author: Elias, Horace J.

1976   **$10.00**

No. 708

Mister Magoo

Illus.: Nofziger, Ed

Author: Newell, Crosby

1958   **$16.00**

No. 709
Quiet Little Indian, The
Illus.: Wood, Ruth
Author: Geis, Darlene
1958   **$6.00**

No. 710
Little Schoolhouse
Illus.: Elgin, Kathleen
Author: Newell, Crosby
1958   **$6.00**

No. 711
Terrytoon Space Train, The
Illus.: Gershen, Irv
Author: Waring, Barbara
1958   **$18.00**

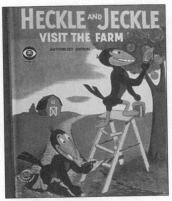

No. 712
Heckle And Jeckle Visit The Farm
Illus.: Gershen, Irv
Author: Waring, Barbara
1958   **$16.00**

No. 713
Tom Corbett: A Trip To The Moon
Illus.: Vaughn, Frank
Author: Martin, Marcia
1953   **$18.00**

No. 714
Ten Little Fingers
Illus.: Pointer, Priscilla
Author: Pointer, Priscilla
1954   **$6.00**

No. 715
Little Red Caboose That Ran Away, The
Illus.: Burchard, Peter
Author: Curren, Polly
1952   **$6.00**

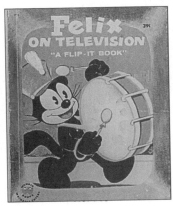

Felix On Television
Illus.: Oriolo, Joe
Author: Shapiro, Irwin
1956   **$14.00**

No. 716
Felix On Television (Second Cover)
Illus.: Oriolo, Joe
Author: Shapiro, Irwin
1956   **$14.00**

No. 717
Mighty Mouse To The Rescue
Illus.: Gershen, Irv
Author: Waring, Barbara
1958   **$17.00**

No. 718
Choo Choo Train, The
Illus.: Kessler, Leonard
Author: Pennington, Lillian Boyer
                                       $6.00

No. 719
There Was Once A Little Boy
Illus.: Cook, Sunny B.
Author: Budney, Blossom
1959   **$6.00**

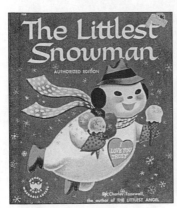

No. 720
Littlest Snowman, The
Illus.: Santis, George De
Author: Tazewell, Charles
1958 $12.00

No. 721
Wonder Book Of Dolls, The
Illus.: Wohlberg, Meg
Author: Hamilton, Antoinette
1959 $10.00

No. 722
Stacks Of Caps
(Monkey See Monkey Do)
Illus.: Moyers, William
Author: Tooze, Ruth
1949 $6.00

No. 723
This Magic World
Illus.: Koehler, Cynthia Iliff
Author: Koehler, Cynthia Iliff
1959 $6.00

No. 724
House That Jack Built, The
Illus.: Wilson, Dagmar
1959 $6.00

No. 725
Nonsense Alphabet, The
Illus.: Seiden, Art
Author: Lear, Edward
1959 $6.00

No. 726
Good Night Fairy Tales
Illus.: Werber, Adele; Heins, Doris
Author: Weigle, Oscar
1959 $6.00

No. 727
Raggedy Ann's Secret
Illus.: Wood, Ruth
Author: Gruelle, Johnny
1959 $15.00

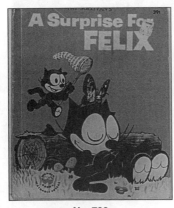

No. 728
Surprise For Felix, A
Illus.: Oriolo, Joe
Author: Sullivan, Pat
1959 $10.00

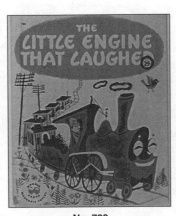

No. 729
Little Engine That Laughed, The
Illus.: Seiden, Art
Author: Evers, Alf
1950 $6.00

No. 730
Wonder Book Of Favorite
Nursery Tales, The
Illus.: Peller, Jackie; Tamburine,
Jean
1953 $6.00

No. 731
Big-Little Dinosaur, The
Illus.: Jones, Bob
Author: Geis, Darlene
1959 $6.00

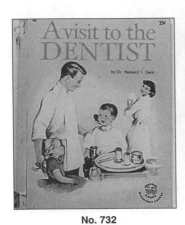

No. 732
Visit To The Dentist, A
Illus.: Wallace, Lucille
Author: Garn, Dr. Bernard J.
1959 $6.00

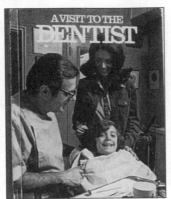

No. 732
Visit To The Dentist, A
(2nd Cover)
Illus.: Wallace, Lucille
Author: Garn, Dr. Bernard J.
1959 $5.00

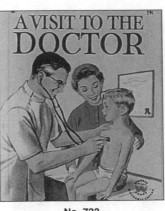

No. 733
Visit To The Doctor, A
Illus.: Dowd, Vic
Authors: Berger, Knute; Tidwell & Haseltine
1960 $6.00

No. 734
Funny Mixed-Up Story, The
Illus.: Wilson, Dagmar
Author: Mcnulty, Faith
1959 $6.00

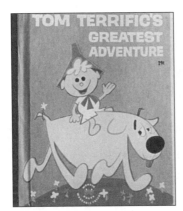

No. 735
Tom Terrific's Greatest Adventure
Illus.: Newell, Crosby
Author: Newell, Crosby
1959 $15.00

No. 736
Joke On Farmer Al Falfa, A
Illus.: Gershen, Irv
Author: Newell, Crosby
1959 $18.00

No. 737
Busy Baby Lion, The
Illus.: Jottier, Rik
Author: Erville, Lucienne
1959 $7.00

No. 738
Baby's First Christmas
Illus.: Dart, Eleanor
1959 $8.00

No. 739
Summer Friends
Illus.: Wood, Ruth
Author: Krinsky, Jeanette
1960 $6.00

No. 740
Blow, Wind, Blow
Illus.: D'amato, Janet and Alex
Authors: D'amato, Janet and Alex
1960 $6.00

No. 741
Bootsy
Illus.: Lear, Mirian
Author: Erville, Lucienne
1959 $6.00

No. 742
Whose Hat Is That?
Illus.: Kessler, Leonard
Author: Kessler, Leonard
1960 $6.00

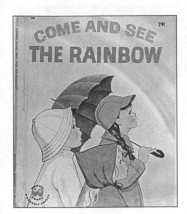

No. 743
Come And See The Rainbow
Illus.: Scholz, Catherine
Author: Walters, Marguerite
1960   **$6.00**

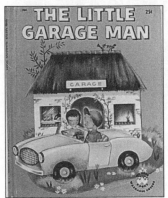

No. 744
Little Garage Man, The
Illus.: Binst, Claire
Authors: Delahaye, Gilgert; Smith, George
1960   **$6.00**

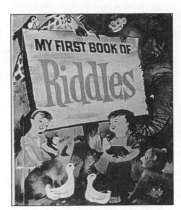

No. 745
My First Book Of Riddles
Illus.: D'amato, Janet and Alex
Authors: D'amato, Janet and Alex
1960   **$6.00**

No. 746
I See The Sky
Illus.: Cook, Sunny B.
Author: Peters, Ann
1960   **$6.00**

No. 747
Insects We Know
Illus.: Koehler, Cynthia Iliff
Author: Rood, Ronald N.
1960   **$6.00**

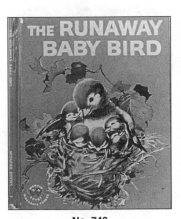

No. 748
Runaway Baby Bird, The
Illus.: Mazza, Adriana
Author: Walters, Marguerite
1960   **$6.00**

No. 749
Cozy Little Farm, The
Illus.: Angela
Author: Bonino, Louise
1946   **$6.00**

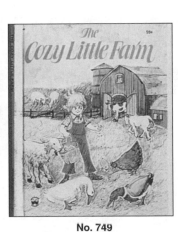

No. 749
Cozy Little Farm, The
(2nd Cover)
Illus.: Angela
Author: Bonino, Louise
1946   **$5.00**

No. 750
House That Popeye Built, The
Illus.: Sagendorf, Bud
Author: Newell, Crosby
1960   **$7.00**

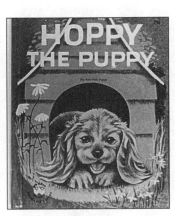

No. 751
Hoppy The Puppy
(The Roly-Poly Puppy)
Illus.: Berthold
Author: Bates, Barbara S.
1950   **$6.00**

No. 752
Let's Give A Party
Illus.: Nigro, Joanne
Author: Newell, Crosby
1960   **$6.00**

No. 752
Let's Give A Party
(2nd Cover)
Illus.: Nigro, Joanne
Author: Newell, Crosby
1960   **$5.00**

No. 753
Songs To Sing And Play
$6.00

No. 754
Horse For Johnny, A
Illus.: Moyers, William
Author: Bookman, Charlotte
1952 **$6.00**

No. 755
Littlest Angel, The
Illus.: Evans, Katherine
Author: Tazewell, Charles
1960 **$8.00**

No. 756
Fixit Man, The
Illus.: Wilde, George
Author: Wilde, Irma
1952 **$6.00**

No. 757
Wonder Book Of Birds, The
Illus.: Koehler, Alvin
Author: Koehler, Cynthia Iliff
1961 **$6.00**

No. 758
Minute-And-A-Half-Man, The
Illus.: Kirkel, Stephen
Author: Newell, Crosby
1960 **$18.00**

No. 759
Little Audrey And The Moon Lady
Illus.: Harvey Cartoon Studios
Author: Harvey Cartoon Studios
1960 **$18.00**

No. 760
Deputy Dog
Illus.: Bezada, Herb; Trombetta, Mario
Author: Newell, Crosby
1960 **$20.00**

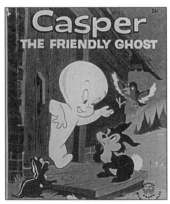

No. 761
Casper, The Friendly Ghost
Illus.: Harvey Cartoon Studios
Author: Harvey Cartoon Studios
1960 **$15.00**

No. 762
Rolling Wheels
Illus.: Dauber, Elizabeth
Author: Elting, Mary
1950 **$6.00**

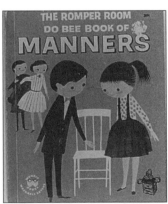

No. 763
Romper Room Do Bee Book Of Manners, The
Illus.: Seiden, Art
Author: Claster, Nancy
1960 **$6.00**

No. 764
Let's Go Fishing
Illus.: Newell, Crosby
Author: Bonsall, George
1955 **$6.00**

No. 765

Uncle Wiggily's Adventures

Illus.: Leone, Sergio

Author: Garis, Howard R.

1961   **$16.00**

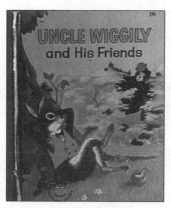

No. 766

Uncle Wiggily And His Friends

Illus.: Leone, Sergio

Author: Garis, Howard R.

1961   **$16.00**

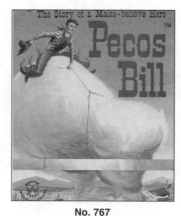

No. 767

Pecos Bill

Illus.: Canizares, Stephenie

Author: Walsh, Henry

1961   **$8.00**

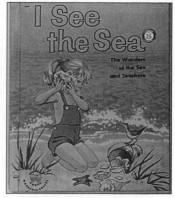

No. 768

I See The Sea

Illus.: Wood, Ruth

Author: Mcgovern, Ann

1961   **$6.00**

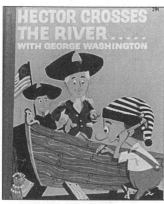

No. 769

Hector Crosses The Rier....With George Washington

Illus.: Crapanzano, Joe; Bezada Jr., Herbert

Author: Newell, Crosby

1961   **$18.00**

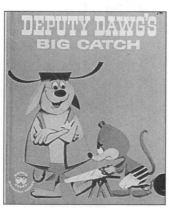

No. 770

Deputy Dawg's Big Catch

Illus.: Bezada, Herb; Crapanzano, Joseph

Author: Newell, Crosby

1961   **$20.00**

No. 771

Donkey Who Wanted To Be Wise, The

Illus.: Marsia, Robert

Author: Delahaye, Gilbert

1961   **$6.00**

No. 772

Peter Hatches An Egg

Illus.: Marlier, Marcel

Author: Brialmont, Louise Bienvenu-

1962   **$6.00**

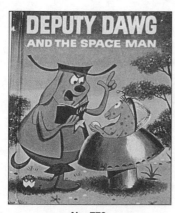

No. 773

Deputy Dawg And The Space Man

Illus.: Bezada, Herb; Crapanzano, Joseph

Author: Sand, Helen

1961   **$18.00**

No. 774

Bunny Sitter, The

Illus.: Meyerhoff, Nancy

Author: Grilley, Virginia

1963   **$6.00**

No. 775

To Market, To Market

Illus.: Seiden, Art

Author: Potter, Miriam Clark

1961   **$6.00**

No. 776

December Is For Christmas

Illus.: Kendrick, Alcy

Author: Scott, Ann

1961   **$6.00**

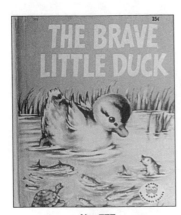

No. 777

Brave Little Duck, The

Illus.: Gayer, Marguerite

Author: Conkling, Fluer

1953 **$6.00**

No. 778

Henry Goes To A Party

Illus.: Anderson, Carl

Author: Anderson, Carl

1955 **$15.00**

No. 779

Who Goes There?

Illus.: D'amato, Janet and Alex

Authors: D'amato, Janet and Alex

1961 **$6.00**

No. 780

Fluffy Little Lamb

Illus.: Baudoin, Simonne

Author: Delahaye, Gilbert

1962 **$6.00**

No. 781

Sheri Lewis Wonder Book, The

Illus.: Wood, Ruth

Author: Newell, Crosby

1961 **$13.00**

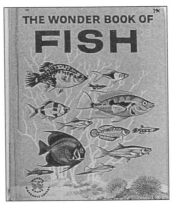

No. 782

Wonder Book Of Fish, The

Illus.: Koehler, Cynthia Iliff and Alvin

Authors: Koehler, Cynthia Iliff and Alvin

1961 **$6.00**

No. 783

Dondi

Illus.: Deson, Gus; Hasen, Erwin

Authors: Deson, Gus; Hasen, Erwin

1961 **$15.00**

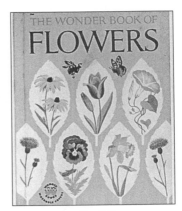

No. 784

Wonder Book Of Flowers, The

Illus.: Koehler, Cynthia Iliff

Author: Koehler, Cynthia Iliff

1961 **$5.00**

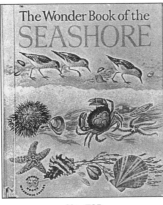

No. 785

Wonder Book Of The Seashore, The

Illus.: Koehler, Alvin

Author: Koehler, Cynthia Iliff

1962 **$5.00**

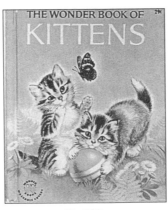

No. 786

Wonder Book Of Kittens, The

Illus.: Koehler, Cynthia Iliff

Author: Waring, Barbara

1963 **$6.00**

No. 787

Baby Huey

Illus.: Harvey Cartoon Studios

Author: Harvey Cartoon Studios

1961 **$20.00**

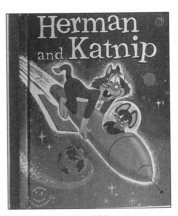

No. 788

Herman And Katnip

Illus.: Harvey Cartoon Studios

Author: Harvey Cartoon Studios

1961 **$17.00**

No. 789

What Is That?

Illus.: Hampson, Denman

Author: Hampson, Denman

1961 **$6.00**

No. 790

Animals' Party, The

Illus.: Brozowska, Elizabeth

Author: Brozowska, Elisabeth

1962 **$6.00**

No. 790

Jetsons The Great Pizza Hunt, The

Illus.: Hanna-Barbera Productions, Inc.

Author: Elias, Horace J.

1976 **$10.00**

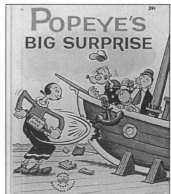

No. 791

Popeye's Big Surprise

Illus.: Sagendorf, Bud

Author: Waring, Barbara

1962 **$8.00**

No. 792

What Are You Looking At?

Illus.: Bonsall, George; Newell, Crosby

Authors: Bonsall, George; Newell, Crosby

1954 **$6.00**

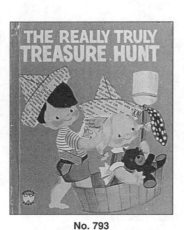

No. 793

Really Truly Treasure Hunt, The

Illus.: Newell, Crosby

Author: Bonsall, George

1954 **$6.00**

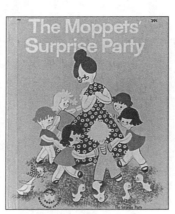

No. 794

Moppets' Surprise Party, The

Illus.: Newell, Crosby

Author: Newell, Crosby

1955 **$6.00**

No. 795

Morning Noises

Illus.: Gree, Alain

Author: Gree, Alain

1962 **$6.00**

No. 796

Over In The Meadow

Illus.: Wood, Ruth

Author: Wadsworth, Olive A.

1962 **$6.00**

No. 797

Baby Raccoon

Illus.: Baudoin, Simonne

Author: Berg, Jean Horton

1963 **$6.00**

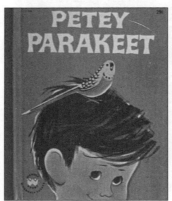

No. 798

Petey Parakeet

Illus.: Cook, Sunny B.

Authors: Bonsall, George; Newell, Crosby

1963 **$6.00**

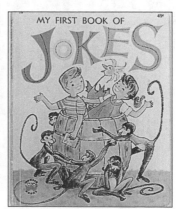

No. 799

My First Book Of Jokes

Illus.: D'amato, Janet and Alex

Authors: D'amato, Janet and Alex

1962 **$6.00**

No. 800
Costume Party, The
Illus.: D'amato, Janet and Alex
Author: Morel, Eve
1962   **$6.00**

No. 801
Who Has My Shoes?
Illus.: Kessler, Leonard
Author: Kessler, Leonard
1963   **$6.00**

No. 802
Doll Family, The
Illus.: Harris, Martin
Author: Wilson, Dorothy
1962   **$6.00**

No. 803
Pelle's New Suit
Illus.: Wilde, George
Author: Beskow, Elsa
1962   **$6.00**

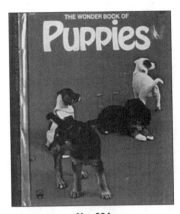

No. 804
Wonder Book Of Puppies, The
Illus.: Koehler, Cynthia Iliff and Alvin
Authors: Koehler, Cynthia Iliff and Alvin
1963   **$6.00**

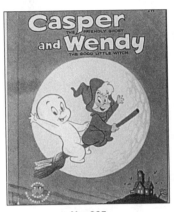

No. 805
Casper And Wendy
Illus.: Harvey Cartoon Studios
Author: Harvey Cartoon Studios
1963   **$8.00**

No. 806
Title Unknown

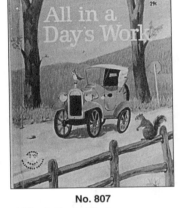

No. 807
All In A Day's Work
Illus.: Leone, Sergio
Author: Emerson, Caroline D.
1964   **$6.00**

No. 808
Romper Room Laughing Book, The
Illus.: Nankivel, Claudine
Author: Claster, Nancy
1963   **$6.00**

No. 809
Can't Verify Title

No. 810
City Boy, Country Boy
Illus.: Weigel, Susi
Author: Lobe, Mira
1963   **$6.00**

No. 811
Rabbits Give A Party, The
Illus.: Baudoin, Simonne
Author: Dermine, Lucie
1963   **$6.00**

No. 811
**Rabbits Give A Party, The
(2nd Cover)**
Illus.: Baudoin, Simonne
Author: Dermine, Lucie
1963   **$5.00**

No. 812
Peter Rabbit
Illus.: Erickson, Phoebe
Author: Potter, Beatrix
1947   **$6.00**

No. 813
Title Unknown

No. 814
Title Unknown

No. 815

Boy Who Wouldn't Eat His Breakfast, The
Illus.: Brozowska, Elizabeth
Author: Brozowska, Elizabeth
1963 **$6.00**

No. 816

Freddy And The Indians
Illus.: Binst, Claire
Author: Delahaye, Gilbert
1963 **$6.00**

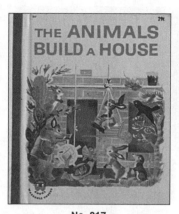

No. 817

Animals Build A House, The
Illus.: Marsia, Robert
Authors: Marsia, Robert; Delahaye, Gilbert
1963 **$6.00**

No. 818

Merry Christmas Mr. Snowman!
Illus.: Wilde, Irma
Author: Wilde, Irma
1951 **$8.00**

No. 819

Polly's Christmas Present
Illus.: Wilde, Irma
Author: Wilde, Irma
1953 **$8.00**

No. 819

Polly's Christmas Present (2nd Cover)
Illus.: Wilde, Irma
Author: Wilde, Irma
1953 **$6.00**

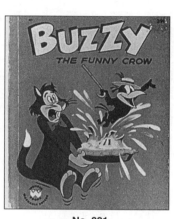

No. 820

Merry Christmas Book
Illus.: Scholz, Catherine
Author: Berg, Jean Horton
1953 **$6.00**

No. 821

Buzzy The Funny Crow
Illus.: Harvey Cartoon Studios
Author: Harvey Cartoon Studios
1963 **$7.00**

No. 822

I Can Do Anything ... Almost
Illus.: Murtagh, Betty
Author: Hartman, Virginia
1963 **$6.00**

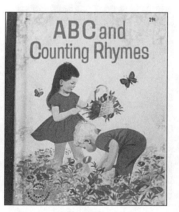

No. 822

I Can Do Anything ... Almost (2nd Cover)
Illus.: Murtagh, Betty
Author: Hartman, Virginia
1963 **$5.00**

No. 823

ABC And Counting Rhymes
Illus.: Horton, Mary
1963 **$6.00**

No. 824

Alvin's Lost Voice
Illus.: Kurtz, Bob
Author: Kurtz, Bob
1963 **$16.00**

No. 825

Animals' Playground, The

Illus.: Seiden, Art

Author: Marshall, Virginia Stone

1964 **$6.00**

No. 826

Around The World Cutout Book

Illus.: Galst, Annie

Author: Galst, Annie

1964 **$6.00**

No. 827

Wonder Book Of Trees, The

Illus.: Koehler, Alvin

Author: Koehler, Cynthia Iliff

1964 **$6.00**

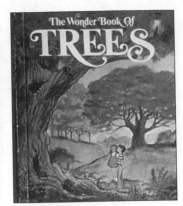

No. 827

Wonder Book Of Trees, The
(2nd Cover)

Illus.: Koehler, Alvin

Author: Koehler, Cynthia Iliff

1964 **$6.00**

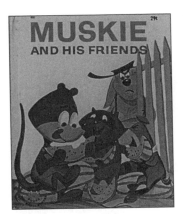

No. 828

Muskie And His Friends

Illus.: Kirkel, Stephen; Bezada,
Herb

Author: Bethell, Jean

1963 **$18.00**

No. 829

Ollie Bakes A Cake

Illus.: Meyerhoff, Nancy

Author: Bethell, Jean

1964 **$20.00**

No. 830

Trick On Deputy Dog, A

Illus.: Kirkel, Stephen; Bezada,
Herb

Author: Bethell, Jean

1964 **$20.00**

No. 831

Luno The Soaring Stallion

Illus.: Kirkel, Stephen; Bezada, Herb

Author: Bethell, Jean

1964 **$14.00**

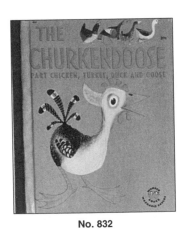

No. 832

Churkendoose, The

Illus.: Cunningham, Dellwyn

Author: Berenberg, Ben Ross

1946 **$10.00**

No. 832

Churkendoose, The

Illus.: Cunningham, Dellwyn

Author: Berenberg, Ben Ross

1946 **$10.00**

No. 832

What Am I?
(Formerly: The Churkendoose)

Illus.: Cunningham, Dellwyn

Author: Berenberg, Ben Ross

1946 **$8.00**

No. 833

What Can We Do With Blocks?

Illus.: Herric, Pru

Author: Shaine, Frances

1964 **$6.00**

No. 834

Look Who's Here!

Illus.: Gaulke, Gloria

Author: Walters, Marguerite

1964 **$6.00**

No. 834

Look Who's Here

(2nd Cover)

Illus.: Gaulke, Gloria

Author: Walters, Marguerite

1964 **$5.00**

No. 835

Diz And Liz

Illus.: Allen, Colin

Author: Key, Ted

1965 **$13.00**

No. 836

Tutu The Little Fawn

Illus.: Morel, Eve

Author: Simon, Romain

1964 **$6.00**

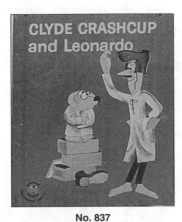

No. 837

Clyde Crashcup And Leonardo

Illus.: Kurtz, Bob

Author: Kurtz, Bob

1965 **$18.00**

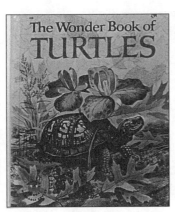

No. 838

Wonder Book Of Turtles, The

Illus.: Koehlerm Cynthia and Alvin

Author: Morel, Eve

1964 **$4.00**

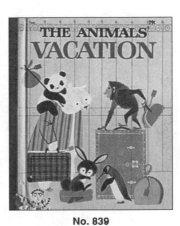

No. 839

Animal's Vacation, The

Illus.: Haber, Shel and Jan

Author: Haber, Shel and Jan

1964 **$4.00**

No. 840

Hector Heathcoat And The Knights

Illus.: Zaffo, George

Author: Bethell, Jean

1965 **$18.00**

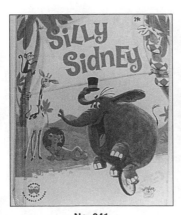

No. 841

Silly Sidney

Illus.: Cummings, Art

Author: Bethell, Jean

1965 **$18.00**

No. 842

Once There Was A House

Illus.: Wood, Ruth

Author: Wynnw, Milton

1965 **$5.00**

No. 843

Peter Cottontail And Reddy Fox

Illus.: Hauge, Carl and Mary

Author: Burgess, Thornton W.

1954 **$5.00**

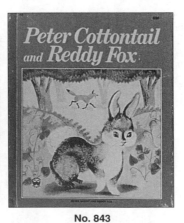

No. 843

Peter Cottontail And Reddy Fox

(Second Cover)

Illus.: Hauge, Carl and Mary

Author: Burgess, Thornton W.

1954 **$5.00**

No. 844
So This Is Spring!
Illus.: Dixon, Rachel Taft
Author: Fritz, Jean
1954   **$5.00**

No. 844
So This Is Spring!
(2nd Cover)
Illus.: Dixon, Rachel Taft
Author: Fritz, Jean
1954   **$5.00**

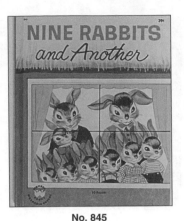

No. 845
Nine Rabbits And Another
Illus.: Dixon, Rachel Taft
Author: Potter, Miriam Clark
1957   **$5.00**

No. 846
What's For Breakfast?
Illus.: Wilde, Irma
Author: Wilde, Irma
1950   **$5.00**

No. 847
Hungry Baby Bunny, The
Illus.: Seiden, Bea Rabin
Author: Evers, Alf
1951   **$5.00**

No. 847
Hungry Baby Bunny, The
(2nd Cover)
Illus.: Seiden, Bea Rabin
Author: Evers, Alf
1951   **$5.00**

No. 848
Sonny The Luck Bunny
Illus.: Seiden, Art
Author: Martin, Marcia
1952   **$5.00**

No. 849
Barbie, The Baby Sitter
Illus.: Nankivel, Claudine
Author: Bethell, Jean
1964   **$15.00**

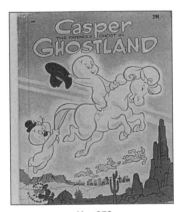

No. 850
Casper The Friendly Ghost In Ghostland
Illus.: Harvey Cartoon Studios
Author: Harvey Cartoon Studios
1965   **$8.00**

No. 851
Puff The Magic Dragon
Illus.: Tallarico, Tony
Author: Newman, Paul
1965   **$7.00**

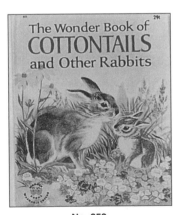

No. 852
Wonder Book Of Cottontails And Other Rabbits, The
Illus.: Koehler, Alvin
Author: Koehler, Cynthia Iliff
1965   **$4.00**

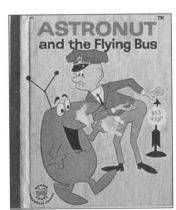

No. 853
Astronut And The Flying Bus
Illus.: Tallarico, Tony
Author: Lenhart, Ellen
1965   **$16.00**

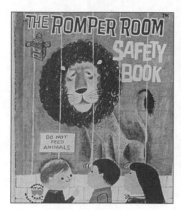

No. 854
Romper Room Safety Book, The
Illus.: Seiden, Art
Author: Claster, Nancy
1965 $6.00

No. 855
Casper And Wendy Adventures
Illus.: Harvey Cartoon Studios
Author: Harvey Cartoon Studios
1969 $12.00

No. 856
Title Unknown

No. 857
Wonder Book Of Horses, The
Illus.: Koehler, Alvin
Author: Koehler, Cynthia Iliff
1965   4.00

No. 858
Night Before Christmas, The
Illus.: Leone, Sergio
Author: Moore, Clement C.
1965 $6.00

No. 858
Night Before Christmas, The
(2nd Cover)
Illus.: Leone, Sergio
Author: Moore, Clement C.
1965 $6.00

No. 860
Soupy Sales And The Talking
Turtle
Illus.: Tallarico, Tony
Author: Bethell, Jean
1965 $8.00

No. 861
Title Unknown

No. 862
Title Unknown

No. 863
Title Unknown

No. 864
Title Unknown

No. 865
Waiting For Santa Claus
Illus.: Cummings, Alison
Author: Martin, Marcia
1952 $7.00

No. 866
How The Rabbit Found Christmas
Illus.: Kendrick, Alcy
Author: Scott, Ann
1961 $6.00

No. 867
Kewtee Bear's Christmas
Illus.: Dixon, Rachel Taft
Authors: Reed, Alan; Stout, Bert;
Quigley, Truman
1965 $10.00

No. 868
Raggedy Ann's Christmas Surprise
Illus.: Sinnickson, Tom
Author: Gruelle, Johnny
1952 $16.00

No. 869
Christmas Favorites
(Formerly: Wonder Christmas
Book)
Illus.: Myers, Lou
1951 $5.00

No. 876

Baby's First Christmas

Illus.: Dart, Eleanor

1959 $6.00

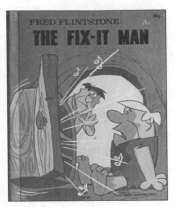

No. 917

Fred Flintstone The Fix-It Man

Illus.: Hanna-Barbera Productions, Inc.

Author: Elias, Horace J.

1976 $8.00

No. 919

Pebbles And Bamm-Bamm Find Things To Do

Illus.: Hanna-Barbera Productions, Inc.

Author: Elias, Horace J.

1976 $10.00

No. 921

Yogi Bear And The Baby Skunk

Illus.: Hanna-Barbera Productions, Inc.

Author: Elias, Horace J.

1976 $8.00

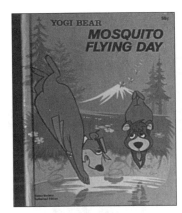

No. 924

Yogi Bear Mosquito Flying Day

Illus.: Hanna-Barbera Productions, Inc.

Author: Elias, Horace J.

1976 $8.00

No. 926

Yogi Bear Playtime In Jelly stone Park

Illus.: Hanna-Barbera Productions, Inc.

Author: Elias, Horace J.

1976 $8.00

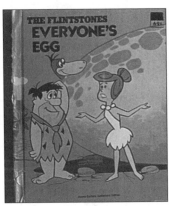

No. 927

Flintstones 'Everyone's Egg'

Illus.: Hanna-Barbera Productions, Inc.

Author: Elias, Horace J.

1976 $8.00

No. 944

Huckleberry Hound 'The Big Blooming Rosebush'

Illus.: Hanna-Barbera Productions, Inc.

Author: Elias, Horace J.

1976 $8.00

Index of Wonder Books

A Brief History of Treasure Books

Treasure Books was a subsidiary of Grosset & Dunlap, the same company that printed Wonder Books. They were printed from 1952 to 1956. You may notice that some Treasure Book titles later appeared—around 1957—as Wonder Books.

The books measured 6-5/8" x 7-7/8" and contained 28 full-color pages. Treasures were similar to Little Golden Books: the front and back covers were stapled together and covered with a paper spine. The spines changes four times over the books' short life—starting as a light tan in 1952, a very pale red in 1953, a very dark red later in 1953, and a yellow with thin colored stripes sometime around 1954.

How to Tell Editions

There are no markings to distinguish a first edition from a reprint, but you can use the last titles on the back of the book to approximate dates. Numbers 850 to 853 only listed four titles. If the last number listed on the back cover is close to the number of the book, you probably have a first edition. The back covers ended in the following numbers:

853, 857, 861, 863, 865, 869, 873, 878, 882, 887, 893, 899, 902, 903, and 906

Treasure Books—By Book Number

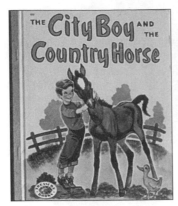

No. 850
City Boy And The Country Horse, The
Illus.: Woyers, William
Author: Bookman, Charlotte
1952   **$15.00**

No. 851
Fixit Man, The
Illus.: Wilde, George
Author: Wilde, Irma
1952   **$12.00**

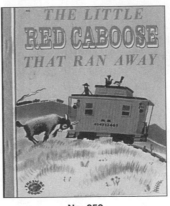

No. 852
Little Red Caboose That Ran Away, The
Illus.: Burchard, Peter
Author: Curren, Polly
1952   **$12.00**

No. 853
Wonderful Treasure Hunt, The
Illus.: Wilde, George
Author: Wilde, Irma
1952   **$12.00**

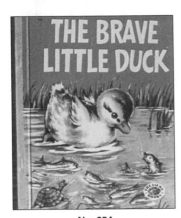

No. 854
Brave Little Duck, The
Illus.: Gayer, Marguerite
Author: Conkling, Fleur
1953   **$12.00**

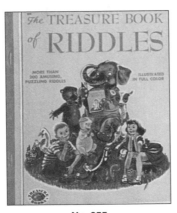

No. 855
Treasure Book Of Riddles, The
Illus.: Wood, Ruth
Author: North, Robert
1950   **$12.00**

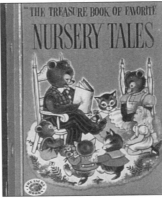

No. 856
Treasure Book Of Favorite Nursery Tales, The
Illus.: Peller, Jackie; Tamburine, Jean
1953   **$12.00**

No. 857
Little Engine That Laughed, The
Illus.: Seiden, Art
Author: Evers, Alf
1950   **$12.00**

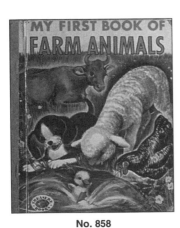

No. 858
My First Book Of Farm Animals
Illus.: Wilde, Irma
Author: Edward, Annette
1953   **$12.00**

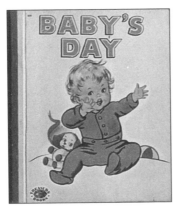

No. 859
Baby's Day
Illus.: Pointer, Priscilla
Author: Edwards, Annette
1953   **$12.00**

No. 860
Mighty Mouse
Illus.: Chad
Author: Sutton, Felix
1953   **$18.00**

No. 861
Dress-Up Parade, The
Illus.: Wilde, George
Author: Wilde, Irma
1953   **$18.00**

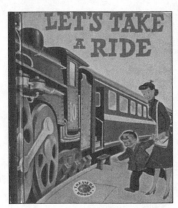

No. 862

Let's Take A Ride
Illus.: Wilde, George
Author: Martin, Marcia
1953   **$12.00**

No. 863

Let's Play Nurse And Doctor
Illus.: Stang, Judy
Author: Stang, Judy
1953   **$12.00**

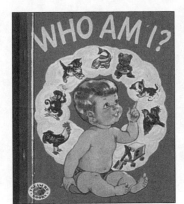

No. 864

Who Am I?
Illus.: Schad, Helen G.
Author: Schad, Helen
1953   **$12.00**

No. 865

Merry Mailman, The
Illus.: Wood, Ruth
Author: Martin, Marcia
1953   **$12.00**

No. 866

Mighty Mouse: Dinky Learns To Fly
Illus.: Chad
Author: Sutton, Felix
1953   **$18.00**

No. 867

Things To Make And Do For Christmas
Illus.: Shelly, Duke
Author: Shelly, Duke
1953   **$20.00**

No. 868

My First Book Of Prayers
Illus.: Ives, Ruth
Author: Juergens, Mary
1953   **$10.00**

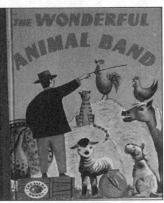

No. 869

Wonderful Animal Band, The
Illus.: Burchard, Peter
Author: Luther, Frank
1953   **$10.00**

No. 870

Let's Play Train
Illus.: Weisgard, Leonard
Author: Weisgard, Leonard
1953   **$25.00**

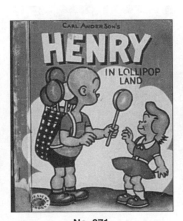

No. 871

Henry In Lollipop Land
Illus.: Anderson, Carl
Author: Anderson, Carl
1953   **$18.00**

No. 872

Felix The Cat
Illus.: Sullivan, Pat
Author: Sullivan, Pat
1953   **$18.00**

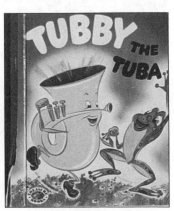

No. 873

Tubby The Tuba
Illus.: Chad
Author: Tripp, Paul
1954   **$16.00**

No. 874
Prince Valiant
Illus.: Foster, Hal
Author: Foster, Hal
1954 **$20.00**

No. 875
Ten Little Fingers
Illus.: Pointer, Priscilla
Author: Pointer, Pricella
1954 **$10.00**

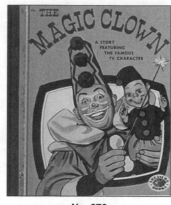

No. 876
Magic Clown, The
Illus.: Schucker, James
Author: Sutton, Felix
1954 **$16.00**

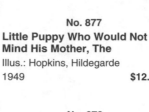

No. 877
Little Puppy Who Would Not Mind His Mother, The
Illus.: Hopkins, Hildegarde
1949 **$12.00**

No. 878
Cozy Little Farm, The
Illus.: Angela
Author: Bonino, Louise
1946 **$10.00**

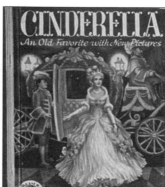

No. 879
Cinderella
Illus.: Ives, Ruth
Author: Andreas, Evelyn
1954 **$10.00**

No. 880
Shy Little Horse, The
Illus.: Robinson
Author: Scott, Therese
1947 **$10.00**

No. 881
Just Like Me
Illus.: Weisgard, Leonard
Author: Weisgard, Leonard
1954 **$12.00**

No. 882
Henny-Penny
Illus.: Ponter, James
1954 **$10.00**

No. 883
Big & Little
Illus.: Hull, John
Author: Hull, John
1954 **$10.00**

No. 884
Mighty Mouse And The Scared Scarecrow
Illus.: Chad
Author: Sutton, Felix
1954 **$18.00**

No. 885
My Own Book Of Fun And Play
$10.00

No. 886
Help Mr. Willy Nilly
Illus.: Tamburine, Jean
Author: Fritz, Jean
1954 **$13.00**

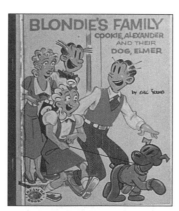

No. 887
Blondie's Family
Illus.: Young, Chic
Author: Young, Chic
1954 **$16.00**

No. 888
Popeye
Illus.: Sagendorf, Bud
1955 **$16.00**

No. 889
What Time Is It?
Illus.: Zabinski, Joseph
Author: Peter, John
1954 **$10.00**

No.890

Let's Take A Trip In Our Car
Illus.: Schucker, James
Author: Sutton, Felix
1954   **$25.00**

No. 891

Really Truly Treasure Hunt, The
Illus.: Newell, Crosby
Author: Bonsall, George
1954   **$13.00**

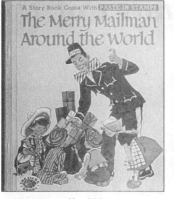

No. 892

Merry Mailman Around The World
Illus.: Wood, Ruth
Author: Martin, Marcia
1955   **$20.00**

No. 893

Let's Go To School
Illus.: Hoecker, Hazel
Author: Edwards, Annette
1954   **$16.00**

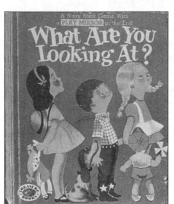

No. 896

Mighty Mouse-Santa's Helper
Illus.: Chad
Author: Sutton, Felix
1955   **$18.00**

No. 897

Henry Goes To A Party
Illus.: Anderson, Carl
Author: Anderson, Carl
1955   **$18.00**

No. 898

Snow White
Illus.: Seiden, Art
1955   **$12.00**

No. 899

It's Fun To Peek
      $10.00

No. 900

Title Unknown

No. 895

What Are You Looking At?
Illus.: Bonsall, George; Newell, Crosby
Authors: Bonsall, George; Newell, Crosby
1954   **$16.00**

No. 894

Title Unknown

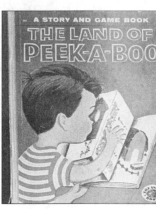

No. 901

Land Of Peek-A-Boo, The
Illus.: Newell, Crosby
Author: Bonsall, George
1955   **$15.00**

No. 902

Sparkie-No School Today
Illus.: Jason, Leon
Author: Jason, Leon
1955   **$16.00**

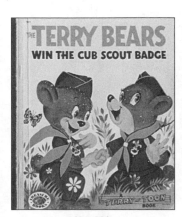

No. 903

Terry Bears Win The Cub Scout Badge, The
Illus.: Moore, Robert J.
Author: Sutton, Felix
1955   **$18.00**

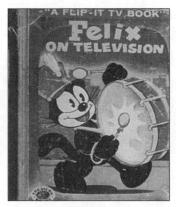

No. 904

Felix On Television
Illus.: Oriolo, Joe
Author: Shapiro, Irwin
1956   **$18.00**

No. 905

Flash Gordon
Illus.: Berger, Alex
1956   **$18.00**

No. 906

Who Is That?
Illus.: Schad, Helen G.
Author: Schad, Helen G.
1956   **$16.00**

Index of Treasure Books

A Brief History of Tell-A-Tale Books

The Tell-A-Tale series was published by Whitman Publishing Company, a subsidiary of Western Publishing Company, Inc., from 1945 to 1984. Since 1985 the series has been published as "A Golden Tell-A-Tale® Book." You will find some Tell-A-Tale titles from the "A Golden Tell-A-Tale® Book" series listed, but I primarily cover the Whitman series.

Whitman first started printing Tell-A-Tale books with number 850, *Poor Kitty*, in 1945. Some, if not all, of the titles printed in 1945 had dust jackets. When the numbers reached 899, somebody at Whitman questioned why the books had started with 850 and not 800. So around 1952, the company went back to 800 and numbered until 848.

Because the company used up all of the 800 numbers, it numbered the books 900 to 966 from 1953 through 1954. Books numbered 2500 through 2600 were published into the 1970s. Books published since 1955 can have more than one title for the same book number. Books with dashes were printed in the "A Golden Tell-A-Tale® Book" series.

Tell-A-Tale books measure 5-5/8" x 6-5/8". The early editions contained 40 pages, including paste-downs, and sold for 15 cents. The exception to this page count was that Authorized titles (books approved by a show or actor) have 32 pages and Flocked titles (books which have a "fuzziness" on the cover and on some of the inside pages) have 20 pages. Later the books were printed with 29 pages.

How to Tell Editions

There is no way to tell a first edition, but you can look at the titles on the back of the book. If you see a TV character listed, you can date the book accordingly.

Tell-A-Tales—Alphabetical Listing

No. 2407-2
1 Is Red
Illus.: Eugenie
Author: Daly, Eileen
1974   **$2.00**

No. 896
ABC
Illus.: Flory, Jane
1949   **$15.00**

No. 896
ABC
(2nd Cover)
Illus.: Flory, Jane
1949   **$12.00**

No. 2658
ABC
Illus.: Nugent, Alys
1956   **$4.00**

No. 808
ABC
Illus.: Vartanian, Raymond
1952   **$6.00**

No. 2554
ABC- A Tale Of A Sale
Illus.: Heckler, William
Author: Hovelsrud, Joyce
1963   **$3.00**

No. 2554
ABC- A Tale Of A Sale
(2nd Cover)
Illus.: Heckler, William
Author: Hovelsrud, Joyce
1963   **$3.00**

No. 2569
Alonzo Purr The Seagoing Cat
Illus.: Hafner, Marylin
Author: Carey, Mary
1966   **$5.00**

No. 2430
Alphabet Rhymes
(Formerly: ABC)
Illus.: Nugent, Alys
1956   **$2.00**

No. 2512
Amy's Long Night
Illus.: Wheeling, Lynn
Author: Carber, Nancy
1970   **$3.00**

No. 2462-46
And So To Bed
Illus.: Orville, Oliver
Author: Orville, Oliver
1989   **$3.00**

No. 2543
Andy
Illus.: Hoecker, Hazel
Author: Michelson, Florence
1966   **$3.00**

No. 906
Andy And Betsy At The Circus
Illus.: Friedel, Violet and Fred
Authors: Friedel, Violet and Fred
1953   **$15.00**

No. 887

Animal ABC

Illus.: Harriett

1949 **$15.00**

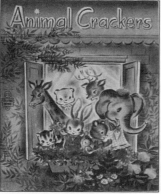

No. 837

Animal Crackers

(Formerly: Animal Jingles)

Illus.: Peller, Jackie

Author: Georgiana

1949 **$15.00**

No. 837

Animal Jingles

Illus.: Peller, Jackie

Author: Georgiana

1951 **$20.00**

No. 2556

Animal Train

Illus.: Williams, Ben D

Author: Roberts, Elizabeth

1969 **$6.00**

No. 2474

Animals In Mother Goose

Illus.: Goldsborough, June

1954 **$3.00**

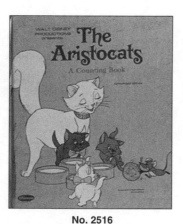

No. 2516

Aristocats 'A Counting Book,' The

Illus.: Walt Disney Studios

Author: Walt Disney Studios

1970 **$4.00**

No. 2524

Around And About Buttercup Farm

Illus.: Miloche, Hilda and Kane, Wilma

Author: Lynn, Patricia

1951 **$6.00**

No. 2493

Baby Goes Around The Block

Illus.: Merkling, Erica

Author: Horn, Gladys M.

1973 **$3.00**

No. 917

Baby Moses

Illus.: Frost, Bruno

Author: Trent, Robbie

1952 **$15.00**

No. 2422

Baby's First Book

Illus.: Allen, Joan

Author: Swetnam, Evelyn

1952 **$2.00**

No. 2548

Bambi

Illus.: Walt Disney Studios

Author: Walt Disney Studios

1972 **$3.00**

No. 2489

Barbie And Skipper Go Camping

Author: Daly, Eileen

1974 **$8.00**

No. 2450-01
Barbie On Skates
Illus.: Tierney, Tom
Author: Balducci, Rita
1992 $2.00

No. 2551
Beany And Cecil Captured For The Zoo
Illus.: Bradbury, Jack; Wolfe, Gene
Author: Hammer, Barbara
1954 $25.00

No. 904
Beany And His Magic Set
Illus.: Armstrong, Samuel; Eisenber, Harvey
Author: Clampett, Bob
1953 $25.00

No. 2455-59
Beauty And The Beast
Illus.: Kicks, Russell
Author: Korman, Justine
1993 $4.00

No. 2554
Bear Country
Illus.: Godwin, Edward and Stephanie
Author: Wright, Betty Ren
1954 $10.00

No. 2554
**Bear Country
(2nd Cover)**
Illus.: Godwin, Edward and Stephani
Author: Wright, Betty Ren
1954 $7.00

No. 2553
Beaver Valley
Illus.: Hartwell, Marjorie
Author: Wright, Betty Ren
1966 $10.00

No. 2553
**Beaver Valley
(2nd Cover)**
Illus.: Hartwell, Marjorie
Author: Wright, Betty Ren
1966 $7.00

No. 2541
Bedknobs And Broomsticks - A Visit To Naboombu
Illus.: Walt Disney Studios
Author: Walt Disney Studios
1971 $5.00

No. 2616
Bedtime Book, The
Illus.: Winship, Florence Sarah
Author: Watts, Mabel
1963 $3.00

No. 825
Beloved Son, The
Illus.: Frost, Bruno
Author: Wagstaff, Blanche Shoemaker
1951 $12.00

No. 2640
Benji 'The Detective'
Illus.: Willis, Werner
Author: Lewis, Jean
1970 $4.00

No. 846

Benny The Bus

Illus.: Vaughan, Eillen Fox

Author: Horn, Gladys M.

1950 **$15.00**

No. 2521

Best Surprise Of All, The

Illus.: D'amato, Alex

Author: Pape, Donna Lugg

1961 **$4.00**

No. 2553

Beware Of The Dog

Illus.: Nagel, Stina

Author: Woyke, Christine

1968 **$4.00**

No. 2474-33

Big And Little Are Not The Same

Illus.: Buckett, George

Author: Ottum, Bob

1972 **$2.00**

No. 2510

Big Bark, The

Illus.: Nagel, Stina

Author: Woyke, Christine

1968 **$2.00**

No. 2452-4

Big Bird Follows The Signs

Illus.: Delaney, A

Author: Kingsley, Emily Perl

1980 **$2.00**

No. 869

Big Game Hunter, The

Illus.: Read, Isobel

Author: Alexander, Florence Bibo

1947 **$17.00**

No. 942

Big Little Kitty

Illus.: Biggers, Jan D.

Author: Biggers, Jan D.

1953 **$8.00**

No. 840

Big Red Pajama Wagon, The

Illus.: Anderson, Betty

Author: Elting, Mary

1949 **$15.00**

No. 2522

Big Whistle, The

Illus.: Myers, Louise

Author: Tompert, Ann

1968 **$4.00**

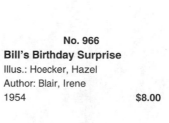

No. 966

Bill's Birthday Surprise

Illus.: Hoecker, Hazel

Author: Blair, Irene

1954 **$8.00**

No. 888

Billy Bunnyscoot - The Lost Bunny

Illus.: Tedder, Elizabeth

Author: Smith, Georgia Tucker

1948 **$16.00**

No. 2560

Bingo
Illus.: Garris, Norma and Dan
Author: Hogstrom, Daphne
1966 **$5.00**

No. 2576

Bingo
(2nd cover)
Illus.: Garris, Norma and Dan
Author: Hogstrom, Daphne
1975 **$4.00**

No. 2510

Box Of Important Things, The
Illus.: Bradfield, Roger
Author: Hellie, Anne
1968 **$4.00**

No. 916

Boy's Friend, A
Illus.: Weiniger, Egon
Author: Trent, Robbie
1952 **$10.00**

No. 2552

Bozo The Clown: King Of The Ring
Illus.: White, Al
1960 **$7.00**

No. 870

Breezy -The Air Minded Pigeon
Illus.: Grider, Dorothy
Author: Grider, Dorothy
1947 **$15.00**

No. 2610

Bremen-Town Musicians, The
Illus.: Mikolaycak, Charles
Author: Zens, Patricia Martin
1964 **$5.00**

No. 2560

Brown Puppy And A Falling Star, A
Illus.: Winship, Florence Sarah
Author: Ross, Elizabeth
1956 **$5.00**

No. 2526

Buffy And The New Girl
Illus.: Mode, Nathalee
Author: Bond, Gladys Baker
1969 **$12.00**

No. 2453-48

Bugs Bunny Calling!
Illus.: Messerli, Joe
Author: Manuchkin, Fran
1988 **$2.00**

No. 2410

Bugs Bunny Hangs Around
Illus.: Abranz, Alfred; Mcgary, Norm
Author: Hoag, Nancy
1957 **$8.00**

No. 2543

Bugs Bunny In Something Fishy
Illus.: Abranz, Alfred; Mcgary, Norm
Author: Warner Bros. Cartoons, Inc.
1956 **$8.00**

No. 2572
Bugs Bunny Keeps A Promise
Illus.: Heimdahl, Ralph; Dempster, Al
1951   **$8.00**

No. 2607
Bugs Bunny Party Pest
Illus.: Andersen, Al; Mekimson, Thomas J.
Author: Johnston, William
1976   **$2.00**

No. 2472-35
Bugs Bunny Rides Again
Illus.: Messerli, Joe
1986   **$2.00**

No. 928
Bugs Bunny's Big Invention
Illus.: Heimdahl, Ralph
Author: Warner Brothers Cartoons
1969   **$8.00**

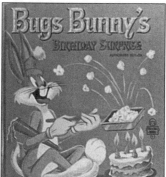

No. 2421
Bugs Bunny's Birthday Surprise
Illus.: Abranz, Alfred; Thomas, Richard
Author: Theresa
1951   **$8.00**

No. 2594
Bullwinkle's Masterpiece
Illus.: Jason, Leon
Author: Lewis, Jean
1976   **$7.00**

No. 923
Bunny Button
Illus.: Myers, Bernice
Author: Revena
1953   **$7.00**

No. 2526
Bunny Button
(2nd Cover)
Illus.: Myers, Bernice
Author: Revena
1953   **$4.00**

No. 834
Buster Bulldozer
Illus.: Stoddard, Maru Alice
Author: Danner, Catherine
1952   **$10.00**
No. 2615
(2nd Cover)
      $4.00

No. 2585
Busy Body Book 'A First Book About You,' The
Illus.: Beylon, Catherine M.
Author: Harrison, David L.
1975   **$2.00**

No. 2473-42
Busy Machines
Illus.: Walz, Richard
Author: Harrison, David
1985   **$2.00**

No. 2474-42
Busy Saturday Word Book, The
Illus.: Dolce, Ellen
1985   **$2.00**

No. 2559
Butterfly 'A Story Of Magic'
Illus.: Winship, Florence Sarah
Author: Daly, Eileen
1969   **$4.00**

No. 2675
Buzzy Beaver
(A Fuzzy Wuzzy Book)
Illus.: Hart, Dick
Author: Sankey, Alice
1951   **$12.00**

No. 2610
Captain Kangaroo 'Tick Tock Trouble'
Illus.: Frost, Bruno
Author: Jones, Mary Voell
1961   **$10.00**

No. 2610
Captain Kangaroo And The Too-Small House
Illus.: Crawford, Mel
Author: Haas, Dorothy
1958   **$10.00**

No. 2547
Captain Kangaroo's Picnic
Illus.: Crawford, Mel
Author: Jones, Mary Voell
1959   **$10.00**

No. 2450
Chicken Little
Illus.: Hartwell, Marjorie
1964   **$4.00**

No. 2519
Child's Friend, A
(Formerly: A Boy's Friend)
Illus.: Weiniger, Egen
Author: Trent, Robbie
1953   **$6.00**

No. 2624
Child's Ten Commandments, A
Illus.: Murray, Marjorie
Author: Regan, Jo B
1959   **$5.00**

No. 889
Chitter Chatter
Illus.: Read, Isobel
Author: Read, Isobel
1948   **$15.00**

No. 2601
Christopher's "Hoppy" Day
Illus.: Winship, Florence Sarah
Author: Elliot, Edith F.
1967   **$6.00**

No. 2672
Christopher John's Fuzzy Blanket
(A Fuzzy Wuzzy Book)
Illus.: Winship, Florence Sarah
Author: Haas, Dorothy
1959   **$12.00**

No. 964
Cinderella
Illus.: Wheeler, George
Author: Walt Disney Studios
1954   **$7.00**

No. 2604

Cinderella
(2nd cover)
Illus.: Wheeler, George
Author: Walt Disney Studios
1954   **$4.00**

No. 2427-2

Cinderella
(3rd cover)
Illus.: Wheeler, George
Author: Walt Disney Studios
1972   **$3.00**

No. 2674

Cinnamon Bear, The
(A Fuzzy Wuzzy Book)
Illus.: Bakacs, George
Author: Hanson, Alice
1961   **$15.00**

No. 2505

Circus Alpahbet ABC
Illus.: Hudson, Patric
1958   **$6.00**

No. 2563

Circus Alphabet
Illus.: Hudson, Patric
1954   **$3.00**

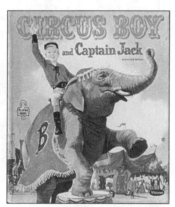

No. 2608

Circus Boy And Captain Jack
Illus.: Boyle, Neil
Author: Snow, Dorothea J.
1957   **$15.00**

No. 2466-40

Circus Mouse
Illus.: Horne, Daniel R.
Author: McGuire, Leslie
1987   **$3.00**

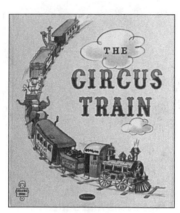

No. 890

Circus Train, The
Illus.: Dorcas
Author: Knittle, Jessie M.
1948   **$16.00**

No. 2492

Clip Clop
Illus.: Winship, Florence Sarah
Author: Hoag, Nancy
1958   **$9.00**

No. 826

Columbus, The Exploring Burro
Illus.: Koering, Ursula
Author: Brewster, Benjamin
1951   **$6.00**

No. 2506

Corey Baker Of Julia And His
Show And Tell
Illus.: Harris, Larry
Author: Bond, Gladys Baker
1970   **$6.00**

No. 2402

Count's Poem, The
(Sesame Street)
Illus.: Cooke, Tom
Author: Sipherd, Ray
1978   **$2.00**

No. 2530
Cousin Matilda And The Foolish Wolf
Illus.: Osborne, Richard
Author: Cole, Joanna
1970   **$4.00**

No. 894
Cradle Rhymes
Illus.: Rachel
Author: Horn, Gladys M.
1949   **$18.00**

No. 2621
Daffy Duck Space Creature
Illus.: Baker, Darrell
Author: Ingoglia, Gina
1977   **$4.00**

No. 2506
Daktari 'Judi And The Kitten'
Illus.: Harris, Larry
Author: Fiedler, Jean
1965   **$6.00**

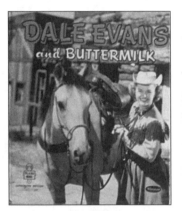

No. 2570
Dale Evans And Buttermilk
Illus.: Wegner, Helmuth G.
Author: Welden, Rose
1956   **$25.00**

No. 802
Dally
Illus.: Clement, Charles
Author: Julian, Lee
1951   **$7.00**

No. 2433
Daniel's New Friend
Illus.: Wilde, Irma
Author: Bach, Hilda
1968   **$3.00**

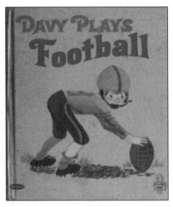

No. 2512
Davy Plays Football
Illus.: Wilde, Carol
Author: Peake, Sylvia
1968   **$5.00**

No. 2513
Davy's Wiggly Tooth
Illus.: Winship, Florence Sarah
Author: Borden, Marion
1964   **$4.00**

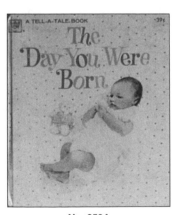

No. 2524
Day You Were Born, The
Illus.: Wood, Muriel
Author: Swetnam, Evelyn
1972   **$2.00**

No. 2451-4
Dennis The Menace 'Takes The Cake'
Illus.: Matchette, Karen
Author: Namm, Diane
1987   **$3.00**

No. 2538
Diddle Daddle Duckling
Illus.: Goldsborough, June
Author: Bennett, Grace Irene
1971   **$3.00**

No. 2615
Digger Dan
(2nd cover)
Illus.: Frankel, Simon
Author: Lynn, Patricia
1953   **$15.00**

No. 908

Digger Dan

Illus.: Frankel, Simon

Author: Lynn, Patricia

1953   **$20.00**

No. 2615

2nd Cover

       $6.00

No. 882

Dipsy Donkey

Illus.: Laurence, Johnny

Author: Laurence, Johnny

1948   **$15.00**

No. 891

Dodo The Little Wild Duck

Illus.: Grider, Dorothy

Author: Scheinert, Carlton A.

1948   **$15.00**

No. 945

Donald Duck And Chip 'n Dale

Illus.: Walsh, Stan and Wolfe, Gene

Author: Walt Disney Studios

1954   **$8.00**

No. 2516

Donald Duck And The New Bird House

Illus.: Moores, Dick and Mcgary, Norm

Author: Walt Disney Studios

1956   **$8.00**

No. 2425-6

Donald Duck And The Super-Sticky Secret

Illus.: Kohn, Arnie

Author: Watts, Mabel

1979   **$3.00**

No. 900

Donald Duck Full Speed Ahead

Illus.: Banta, Milton; Mac Laughlin, Don

1953   **$10.00**

No. 2609

Donald Duck Goes Camping

Illus.: Walt Disney Studios

Author: Walt Disney Studios

1977   **$4.00**

No. 2559

Donald Duck Goes To Disneyland

Illus.: Banta, Milton; Boyle, Neil

Author: Walt Disney Studios

1955   **$11.00**

No. 2520

Donald Duck In Frontierland

Illus.: Boyle, Neil

Author: Walt Disney Studios

1957   **$8.00**

No. 2409

Donald Duck On Tom Sawyer's Island

Illus.: Strobl, Tony and The Mattinsons

Author: Snow, Dorothea J.

1960   **$7.00**

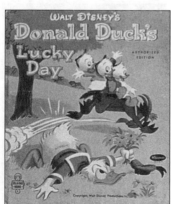

No. 827

Donald Duck's Lucky Day

Illus.: Walt Disney Studios

Author: Walt Disney Studios

1951   **$7.00**

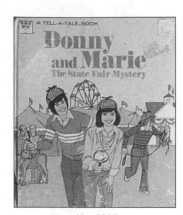

No. 2635

Donnie And Marie The State Fair Mystery

Illus.: Giacomini, Olindo

Author: Daly, Eileen

1977 **$5.00**

No. 841

Dr. Goat

Illus.: Clement, Charles

Author: Georgiana

1950 **$40.00**

No. 841

Dr. Goat

(2nd cover)

Illus.: Clement, Charles

Author: Georgiana

1950 **$25.00**

No. 2463

Dr. Hilda Makes House Calls

Illus.: Petruccio, Steven

Author: Watts, Mabel

1988 **$3.00**

No. 2454

Duck Tales 'Silver Dollars For Uncle Scrooge'

Illus.: Ito, Willy

Author: Weiner, Gina

1988 **$3.00**

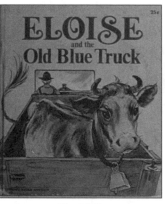

No. 2454

Eloise And The Old Blue Truck

Illus.: Winship, Florence Sarah

Author: Graham, Kennon

1971 **$7.00**

No. 2561

Elves And The Shoemaker, The

Illus.: Miloche, Hilda

1958 **$6.00**

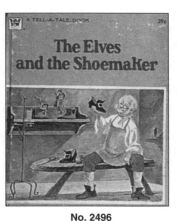

No. 2496

Elves And The Shoemaker, The

Illus.: Robison, Jim

1973 **$3.00**

No. 2604

Ernie The Cave King And Sherlock The Smart Person in The Invention of Paper

Illus.: Children's Television Workshop

Author: Wilcox, Daniel

1975 **$2.00**

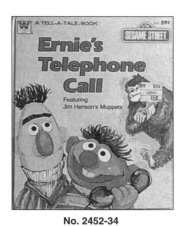

No. 2452-34

Ernie's Telephone Call

Illus.: Duga, Irra

Author: Sipherd, Ray

1978 **$2.00**

No. 2527

Especially From Thomas

Illus.: Ker, Edith M. Photos By Duesseldorf

Author: Haas, Dorothy

1965 **$4.00**

No. 2462-43

Evening Walk, The

Illus.: Durrell, Julie

Author: Ryder, Joanne

1985 **$2.00**

No. 862

Fanny Forgot

Illus.: Flory, Jane

Author: Flory, Jane

1946 **$15.00**

No. 2468

Farm ABC

Illus.: Michell, Gladys Turley

Author: Lynn, Patricia

1954 **$3.00**

No. 2464-50

Farm Animals

Illus.: Krupp, Marion

Author: Relf, Patricia

1992 **$1.00**

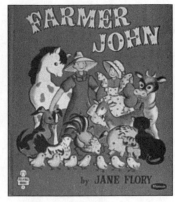

No. 838

Farmer John

Illus.: Flory, Jane

Author: Flory, Jane

1950 **$15.00**

No. 2412

Fire Dog

Illus.: Clement, Charles

Author: Julian, Lee

1960 **$6.00**

No. 2552

Flintstones At The Circus, The

Illus.: McSavage, Frank; Heiner, Robert

Author: Lewis, Jean

1963 **$15.00**

No. 872

Fluffy And Tuffy The Twin Ducklings

Illus.: McKean, Emma C.

Author: McKean, Emma C.

1947 **$15.00**

No. 820

Flying Sunbeam, The

Illus.: Anderson, Betty

Author: Fairbairn, D. N.

1950 **$16.00**

No. 820

Franky, The Fuzzy Goat (A Fuzzy Wuzzy Book)

Illus.: Suzanne

Author: Horn, Gladys M.

1951 **$15.00**

No. 2660

Frisker

Illus.: Shortall, Leonard

Author: Nowak, Mary Lauer

1956 **$6.00**

No. 2567

Funny Company, The

Illus.: Fletcher, James

Author: Patrick, Lenore

1965 **$8.00**

No. 2647

Funny Friends In Mother Goose Land

Illus.: Ford, Pam

1978 **$2.00**

No. 2611

Fury

Illus.: Bartram, Bob

Author: Haas, Dorothy

1958 **$15.00**

No. 821

Fuzzy Dan

(A Fuzzy Wuzzy Book)

Illus.: Biers, Clarence

Author: Whitehead, Jane

1951 **$16.00**

No. 912

Fuzzy Duckling

(A Fuzzy Wuzzy Book)

Illus.: Banigan, Sharon

1952 **$15.00**

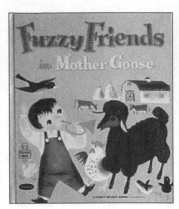

No. 914

Fuzzy Friends In Mother Goose Land

(A Fuzzy Wuzzy Book)

Illus.: Cunningham, Dellwyn

1952 **$15.00**

No. 954

Fuzzy Joe Bear

(A Fuzzy Wuzzy Book)

Illus.: Berry, Anne Scheu

Author: Horn, Gladys M.

1954 **$15.00**

No. 823

Fuzzy Mittens For Three Little Kittens

(A Fuzzy Wuzzy Book)

Illus.: Laqueur, Alys

1951 **$12.00**

No. 2671

Fuzzy Pet, A

(A Fuzzy Wuzzy Book)

Illus.: Hartwell, Marjorie

Author: Hanson, Alice

1960 **$13.00**

No. 915

Fuzzy Wuzzy Puppy, The

(A Fuzzy Wuzzy Book)

Illus.: Suzanne

Author: Winship, Florence Sarah

1954 **$12.00**

No. 800

Gene Autry 'Makes A New Friend'

Illus.: Case, Richard

Author: Beecher, Elizabeth

1952 **$22.00**

No. 932

Gene Autry And The Lost Doggie

Illus.: Armstrong, Samuel

1953 **$22.00**

No. 2566

Gene Autry Goes To The Circus

Illus.: Ushler, John

1950 **$22.00**

No. 2552

Gentle Ben And The Pesky Puppy

Illus.: Harris, Larry

Author: Fiedler, Jean

1969 **$7.00**

No. 2530

Getting Ready For Roddy

Illus.: Helwig, Hans

Author: Lynn, Patricia

1955 **$8.00**

No. 2596

Gingerbread Man, The

Illus.: Lesko, Zillah

1953 **$6.00**

No. 2504

Gingerbread Man, The

Illus.: Sari

1958 **$4.00**

No. 2619

Ginghams, The Ice-Cream Parade, The

Illus.: Land, Kate

Author: Bowden, Joan Chase

1976 **$3.00**

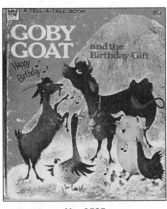

No. 2595

Goby Goat And The Birthday Gift

Illus.: Rutherford, Bonnie and Bill

Authors: Russell, Solveig Paulson

1975 **$2.00**

No. 955

Good Night 'A Flocked Book' (A Fuzzy Wuzzy Book)

Illus.: Paflin, Roberta

Author: Burrowes, Elizabeth

1954 **$15.00**

No. 2487

Goodnight Book, The

Illus.: Karch, Pat and Paul

Authors: Well, Lynn and Mandy

1969 **$3.00**

No. 2552

Goofy And The Tiger Hunt

Illus.: Moores, Dick and Armstrong, Samuel

Author: Walt Disney Studios

1964 **$6.00**

No. 2447

Goofy And His Wonderful Cornet

Illus.: Alvarado, Peter and Lorencz, William

Author: Brightman, Homer

1973 **$4.00**

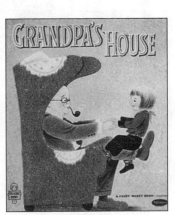

No. 2670

Grandpa's House (A Fuzzy Wuzzy Book)

Illus.: Stang, Judy

Author: Wright, Betty Ren

1969 **$14.00**

No. 2665

Grandpa's Policemen Friends

Illus.: Winship, Florence Sarah

Author: Frankel, Bernice

1967 **$4.00**

No. 2564

Great Fort, The

Illus.: Oechsli, Kelly

Author: Garber, Nancy

1970 **$3.00**

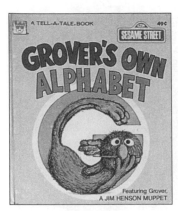

No. 2402-6
Grover's Own Alphabet
Illus.: Murdocca, Sal
1978 **$2.00**

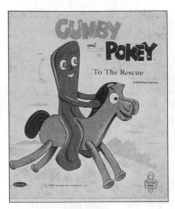

No. 2552
Gumby And Gumby's Pal Pokey To The Rescue
Illus.: Santis, George De
Author: Lewis, Jean
1969 **$15.00**

No. 2506
Gumby And Gumby's Pal Pokey
Illus.: Santis, George De
Author: Biesterveld, Betty
1968 **$15.00**

No. 2624
H.R. Pufnstuf
Illus.: Moore, Sparky; Totten, Bob
Author: Lewis, Jean
1970 **$6.00**

No. 2580
Handy Andy
Illus.: Dreany, E. Joseph
Author: Lynn, Patricia
1953 **$7.00**

No. 2516
Happiest Christmas, The
Illus.: Wilde, Irma
Author: Fairweather, Jessie Home
1955 **$12.00**

No. 2516
Happiest Christmas, The
Illus.: Wilde, Irma
Author: Fairweather, Jessie Home
1955 **$8.00**

No. 2631
Happy
Illus.: Garris, Norma and Dan
Author: Bordon, Marion
1964 **$4.00**

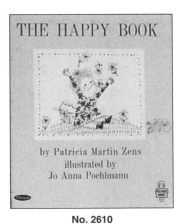

No. 2610
Happy Book, The
Illus.: Poehlmann, Jo Anna
Author: Zens, Patricia Martin
1965 **$3.00**

No. 2535
Have You Seen A Giraffe Hat?
Illus.: Storms, Robert
Author: Joyce, Irma
1969 **$4.00**

No. 2510
Hello, Joe
Illus.: Corrigan, Barbara
Author: Stempel, Ruth
1961 **$6.00**

No. 2616
Hello, Rock
Illus.: Bradfield, Roger
Author: Bradfield, Roger
1965 **$6.00**

No. 2472-42
Henrietta And The Hat
Illus.: Schweninger, Ann
Author: Watts, Mabel
1985 $2.00

No. 855
**Henry The Helicopter
(Previously Little Henry)**
Illus.: Williams, Ben D.
Author: Graham, Eleanor
1945 $15.00

No. 2602
"Hey There It's Yogi Bear!"
Illus.: McSavage, Frank and Young,
Harland
Author: Daly, Eileen
1964 $17.00

No. 847
Hi! Cowboy
Illus.: Williams, Ben D.
Author: Horn, Gladys M.
1950 $15.00

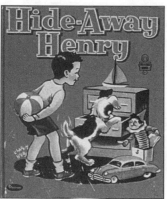

No. 938
Hide-Away Henry
Illus.: Biers, Clarence
Author: Sankey, Alice
1953 $6.00

No. 2553
Hiding Place, The
Illus.: O'Sullivan, Tom
Author: Meek, Pauline Palmer
1971   2.00

No. 924
Hippety Hop Around The Block
Illus.: Dorcas
Author: Horn, Gladys M.
1953 $7.00

No. 2553
Ho-Hum
Illus.: Myers, Jack and Louise
Author: Lynn, Patricia
1957 $10.00

No. 2510
**Ho-Hum
(2nd Cover)**
Illus.: Meyers, Jack and Louise
Author: Lynn, Patricia
1957 $5.00

No. 2466-46
Honey Bear Finds A Friend
Illus.: Orville, Oliver
Author: Pepper, Alice
1990 $2.00

No. 2503
Hooray For Lassie!
Illus.: Marshall, Carol
Author: Borden, Marion
1964 $6.00

No. 866
Hop, Skippy And Jump
Illus.: Vivienne
Author: Vivienne
1947 $15.00

No. 2552
Hoppity Hooper Vs. Skippity Snooper
Illus.: Santis, George De
Author: Lewis, Jean
1966   **$8.00**

No. 2411-1
Horse For Charlie, A
Illus.: Elfrieda
Author: Tompert, Ann
1970   **$3.00**

No. 2530
House My Grandpa Built, The
Illus.: Rutherford, Bonnie and Bill
Author: Gohn, Geraldine Everett
1971   **$3.00**

No. 2480
House That Jack Built, The
Illus.: Suzanne
1961   **$4.00**

No. 2601
How Big Is A Baby?
Illus.: Garris, Norma and Dan
Author: Holmgren, Virginia C.
1966   **$2.00**

No. 2660
How Can We Get To The Zoo?
Illus.: Rutherford, Bonnie and Bill
Author: Joyce, Irma
1966   **$2.00**

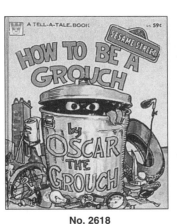

No. 2521
How Does Your Garden Grow?
Illus.: Goldsborough, June
Author: Benton, William and Elizabeth
1969   **$2.00**

No. 2618
How To Be A Grouch (Sesame Street)
Illus.: Bathman, Ed
Author: Spinney, Carol
1976   **$2.00**

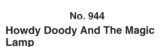

No. 944
Howdy Doody And The Magic Lamp
Illus.: Crawford, Mel
Author: Coppersmith, Jerry
1954   **$20.00**

No. 902
Howdy Doody And The Monkey Tale
1953   **$20.00**

No. 934
Howdy Doody's Clarabell And Pesky Peanut
Illus.: Kagran, Corporation
Author: Kagran Corporation
1953   **$20.00**

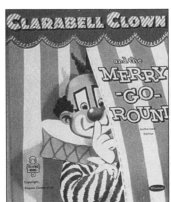

No. 2558
Howdy Doody's Clarabell Clown And The Merry-Go-Round
Illus.: Crawford, Mel
Author: Barron, John
1955   **$20.00**

No. 2611
Huckleberry Hound The Rainmaker
Illus.: Daly, Eileen
Author: Fletcher, Jim
1963   **$18.00**

No. 2421-2
Huffin Puff Express, The
Illus.: Seiden, Art
Author: Harrison, David L.
1974   **$5.00**

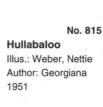

No. 815
Hullabaloo
Illus.: Weber, Nettie
Author: Georgiana
1951   **$8.00**

No. 2659
Hungry Lion, The
Illus.: Stang, Judy
Author: Fletcher, Steffi
1960   **$7.00**

No. 2616
Hurry, Scurry
Illus.: Tomes, Jackie
Authors: Putnam, Nina; Williams, Gretchen
1963   **$3.00**

No. 2527
I Know What A Farm Is
Illus.. Crawford, Mel
Author: Fiedler, Jean
1969   **$3.00**

No. 2522
I Like The Farm
Illus.: Depper, Hertha
Author: Wolf, Nancy Hoag
1961   **$3.00**

No. 2615
I Like To Be Little
Illus.: Mill, Eleanor
Author: Matthews, Ann
1976   **$2.00**

No. 2443
I Like To See 'A Book About The Five Senses'
Illus.: Goldsborough, June
Author: Tymms, Jean
1973   **$2.00**

No. 2554
I Live In The City ABC
Illus.: O'Sullivan, Tom
Author: Moore, Lou
1969   **$3.00**

No. 2671
I Love My Grandma
(A Fuzzy Wuzzy Book)
Illus.: Wilson, Dagmar
Author: Hoag, Florence Jenkins
1960   **$12.00**

No. 2510
I Play In The Snow
Illus.: Rutherford, Bonnie and Bill
Author: Pape, Donna Lugg
1967   **$4.00**

No. 2616
I Walk To The Park
Illus.: Nagel, Stina
Author: Schwalj, Marjory
1966   **$4.00**

No. 2462-42
I'm Not Sleepy
Illus.: Beylon, Catherine M.
Author: Ryder, Joanne
1986   **$2.00**

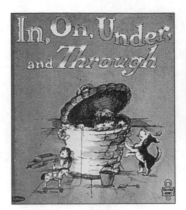

No. 2666
In, On, Under, And Through
Illus.: Nagel, Stina
Author: Elwart, Joan Potter
1965   **$4.00**

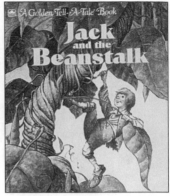

No. 2461-51
Jack And The Beanstalk
Illus.: Walz, Richard
Author: Balducci, Rita
1992   **$2.00**

No. 898
Jasper Giraffe
Illus.: Myers, Louise W.
Author: Ferrell, Polly
1949   **$18.00**

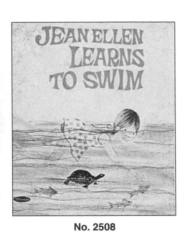

No. 2508
Jean Ellen Learns To Swim
Illus.: Wilde, Carol
Author: Swetnam, Evelyn
1970   **$2.00**

No. 2601
Jerry And Dr. Dave
Illus.: Nankivel, Claudine
Author: Bordon, Marion
1964   **$2.00**

No. 2527
Jim Jump
Illus.: Banigan, Sharon
Author: Wright, Betty Ren
1954   **$6.00**

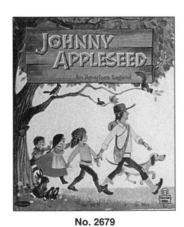

No. 2679
Johnny Appleseed
Illus.: Elfrieda
Author: Russell, Solveig Paulson
1967   **$4.00**

No. 2525
Johnny Go Round
Illus.: Walz, Richard
Author: Wright, Betty Ren
1960   **$8.00**

No. 899
Jolly Jingles
Illus.: Williams, Ben D.
Author: Alexander, Florence Bibo
1949   **$13.00**

No. 2610
Jumpty Dumpty And Other Nursery Rhymes
Illus.: Ruth, Rod
1976   **$2.00**

No. 2488
Jumpy, Humpy, Fuzzy, Buzzy, Animal Book, The
Illus.: Stone, David K.
Author: Davis, Douglas
1974   **$2.00**

No. 2607
Jungle Book, The
Illus.: Walt Disney Studios
Author: Adapted from Kipling,
Rudyard
1967 **$6.00**

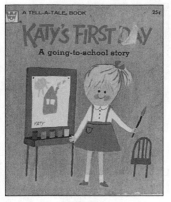

No. 2512
Katy's First Day
(Formerly: Katy Did)
Illus.: Aliki
Author: Soule, Jean Conder
1972 **$3.00**

No. 2521
Kobo The Koala Bear
Illus.: Sampson, Katherine
Author: Schwaljé, Marjory
1968 **$4.00**

No. 2552
Lady
Illus.: Hubbard, Allen and Wolfe,
Gene
Author.: Walt Disney Studios
1954 **$8.00**

No. 2617
Lambikin, The
Illus.: Myers, Jack and Louise
Author: Hansen, Helen S.
1962 **$15.00**

No. 2607
Land Of The Lost The Dinosaur
Adventure
Illus.: Purtle, John
Author: Godfry, Jane
1975 **$5.00**

No. 2503
Lassie And The Cub Scout
Illus.: Andersen, Al
Author: Michelson, Florence
1966 **$8.00**

No. 2462
Lassie And The Fire Fighters
Illus.: Harris, Larry
Author: Michelson, Florence
1968 **$4.00**

No. 2503
Lassie And The Kittens
Illus.: Andersen, Al
Author: Michelson, Florence
1966 **$8.00**

No. 2406
Lassie Finds A Friend
Illus.: Andersen, Al
Author: Theresa
1960 **$5.00**

No. 2571
Lassie's Brave Adventure
Illus.: Bartram, Bob
1958 **$8.00**

No. 2484
Lassie: The Busy Morning
Illus.: Harris, Larry
Author: Lewis, Jean
1973 **$4.00**

No. 2603
Lazy Fox And Red Hen
Illus.: Suzanne
1957 $5.00

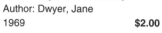

No. 2485
Lazy Fox And Red Hen
Illus.: Hauge, Carl and Mary
Author: Dwyer, Jane
1969 $2.00

No. 2555
Learning To Count With Twelve Elves
Illus.: Giordano, Joseph
Author: Wylie, Joanne
1972 $2.00

No. 2615
Let Me See
Illus.: Stang, Judy
Author: Hilt, Mary L.
1963 $4.00

No. 2407-4
Let's Count All The Animals
Illus.: Wickart, Terry
Author: Lulas, Jim E.
1979 $2.00

No. 907
Let's Play
Illus.: Gavy
Author: Georgiana
1952 $6.00

No. 876
Let's Visit The Farm
Illus.: Keyser, Evelyn
Author: Cunningham, Virginia
1948 $15.00

No. 2567
Linus 'A Smile For Grouse'
Illus.: Carleton, James F
Author: Patrick, Lenore
1966 $15.00

No. 2519
Lion's Haircut, The
Illus.: Eugenie
Author: Giddings, Jennifer
1969 $4.00

No. 2526
Little Bear And The Beautiful Kite
Illus.: Depper, Hertha
Author: Udry, Janice
1955 $5.00

No. 2548
Little Bear And The Beautiful Kite (2nd Cover)
Illus.: Depper, Hertha
Author: Udry, Janice
1955 $6.00

No. 935
Little Beaver
Author: Beecher, Elizabeth
1954 $15.00

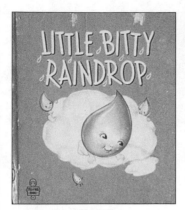

No. 875
Little Bitty Raindrop
Illus.: Usher, Peggy
Author: Usher, Peggy
1948   **$18.00**

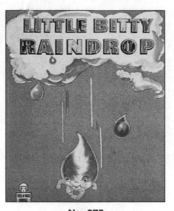

No. 875
Little Bitty Raindrop
(2nd Cover)
Illus.: Usher, Peggy
Author: Usher, Peggy
1948   **$15.00**

No. 812
Little Black Sambo
Illus.: Suzanne
1950   **$40.00**

No. 2661
Little Black Sambo
Illus.: Michell, Gladys Turley
1953   **$34.00**

No. 2661
Little Black Sambo
Illus.: Lamont, Violet
1959   **$22.00**

No. 2553
Little Boy In The Forest, The
Illus.: Osborne, Richard
Author: Harrison, David
1969   **$4.00**

No. 817
Little Caboose, The
Illus.: Flory, Jane
Author: O'Hearn, Nila
1951   **$15.00**

No. 843
Little Chuff Chuff And Big Streamline
     $15.00

No. 863
Little Folks in Mother Goose
Illus.: Rachel
1946   **$15.00**

No. 2651
Little Gray Rabbit
Illus.: Cauley, Lorinda Bryan
Author: Bowden, Joan Chase
1979   **$2.00**

No. 883
Little Hank
Illus.: Williams, Ben D.
Author: Sankey, Alice
1948   **$15.00**

No. 2604
Little Henry To The Rescue
Illus.: Williams, Ben D.
Author: Graham, Eleanor
1945   **$15.00**

No. 2560
Little Joe's Puppy
Illus.: Winship, Florence Sarah
Author: Haas, Dorothy
1957 **$12.00**

No. 2622
Little Lulu 'Has An Art Show'
Illus.: Buell, Marjorie Henderson
Author: Buell, Marjorie Henderson
1964 **$10.00**

No. 2502
Little Lulu And The Birthday Mystery
Illus.: Baker, Darrell; Jason Studios
Author: Drake, Arnold
1974 **$8.00**

No. 2437
Little Lulu Lucky Landlady!
1973 **$8.00**

No. 2552
Little Lulu Uses Her Head
Illus.: Buell, Marjorie Henderson
Author: Buell, Marjorie Henderson
1955 **$17.00**

No. 2483
Little Miss Muffet And Other Nursery Rhymes
Illus.: Scott, Marguerite K.
1973 **$3.00**

No. 806
Little Pony, The
Illus.: Hartwell, Marjorie
Author: Hawley, Mary Alice
1952 **$5.00**

No. 2585
Little Red Bicycle, The
Illus.: King, Dorothy Urfer
Author: King, Dorothy Urfer
1953 **$6.00**

No. 2431
Little Red Hen
Illus.: Wilson, Beth
1953 **$6.00**

No. 937
Little Red Riding Hood
Illus.: Stella
1953 **$7.00**

No. 2651
Little Red Riding Hood
Illus.: Depper, Hertha
1959 **$4.00**

No. 2606
Little Red Riding Hood
Illus.: Lesko, Zillah
1957 **$8.00**

284

No. 2670
Little Red Riding Hood
(A Fuzzy Wuzzy Book)
Illus.: Carroll, Nancy
1960 **$15.00**

No. 2651
Little Red Riding Hood
Illus.: Goldsborough, June
1964 **$3.00**

No. 2507
Little Red Riding Hood
Illus.: Dettmer, Mary Lou
1971 **$2.00**

No. 2461-44
Little Red Riding Hood
Illus.: Dolce, Ellen
1989 **$2.00**

No. 814
Little Tweet
Illus.: Gehr, Mary
Author: Holloway, Charles W.
1951 **$15.00**

No. 2561
**Lone Ranger And The Ghost
Horse, The**
Illus.: Totten, Bob
Author: Sankey, Alice
1955 **$20.00**

No. 2622
Lone Ranger Desert Storm, The
Illus.: Wenzel, Paul
Author: Revena
1957 **$18.00**

No. 2418-1
Longest Birthday, The
Illus.: Leiner, Alan
Author: Garber, Nancy
1975 **$2.00**

No. 2473-46
Look For Boats
Illus.: Nez, John
Author: Bell, Sally
1991 **$2.00**

No. 2473-25
Look For Trucks
Illus.: La Padu La, Thomas
Author: Weiner, Gina (Ingoglia)
1989 **$$2.00**

No. 2611
Loopy De Loop 'Odd Jobber'
Illus.: Frost, Bruno
Author: Hagen, Patrick
1964 **$16.00**

No. 893
Lucky Four Leaf Clover
Illus.: Peller, Jackie
Author: Antonie, Rosalind Lane
1949 **$12.00**

No. 2476-39
Maggie To The Rescue
Illus.: Hunt, Judith
Author: Hill, Ari
1986 **$2.00**

No. 2544

Magic Clothes Basket, The

Illus.: Rutherford, Bonnie and Bill

Author: Thomas, Sharon

1969 **$4.00**

No. 2565

Magic Zoo - Or How To Tell Time, The

Illus.: Wylie, Joanne

Author: Mowers, Patricia

1972 **$3.00**

No. 2552

Magilla Gorilla Takes A Banana Holiday

Illus.: Jason Art Studios

Author: Johnston, William

1965 **$16.00**

No. 2521

Manuel's Cat

Illus.: Stone, David K.

Author: Fein, Dorothy A.

1971 **$3.00**

No. 2632

Marvelous Monster

Illus.: Ruth, Rod

Author: Joyce, Carolyn

1977 **$3.00**

No. 836

Matilda, MacElroy, And Mary

Illus.: Robison, I. E.

Author: Fairweather, Jessie Home

1950 **$13.00**

No. 2436

Mee-Yow

1968 **$4.00**

No. 2616

Me Too!

Illus.: Zemsky, Jessica

Author: Nathan, Stella Williams

1962 **$6.00**

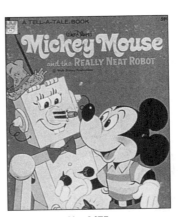

No. 2633

Merton And His Moving Van

Illus.: Seiden, Art

Author: Watts, Mabel

1970 **$2.00**

No. 2454-45

Mickey Mouse And The Lucky Goose Chase

Illus.: Wilson, Roy; William, Arthur; McGuire

Author: Scooter, M. J.

1986 **$3.00**

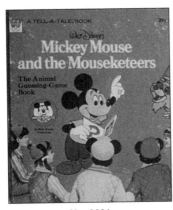

No. 2631

Mickey Mouse And The Mouse-keteers - The Animal Guessing

Illus.: Walt Disney Studios

Author: Walt Disney Studios

1977 **$3.00**

No. 2454-2

Mickey Mouse And The Pet Show

Illus.: Walt Disney Studios

Author: Walt Disney Studios

1976 **$3.00**

No. 2475

Mickey Mouse And The Really Neat Robot

Illus.: Walt Disney Studios

Author: Walt Disney Studios

1970 **$3.00**

No. 2418

Mickey Mouse And The Second Wish

Illus.: Walt Disney Studios

Author: Walt Disney Studios

1973 **$3.00**

No. 2424-2

Mickey Mouse And The World's Friendliest Monster

Illus.: Walt Disney Studios
Author: Walt Disney Studios
1976 **$3.00**

No. 2467

Mimi The Merry-Go-Round Cat

Illus.: Winship, Florence Sarah
Author: Haas, Dorothy
1958 **$7.00**

No. 2599

Mister Rogers Neighborhood Everyone Is Special

Illus.: Jason Art Studios
Author: Rogers, Fred M.
1975 **$4.00**

No. 2452-39

Monsters Come In Many Colors! (Sesame Street)

Illus.: McLean, Sammis
Author: Stevenson, Joyce
1980 **$3.00**

No. 2523

More The Merrier, The

Illus.: Magagna, Anna Marie
Author: Michelson, Florence
1964 **$4.00**

No. 825

Mother Goose

Illus.: Vaughan, Eillen Fox
1950 **$6.00**

No. 925

Mother Goose

Illus.: Lesko, Zillah
1961 **$5.00**

No. 2511

Mother Goose

Illus.: Wallace, Lucille
1958 **$6.00**

No. 2511

Mother Goose

Illus.: Clement, Charles
1955 **$6.00**

No. 2417

Mother Goose

Illus.: Scott, Marguerite K.
1973 **$3.00**

No. 2587

Mother Goose On The Farm

Illus.: Goldsborough, June
1975 **$3.00**

No. 2464-44

Mother Goose On The Farm

Illus.: Aitken, Amy
Author: Muldrow, Diane
1989 **$3.00**

No. 2464-36

Mother Goose Rhymes

Illus.: Nez, John
1985 **$3.00**

No. 2649

Mouseketeers Tryout Time, The

Illus.: Satterfield, Charles
Author: Revena
1956 **$5.00**

No. 816

Mr. Grabbit

Illus.: Charlie
Author: Hoff, Virginia
1952 **$18.00**

No. 2526

Mr. Grabbit

Illus.: Charlie

Author: Hoff, Virginia

1952 **$15.00**

No. 868

Mr. Jolly

Illus.: Spicer, Jesse

Author: Mathison, Jane

1948 **$15.00**

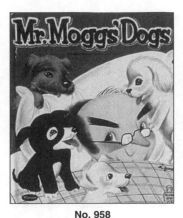

No. 958

Mr. Mogg's Dogs

(A Fuzzy Wuzzy Book)

Illus.: Frankel, Simon

Author: Revena

1954 **$15.00**

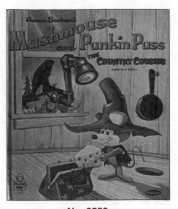

No. 2552

Mushmouse And Punkin Puss 'The Country Cousins'

Illus.: Alvarado, Peter; Jacobs, Raymond

Author: Freman, Jay

1964 **$18.00**

No. 2414-3

My Big Book Of Big Machines

Illus.: Andersen, Al

Author: Ottum, Bob

1975 **$2.00**

No. 2536

My Little ABC

Illus.: Ericksen, Barbara

Author: Vogels, Mary Prescott

1971 **$2.00**

No. 2578

My Little Book About Our Flag

Illus.: Karch, Pat and Paul

Author: Mrowski, Jan

1975 **$2.00**

No. 2466-4

My Little Book Of Big Animals

Illus.: Burridge, Marge Opitz

Author: Kulas, Jim E.

1978 **$2.00**

No. 2589

My Little Book Of Big Machines

Illus.: Andersen, Al

Author: Ottum, Bob

1975 **$2.00**

No. 2490

My Little Book Of Birds

Illus.: Dunnington, Tom

Author: Ray, Ora

1973 **$2.00**

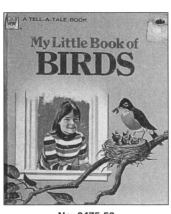

No. 2475-50

My Little Book Of Birds

Illus.: Solomon, Rosiland

Author: Ingoglia, Gina

1991 **$2.00**

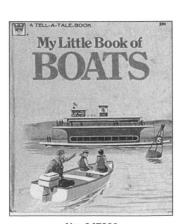

No. 247332

My Little Book Of Boats

Illus.: Dunnington, Tom

Author: Hanrahan, Mariellen

1974 **$2.00**

No. 24750
My Little Book Of Bugs
Illus.: Solomon, Rosiland
Author: Silverman, Maida
1993 $2.00

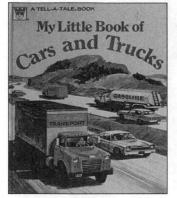

No. 2473
My Little Book Of Cars And Trucks
Illus.: Korta, Bob
Author: Graham, Kennon
1974 $2.00

No. 2482
My Little Book Of Dinosaurs
Illus.: Ruth, Rod
Author: Daly, Eileen
1972 $2.00

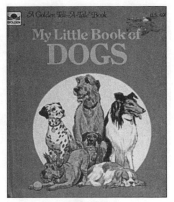

No. 2476-93
My Little Book Of Dogs
Illus.: Stone, David K.
Author: Draper, Delores
1976 $2.00

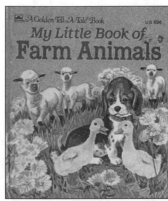

No. 2559
My Little Book Of Farm Animals
Illus.: Hauge, Carl and Mary
Author: Hogstrom, Daphne
1972 $2.00

No. 2414-4
My Little Book About Flying
Illus.: Irvin, Fred
Author: Graham, Kennon
1978 $2.00

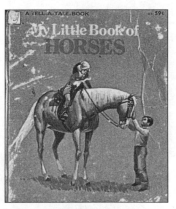

No. 2466-3
My Little Book Of Horses
Illus.: Dunnington, Tom
Author: Walrath, Jane Dwyer
1974 $2.00

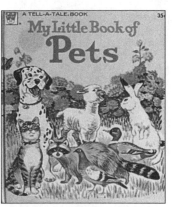

No. 2401
My Little Book Of Pets
Illus.: Hauge, Carl and Mary
Author: Sukus, Jan
1972 $2.00

No. 2407-3
My Little Counting Book
Illus.: Ruhman, Ruth
Author: Yerian, Margaret
1967 $2.00

No. 2525
Nancy And Sluggo 'The Big Surprise'
                       $8.00

No. 2538
Nibbler
Illus.: Winship, Florence Sarah
Author: Watts, Mabel
1973 $5.00

No. 839
Night Before Christmas, The
Illus.: Newton, Ruth E.
Author: Moore, Clement C.
1937 $18.00

No. 839

Night Before Christmas, The

Illus.: Lesko, Zillah

Author: Moore, Clement C.

1953   **$16.00**

No. 2517

Night Before Christmas, The

(2nd cover)

Illus.: Lesko, Zillah

Author: Moore, Clement C.

1953   **$8.00**

No. 2517

Night Before Christmas, The

Illus.: Munshi, Carol

Author: Moore, Clement C.

1963   **$6.00**

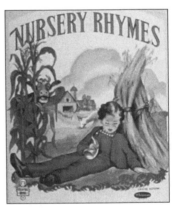

No. 2517

Night Before Christmas, The

Illus.: Winship, Florence Sarah

Author: Moore, Clement C.

1963   **$6.00**

No. 2558

Noah And The Ark

Illus.: Gray, Leslie

Author: Ramsay, Devere

1967   **$5.00**

No. 920

Nobody's Puppy

Illus.: Winship, Florence Sarah

Author: Lynn, Patricia

1953   **$6.00**

No. 962

Not Quite Three

Illus.: Castagnoli, Martha

Author: Wolf, Helen

1954   **$7.00**

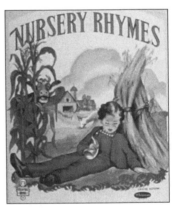

No. 857

Nursery Rhymes

Illus.: Altson, Louise

1945   **$8.00**

No. 2672

Oh, Look!

(A Fuzzy Wuzzy Book)

Illus.: Myers, Jack and Louise

Author: Haas, Dorothy

1961   **$10.00**

No. 2589

Old MacDonald Had A Farm

Illus.: Hauge, Carl and Mary

Illus.: 1975   **$3.00**

NO. 2610

Old Woman And Her Pig, The

Illus.: Mars, W. T.

1964   **$4.00**

No. 2512

Once I Had A Monster

Illus.: Rutherford, Bonnie and Bill

Author: Hellie, Anne

1969   **$4.00**

No. 865

Once Upon A Windy Day

Illus.: Flory, Jane

Author: Flory, Jane

1947 **$15.00**

No. 2622

One Hundred And One Dalmatians

Illus.: Fletcher, James

Author: Walt Disney Studios

1960 **$7.00**

No. 807

One Two Buckle My Shoe

Illus.: Kaula, Edna M.

1951 **$12.00**

No. 926

One Two Three

Illus.: CharlieAuthor: Charlie

1953 **$8.00**

No. 2616

One Two Three

(2nd cover)

Illus.: CharlieAuthor: Charlie

1953 **$5.00**

No. 2440

One Two Three

(3rd cover)

Illus.: CharlieAuthor: Charlie

1953 **$2.00**

No. 2546

Outside With Baby

Illus.: Skibinski, Ray

Author: Swetnam, Evelyn

1974 **$2.00**

No. 2544

Pals

Illus.: O'Sullivan, Tom

Author: Funk, Melissa Don

1966 **$3.00**

No. 2424

Pamela Jane's Week 'A Story About Days Of The Week'

Illus.: Ike, Jane

Author: Robinson, Alberta

1973 **$2.00**

No. 2562

Parade For Chatty Baby, A

Illus.: Mode, Nathalee

Author: Schwalj, Marjory

1965 **$15.00**

No. 2475-4

Patsy The Pussycat

Illus.: Super, Terri

Author: Watts, Mabel

1986 **$2.00**

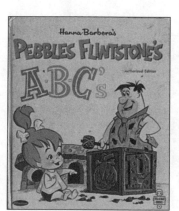

No. 2622

Pebbles Flintstone's ABCs

Illus.: Lorencz, Bill; Strobl, Anthony

Author: Daly, Eileen

1966 **$18.00**

No. 2657

Pebbles Flintstone 'Daddy's Little Helper'

Illus.: Storms, Robert

Author: Hagen, Patrick

1964 **$18.00**

No. 848
Peppermint, The Story Of A Kitten
Illus.: Grider, Dorothy
Author: Grider, Dorothy
1950   **$20.00**

No. 2502
Peppermint, The Story Of A Kitten (2nd Cover)
Illus.: Burns, Raymond
Author: Grider, Dorothy
1966   **$8.00**

No. 2405
Peppermint, The Story Of A Kitten (3rd cover)
Illus.: Burns, Raymond
Author: Grider, Dorothy
1966   **$10.00**

No. 2637
Pete's Dragon 'The Best Of Friends'
Illus.: Walt Disney Studios
Author: Walt Disney Studios
1977   **$6.00**

No. 2616
Peter Pan And The Tiger
Illus.: McNatt Jr., Rich; Totten, Bob
Author: Carey, Mary
1976   **$8.00**

No. 2506
Peter Potamus 'Meets The Black Knight'
Illus.: Strobl, Anthony; Jancar, Milli
Author: Freeman, Jane
1965   **$15.00**

No. 884
Peter Rabbit
Illus.: Snow, Dorthea
1948   **$8.00**

No. 929
Peter Rabbit
Illus.: Wilson, Beth
1953   **$7.00**

No. 2515
Peter Rabbit
Illus.: Winship, Florence Sarah
1955   **$6.00**

No. 2539
Peter Rabbit
Illus.: Myers, Jack and Louise
1959   **$5.00**

No. 884
Peter The Lonesome Hermit
Illus.: Snow, Dorothea J.
Author: Snow, Dorothea J.
1948   **$18.00**

No. 927
Peter's Pencil
Illus.: Butler, Paula Hurley
Author: Butler, Paula Hurley
1953   **$12.00**

No. 2463-38
Peter's Welcome
Illus.: Schweninger, Ann
1985 $7.00

No. 885
Petunia
Illus.: Williams, Ben D.
Author: Sankey, Alice
1948 $16.00

No. 2475-48
Pig And The Witch, The
Illus.: Severn, Jeffery
Author: Goldsmith, Howard
1990 $2.00

No. 2628
Pink Panther Rides Again, The
Illus.: Jason Art Studios
Author: Graham, Kennon
1976 $3.00

No. 2428-2
Pinocchio
Illus.: McSavage, Frank and Fisher, Frank
Author: Hass, Dorothy
1961 $6.00

No. 2614
Pippi Longstocking And The South Sea Pirates
Illus.: Baker, Darrell
Author: Carey, Mary
1976 $3.00

No. 2641
Pitty Pat
(A Fuzzy Wuzzy Book)
Illus.: Winship, Florence Sarah
Author: Horn, Gladys M.
1954 $15.00

No. 2471-46
Play School ABC
Illus.: Stellerman, Robbie
1985 $2.00

No. 803
Playmate For Peter
Illus.: Myers, Louise W.
Author: Maritano, Adela Kay
1951 $8.00

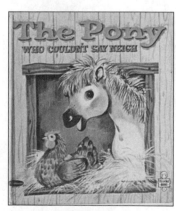

No. 2509
Pluto
Illus.: Strobl, Tony and Boyle, Neil
Author: Revena
1957 $7.00

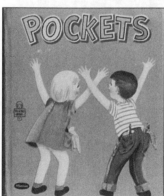

No. 2616
Pockets
Illus.: Ozone, Lucy
Author: Ozone, Lucy
1955 $6.00

No. 864
Polka Dot Tots
Illus.: Tedder, Elizabeth
Author: Lieberman, Nina Belle
1946 $15.00

No. 2527
Pony
Illus.: Crawford, Mel; Photo's Haas, Arthur
Author: Merow, Erva Loomis
1965 $4.00

No. 2543
Pony Who Couldn't Say Neigh, The
Illus.: Thomas, Stephen
Author: Schwaljé, Marjory
1964 $4.00

No. 850
Poor Kitty
Illus.: Tedder, Elizabeth
Author: Tedder, Elizabeth
1945 **$15.00**

No. 844
Pop-O The Clown
Illus.: Cummings, Alison
Author: Whitteberry, Caroline
1950 **$15.00**

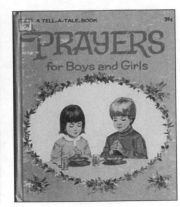

No. 918
Prayers For Boys And Girls
Illus.: Cummings, Alison
1953 **$5.00**

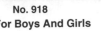

No. 2523
Prayers For Boys And Girls
(2nd Cover)
Illus.: Cummings, Alison
1953 **$2.00**

No. 2508
Prickly Tale, A
Illus.: Hauge, Carl and Mary
Author: Begley, Evelyn M.
1965 **$5.00**

No. 2610
Princess And The Pea, The
Illus.: Herric, Pru
1961 **$4.00**

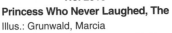

No. 2610
Princess Who Never Laughed, The
Illus.: Grunwald, Marcia
1961 **$7.00**

No. 2641
Prrrtt
Illus.: Hartwell, Marjorie
Author: Hartwell, Marjorie
1952 **$6.00**

No. 819
Puffy
Illus.: Porter, Genevieve
Author: Georgiana
1952 **$8.00**

No. 2476-45
Puppies On Parade
Illus.: Eubank, Mary Grace
Author: Helfand, Karen
1989 **$2.00**

No. 895
Pussy Cat's Secret
Illus.: Spicer, Jessie
Author: Elting, Mary
1949 **$15.00**

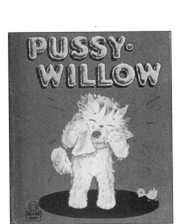

No. 873
Pussy Willow
Illus.: MacKean, Emma C.
Author: MacKean, Emma C.
1948 **$15.00**

No. 2615
Quiet Quincy And The Delivery
Truck
Illus.: Steigerwald, Beverly
Author: Kemp, Polly G.
1961 **$6.00**

No. 893
Rackety-Boom
Illus.: Florian
Author: Wright, Betty Ren
1953 **$15.00**

No. 2557
Rackety-Boom
(2nd cover)
Illus.: Florian
Author: Wright, Betty Ren
1953 **$10.00**

No. 2641

Raggedy Andy And The Jump-Up Contest

Illus.: Goldsborough, June
Author: Schwaljé, Marjory
1978   **$6.00**

No. 2417-2

Raggedy Andy's Treasure Hunt

Illus.: Goldsborough, June
Author: Schwaljé, Marjory
1973   **$5.00**

No. 2596

Raggedy Ann And Andy On The Farm

Illus.: Goldsborough, June
Author: Daly, Eileen
1958   **$5.00**

No. 2417-1

Raggedy Ann And The Tagalong Present

Illus.: Krehbiel, Becky
Author: Schwaljé, Marjory
1978   **$5.00**

No. 2498

Raggedy Ann's Cooking School

Illus.: Goldsborough, June
Author: Schwaljé, Marjory
1974   **$5.00**

No. 2451-4

Rainbow Brite And The Magic Belt

Illus.: Costanza, John
Author: Grunewalt, Pine
1985   **$4.00**

No. 2474-44

Rainbow Circus Comes To Town

Illus.: Steadman, Barbara
Author: Ryder, Joann C.
1986   **$2.00**

No. 858

Rainy Day Story On The Farm

Illus.: Matson, Elizabeth
Author: Little, Irene
1944   **$15.00**

No. 2429-3

Rescuers ABC, The

Illus.: Walt Disney Studios
Author: Walt Disney Studios
1977   **$6.00**

No. 2622

Ricochet Rabbit 'Showdown At Gopher Gulch Bakery'

Illus.: Andersen, Al; Alvarado, Peter
Author: Hagen, Patrick
1964   **$14.00**

No. 2571

Rinty And Pals For Rusty

Illus.: Bartram, Bob
Author: Francis, Dee
1957   **$10.00**

No. 2466

Road Runner, The 'Tumbleweed Trouble'

Illus.: Leon Jason Studios
Author: Woolgar, Jack
1971   **$3.00**

No. 2408

Road Runner: Bird Watchers

Illus.: De Lara, Phil
Author: Lewis, Jean
1968   **$3.00**

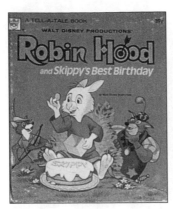

No. 2441
Robin Hood And Skippy's Best Birthday
Illus.: Walt Disney Studios
Author: Walt Disney Studios
1973 $5.00

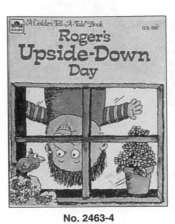

No. 2463-4
Roger's Upside-Down Day
Illus.: Lee, Jared D.
Author: Wright, Betty Ren
1979 $3.00

No. 936
Rootie Kazootie And The Pineapple Pies
Illus.: Crawford, Mel
Author: Barrow, John
1953 $25.00

No. 2436
Roundabout Train
Illus.: Clement, Charles
Author: Wright, Betty Ren
1953 $5.00

No. 861
Rowdy
Illus.: Scott, Janet Laura
Author: Wyatt, Jane
1946 $15.00

No. 811
Roy Rogers And The Lane Ranch
Illus.: La Grotta, J. M.
1950 $25.00

No. 801
Roy Rogers And The Sure 'Nough Cowpoke
Illus.: Steffen, Randy
Author: Beecher, Elizabeth
1952 $22.00

No. 2567
Roy Rogers' Bullet Leads The Way
Illus.: Doe, Bart
Author: Wood, Frances
1953 $18.00

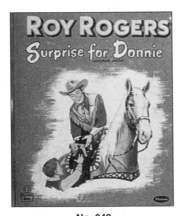

No. 943
Roy Rogers' Surprise For Donnie
Illus.: Steel, John
Author: Sankey, Alice
1954 $17.00

No. 2622
Rubbles And Bamm-Bamm, The 'Problem Present'
Illus.: Storms, Robert
Author: Carey, Mary
1965 $18.00

No. 2517-2
Rudolph The Red-Nosed Reindeer
Illus.: Miyake, Yoshi
Author: Daly, Eileen
1980 $4.00

No. 2483-02
Rudolph The Red-Nosed Reindeer
Illus.: Ortiz, Phil and Cuddy, Robbin
Author: Cohen, Robin
1993 $2.00

No. 2567
Ruff And Reddy Go To A Party
Illus.: Eisenberg, Harvey; Boyle, Neil
1958 $20.00

No. 897
Runaway Ginger
Illus.: Lesko, Zillah
Author: Elting, Mary
1949 **$15.00**

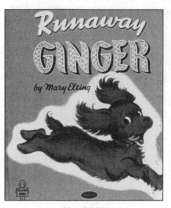

No. 2537
Runaway Ginger
(2nd Cover)
Illus.: Lesko, Zilah
Author: Elting, Mary
1949 **$10.00**

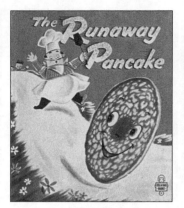

No. 2465
Runaway Pancake, The
Illus.: Williams, Ben D.
1956 **$8.00**

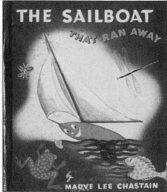

No. 842
Sailboat That Ran Away, The
Illus.: Chastain, Madye Lee
Author: Chastain, Madye Lee
1950 **$15.00**

No. 2570
Scooby Doo At The Zoo
Illus.: Szwejkowski, Adam and
Totten, Bob
Author: Nathan, Williams
1974 **$4.00**

No. 805
See It Goes!
Illus.: Wilde, George and Wilma
Authors: Wilde, George and Wilma
1953 **$8.00**

No. 2471-43
Sesame Street ABC
Illus.: Nez, John
Author: Calmenson, Stephanie
1987 **$2.00**

No. 2402-8
Sesame Streets Cookie Monster's Book Of Cookie Shapes
Illus.: Brown, Richard
1979 **$2.00**

No. 2465-43
Sesame Streets First Times
Illus.: Delaney, Toni
Author: Calmenson, Stephanie
1987 **$2.00**

No. 2606
Seven Wishes, The
Illus.: Miyake, Yoshi
Author: Cowles, Kathleen
1976 **$3.00**

No. 2564
Sherlock Hemlock And The Great Twiddlebug Mystery
Illus.: Children's Television Workshop
Author: Children's Television Workshop
1972 **$2.00**

No. 2649
Sleeping Beauty
Author: McGary, Norm
1959 **$10.00**

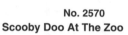

No. 2462
Sleepy Puppy, The
Illus.: Winship, Florence Sarah
Author: Chamberlin, Mary Jo
1961 **$4.00**

No. 2457
Slowpoke At The Circus
Illus.: Ruhman, Ruth
Author: Richardson, Kay
1973 **$3.00**

No. 2463
Smokey Bear 'Saves The Forest'
Illus.: Gantz, David
Author: Graham, Kennon
1971 **$8.00**

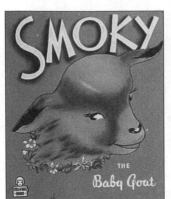

No. 867
Smoky The Baby Goat
Illus.: Reed, Veronica
Author: Elting, Mary
1947 **$15.00**

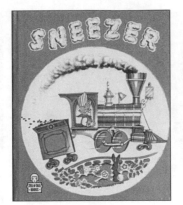

No. 854
Sneezer
Illus.: Williams, Ben D.
Author: Upson, Estelle McInnes
1945 **$15.00**

No. 851
Snooty
Illus.: Flory, Jane
Author: Flory, Jane
1944 **$15.00**

No. 2578
Snow White And The Seven Dwarfs
Illus.: Wegner, Helmuth G.
Author: Walt Disney Studios
1957 **$12.00**

No. 2427-4
Snow White And The Seven Dwarfs
(2nd cover)
Illus.: Wegner, Helmuth G.
Author: Walt Disney Studios
1957 **$3.00**

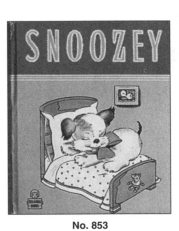

No. 853
Snoozey
Illus.: McKean, Emma C.
Author: McKean, Emma C.
1944 **$15.00**

No. 2538
Snoozey
(2nd cover)
Illus.: McKean, Emma C.
Author: McKean, Emma C.
1944 **$8.00**

No. 886
Socks
Illus.: Winship, Florence Sarah
Author: Ryan, Betty Molgard
1949 **$15.00**

No. 963
Somebody Forgot
Illus.: Stang, Judy
Author: Horn, Gladys M.
1954 **$8.00**

No. 2659
Someplace For Sparky
Illus.: Walters, Audry
Author: Beatie, Bernadine
1965 **$4.00**

No. 2521
Special Pet, A
Illus.: Giacomini, Olindo
Author: Schwaljé, Marjory
1968 **$2.00**

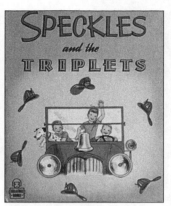

No. 874
Speckles And The Triplets
Illus.: Stevens, Mary
Author: Elting, Mary
1949 **$18.00**

No. 2526
Splish Splash, And Splush
Illus.: Wilde, Irma
Author: Pape, Donna Lugg
1962 **$7.00**

No. 2560
Spotted Dotted Puppy, The
Illus.: Seiden, Art
Author: Fletcher, Steffi
1961 **$3.00**

No. 2472-41
Spoon Necklace, The
Illus.: De Moth, Vivienne
Author: Young, Opal Dean
1986 **$2.00**

No. 2615
Stubby
Illus.: Seiden, Art
Author: Borden, Marion
1963 **$4.00**

No. 2463-44
Stuck In The Tub
Illus.: Orville, Oliver
Author: Hylst, Marguerite Van
1988 **$2.00**

No. 824
Sunny, Honey, And Funny
(A Fuzzy Wuzzy Book)
Illus.: Lesko, Zillah
Author: Horn, Gladys M.
1951 **$15.00**

No. 2573
Surprise For Howdy Doody
Illus.: Kean, Edward
1951 **$20.00**

No. 2543
Surprise In The Barn
Illus.: Flory, Jane
Author: Flory, Jane
1955 **$6.00**

No. 2543
Surprise In The Barn
(2nd cover)
Illus.: Flory, Jane
Author: Flory, Jane
1955 **$5.00**

No. 2509
Swiss Family Duck
Illus.: Strobl, Anthony; Irvin, Fred
Author: Hagen, Patrick
1964 **$6.00**

No. 879
Susan And The Rain
Illus.: Chastain, Madye Lee
Author: Chastain, Madye Lee
1947 **$10.00**

No. 2476-44

Tabitha Tabby's Fantastic Flavor

Illus.: Peltier, Phyllis A.

Author: Lewis, Jean

1988   **$2.00**

No. 2601

Tag-Along Shadow

Illus.: Macpherson, Ruth Rosamond

Author: Macpherson, Ruth Rosamond

1959   **$7.00**

No. 2488-02

Tale Of Peter Rabbit, The

Illus.: Schweninger, Ann

1992   **$2.00**

No. 2534

Tall Tree Small Tree

Illus.: Winship, Florence Sarah

Author: Watts, Mabel

1970   **$3.00**

No. 809

Teddy's Surprise

Illus.: SuzanneAuthor: Georgiana

$15.00

No. 2423

Teena And The Magic Pot

Illus.: Myers, Louise And Jack

1961   **$4.00**

No. 2513

Teeny-Tiny Tale, A

Illus.: Williams, Ben D.

1955   **$10.00**

No. 2502

That Donkey

Illus.: Grider, Dorothy

Author: Georgiana

1954   **$8.00**

No. 2675

That Puppy

(A Fuzzy Wuzzy Book)

Illus.: Zemsky, Jessica

Author: Haas, Dorothy

1961   **$10.00**

No. 2534

That's Where You Live

Illus.: Fraser, Betty

Author: Vogels, Mary Prescott

1970   **$3.00**

No. 2691

Thin Arnold

Illus.: Heckler, William

Author: Bacon, Joan Chase

1970   **$5.00**

No. 2643

This Room Is Mine

Illus.: Stang, Judy

Author: Wright, Betty Ren

1977   **$3.00**

No. 877
This Way To The Zoo
Illus.: Weber, Nettie
Author: Cunningham, Virginia
1948 **$10.00**

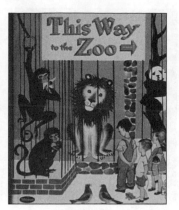

No. 2536
This Way To The Zoo
(2nd Cover)
Illus.: Weber, Nettie
Author: Cunningham, Virginia
1948 **$6.00**

No. 859
Three Bears, The
Illus.: Yeakey, Carol
1945 **$15.00**
Three Bears, The
(2nd Cover)
$10.00

No. 909
Three Bears, The
Illus.: Rowland, Helen
1952 **$5.00**

No. 2512
Three Bears, The
Illus.: Sari
1955 **$6.00**

No. 2512
Three Bears, The
Illus.: Suzanne
1955 **$7.00**

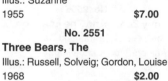

No. 2551
Three Bears, The
Illus.: Russell, Solveig; Gordon, Louise
1968 **$2.00**

No. 2515
Three Billy Goats Gruff
Illus.: Ames, Lee J.
1954 **$5.00**

No. 836
Three Little Mice
(Formerly: Matilda MacElroy
And Mary)
Illus.: Robison, I. E.
Author: Fairweather, Jessie Home
1950 **$8.00**

No. 860
Three Little Pigs, The
Illus.: Irwin, Josephine
1944 **$15.00**

No. 2547
Three Little Pigs, The
Illus.: Myers, Louise W
1953 **$6.00**

No. 2542
Three Little Pigs, The
Illus.: Miloche, Hilda
1956 **$5.00**

No. 2547
Three Little Pigs, The
Illus.: Williams, Ben D.
1959 **$4.00**

No. 2501
Three Little Pigs, The
Illus.: Bracke, Charles
Author: Wood, Jo Anne
1969 $5.00

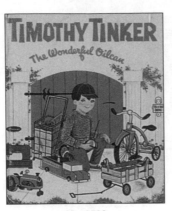

No. 2522
Timothy Tinker 'The Wonderful Oilcan'
Illus.: Stang, Judy
Author: Watts, Mabel
1968 $4.00

No. 856
Timothy's Shoes
Illus.: Schad, Helen G.
1946 $15.00

No. 2615
Tiny Tots 1-2-3
Illus.: Murray, Marjorie
1958 $6.00

No. 2555
Tip-Top Tree House
Illus.: Wilde, Carol
Author: Tucker, Daisy
1969 $3.00

No. 2465-44
Toby Bunny's Secret Hiding Place
Illus.: Spence, James
Author: Werner, Dave
1988 $1.00

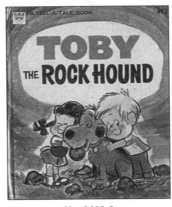

No. 2408-6
Toby The Rock Hound
Illus.: Bradfield, Roger
Author: Walrath, Jane Dwyer
1979 $3.00

No. 2505
Toby Zebra And The Lost Zoo
Illus.: Garris, Norma and Dan
Author: Pape, Donna Lugg
1963 $4.00

No. 2509
Tom And Jerry And The Toy Circus
Illus.: Armstrong, Samuel; Ray, Tom
1953 $8.00

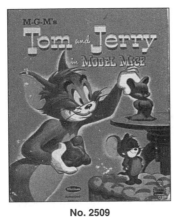

No. 2509
Tom And Jerry In Model Mice
Illus.: Eisenberg, Harvey; Dempster, Al
Author: M-G-M Cartoons
1951 $10.00

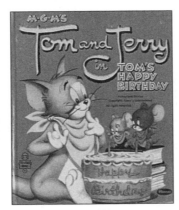

No. 2611
Tom And Jerry In Tom's Happy Birthday
Illus.: Eisenberg, Harvey and Wolfe, Gene
Author: M-G-M Cartoons, Inc.
1955 $8.00

No. 2451-38
Tom And Jerry's Big Move
Illus.: Messerli, Joe
Author: Lewis, Jean
1985 $2.00

No. 822
Tommy And Timmy (A Fuzzy Wuzzy Book - Black)
Illus.: Berry, Anne Scheu
Author: Sankey, Alice
1951 $15.00

No. 2644
Tommy And Timmy
(A Fuzzy Wuzzy Book - Yellow)
Illus.: Berry, Anne Scheu
Author: Sankey, Alice
1951 **$15.00**

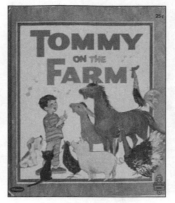

No. 2557
Tommy On The Farm
Illus.: Elfrieda
Author: Russell, Solveig Paulson
1968 **$3.00**

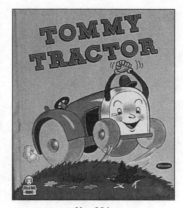

No. 881
Tommy Tractor
Illus.: Buehrig, Rosemary
Author: Mcpherson, Ge
1947 **$12.00**

No. 2525
Too Many Kittens
Illus.: Suzanne
Author: Watts, Mabel
1963 **$8.00**

No. 2614
Too Small Names!
Illus.: Eugenie
Author: Peterson, Jeri
1970 **$3.00**

No. 2561
Town Mouse And The Country Mouse, The
Illus.: Stang, Judy
Author: Horn, Gladys M.
1954 **$7.00**

No. 878
Toy Party, The
Illus.: Wysse
Author: Christopher, Til B.
1948 **$15.00**

No. 2518
Toy That Flew, The
Illus.: Depper, Hertha
Author: Smaridge, Nora
1974 **$4.00**

No. 2556
Train Coming!
Illus.: Florian
Author: Wright, Betty Ren
1954 **$6.00**

No. 813
Truck That Stopped At Village Small, The
Illus.: Dorcas
Author: Knittle, Jessie M.
1951 **$8.00**

No. 931
Trumpet
Illus.: Myers, Bernice
Author: Lynn, Patricia
1953 **$6.00**

No. 2460
Try Again, Sally!
Illus.: Tsambon, Athena
Author: Laughlin, Florence
1969 **$3.00**

No. 2552
Tubsy And The Picnic Tree
(Ideal Doll)
Illus.: Sampson, Katherine
Author: Daly, Eileen
1968 **$12.00**

No. 2672

**Tuffer
(A Fuzzy Wuzzy Book)**
Illus.: Rutherford, Bonnie and Bill
Author: Wright, Betty Ren
1959   **$12.00**

No. 880

Tuffy The Tugboat
Illus.: Williams, Ben D.
Author: Sankey, Alice
1947   **$15.00**

No. 901

Tweety
Illus.: Abranz, Fred; Maclaughlin
Author: Warner Bros., Inc.
1953   **$10.00**

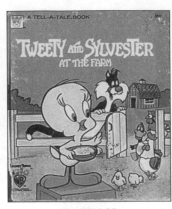

No. 2453-35

Tweety And Sylvester At The Farm
Illus.: Barto, Renzo
Author: Hogan, Cecily Ruth
1978   **$4.00**

No. 2453-47

Tweety And Sylvester 'A Visit To The Vet'
Illus.: Messerli, Joe
Author: Lewis, Jean
1988   **$4.00**

No. 2448

Tweety And Sylvester 'Picnic Problems'
Illus.: Leon Jason Studios
Author: Biesterveld, Betty
1970   **$3.00**

No. 2525

Two Kittens
Illus.: Zfa-Duesseldorf
Author: Tiffany, Virginia
1966   **$4.00**

No. 2526

Two Stories About Chap And Chirpy
Illus.: Wilde, Irma
Author: Bond, Gladys Baker
1965   **$4.00**

No. 2510

Two Stories About Kate and Kitty
Illus.: Schlesinger, Alice
Author: Priestly, Lee
1968   **$4.00**

No. 2683

Two Stories About Lollipop
Illus.: Eugenie
Author: Bell, Luann Stull
1969   **$4.00**

No. 2601

Two Stories About Ricky
Illus.: Goldsborough, June
Author: Frankel, Bernice
1966   **$4.00**

No. 2560

Two Stories About Wags
Illus.: Garris, Norma and Dan
Author: Biesterveld, Betty
1966   **$4.00**

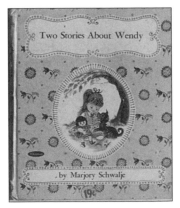

No. 2659

Two Stories About Wendy
Illus.: Nagel, Stina
Author: Schwaljé, Marjory
1965   **$4.00**

No. 2543

Two To Twins, The

Illus.: Goldsborough, June

Author: Priestly, Lee

1966   **$5.00**

No. 2552

Uncle Scrooge 'The Winner'

Illus.: Strobl, Anthony; Andersen, Al

Author: Carter, Katherine

1964   **$15.00**

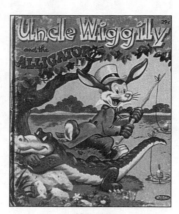

No. 903

Uncle Wiggily And The Alligator

Illus.: Weaver, William

Author: Turner, Gill; Garis, Howard

1953   **$7.00**

No. 2611

Under Dog

Illus.: Jason Art Studios

Author: Johnston, William

1966   **$10.00**

No. 2543

Under The Saskatoon Tree

Illus.: Rutherford, Bonnie and Bill

Author: Russell, Solveig Paulson

1966   **$4.00**

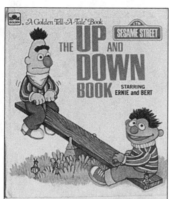

No. 2402-7

Up And Down Book Staring Ernie And Bert, The

Illus.: Swanson, Maggie

1979   **$2.00**

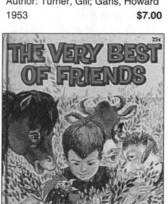

No. 2559

Very Best Of Friends, The

Illus.: Hauge, Carl and Mary

Author: Fletcher, Steffi

1963   **$3.00**

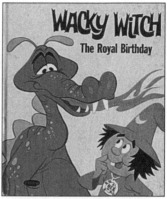

No. 2546

Wacky Witch: The Royal Birthday

Illus.: Arens, Michael; Toten, Bob

Author: Lewis, Jean

1971   **$6.00**

No. 2688

Waldo, The Jumping Dragon

Illus.: Oechsli, Kelly

Author: Detiege, Dave

1964   **$5.00**

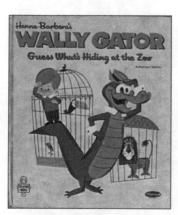

No. 2506

Wally Gator 'Guess What's Hiding At The Zoo'

Illus.: Crawford, Mel

Author: Daly, Eileen

1963   **$8.00**

No. 2471-47

Walt Disney Babies 1 To 10 Again

Illus.: Baker, Darrell

1988   **$3.00**

No. 2533

Walt Disney World - Big Albert Moves In

Illus.: Walt Disney Studios

Author: Walt Disney Studios

1971   **$6.00**

No. 2564

Water Birds
(Walt Disney Productions)

Illus.: Hartwell, Marjorie

Authors: Wright, Betty Ren; Hanson, Alice

1955   **$10.00**

No. 2577

Winnie-The-Pooh 'The Blustery Day'

Illus.: Walt Disney Studios

Author: Milne, A.A.

1975 $4.00

No. 2620

Winnie-The-Pooh And Eeyore's House

Illus.: Walt Disney Studios

Author: Milne, A.A.

1976 $4.00

No. 2526

Winnie-The-Pooh And The Unbouncing of Tigger

Illus.: Walt Disney Studios

Author: Milne, A.A.

1974 $4.00

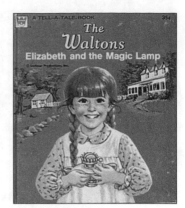

No. 2579

Walton's The 'Elizabeth And The Magic Lamp'

Illus.: Neely, Jan

Author: Graham, Charlotte

1975 $4.00

No. 2404-3

We Talk With God

Illus.: McElwain, Diane

Author: Burdick, Faith Oliver

1979 $3.00

No. 2541-41

We're Busy Charlie Brown

Illus.: Schulz, Charles; Ellis, Art

Author: Namm, Diane

1987 $3.00

No. 2425

What Makes My Cat Purr?

Illus.: Elfrieda

Author: Tompert, Ann

1965 $4.00

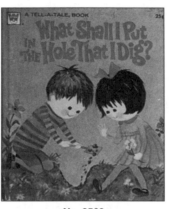

No. 2563

What Shall I Put In The Hole That I Dig?

Illus.: Aliki

Author: Thompson, Eleanor

1972 $4.00

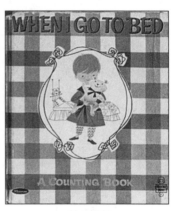

No. 2542

When I Go To Bed

Illus.: Ruhman, Ruth

Author: Yerian, Margaret

1967 $4.00

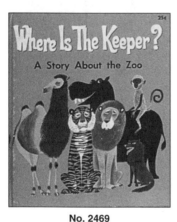

No. 2469

Where Is The Keeper?

Illus.: Seiden, Art

Author: Watts, Mabel

1966 $4.00

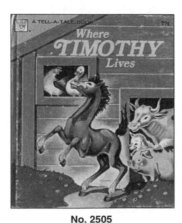

No. 2505

Where Timothy Lives

Illus.: Frost, Bruno

Author: Wright, Betty Ren

1953 $6.00

No. 2546

Where's Harry?

Illus.: Stirnweis, Shannon

Author: Meek, Pauline Palmer

1969 $3.00

No. 2521

Who Are You?

Illus.: Fitch, Winnie

Author: Bradfield, Joan and Rogers

1966 $4.00

No. 2557

Whoa, Joey!

Illus.: Bracke, Charles

Author: Hogstrom, Daphne

1968 $4.00

No. 884

Whoop-ee, Hunkydory!

Illus.: Vaughan, Eillen Fox

Author: Justus, May

1952 $7.00

No. 2553

Whose Baby Is That?

Illus.: Nagel, Stina

Author: Jones, Clair

1969 $4.00

No. 2428

Why Do You Love Me?

Illus.: Sampson, Katherine

Author: Watts, Mabel

1970 $3.00

No. 892

Why Roosty Sang

Illus.: Winship, Florence Sarah

Author: Page, Marguerita

1948 $15.00

No. 852

Wiggletail

Illus.: Charlie

Author: Charlie

1944 $15.00

No. 2475-3

Wild Animal Babies

Illus.: Hauge, Carl and Mary

1973 $2.00

No. 2625

Wild Kingdom 'A Trip To A Game Park'

Illus.: Seward, James/Creative Studios

Author: Dinneen, Betty

1976 $3.00

No. 818

Willy Woo-Oo-Oo

Illus.: Winship, Florence Sarah

Author: Wright, Belly Ren

1951 $15.00

No. 2627

Wilmer The Watchdog

Illus.: Giacomini, Olindo

Author: Kittke, Lae

1970 $2.00

No. 2561

Wolf And The Seven Kids

Illus.: Sondern, Ferdinand A.

Author: Hansen, Gretchen

1969 $3.00

No. 871

Wonderful Tony

Illus.: Berry, Anne Scheu

Author: Page, Marguerita

1947 $15.00

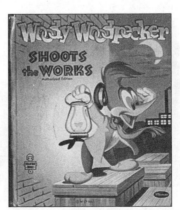

No. 2439

Woody Woodpecker 'Shoots The Works'

Illus.: McSavage, Frank and Armstrong, Sam

Author: Walter Lantz Studios

1955 $7.00

No. 2562

Woody Woodpecker's 'Pogo Stick Adventures'

Illus.: Abranz, Alfred; Knight, John

Author: Walter Lantz Studios

1954 $8.00

No. 831

Woody Woodpecker's 'Peck Of Trouble'

Illus.: Thompson, Riley and Armstrong, Sam

Author: Watts, Mabel

1951 **$10.00**

No. 2523

Wrong-Way Howie Learns To Slide

Illus.: Wilde, Carol

Author: Peake, Sylvia

1969 **$3.00**

No. 911

**Yellow Cat, The
(A Fuzzy Wuzzy Book)**

Illus.: Sari

Author: Wright, Betty Ren

1952 **$15.00**

No. 940

Yippie Kiyi

Illus.: Munson, Floyd

Author: Rose, Florella

1953 **$18.00**

No. 2514

Yippie Kiyi And Whoa Boy

Illus.: Sari

Author: Rose, Florella

1955 **$15.00**

No. 2642

Yogi Bear, And The Super Scooper

Illus.: Hooper, L.; and Thomas, R.

Author: Hoag, Nancy

1961 **$16.00**

No. 2608

Yogi Bear's Secret

Illus.: Jason, Leon

Author: Jones, Mary Voell

1963 **$18.00**

No. 2423

Zoo Friends Are At Our School Today!

Illus.: Brewer, Sally King

Author: Watts, Mabel

1979 **$3.00**

**Knott's Berry Farm Burro In Ghost Town
(Knott's Berry Farm Promotion)**

Illus.: Alvarado, Peter

Author: Klinordlinger, Jean

1955 **$15.00**

**Search for Santa Claus, A
(Santa's Village Promotion)**

Illus.: Boyle, Neil

Author: Nast, Elsa Ruth

1958 **$12.00**

Free Public Library of Monroe Township
306 S. Main Street
Williamstown, N.J. 08094-1727

8 6 3 3 1

Index of Tell-A-Tale Books (Numerical)

For those of you who collect numerically, the following listing is for you. Because the early editions had only three digits, they are easy to organize. After the three digits, the books were done with four, and most of these had multiple titles through the years. Tell-A-Tales with dashes have no numerical significance. It is possible you may have a book with different numbers than are listed here.

Index of Book Types and Subjects

Hector Heathcoat And The Knights	Wonder	840
Minute-And-A-Half-Man	Wonder	758

Felix The Cat

Felix On Television	Treasure	904
Felix On Television	Wonder	716
Felix The Cat	Wonder	665
Felix The Cat	Treasure	872
Surprise For Felix A	Wonder	728

Flintstones

Bamm-Bamm	LGB	540
Cave Kids	LGB	539
Flintstones, The	LGB	450
Flintstones 'Everyone's Egg'	Wonder	927
Flintstones At The Circus, The	TellTale	2552
Pebbles Flintstone	LGB	531
Pebbles And Bamm-Bamm Find Things To Do	Wonder	919
Pebbles Flintstone A B C's	TellTale	2622
Pebbles Flintstone 'Daddy's Little Helper'	TellTale	2657
Rubbles And Bamm-Bamm, The 'Problem Present'	TellTale	2622

Garfield

Garfield 'The Cat Show' LGB		110-61
Garfield And The Space Cat	LGB	107-65

Gumby And Pokey

Gumby And Gumby's Pal Pokey To The Rescue	TellTale	2552
Gumby And Gumby's Pal Pokey	TellTale	2506

Henry

Henry Goes To A Party	Wonder	778
Henry Goes To A Party	Treasure	897
Henry In Lollipop Land	Treasure	871
Henry In Lollipop Land	Wonder	664

Hong Kong Phooey

Hong Kong Phooey And The Bird Nest Snatchers	Elf'	
Hong Kong Phooey And The Fire Engine Mystery	Elf	
Hong Kong Phooey And The Fortune Cookie Caper	Elf	

Huckleberry Hound

Huckleberry Hound Builds A House	LGB	3 76
Huckleberry Hounds And The Christmas Sleigh	LGB	403
Huckleberry Hound And His Friends	LGB	406
Huckleberry Hound Safety Signs	LGB	458
Huckleberry Hound 'The Big Blooming Rosebush'	Wonder	944
Huckleberry Hound The Rainmaker	TellTale	2611

Jetsons

Jetsons, The	LGB	500
Jetsons, The 'Great Pizza Hunt, The'	Wonder	790

Little Lulu

Little Lulu	LGB	476
Little Lulu And Her Magic Tricks	LGB	203
Little Lulu And The Birthday Mystery	TellTale	2502
Little Lulu 'Has An Art Show'	TellTale	2622
Little Lulu Lucky Landlady!	TellTale	2437
Little Lulu Uses Her Head	TellTale	2552

Loopy De Loop

Loopy De Loop Goes West	LGB	417
Loopy De Loop 'Odd Jobber'	TellTale	2611

Magilla Gorilla

Magilla Gorilla	LGB	547
Magilla Gorilla And The Super Kite	Wonder	707
Magilla Gorilla Takes A Banana Vacation	TellTale	2552

Mighty Mouse

Mighty Mouse-Dinky Learns To Fly	Wonder	677
Mighty Mouse-Santa's Helper	Treasure	896
Mighty Mouse-Santas Helper	Wonder	662
Mighty Mouse And The Scarecrow	Wonder	678
Mighty Mouse And The Scared Scarecrow	Treasure	884
Mighty Mouse To The Rescue	Wonder	717
Mighty Mouse- Dinky Learns To Fly	Treasure	866

Peter Potamus

Peter Potamus	LGB	556
Peter Potamus 'Meets The Black Knight'	TellTale	2506

Pink Panther

Pink Panther In The Haunted House, The	LGB	140*
Pink Panther And Sons Fun At The Picnic	LGB	111-60
Pink Panther Rides Again, The	TellTale	2628

Pound Puppies

Pound Puppies 'Problem Puppies'	LGB	111-61
Pound Puppies In Pick Of The Litter	LGB	110-59

Popeye

House That Popeye Built, The	Wonder	750
Popeye	Treasure	888
Popeye	Wonder	667
Popeye Goes On A Picnic	Wonder	697
Popeye's Big Surprise	Wonder	791

Rainbow Brite

Rainbow Brite And The Brook Meadow Deer	LGB	107-48
Rainbow Brite And The Magic Belt	TellTale	2451-4

Road Runner

Road Runner 'Bird Watchers'	TellTale	2408
Road Runner The 'A Very Scary Lesson'	LGB	122*
Road Runner The 'Mid-Mesa Marathon'	LGB	110-57
Road Runner The 'Tumbleweed Trouble'	TellTale	2466

Rocky And Bullwinkle

Rocky And Bullwinkle	TellTale	2451-38

Rocky And His Friends	LGB	408
Bullwinkle	LGB	462
Bullwinkle's Masterpiece	TellTale	2594

Ruff And Reddy

Ruff And Reddy	LGB	378
Ruff And Reddy	LGB	477
Ruff And Reddy Go To A Party	TellTale	2567

Scooby Doo

Scooby Doo At The Zoo	TellTale	2570
Scooby Doo And The Pirate Treasure	LGB	126*
Scooby-Doo And The Case Of The Counterfeit Money	Elf	
Scooby-Doo And The Haunted Doghouse	Elf	
Scooby-Doo And The Headless Horseman	Elf	
Scooby-Doo And The Mystery Monster	Elf	
Scooby-Doo And The Old Ship Mystery	Elf	

Storytoon Express

Three Pigs, The	Elf	8430
Tortoise And The Hare, The	Elf	8431
Sugarplum Tree, The	Elf	8432
Magic Pot The	Elf	8433
Silly Joe	Elf	8434
Lazy Jack	Elf	8435

Tom And Jerry

Tom And Jerry	LGB	117
Tom And Jerry Photo Finish	LGB	124*
Tom And Jerry Meet Little Quack	LGB	181
Tom And Jerry's Merry Christmas	LGB	197
Tom And Jerry's Party	LGB	235
Tom And Jerry Meet Little Quack	LGB	311
Tom And Jerry	LGB	561
Tom And Jerry's Merry Christmas	LGB	457-42
Tom And Jerry And The Toy Circus	TellTale	2509
Tom And Jerry In Model Mice	TellTale	2509
Tom And Jerry In Tom's Happy Birthday	TellTale	2611
Tom And Jerry's Big Move		

Tom Terrific

Tom Terrific With Mighty Manfred The Wonder Dog	Wonder	703
Tom Terrific's Greatest Adventure	Wonder	735

Tweety And Sylvester

Tweety Plays Catch The Puddy Cat	LGB	141*
Tweety And Sylvester In 'Birds Of A Feather'	LGB	1 10-78
Tweety Global Patrol	LGB	110-82
Tweety	TellTale	901
Tweety And Sylvester At The Farm	TellTale	2453-35
Tweety And Sylvester 'A Visit To The Vet'	TellTale	2453-47
Tweety And Sylvester 'Picnic Problems'	TellTale	2448

Tiny Toon Adventures

Tiny Toon Adventures 'Happy Birthday Babs'	LGB	111-67
Tiny Toon Adventures 'Lost In The Funhouse'	LGB	111-68
Tiny Toon Adventures 'The Adventures Of Buster Hood	LGB	111-72
Buster Bunny And The Best Friends Ever	LGB	111-76

Under Dog

Underdog And The Disappearing Ice Cream	LGB	135*
Under Dog	TellTale	2611

Woody Woodpecker

Woody Woodpecker	LGB	145
Woody Woodpecker	LGB	330
Woody Woodpecker At The Circus	LGB	149
Woody Woodpecker Steps To Drawing	LGB	372
Woody Woodpecker Takes A Trip	LGB	445
Woody Woodpecker's 'Peck Of Trouble'	TellTale	831
Woody Woodpecker's 'Pogo Stick Adventures'	TellTale	2562
Woody Woodpecker 'Shoots The Works'	TellTale	2439

Yogi Bear

Cindy Bear	LGB	442
Hey There It's Yogi Bear!	LGB	542
Hey There It's Yogi Bear!	TellTale	2602
Yogi Bear And The Super Scooper	TellTale	2642
Yogi Bears Secret	TellTale	2608
Yogi Bear	LGB	395
Yogi Bear And The Baby Skunk	Wonder	921
Yogi Bear Mosquito Flying Days	Wonder	924
Yogi Bear Playtime In Jellystone Park	Wonder	926
Yogi-A Christmas Visit	LGB	433

Misc. Characters

Clyde Crashcup And Leonardo	Wonder	837
Crusader Rabbit	Wonder	698
Dally Duck Space Creature	TellTale	2621
Dick Tracy	LGB	497
Diz And Liz	Wonder	835
Dondi	Wonder	783
Family Circus Daddy's Surprise Day	LGB	111-29
Fireball X-L5	LGB	546
Funny Company, The	TellTale	2567
Gay Purr-ee	LGB	488
Inspector Gadget In Africa	LGB	107-49
Lady Lovely Locks Silkypup Saves The Day	LGB	107-57
Linus' A Smile For Grouse'	TellTale	2567
Luno The Soaring Stallion	Wonder	831
Mister Magoo	Wonder	708
Mrs. Brisby And The Magic Stone	LGB	110-3 8
Nancy And Sluggo 'The Big Surprise'	TellTale	2525
Quints 'The Cleanup'	LGB	107-72
Robotman & His Friends At School	LGB	110-58
Shazam! A Circus Adventure	LGB	155*

Supercar		LGB492
Tom Thumb		LGB353

Misc. Harvey Cartoon Characters

Baby Huey	Wonder	787
Buzzy The Funny Crow	Wonder	821
Herman And Katnip	Wonder	788
Little Audrey And The Moon Lady	Wonder	759
Woodsy Owl And The Trail Bikers	LGB	107*

Misc. Hanna Barbera Characters

Bisketts In Double Trouble	LGB	111-49
Clue Club The Case Of The Missing Racehorse	Elf	
Devlin	Elf	
Dynomutt And The Pie In The Sky Caper	Elf	
Great Grape Ape At The Circus	Elf	
Hokey Wolf And Ding-A-Ling	LGB	444
Jabberjaw Out West	Elf	
Josie And The Pussycats/ The Bag Factory Detour	Elf	
Lippy The Lion And Hardy Har Har	LGB	508
Mumbly To The Rescue	Elf	
Mushmouse And Punkin Puss 'The Country Cousins'	TellTale	2552
Pixi Dixi & Mr. Jinx	LGB	454
Quick Draw McGraw	LGB	398
Ricochet Rabbit 'Showdown At Gopher Gulch Bakery'	TellTale	2622
Speed Buggy And The Secret Message	Elf	
Top Cat	LGB	453
Touché Turtle	LGB	474
Valley Of The Dinosaurs	Elf	
Wally Gator	LGB	502
Wally Gator 'Guess What's Hiding At The Zoo'	TellTale	2506
Wheelie And The Chopper Bunch	Elf	
Yacky Doodle And Chopper	LGB	449

Misc. King Features

Blondie's Family Cookie Alexander And Dog Elmer	Wonder	666
Blondie's Family	Treasure	887
Flash Gordon	Treasure	905
Flash Gordon And The Baby Animals	Wonder	684
Prince Valiant	Treasure	874

Misc. Terrytoon Characters

Astronut And The Flying Bus	Wonder	853
Gandy Goose	Wonder	695
Heckle And Jeckle	Wonder	694
Heckle And Jeckle Visit The Farm	Wonder	712
Joke On Farmer Al Falfa, A	Wonder	736
Silly Sidney	Wonder	841
Terry Bears Win The Cub Scout Badge, The	Treasure	903
Terrytoon Space Train, The	Wonder	711

Christmas .Titles

12 Days Of Christmas, The	LGB	526
ABC Is For Christmas	LGB	108*
Animals' Merry Christmas, The	LGB	329
Animals Christmas Eve, The	LGB	154*

Babar And Father Christmas	Wonder	592
Baby's Christmas	LGB	460-08
Baby's First Christmas	LGB	368
Baby's First Christmas	Wonder	738
Baby's First Christmas	Wonder	876
Biggest Most Beautiful Christmas Tree, The	LGB	459-8
Cat That Climbed The Christmas Tree, The	LGB	458-03
Chipmunk's Merry Christmas The	LGB	375
Christmas ABC		LGB478
Christmas Bunny, The	LGB	450-13
Christmas Carols	LGB	26
Christmas Carols	LGB	595
Christmas Donkey, The	LGB	460- 9
Christmas Favorites	Wonder	869
Christmas In Song And Story	Wonder	586
Christmas In The Country	LGB	95
Christmas Is Coming	Wonder	593
Christmas Manger, The	LGB	176
Christmas Puppy, The	Wonder	585
Christmas Story, The	LGB	158
Christmas Tree That Grew, The	LGB	458-1
December Is For Christmas	Wonder	776
Dennis The Menace Waits For Santa Claus	LGB	432
Donald Duck's Christmas Tree	LGB	460-13
Donald Duck's Christmas, Tree	LGB	D 39
Donald Duck And The Christmas Carol	LGB	D 84
Frosty The Snowman	LGB	142
Frosty The Snowman	LGB	451-15
Happiest Christmas The	TellTale	2516
How The Rabbit Found Christmas	Wonder	866
Huckleberry Hounds And The Christmas Sleigh	LGB	403
I Can't Wait Until Christmas	LGB	456-10
Jingle Bells	LGB	458*
Jingle Bells	LGB	55.3
Kewtee Bear's Christmas	Wonder	867
Kewtee Bear-Santa's Helper	Wonder	652
Little Cowboy's Christmas A	Wonder	570
Little Lost Angel	Elf	580
Little Lost Angel	Elf	483
Little Lost Angel	Elf	8376
Little Lost Angel	Elf	8680
Littlest Christmas Elf, The	LGB	459-00
Littlest Christmas Tree, The	Wonder	625
Littlest Snowman, The	Wonder	720
Merry Christmas Book	Wonder	820
Merry Christmas Mr. Snowman	Wonder	818
Mickey Mouse Flies The Christmas Mail	LGB	D 53
Mickey Mouse Goes Christmas Shopping	LGB	D 33
Mighty Mouse-Santa's Helper	Treasure	896
Mighty Mouse-Santas Helper	Wonder	662
Most Beautiful Tree In The World, The	Wonder	653
My Christmas Book	LGB	298
My Christmas Treasury	LGB	144*
My Christmas Treasury	LGB	455*
My Christmas Treasury	LGB	5003
Night Before Christmas, The	LGB	20

Night Before Christmas, The	LGB	241
Night Before Christmas, The	LGB	450*
Night Before Christmas, The	LGB	450-10
Night Before Christmas, The	TellTale	839
Night Before Christmas, The	TellTale	839
Night Before Christmas, The	TellTale	2517
Night Before Christmas, The	TellTale	2517
Night Before Christmas, The	Wonder	858
Night Before Christmas, The	TellTale	2517
Noel	LGB	456-16
Nutcracker The	LGB	460-15
Parade For Chatty Baby A	TellTale	2562
Poky Little Puppy's First Christmas, The	LGB	461-01
Polly's Christmas Present	Wonder	819
Roly-Poly Puppy, The	Wonder	549
Rudolph The Red-Nosed Reindeer	TellTale	2517-2
Rudolph The Red-Nosed Reindeer	TellTale	2483-02
Rudolph The Red-Nosed Reindeer	LGB	3 31
Rudolph The Red-Nosed Reindeer Shines Again	LGB	452- 8
Santa's Rocket Sleigh	Elf	568
Santa's Surprise Book	LGB	121*
Snowman's Christmas Present, The	Wonder	572
Things To Make And Do For Christmas	Treasure	867
Tom And Jerry's Merry Christmas	LGB	457-42
Trim The Christmas Tree	LGB	A 15
Trim The Christmas Tree	LGB	A 50
Twelve Days Of Christmas, The	LGB	454-42
Twelve Days Of Christmas, The	LGB	451 - 16
Twelve Days Of Christmas, The	Wonder	651
Waiting For Santa Claus	Wonder	865
Wonder Book Of Christmas, The	Wonder	575
Yogi-A Christmas Visit	LGB	433

Company Products and or Corporate Characters

American Airlines

Gordon's Jet Flight	LGB	A48

Campbell Soup

Campbell Kids At Home, The	Elf	493
Campbell Kids Have A Party, The	Elf	494

Fort Chimo Co-Operative Association

Ookpik, The Arctic Owl	LGB	579

Good Humor Ice Cream

Good Humor Man	LGB	550

International Harvester

Trucks	LGB	A6

Johnson & Johnson (Band-Aids)

Doctor Dan At The Circus	LGB	399
Doctor Dan The Bandage Man	LGB	295
Doctor Dan The Bandage Man	LGB	312-07
Doctor Dan The Bandage Man	LGB	111
Nurse Nancy	LGB	154
Nurse Nancy	LGB	346
Nurse Nancy	LGB	473

Marshal Field & Co.

Uncle Mistletoe	LGB	175

McDonalds

Ronald McDonald And The Tale Of The Talking Plant	LGB	111-50

Meyercord Decals

Fun With Decals	LGB	139

Texel Cellophane Tape

Tex And His Toys	LGB	129

Dolls

Baby Dear	LGB	466
Betsy Mc Call	LGB	559
Busy Timmy	LGB	50
Busy Timmy	LGB	452
Cabbage Patch Kids 'Xavier's Birthday Surprise!'	LGB	107-64
Charmin' Chatty	LGB	554
Kewtee Bear-Santa's Helper	Wonder	652
Kewtee Bear's Christmas	Wonder	867
Parade For Chatty Baby, A	TellTale	2562
Pepper Plays Nurse	LGB	555
So Big	LGB	574
Tubsy And The Picnic Tree	TellTale	2552

Fuzzy Wuzzy Books

Buzzy Beaver	TellTale	2675
Christopher John's Fuzzy Mittens	TellTale	2672
Cinnamon Bear, The	TellTale	2674
Franky The Fuzzy Goat	TellTale	820
Fuzzy Dan	TellTale	821
Fuzzy Duckling	TellTale	912
Fuzzy Friends In Mother Goose Land	TellTale	914
Fuzzy Joe Bear	TellTale	954
Fuzzy Mittens For Three Little Kittens	TellTale	823
Fuzzy Pet A	TellTale	2671
Fuzzy Wuzzy Puppy The	TellTale	915
Good Night 'A Flocked Book'	TellTale	955
Grandpa's House	TellTale	2670
I Love My Grandma	TellTale	2671
Little Red Riding Hood	TellTale	2670
Mr. Mogg's Dogs	TellTale	958
Oh Look!	TellTale	2672
Pitty Pat	TellTale	2641
Snowball	TellTale	2670
Sunny Honey And Funny	TellTale	824
That Puppy	TellTale	2675
Tommy And Timmy	TellTale	822
Tommy And Timmy	TellTale	2644
Tuffer	TellTale	2672
Yellow Cat The	TellTale	911

Howdy Doody

Howdy Doody's Animal Friends	LGB	252
Howdy Doody's Circus	LGB	99
Howdy Doody's Clarabell And Pesky Peanut	TellTale	934
Howdy Doody's Clarabell Clown And The Merry-Go-Round	TellTale	2558
Howdy Doody's Lucky Trip	LGB	171
Howdy Doody And Clarabell	LGB	121

The Cookie Snatcher	LGB	262
Raggedy Ann And The Tagalong Present	TellTale	2417-1

Religious Titles

Angel Child	Elf	8373
Angel Child	Elf	8715
Baby Jesus Stamps	LGB	A 12
Baby Jesus The	Elf	8556
Baby Moses	TellTale	917
Beloved Son, The	TellTale	825
Bible Stories	LGB	174
Bible Stories From The Old Testament	LGB	153*
Bible Stories: Old Testament	Elf	491
Bible Stories: Old Testament	Elf	8613
Bible Treasures	Wonder	643
Book Of God's Gifts A	LGB	112
Child's Friend A	TellTale	2519
Child's Ten Commandments A	TellTale	2624
Daniel In The Lions' Den	LGB	311-62
David And Goliath	LGB	110*
First Book Of Bible Stories	LGB	198
Heroes Of The Bible	LGB	236
I Think About Jesus	Elf	8652
Little Lost Angel	Elf	580
Little Lost Angel	Elf	483
Little Lost Angel	Elf	8376
Little Lost Angel	Elf	8680
Littlest Angel, The	Wonder	755
Lord's Prayer, The	Wonder	647
Lord Is My Shepherd, The 'The twenty-third Psalm'	LGB	311-60
My Bible Book	Elf	8696
My Book About God	Wonder	644
My First Book Of Bible Stories	LGB	19
My First Book Of Prayers	Treasure	868
My Prayer Book	Elf	8697
Noah's Ark	LGB	109
Noah's Ark	LGB	311-64
Noah's Ark	LGB	D 28
Noah's Ark	Elf	461
Noah's Ark	Elf	1020
Noah's Ark	Elf	8424
Noah's Ark	Elf	8648
Noah And The Ark	TellTale	2558
Prayers And Graces For A Small Child	Elf	502
Prayers And Graces For A Small Child	Elf	8609
Prayers For Boys And Girls	TellTale	918
Prayers For Boys And Girls	TellTale	2523
Prayers For Children	LGB	205
Prayers For Children	LGB	301-10
Prayers For Little Children	Elf	8557
Stories Of The Christ Child	Elf	484
Stories Of The Christ Child	Elf	8612
Story Of David The	Elf	8725
Story Of Jesus, The	LGB	27
Story Of Jonah, The	LGB	311-61
Story Of Joseph The	Elf	8724
Story Of The Christ Child, The	Wonder	587
Ten Commandments For Children, The	Elf	543

Ten Commandments For Children, The	Elf	8604
twenty-third Psalm, The	Elf	8698
We Talk With God	TellTale	2404-3
Where Jesus Lived	LGB	147
Wonder Book Of Bible Stories, The	Wonder	577

Romper Room

Romper Room Do Bee Book Of Manners, The	Wonder	763
Romper Room Do Bees	LGB	273
Romper Room Exercise Book, The	LGB	527
Romper Room Laughing Book	Wonder	808
Romper Room Safety Book, The	Wonder	854

Rootie Kazootie

Rootie Kazootie	LGB	150
Rootie Kazootie Baseball Star	LGB	190
Rootie Kazootie Joins The Circus	LGB	226
Rootie Kazootie And The Pineapple Pies	TellTale	936

Scouting Books

Brownie Scouts	LGB	409
Cub Scouts	LGB	5022
Little Cub Scout	Elf	8665

Sesame Street/Muppets

Amazing Mumford Forgets The Magic Word	LGB	108- 5
Bert's Hall Of Great Inventions	LGB	321*
Big Bird's Day On The Farm	LGB	107-61
Big Bird's Red Book	LGB	157*
Big Bird Brings Spring To Sesame Street	LGB	108-57
Big Bird Follows The Signs	TellTale	2452-4
Big Bird Visits Navajo Country	LGB	108-68
Cookie Monster And The Cookie Tree	LGB	159
Cookie Monster And The Cookie Tree	LGB	109-52
Count's Poem, The	TellTale	2402
Count All The Way To Sesame Street	LGB	203-56
Day Snuffy Had The Sniffles, The	LGB	108-59
Ernie's Telephone Call	TellTale	2452-34
Ernie's Work Of Art	LGB	109- 5
Four Seasons, The	LGB	108- 4
Fozzie's Funnies	LGB	111-87
From Trash To Treasure	LGB	108-70
Grover's Guide To Good Manners	LGB	109-66
Grover's Own Alphabet	LGB	108-46
Grover's Own Alphabet	TellTale	2402-6
Grover Takes Care Of Baby	LGB	109-57
Happy And Sad Grouch And Glad	LGB	108-67
How To Be A Grouch	TellTale	2618
I Think That It Is Wonderful	LGB	109-47
Kermit Saves The Swamp!	LGB	111-84
Many Faces Of Ernie The	LGB	109- 4
"Me Cookie"	LGB	109-69
Monster At The End Of This Book, The	LGB	316*
Monsters' Picnic, The	LGB	109-59
Muppet -Treasure Island	LGB	111-88
Oscar's Book	LGB	120*

Oscar's New Neighbor	LGB	109-67
Puppy Love	LGB	109-46
Ready Set Go! A Counting Book	LGB	109-71
Sesame Street 'Mother Goose Rhymes'	LGB	108-69
Sesame Street 'The Together Book'	LGB	315*
Sesame Street ABC	TellTale	2471-43
Sesame Streets Cookie Monster's Book Of Cookie Shapes	TellTale	2402-8
Sesame Streets First Times	TellTale	2465-43
Sherlock Hemlock And The Great Twiddlebug Mystery	TellTale	2564
What's Up In The Attic?	LGB	108-58
Which Witch Is Which?	LGB	98770-01

Shari Lewis

Party In Shariland	LGB	360
Shari Lewis Wonder Book, The	Wonder 781	

Smokey The Bear

Smokey And His Animal Friends	LGB	387
Smokey Bear 'Saves The Forest'	TellTale	2463
Smokey Bear And The Campers	LGB	423
Smokey The Bear	LGB	224
Smokey The Bear	LGB	481
Smokey The Bear Finds A Helper	LGB	345

TV Shows (Misc.)

Adventures Of Robin Hood And His Merry Men	Elf	532
Barney 'Sharing Is Caring'	LGB	98790
Benji 'Fastest Dog In The West'	LGB	165*
Benji 'The Detective'	TellTale	2640
Buck Rogers And The Children Of Hopetown	LGB	500*
Bully And The New Girl	TellTale	2526
Circus Boy	LGB	290
Circus Boy And Captain Jack	TellTale	260
Cleo	LGB	287
Corey Baker Of Julia And His Show And Tell	TellTale	2506
Daktari 'Judi And The Kitten'	TellTale	2506
Donnie And Marie The Top Secret Project	LGB	160*
Donnie And Marie The State Fair Mystery	TellTale	2635
Emmett Kelly In Willie The Clown	Elf	573
Gentle Ben And The Pesky Puppy	TellTale	2552
H.R. Pufnstuf	TellTale	2624
J. Fred Muggs	LGB	234
Land Of The Lost The Dinosaur Adventure	TellTale	2607
Land Of The Lost The Surprise	LGB	136*
Leave It To Beaver	LGB	347
Little Beaver	TellTale	2611
Magic Clown, The	Treasure	876
Mister Rogers Neighborhood Everyone Is Special	TellTale	2599
Mr. Ed	LGB	483
Mr. Rogers Neighborhood 'Henrietta Meets Someone New'	LGB	133*
National Velvet	LGB	431
Ollie Bakes A Cake	Wonder	829
Runaway Squash, The	LGB	143*
Sergeant Preston And Rex	Elf	569

Sergeant Preston And The Yukon King	Elf	500
Silver Chief	Wonder	650
Soupy Sales And The Talking Turtle	Wonder	860
Sparkie-No School Today	Treasure	902
Super Circus	Elf	503
Walton's Birthday Present, The	LGB	134*
Walton's, The 'Elizabeth And The Magic Lamp'	TellTale	2579
Whistling Wizard	LGB	132
Wild Kingdom 'A Trip To A Game Park'	TellTale	2625
Wild Kingdom	LGB	151*
Winky Dink	LGB	266

Tom Corbett

Tom Corbett's Wonder Book Of Space	Wonder	603
Tom Corbett: A Trip To The Moon	Wonder	713

Uncle Wiggily

Uncle Wiggily	LGB	148
Uncle Wiggily's Adventures	Wonder	765
Uncle Wiggily And His Friends	Wonder	766
Uncle Wiggily And The Alligator	TellTale	903

Walt Disney
(Excluding Little Golden Books)

Aristocats 'A Counting Book,' The	TellTale	2516
Bambi	TellTale	2548
Beauty And The Beast	TellTale	2455-59
Bedknobs And Broomsticks - A Visit To Naboombu	TellTale	2541
Cinderella	TellTale	2427-2
Donald Duck's Lucky Day	TellTale	827
Donald Duck And Chip 'n Dale	TellTale	945
Donald Duck And The New Bird House	TellTale	2516
Donald Duck And The Super-Sticky Secret	TellTale	2425-6
Donald Duck Full Speed Ahead	TellTale	900
Donald Duck Goes Camping	TellTale	2609
Donald Duck Goes To Disneyland	TellTale	2559
Donald Duck In Frontierland	TellTale	2520
Donald Duck On Tom Sawyer's Island	TellTale	2409
Duck Tales 'Silver Dollars For Uncle Scrooge'	TellTale	2454
Ernie The Cave King And Sherlock The Smart Person	TellTale	2604
Mickey Mouse And The Lucky Goose Chase	TellTale	2454-45
Mickey Mouse And The Mouseketeers - The Animal Guessing	TellTale	2631
Mickey Mouse And The Pet Show	TellTale	2454-45
Mickey Mouse And The Really Neat Robot	TellTale	2475
Mickey Mouse And The Second Wish	TellTale	2418
Mickey Mouse And The World's Friendliest Monster	TellTale	2424-2
Pinocchio	TellTale	2428-2
Rescuers ABC, The	TellTale	2429-3
Robin Hood And Skippy's Best Birthday	TellTale	2441

Snow White And The Seven Dwarfs	TellTale	2578
Snow White And The Seven Dwarfs	TellTale	2427-4
Sword In The Stone, The	TellTale	2459
Uncle Scrooge 'The Winner'	TellTale	2552
Wait Disney Babies 1 To 10 Again	TellTale	2471-47
Walt Disney World - Big Albert Moves In	TellTale	2533
Winnie-The-Pooh 'The Blustery Day'	TellTale	2577
Winnie-The-Pooh And Eeyore's House	TellTale	2620
Winnie-The-Pooh And The Unbouncing Tigger	TellTale	2526

Western TV Shows

Gene Autry

Gene Autry	LGB	230
Gene Autry And Champion	LGB	267
Gene Autry 'Makes A New Friend'	TellTale	800
Gene Autry And The Lost Doggie	TellTale	932
Gene Autry Goes To The Circus	TellTale	2566

Lone Ranger

Lone Ranger & Tonto, The	LGB	297
Lone Ranger And The Ghost Horse, The	TellTale	2561
Lone Ranger And The Talking Pony, The	LGB	310
Lone Ranger Desert Storm, The	TellTale	2622
Lone Ranger, The	LGB	263

Rin Tin Tin

Rin Tin Tin And Rusty	LGB	246
Rin Tin Tin And The Last Indian	LGB	276
Rin Tin Tin & The Outlaw	LGB	304
Rinty And Pals For Rusty	TellTale	2571

Roy Rogers & Dale Evans

Dale Evans And Buttermilk	TellTale	2570
Dale Evans And The Coyote	LGB	253
Dale Evans And The Lost Goldmine	LGB	213
Roy Rogers' Bullet Leads The Way	TellTale	2567
Roy Rogers' Surprise For Donnie	TellTale	943
Roy Rogers	LGB	177
Roy Rogers And Cowboy Toby	LGB	195
Roy Rogers And The Indian Sign	LGB	259
Roy Rogers And The Lane Ranch	TellTale	811
Roy Rogers And The Mountain Lion	LGB	231
Roy Rogers And The Sure'Nough Cowpoke	TellTale	801

Wild Bill Hickok

Wild Bill Hickok	Wonder	649
Wild Bill Hickok And Deputy Marshall Joey	Elf	496
Wild Bill Hickok And The Indians	Elf	570

Misc. Television Westerns

Annie Oakley	LGB	221
Annie Oakley Sharpshooter	LGB	275
Brave Eagle	LGB	294
Broken Arrow	LGB	299
Buffalo Bill Jr.	LGB	254
Cheyene	LGB	318
Fury	TellTale	2611

Fury	LGB	286
Fury Takes The Jump	LGB	336
Gunsmoke	LGB	320
Hopalong Cassidy And The Bar 20 Cowboys	LGB	147
Life And Legend Of Wyatt Earp, The	LGB	315
Maverick	LGB	354
Tales Of Wells Fargo	LGB	328
Wagon Train	LGB	326

Wizard Of Oz

Cowardly Lion, The	Wonder	642
Emerald City Of Oz	LGB	151
Road To Oz, The	LGB	144
Tin Woodsman Of Oz, The	LGB	159
Wizard Of Oz, The	LGB	119
Wizard Of Oz, The	Wonder	543

Zippy

Zippy's Birthday Party	Elf	506
Zippy Goes To School	Elf	489
Zippy The Chimp	Elf	487
Zippy The Chimp	Elf	8306
Zippy The Chimp	Elf	8705

INDEX OF ILLUSTRATORS

Those who illustrated only one title are not listed.

Bugs Bunny, Pioneer	Golden	161*
Chip 'n Dale Rescue Rangers 'The Big Cheese Caper'	Golden	105-78
Daffy Duck Space Creature	TellTale	2621
Grand And Wonderful Day, The	Golden	98737-01
Little Lulu And The Birthday Mystery	TellTale	2502
Pink Panther In The Haunted House, The	Golden	140*
Pippi Longstocking And The South Sea Pirates	TellTale	2614
Rudolph The Red-Nosed Reindeer Shines Again	Golden	452- 8
Walt Disney Babies 1 To 10 Again	TellTale	2471-47

Banigan, Sharon

Fuzzy Duckling	TellTale	912
Jim Jump	TellTale	2527

Banta, Milton

Donald Duck Full Speed Ahead	TellTale	900
Donald Duck Goes To Disneyland	TellTale	2559
Mickey Mouse And His Space Ship	Golden	D 29
Mickey Mouse And His Space Ship	Golden	D108
Three Little Pigs	Golden	D 10
Three Little Pigs	Golden	D 78

Barbaresi, Nina

Fox Jumped Up One Winters Night, A	Golden	300-53

Bartram, Bob

Fury	TellTale	2611
Lassie's Brave Adventure	TellTale	2571
Rinty And Pals For Rusty	TellTale	2571

Battaglia, Aurelius

Baby's Mother Goose	Golden	303
Baby's Mother Goose	Golden	422
Hiram's Red Shirt	Golden	204-43
Little Boy With A Big Horn	Golden	100
Mr. Bell's Fixit Shop	Golden	204-42
Old Mother Hubbard	Golden	591
Pat-A-Cake	Golden	54
Pets For Peter	Golden	82
Pets For Peter (Puzzle Edition)	Golden	82

Baudoin, Simonne

Baby Raccoon	Wonder	797
Fluffy Little Lamb	Wonder	780
Rabbits Give A Party, The	Wonder	811

Beckett, Sheilah

My Christmas Book	Golden	298
Rapunzel	Golden	207-57
Twelve Dancing Princesses, The	Golden	194
Twelve Days Of Christmas, The	Golden	451-16

Bemelmans, Ludwig

Madeline	Golden	186

Bendel, Ruth

Lucky Rabbit	DingDong	221
Lucky Rabbit	DingDong	DIN 7
Puppy Twins, The	Elf	8420
Puppy Twins, The	Elf	8603

Berger, Alex

Flash Gordon	Treasure	905
Flash Gordon And The Baby Animals	Wonder	684

Berlin, Rose Mary

Buster Cat Goes Out	Golden	302-57
But, You're A Duck	Golden	206-58

Berry, Anne Scheu

Fuzzy Joe Bear	TellTale	954
Tommy And Timmy	TellTale	822
Tommy And Timmy	TellTale	2644
Wonderful Tony	TellTale	871

Berthold

Hoppy The Puppy	Wonder	751
Roly-Poly Puppy, The	Wonder	549

Bester, Don

Lucky Puppy, The	Golden	D 89

Beylon, Catherine

Busy Body Book 'A First Book About You', The	TellTale	2585
I'm Not Sleepy	TellTale	2462-42

Bezada, Herb

Deputy Dawg And The Space Man	Wonder	773
Deputy Dawg's Big Catch	Wonder	770
Deputy Dog	Wonder	760
Hector Crosses The River.... With George Washington	Wonder	769
Luno The Soaring Stallion	Wonder	831
Muskie And His Friends	Wonder	828
Trick On Deputy Dog	Wonder	830

Biers, Clarence

Fuzzy Dan	TellTale	821
Hide-Away Henry	TellTale	938

Bilder, A.K.

Space Ship To The Moon	Elf	473
Superliner United States, The: World's Fastest Liner	Elf	474

Binst, Claire

Freddy And The Indian	Wonder	816
Little Garage Man, The	Wonder	744

Blair, Mary

Baby's House	Golden	80
Baby's House (Puzzle Edition)	Golden	80
I Can Fly	Golden	92

Blake, Vivienne Leah

Alphabet A-Z, The	Golden	3
Lion And The Mouse, The	Elf	8569
Peppy, The Lonely Little Puppy	Elf	425

Dolce, Ellen J.

Busy Saturday Word Book	TellTale	2474-42
Little Red Riding Hood	TellTale	2461-44

Dorcas

Circus Train, The	TellTale	890
Hippety Hop Around The Block	TellTale	924
Truck That Stopped At Village Small, The	TellTale	813

Dottie

Hide-Away Puppy	Elf	8587
Hide-Away Puppy	Elf	466
Hide-Away Puppy	Elf	587
Hide-Away Puppy	Elf	8357

Dreany, E. Joseph

Adventures Of Lassie:	Golden	5012
Annie Oakley Sharpshooter	Golden	275
Car And Truck Stamps	Golden	A 20
Dale Evans And The Coyote	Golden	253
Gunsmoke	Golden	320
Handy Andy	TellTale	2580
Lassie And The Daring Rescue	Golden	277
Lone Ranger, The	Golden	263
Train Stamps	Golden	A 26

Dugan, William J.

Animal Stamps	Golden	A 7
Book Of A, The	Golden	615
Book Of B, The	Golden	616
Book Of C, The	Golden	617
Book Of D E, The	Golden	618
Book Of F, The	Golden	619
Book Of G H, The	Golden	620
Book Of I J K, The	Golden	621
Book Of L, The	Golden	622
Book Of M, The	Golden	623
Book Of N O, The	Golden	624
Book Of P Q, The	Golden	625
Book Of R, The	Golden	626
Book Of T U V, The	Golden	629
Book Of W X Y Z, The	Golden	630
Cars	Golden	251
I'm An Indian Today	Golden	425
Let's Go Trucks!	Golden	185*
Machines	Golden	455
My Magic Slate Book	Golden	5025
Red Book Of Fairy Tales, The	Golden	306
Rumpelstiltskin And The Princess And The Pea	Golden	498
Second Book Of S, The	Golden	628
Tom Thumb	Golden	353
Rumpelstiltskin	Golden	300-56

Dunnington, Tom

My Little Book Of Birds	TellTale	2490
My Little Book Of Boats	TellTale	247332
My Little Book Of Horses	TellTale	2466-3

Durrell, Julie

Colorful Mouse, The	Golden	211-71
Evening Walk, The	TellTale	2462-43
Little Mouse's Book Of Colors	Golden	211-74
Tickety-Tock, What Time Is It?	Golden	308-51

Edwards, Beverly

Mary Poppins, A Jolly Holiday	Golden	D112
Ookpik, The Arctic Owl	Golden	579

Eisenberg, Harvey

Beany And His Magic Set	TellTale	904
Cindy Bear	Golden	442
Huckleberry Hound Builds A House	Golden	376
Ruff And Reddy Go To A Party	TellTale	2567
Tom And Jerry	Golden	117
Tom And Jerry	Golden	561
Tom And Jerry In Model Mice	TellTale	2509
Tom And Jerry In Tom's Happy Birthday	TellTale	2611
Tom And Jerry Meet Little Quack	Golden	311
Tom And Jerry Meet Little Quack	Golden	181
Tom And Jerry's Merry Christmas	Golden	457-42
Tom And Jerry's Party	Golden	235
Woody Woodpecker, Steps To Drawing	Golden	372
Ruff And Reddy	Golden	378
Ruff And Reddy	Golden	477
Tom And Jerry's Merry Christmas	Golden	197

Elfrieda

Gingerbread Man, The	Golden	182*
Horse For Charlie, A	TellTale	2411-1
Johnny Appleseed	TellTale	2679
Tommy On The Farm	TellTale	2557
What Makes My Cat Purr?	TellTale	2425

Elliott, Gertrude

First Little Golden Book Of Fairy Tales, The	Golden	9
Gingerbread Shop, The	Golden	126
Happy Family, The	Golden	35
Little Golden Book Of Words, The	Golden	45
Magic Compass, The	Golden	146
Mother Goose	Golden	4
Mother Goose	Golden	240
Mr. Wigg's Birthday Party	Golden	140
Nursery Rhymes	Golden	59
Two Little Gardeners	Golden	108
Words	Golden	A 1
Words	Golden	A 30
Words	Golden	A 45

Ellis, Art & Kim

Barbie 'A Picnic Surprise'	Golden	107-70
Tawny Scrawny Lion 'Saves The Day'	Golden	GBL377
We're Busy Charlie Brown	TellTale	2541-41
Where's Woodstock?	Golden	111-63

Emslie, Peter

Beauty And The Beast 'The Teapot's Tale'	Golden	104-70
Pocahontas 'The Voice Of The Wind'	Golden	104-72
Sorcerer's Apprentice, The	Golden	100-79

Endred, Helen

Bunny Tales	Elf	574
Bunny Tales	Elf	8406
Bunny Tales	Elf	8641
Cinderella	Elf	551
Cinderella	Elf	8417
Cinderella	Elf	8644

Erickson, Phoebe

Baby Animal Friends	Wonder	608
Little Peter Cottontail	Wonder	641
Peter Rabbit And Other Stories	Wonder	513

Esley, Joan

Jenny's New Brother	Golden	596
New Brother, New Sister	Golden	564
Play Street	Golden	484

Eugenie

1 Is Red	TellTale	2407-2
Good-Bye Day, The	Golden	209-57
Jenny's Surprise Summer	Golden	204-39
Lion's Haircut, The	TellTale	2519
Moving Day	Golden	209-57
Too Small Names!	TellTale	2614
Two Stories About Lollipop	TellTale	2683

Evans, Katherine

Dressing Up	DingDong	206
Jingle Bell Jack	DingDong	219
Jingle Bell Jack	DingDong	DIN 1
Littlest Angel, The	Wonder	755
Peek Fish	DingDong	209

Evers, Helen & Alf

Chatterduck	Elf	8576
Copy-Kitten	Elf	584
Copy-Kitten	Elf	8370
Copy-Kitten	Elf	8689
Crosspatch	Elf	8442
Crosspatch	Elf	8675
Crybaby Calf	Elf	547
Crybaby Calf	Elf	8426
Crybaby Calf	Elf	8606
Day On The Farm, A	Elf	8586
Fussbunny	Elf	530
Fussbunny	Elf	8405
Fussbunny	Elf	8642
Moonymouse	Elf	1021
Moonymouse	Elf	8400
Moonymouse	Elf	8639
Plump Pig, The	Elf	542
Plump Pig, The	Elf	8309
Plump Pig, The	Elf	8592
Pokey Bear	Elf	8451
Pokey Bear	Elf	8720
So Long	Elf	1036
So Long	Elf	8342
So Long	Elf	8622

Ewers, Joe

From Trash To Treasure	Golden	108-70
I Can't Wait Until Christmas	Golden	456-10
Little Red Riding Hood	Golden	300-65
Monsters' Picnic, The	Golden	109-59

Fleishman, Seymour

Hop-Away Joey	Elf	8572
Trip In Space, A	Elf	8566

Fletcher, James

Funny Company, The	TellTale	2567
One Hundred And One Dalmatians	TellTale	2622

Florian

Rackety-Boom	TellTale	893
Rackety-Boom	TellTale	2557
Train Coming	TellTale	2556

Flory, Jane

ABC	TellTale	896
Dolls Of Other Lands	DingDong	213
Fanny Forgot	TellTale	862
Farmer John	TellTale	838
Little Caboose, The	TellTale	817
Once Upon A Windy Day	TellTale	865
Snooty	TellTale	851
Surprise In The Barn	TellTale	2543
Surprise In The Barn (Second Cover)	TellTale	2543
Too-Little Fire Engine, The	Wonder	526

Frame, Paul

Building A Skyscraper	Elf	8552
Turtles Turn Up On Tuesday	Elf	8561

Frankel, Simon

Digger Dan	TellTale	2615
Digger Dan	TellTale	908
Four Puppies Who Wanted A Home, The	Wonder	530
Jolly Jumping Man, The	Wonder	537
Mr. Mogg's Dogs	TellTale	958

Franzen, Jim

Clue Club The Case Of The Missing Racehorse	Elf	
Jabberjaw Out West	Elf	
Josie And The Pussycats/ The Bag Factory Detour	Elf	

Frees, Harry Whittier

Four Little Kittens	Elf	566
Four Little Kittens	Elf	8336
Four Little Kittens	Elf	8718
Four Little Puppies	Elf	578
Four Little Puppies	Elf	8335
Four Little Puppies	Elf	8597
Little Kittens' Nursery Rhymes	Elf	440
Little Kittens' Nursery Rhymes	Elf	8311
Snuggles	Elf	1005
Yip And Yap	Elf	1022
Yip And Yap	Elf	8380
Yip And Yap	Elf	8690

Freund, Rudolf

Animals Of Farmer Jones, The	Golden	11
Little Red Hen, The	Golden	6
Little Red Hen, The (Second Cover)	Golden	6

Little Majorette	Elf	8410
Little Majorette	Elf	8605
Little Skater	Elf	8389
Little Skater	Elf	8610
Little Swimmers	Elf	8416
Little Swimmers	Elf	8633
Looking In And Other Poems	Elf	8568
Moving Day	Elf	588
My Truck Book	Elf	431
Nancy Plays Nurse	Elf	8726
Our Auto Trip	Elf	457
Our Auto Trip	Elf	8339
Parakeet Peter	Elf	490
Parakeet Peter	Elf	591
Parakeet Peter	Elf	8374
Peppermint, The Story Of A Kitten	TellTale	848
Pink Lemonade (And Other Peter Patter Rhymes)	Elf	8452
That Donkey	TellTale	2502
That Funny Hat	Elf	8314
We Love Grandpa	DingDong	225
We Love Grandpa	DingDong	DIN 4

Guenther, Annie

Duck Tales 'The Secret City Under The Sea'	Golden	102-57
Dumbo	Golden	104-59

Hanna-Barbera Productions, Inc.

Flintstones 'Everyone's Egg'	Wonder	927
Huckleberry Hound 'The Big Blooming Rosebush'	Wonder	944
Jetsons The Great Pizza Hunt, The	Wonder	790
Magilla Gorilla And The Super Kite	Wonder	707
Pebbles And Bamm-Bamm Find Things To Do	Wonder	919
Yogi Bear And The Baby Skunk	Wonder	921
Yogi Bear Mosquito Flying Days	Wonder	924
Yogi Bear Playtime In Jellystone Park	Wonder	926

Harris, Larry

Corey Baker Of Julia And His Show And Tell	TellTale	2506
Daktari 'Judi And The Kitten'	TellTale	2506
Gentle Ben And The Pesky Puppy	TellTale	2552
Lassie And The Fire Fighters	TellTale	2462
Lassie: The Busy Morning	TellTale	2484

Hartwell, Marjorie

Beaver Valley	TellTale	2553
Beaver Valley (Second Cover)	TellTale	2553
Bible Stories	Golden	174
Chicken Little	TellTale	2450
Fuzzy Pet, A	TellTale	2671
Little Pony, The	TellTale	806
Prrrtt	TellTale	2641
Water Babies	TellTale	2564

Harvey Cartoon Studios

Baby Huey	Wonder	787
Buzzy The Funny Crow	Wonder	821
Casper And Wendy	Wonder	805
Casper And Wendy Adventures	Wonder	855
Casper The Friendly Ghost In Ghostland	Wonder	850
Casper, The Friendly Ghost	Wonder	761
Herman And Katnip	Wonder	788
Little Audrey And The Moon Lady	Wonder	759

Hauge, Carl & Mary

Lazy Fox And Red Hen	TellTale	2485
Little Red Hen, The	Golden	438
Littlest Christmas Tree, The	Wonder	625
My Little Book Of Farm Animals	TellTale	2559
My Little Book Of Pets	TellTale	2401
Old Mac Donald Had A Farm	Golden	200-55
Old Mac Donald Had A Farm	Golden	200-65
Old Mac Donald Had A Farm	TellTale	2589
Peter Rabbit	TellTale	2493
Peter Rabbit And Reddy Fox	Wonder	611
Peter Cottontail And Reddy Fox	Wonder	843
Prickly Tale, A	TellTale	2508
Silver Chief	Wonder	650
Tuggy The Tugboat	Wonder	696
Very Best Of Friends, The	TellTale	2559
What Happened To Piggy?	Wonder	629
Wild Animal Babies	TellTale	2475-3

Heckler, William

ABC - A Tale Of A Sale	TellTale	2554
Thin Arnold	TellTale	2691

Heimdahl, Ralph

Bugs Bunny Keeps A Promise	TellTale	2572
Bugs Bunny's Big Invention	TellTale	928

Helweg, Hans

Animal Paintbook	Golden	A 4
Getting Ready For Roddy	TellTale	2530

Henderson, Doris & Marion

Party In Shariland	Golden	360
Trim The Christmas Tree	Golden	A 15
Trim The Christmas Tree	Golden	A 50

Herric, Pru

Princess And The Pea, The	TellTale	2610
What Can We Do With Blocks?	Wonder	833

Hess, Lowell

Aladdin	Golden	371
Ali Baba	Golden	323
Fairy Tales	Golden	5020
My Christmas Treasury	Golden	5003

Hicks, Russell

Winnie The Pooh And The Honey Tree	Golden	101-63
Winnie The Pooh And The Honey Tree	Golden	98267-01

Hockerman, Dennis

Giant Who Wanted

333

Lapadula, Tom

Daniel In The Lions' Den	Golden	311-62
Lord Is My Shepherd, The 'The Twenty-Third Psalm'	Golden	311-60

Le Grand

Are Dogs Better Than Cats?	Wonder	56
Boy Who Wanted To Be A Fish, The	Wonder	55

Leaf, Anne Sellers

Aesop's Fables	Elf	463
Aesop's Fables	Elf	1019
Aesop's Fables	Elf	8440
Aesop's Fables	Elf	8615
Emperor's New Clothes, The	Elf	8567
Gingerbread Man, The	Elf	8457
Gingerbread Man, The	Elf	8599
Goody: A Mother Cat Story	Elf	470
Goody: A Mother Cat Story	Elf	545
Goody: A Mother Cat Story	Elf	8310
House That Jack Built, The	Elf	8312
House That Jack Built, The	Elf	8681
Jack And Jill	Elf	1001
Jack And Jill	Elf	8395
Jack And Jill	Elf	8625
Jack And The Beanstalk	Elf	8372
Jack And The Beanstalk	Elf	8668
Little Boy Blue And Other Nursery Rhymes	Elf	8366
Little Boy Blue And Other Nursery Rhymes	Elf	555
Little Boy Blue And Other Nursery Rhymes	Elf	8711
Little Red Riding Hood	Elf	1037
Little Red Riding-Hood	Elf	8419
Little Red Riding-Hood	Elf	8646
Muggins Becomes A Hero	Elf	8448
Muggins Becomes A Hero	Elf	8702
Muggins Big Balloon	Elf	8447
Muggins Big Balloon	Elf	8701
Muggins Mouse	Elf	8444
Muggins Mouse	Elf	8673
Muggins Takes Off	Elf	8700
Old Mother Hubbard	Elf	1007
Old Mother Hubbard	Elf	8413
Old Mother Hubbard	Elf	8624
Princess And The Pea	Elf	8727
Rip Van Winkle	Elf	8383
Rip Van Winkle	Elf	8671

Leder, Dora

Jack And The Beanstalk	Golden	545
Jack And The Beanstalk	Golden	207-54
Mother Goose In The City	Golden	336*
My Little Golden Book About Cats	Golden	309-57

Lee, Manning De V

Bugle, A Puppy In Old Yorktown	Elf	8618
Elves And The Shoemaker, The	Elf	8315
Elves And The Shoemaker, The	Elf	8682
Little Lost Kitten: Story Of Williamsburg	Elf	544
Little Lost Kitten: Story Of Williamsburg	Elf	8600
Pocahontas, A Little Indian Girl Of Jamestown	Elf	575
Pocahontas, A Little Indian Girl Of Jamestown	Elf	8601
Story Of David, The	Elf	8725
Story Of Joseph, The	Elf	8724
Twenty-Third Psalm, The	Elf	8698

Leone, John

Maverick	Golden	354
Tales Of Wells Fargo	Golden	328

Leone, Sergio

All In A Day's Work	Wonder	807
Night Before Christmas, The	Wonder	858
Romper Room Exercise Book, The	Golden	527
Uncle Wiggily And His Friends	Wonder	766
Uncle Wiggily's Adventures	Wonder	765

Lerch, Steffie

Christmas Manger, The	Golden	176
Heidi: Child Of The Mountain	Wonder	532
Story Of Jesus, The	Golden	27
Surprise Doll, The	Wonder	519
We Like To Do Things	Golden	62

Lesko, Zillah

Gingerbread Man, The	TellTale	2596
Little Red Riding Hood	TellTale	2606
Mother Goose	TellTale	925
Night Before Christmas, The	TellTale	839
Night Before Christmas, The	TellTale	2517
Runaway Ginger	TellTale	897
Sunny, Honey, And Funny	TellTale	824

Lorencz, William

Beany Goes To Sea	Golden	537
Pebbles Flintstone ABCs	TellTale	2622
Scooby Doo And The Pirate Treasure	Golden	126*
Touché Turtle	Golden	474
Tweety Plays Catch The Puddy Cat	Golden	141*
Wally Gator	Golden	502

Lowe, Richard

Scooby-Doo And The Case Of The Counterfeit Money	Elf	
Scooby-Doo And The Haunted Doghouse	Elf	
Scooby-Doo And The Headless Horseman	Elf	

MacLaughlin, Don

Bugs Bunny Gets A Job	Golden	136
Donald Duck Full Speed Ahead	TellTale	900
Tom And Jerry	Golden	117
Tom And Jerry	Golden	561
Tom And Jerry Meet Little Quack	Golden	181
Tom And Jerry Meet Little Quack	Golden	311
Ugly Duckling, The	Golden	D 22

Malvern, Corinne

5 Pennies To Spend	Golden	238
All Aboard	Golden	152
Christmas Carols	Golden	26
Christmas Carols (Second Cover)	Golden	26
Christmas Carols	Golden	595
Christmas Carols (Second Cover)	Golden	595
Counting Rhymes	Golden	257
Day At The Beach, A	Golden	110
Doctor Dan The Bandage Man	Golden	111
Doctor Dan, The Bandage Man	Golden	295
Doctor Dan, The Bandage Man (Without Band-Aids)	Golden	295
Doctor Dan, The Bandage Man	Golden	312-07
Frosty The Snowman	Golden	142
Fun With Decals	Golden	139
Happy Family, The	Golden	216
Heidi	Golden	192
Heidi	Golden	258
Heidi	Golden	470
How Big	Golden	83
How Big (Second Cover)	Golden	83
Jerry At School	Golden	94
Jerry At School (Puzzle Edition)	Golden	94
Little Golden Book Of Hymns, The	Golden	34
Little Golden Book Of Hymns, The	Golden	392
Little Golden Book Of Poetry, The	Golden	38
Little Golden Book Of Singing Games, The	Golden	40
Night Before Christmas, The	Golden	20
Night Before Christmas, The (Second Cover)	Golden	20
Night Before Christmas, The	Golden	450*
Nurse Nancy	Golden	154
Nurse Nancy	Golden	346
Nurse Nancy	Golden	473
Nursery Rhymes	Golden	529
Nursery Songs	Golden	7
Nursery Songs (Second Cover)	Golden	7
Off To School	Golden	5015
Open Up My Suitcase	Golden	207
Rainy Day Play Book, The	Golden	133
Robert And His New Friends	Golden	124
Surprise For Sally	Golden	84
Susie's New Stove	Golden	85
Tex And His Toys	Golden	129
Uncle Mistletoe	Golden	175
Up In The Attic	Golden	53
When I Grow Up	Golden	96
When I Grow Up (Puzzle Edition)	Golden	96
When You Were A Baby	Golden	70
When You Were A Baby	Golden	435

Marsia, Robert

Animals Build A House, The	Wonder	817
Donkey Who Wanted To Be Wise, The	Wonder	771

Martin, Judy & Barry

Bunny's Magic Tricks	Golden	441
Hansel & Gretel	Golden	A 41

Masha

Bedtime Stories		
Wonder		507
Nursery Tales	Golden	14
Three Little Kittens	Golden	1
Three Little Kittens	Golden	225
Three Little Kittens	Golden	288
Three Little Kittens	Golden	381
Toys	Golden	22

Mastri, Fiore & Jackie

Wonderful Plane Ride, The	Elf	433
Wonderful Train Ride, The	Elf	427

Mateu, Franc

Alice In Wonderland	Golden	105-77
Rescuers Down Under, The	Golden	105-70
Welcome To Little Golden Book Land	Golden	GBL370

Mathieu, Joe

Cookie Monster And The Cookie Tree	Golden	159*
Cookie Monster And The Cookie Tree	Golden	109-52
Ernie's Work Of Art	Golden	109- 5

Mattinson, Sylvia & Burne

Pixi, Dixi & Mr. Jinx	Golden	454
Yogi-A Christmas Visit	Golden	433

McCue Karsten, Lisa

Timothy Tiger's Terrible Toothache	Golden	209-60
Arthur's Good Manners	Golden	305-58
Puppy On The Farm	Golden	304-52
Ugly Duckling, The	Golden	207-72

McGary, Norman

Bugs Bunny Hangs Around	TellTale	2410
Bugs Bunny In Something Fishy	TellTale	2543
Donald Duck And The Christmas Carol	Golden	D 84
Scamp	Golden	D 63
Woody Woodpecker, Steps To Drawing	Golden	372

McKean, Emma C.

Pussy Willow	TellTale	873
Snoozey	TellTale	853
Snoozey	TellTale	2538
Fluffy And Tuffy The Twin Ducklings	TellTale	872

McKimson, Thomas J.

Bugs Bunny 'Party Pest'	Golden	111-69
Bugs Bunny And The Indians	Golden	430

McKinley, Clare

Amos Learns To Talk: The Story Of A Little Duck	Elf	446

Miyake, Yoshi

Rudolph The Red-Nosed Reindeer	TellTale	2517-2
Seven Wishes, The	TellTale	2606

Mode, Nathalee

Buffy And The New Girl	TellTale	2526
Parade For Chatty Baby, A	TellTale	2562

Mones, Isidre

Mickey Mouse 'Those Were The Days'	Golden	100-61
Tootle And Katy Caboose 'A Special Treasure'	Golden	GBL374

Moore, Robert J.

Donald Duck's Christmas Tree	Golden	D 39
Mickey Mouse Goes Christmas Shopping	Golden	D 33
Peter Pan And The Pirates	Golden	D 25
Peter Pan And The Pirates	Golden	D 73
Terry Bears Win The Cub Scout Badge, The	Treasure	903

Moores, Dick

Donald Duck And The New Bird House	TellTale	2516
Goofy And The Tiger Hunt	TellTale	2552

Moyers, William

Horse For Johnny, A	Wonder	754
Monkey See, Monkey Do	Wonder	521
Stacks Of Caps	Wonder	722

Murdocca, Sal

Grover's Own Alphabet	Golden	108-46
Grover's Own Alphabet	TellTale	2402-6

Murray, Marjorie

Child's Ten Commandments, A	TellTale	2624
Tiny Tots 1-2-3	TellTale	2615

Myers, Bernice & Lou

Billy And His Steam Roller	Wonder	557
Brave Little Steam Shovel, The	Wonder	555
Bunny Button	TellTale	2526
Bunny Button	TellTale	923
Christmas Favorites	Wonder	869
It's A Secret	Wonder	540
Picnic At The Zoo	Wonder	613
Puss-In-Boots	Elf	507
Puss-In-Boots	Elf	513
Puss-In-Boots	Elf	8356
Puss-In-Boots	Elf	8573
Sailing On A Very Fine Day	Elf	497
Trumpet	TellTale	931
Wonder Book Of Christmas, The	Wonder	575

Myers, Jack & Louise

Big Whistle, The	TellTale	2522
Ho-Hum	TellTale	2553
Jasper Giraffe	TellTale	898
Lambikin, The	TellTale	2617
Oh, Look!	TellTale	2672

Peter Rabbit	TellTale	2539
Playmate For Peter	TellTale	803
Teena And The Magic Pot	TellTale	2423
Three Little Pigs, The	TellTale	2547

Nagel, Stina

Beware Of The Dog	TellTale	2553
Big Bark, The	TellTale	2510
I Walk To The Park	TellTale	2616
In, On, Under, And Through	TellTale	2666
Magic Friend Maker, The	Golden	137*
Two Stories About Wendy	TellTale	2659
Whose Baby Is That?	TellTale	2553

Nankivel, Claudine

Barbie, The Baby Sitter	Wonder	849
Jerry And Dr. Dave	TellTale	2601
Romper Room Laughing Book	Wonder	808

Nebbe, William

Bunny Tales	Elf	8406
Sergeant Preston And The Yukon King	Elf	500
Seven Wonderful Cats, The	Elf	8411
Baby Chipmunk, The	DingDong	208
Mr. Meyer's Cow	DingDong	DIN 2
Three Billy Goats Gruff, The	Elf	8368
Big Coal Truck, The	DingDong	203
Bunny Tales	Elf	574
Bunny Tales	Elf	8641
Cinderella	Elf	551
Cinderella	Elf	8417
Cinderella	Elf	8644
Mr. Meyer's Cow	DingDong	220
Sergeant Preston And Rex	Elf	569
Seven Wonderful Cats, The	Elf	548
Seven Wonderful Cats, The	Elf	8607
Slowpoke, The Lazy Little Puppy	Elf	582
Snoopy, The Nosey Little Puppy	Elf	509
Three Billy Goats Gruff, The	Elf	583
Your Friend, The Policeman	DingDong	200

Neely, Jan

Donnie And Marie, The Top Secret Project	Golden	160*
New Friends For The Saggy Baggy Elephant	Golden	131*
Walton's The 'Elizabeth And The Magic Lamp'	TellTale	2579

Newell, Crosby

Big Joke, The	Wonder	628
Helpful Friends, The	Wonder	631
I Love You	Wonder	657
Land Of Peek-A-Boo, The	Treasure	901
Let's Go Fishing	Wonder	764
Make-Believe Book, The	Wonder	634
Moppets' Surprise Party, The	Wonder	794
Really Truly Treasure Hunt, The	Wonder	793
Really Truly Treasure Hunt, The	Treasure	891
Surprise Party, The	Wonder	620
Tom Terrific's Greatest Adventure	Wonder	735

What Are You Looking At?	Wonder	792
What Are You Looking At?	Treasure	895

Nez, John

Baby Brown Bear's Big Bellyache	Golden	304-64
Look For Boats	TellTale	2473-46
Mother Goose Rhymes	TellTale	2464-36
My First Book Of Planets	Golden	308-56
Sesame Street ABC	TellTale	2471-43
Tortoise And The Hare, The	Golden	207-56

Nicklaus, Carol

Mrs. Brisby And The Magic Stone	Golden	110-38
Puppy Love	Golden	109-46

Nielsen, Jon

Camping Trip With The Range Rider, A	Wonder	681
Wild Bill Hickok	Wonder	649

Nugent, Alys

ABC	TellTale	2658
Alphabet Rhymes	TellTale	2430

O'Brien, John

Little Golden Book Of Jokes & Riddles	Golden	211-45
Snow White	Golden	D 66
Snow White And The Seven Dwarfs	Golden	D 4

O'Sullivan, Tom

Big Enough Helper, The	Golden	152*
Cat Who Stamped His Feet	Golden	806
Corkey's Hic-Cup	Golden	503
Hiding Place, The	TellTale	2553
I Live In The City ABC	TellTale	2554
Pals	TellTale	2544
Who Comes To Your House	Golden	575

Obligado, Lilian

Animals And Their Babies	Golden	A 29
Charlie	Golden	587
Charlie	Golden	302-44
Four Puppies	Golden	405
Golden Egg Book, The	Golden	456
Golden Egg Book, The	Golden	307-69
I Like To Live In The City	Golden	593
If I Had A Dog	Golden	205-40
Little Black Puppy	Golden	804
Little Cottontail	Golden	414
Little Cottontail	Golden	304-73
New Puppy, The	Golden	370
New Puppy, The	Golden	203-55
Pussycat Tiger	Golden	362
Reading, Writing & Spelling Stamps	Golden	A 24
Willie Found A Wallet	Golden	205-56
Wait-For-Me-Kitten	Golden	463

Oechsli, Kelly

Great Fort, The	TellTale	2564
Peaky Beaky	Elf	8598
Waldo, The Jumping Dragon	TellTale	2688

Opitz, Marge

I Decided	DingDong	204
Ugly Duckling, The	Elf	8327
Ugly Duckling, The	Elf	8590
What Happened To George?	Elf	1006
What Happened To George?	Elf	8409

Oriolo, Joe

Felix On Television	Treasure	904
Felix On Television	Wonder	716
Surprise For Felix, A	Wonder	728

Orville, Oliver

And So To Bed	TellTale	2462-46
Honey Bear Finds A Friend	TellTale	2466-46
Stuck In The Tub	TellTale	2463-44

Osborne, Richard N.

Cousin Matilda And The Foolish Wolf	TellTale	2530
Little Boy In The Forest, The	TellTale	2553

Ostapczuk, Phil

Hong Kong Phooey And The Bird Nest Snatchers	Elf
Hong Kong Phooey And The Fire Engine Mystery	Elf

Ozone, Lucy

Pockets	TellTale	2616
Robin Family, The	DingDong	215
Surprise!	Elf	562
Surprise!	Elf	8384

Paflin, Roberta

Counting Rhymes	Golden	12
Good Night 'A Flocked Book'	TellTale	955
This Little Piggy Counting Rhymes	Golden	12
Uncle Remus	Golden	D 6

Parsons, Virginia

Fly High	Golden	597
Sam The Firehouse Cat	Golden	580
Wonder Book Of Counting Rhymes, The	Wonder	682

Peet, Bill

Golliath II	Golden	D 83

Peller, Jackie

Animal Crackers	TellTale	837
Animal Jingles	TellTale	837
Lucky Four Leaf Clover	TellTale	893
Three Little Pigs And Little Red Riding Hood	Wonder	609
Treasure Book Of Favorite Nursery Tales	Treasure	856
Wonder Book Of Favorite Nursery Tales, The	Wonder	730

Pfloog, Jan

Animals On The Farm	Golden	573
Sly Little Bear	Golden	411
Tiny-Tawny Kitten, The	Golden	590

Phillips, Katherine L.

Mr. Punnymoon's Train	Elf	449
Mr. Punnymoon's Train	Elf	557

Hop, Little Kangaroo	Golden	558
Kitten's Surprise	Golden	107
Kitty On The Farm	Golden	200-57
Little Golden Mother Goose, The	Golden	390
Little Golden Mother Goose, The	Golden	472
Little Lost Kitten	Golden	302-56
More Mother Goose Rhymes	Golden	317
Mother Goose	Golden	283
Mother Goose	Golden	5007
Mother Goose Rhymes	Golden	5016
Name For Kitty, A	Golden	55
Our Puppy	Golden	56
Our Puppy	Golden	292
Ten Little Animals	Golden	451
Three Bears, The	Golden	47
Three Bears, The (Second Cover)	Golden	47
What's Next Elephant?	Golden	206-61
White Bunny And His Magic Nose, The	Golden	305
Wild Animal Babies	Golden	332
Wild Animals	Golden	394
Wild Animals	Golden	499

Rooks, Dale & Sally

Three Little Bunnies	Elf	443
Three Little Bunnies	Elf	589
Three Little Bunnies	Elf	8388
Three Little Puppies	Elf	447
Three Little Puppies	Elf	598
Three Little Puppies	Elf	8363
Three Little Puppies	Elf	8745

Rosenberg, Amye

Biggest, Most Beautiful Christmas Tree, The	Golden	459- 8
I Don't Want To Go	Golden	208-59
Lily Pig's Book Of Colors	Golden	205-58
Polly's Pet	Golden	302-55

Ruhman, Ruth

Gandy Goose	Wonder	695
Jingle Dingle Book, The	Wonder	675
My Little Counting Book	TellTale	2407-3
Slowpoke At The Circus	TellTale	2457
When I Go To Bed	TellTale	2542

Russell, H. R.

Lion King, The	Golden	107-93
Lion King, The 'No Worries'	Golden	107-97

Ruth, Rod

Feelings From A To Z	Golden	200-6
Jumpty Dumpty And Other Nursery Rhymes	TellTale	2610
Marvelous Monster	TellTale	2632
My Little Book Of Dinosaurs	TellTale	2482
Whales	Golden	171*

Rutherford, Bonnie & Bill

Goby Goat And The Birthday Gift	TellTale	2595
House My Grandpa Built	TellTale	2530

How Can We Get To The Zoo?	TellTale	2660
I Play In The Snow	TellTale	2510
Magic Clothes Basket, The	TellTale	2544
Once I Had A Monster	TellTale	2512
Tuffer	TellTale	2672
Under The Saskatoon Tree	TellTale	2543

Sagendorf, Bud

House That Popeye Built, The	Wonder	750
Popeye	Wonder	667
Popeye	Treasure	888
Popeye Goes On A Picnic	Wonder	697
Popeye's Big Surprise	Wonder	791

Sampson, Katherine

Doctor Dan At The Circus	Golden	399
Kobo The Koala Bear	TellTale	2521
Tubsy And The Picnic Tree (Ideal Doll)	TellTale	2552
Why Do You Love Me?	TellTale	2428

Sanderson, Ruth

One Of The Family	Golden	208-42
Owl And The Pussy Cat	Golden	300-41
Store Bought Doll, The	Golden	204-54
When You Were A Baby	Golden	306-41

Santis, George De

Gumby And Gumby's Pal Pokey To The Rescue	TellTale	2552
Gumby And Gumby's Pal Pokey	TellTale	2506
Hoppity Hooper Vs Skippity Snooper	TellTale	2552
Littlest Snowman, The	Wonder	720

Santoro, Christopher

Cat That Climbed The Christmas Tree, The	Golden	458-03
Lion's Mixed-Up Friends	Golden	304-62

Santos, George

Black Beauty	Wonder	595
Loopy De Loop Goes West	Golden	417

Sari

Gingerbread Man, The	TellTale	2504
Three Bears, The	TellTale	2512
Why The Bear Has A Short Tail	Wonder	508
Yellow Cat, The	TellTale	911
Yippie Kiyi And Whoa Boy	TellTale	2514

Satterfield, Charles

Bozo The Clown	Golden	446
Huckleberry Hounds And The Christmas Sleigh	Golden	403
Mouseketeers Tryout Time, The	TellTale	2649

Saviozzi, Adriana Mazza

Farm Stamps	Golden	A 19
Four Little Kittens	Golden	322
Four Little Kittens	Golden	530
Ginger Paper Doll	Golden	A 14
Ginger Paper Doll	Golden	A 32
Mike And Melissa (Paper Dolls)	Golden	A 31
Nursery Songs	Golden	348

Let's Play Nurse And Doctor	Treasure	863
Magic Next Door, The	Golden	106*
Pet In The Jar, The	Golden	801
Somebody Forgot	TellTale	963
This Room Is Mine	TellTale	2643
Timothy Tinker 'The Wonderful Oilcan'	TellTale	2522
Town Mouse And The Country Mouse, The	TellTale	2561

Steadman, Barbara

Bettina The Ballerina	Golden	211-69
Rainbow Circus Comes To Town	TellTale	2474-44

Steel, John

Roy Rogers' Surprise For Donnie	TellTale	943
Zorro	Golden	D 68
Zorro (Yellow Background)	Golden	D 68

Steigerwald, Beverly

Quiet Quincy And The Delivery Truck	TellTale	2615

Steiner, Charlotte

Copycat Colt, The	Wonder	545
Five Little Finger Playmates	Wonder	522
Frisky, The Black Colt	Wonder	699
Little John Little	Wonder	558
Little Train That Saved The Day, The	Wonder	571
Surprise For Mrs. Bunny, A	Wonder	601

Stone, David K.

Jumpy, Humpy, Fuzzy, Buzzy, Animal Book, The	TellTale	2488
Manuel's Cat	TellTale	2521
My Little Book Of Dogs	TellTale	2476-93

Storms, Robert

Have You Seen A Giraffe Hat?	TellTale	2535
Pebbles Flintstone 'Daddy's Little Helper'	TellTale	2657
Rubbles And Bamm-Bamm, The 'Problem Present'	TellTale	2622

Strobe, Dorothy

Sleeping Beauty & The Fairies	Golden	D 71
Bugs Bunny At The Easter Party	Golden	183
Bugs Bunny Gets A Job	Golden	136
Donald Duck On Tom Sawyer's Island	TellTale	2409
Pebbles Flintstone ABCs	TellTale	2622
Peter Potamus 'Meets The Black Knight'	TellTale	2506
Pluto	TellTale	2509
Swiss Family Duck	TellTale	2509
Uncle Scrooge 'The Winner'	TellTale	2552

Sullivan, Pat

Felix The Cat	Wonder	665
Felix The Cat	Treasure	872

Super, Terri

First Airplane Ride, A	Golden	310-57

Flying Is Fun	Golden	310-53
Frosty The Snowman	Golden	451-11
Grandma And Grandpa Smith	Golden	305-55
Littlest Christmas Elf, The	Golden	459-00
Patsy The Pussycat	TellTale	2475-4
Ten Items Or Less	Golden	203-54

Suzanne

Franky, The Fuzzy Goat	TellTale	820
Fuzzy Wuzzy Puppy, The	TellTale	915
House That Jack Built, The	TellTale	2480
Lazy Fox And Red Hen	TellTale	2603
Little Black Sambo	TellTale	812
Teddy's Surprise	TellTale	809
Three Bears, The	TellTale	2512
Too Many Kittens	TellTale	2525

Svendsen, Julius

Mickey Mouse And The Missing Mouseketeers	Golden	D 57
Mickey Mouse Club Stamp Book	Golden	A 10
Mickey Mouse Flies The Christmas Mail	Golden	D 53
Seven Dwarfs Find A House, The	Golden	D 35
Seven Dwarfs Find A House, The	Golden	D 67
Sleeping Beauty	Golden	D 61
Sleeping Beauty	Golden	A 33
Sleeping Beauty & The Fairies	Golden	D 71

Swanson, Maggie

Big Bird Visits Navajo Country	Golden	108-68
Big Bird's Day On The Farm	Golden	107-61
Curious Little Kitten Around The House	Golden	206-57
"Me Cookie"	Golden	109-69
Rabbit's Adventure, The	Golden	164*
Sesame Street 'Mother Goose Rhymes'	Golden	108-69
Up And Down Book Staring Ernie And Bert, The	TellTale	2402-7

Szekeres, Cyndy

Tale Of Peter Rabbit, The	Golden	307-11
Whispering Rabbit, The	Golden	313-03

Szepelak, Helen

Busy Book, The (Rhymes & Riddles & Things To Do)	Elf	462
Busy Book, The (Rhymes & Riddles & Things To Do)	Elf	1038
Busy Book, The (Rhymes & Riddles & Things To Do)	Elf	8402
Busy Book, The (Rhymes & Riddles & Things To Do)	Elf	8623
Funland Party	Elf	478
Popcorn Party	Elf	468
Popcorn Party	Elf	8303
Popcorn Party	Elf	8743
Sleepy-Time Rhymes	Elf	8346
Sleepy-Time Rhymes	Elf	8664

Tallarico, Tony

Astronaut And The Flying Bus	Wonder	853

Puff The Magic Dragon	Wonder	851
Soupy Sales And The Talking Turtle	Wonder	860

Tamburine, Jean

Billy Whiskers' Twins	Elf	538
Billy Whiskers' Twins	Elf	8333
Five Busy Bears, The	Elf	498
Five Busy Bears, The	Elf	8404
Five Busy Bears, The	Elf	8629
Fraidy Cat	Elf	8319
Goat That Went To School, The	Elf	469
Goat That Went To School, The	Elf	594
Goat That Went To School, The	Elf	8386
Goat That Went To School, The	Elf	8594
Help Mr. Willy Nilly	Treasure	886
Outdoor Fun	Elf	479
Pillowtime Tales	Elf	552
Pillowtime Tales	Elf	8338
Pillowtime Tales	Elf	8740
Pudgy The Little Bear	Elf	8441
Pudgy The Little Bear	Elf	8674
Scamper	Elf	8326
Scamper	Elf	8716
Three Little Pigs And Little Red Riding Hood	Wonder	609
Treasure Book Of Favorite Nursery Tales	Treasure	856
Wonder Book Of Favorite Nursery Tales, The	Wonder	730

Tedder, Elizabeth

Billy Bunnyscoot - The Lost Bunny	TellTale	888
Polka Dot Tots	TellTale	864
Poor Kitty	TellTale	850

Tellingen, Ruth Van

Bertram And The Ticklish Rhinoceros	Elf	430
Daddy's Birthday Cakes	DingDong	207
Grandmother Is Coming	DingDong	216
Growing Things	DingDong	210
Suitcase With A Surprise, A	DingDong	202

Tenggren, Gustaf

Bedtime Stories	Golden	2
Bedtime Stories	Golden	239
Bedtime Stories	Golden	364
Bedtime Stories	Golden	538
Bedtime Stories (Second Cover)	Golden	538
Big Brown Bear, The	Golden	89
Big Brown Bear, The	Golden	335
Five Bedtime Stories	Golden	5002
Giant With Three Golden Hairs, The	Golden	219
Golden Goose, The	Golden	200
Golden Goose, The	Golden	487
Jack And The Beanstalk	Golden	179
Jack And The Beanstalk	Golden	281
Jack And The Beanstalk	Golden	420

Kittens	Golden	5013
Lion's Paw, The	Golden	367
Little Black Sambo (42 page)	Golden	57
Little Black Sambo (28 page)	Golden	57
Little Black Sambo (24 page)	Golden	57
Little Trapper, The	Golden	79
Lively Little Rabbit, The	Golden	15
Lively Little Rabbit, The (Second Edition)	Golden	15
Lively Little Rabbit, The	Golden	551
Poky Little Puppy, The	Golden	8
Poky Little Puppy, The	Golden	271
Poky Little Puppy, The	Golden	506
Saggy Baggy Elephant, The	Golden	36
Saggy Baggy Elephant, The	Golden	385
Shy Little Kitten, The	Golden	23
Shy Little Kitten, The	Golden	248
Shy Little Kitten, The	Golden	494
Snow White And Rose Red	Golden	228
Tawny Scrawny Lion	Golden	138
Thumbelina	Golden	153
Thumbelina	Golden	514
Thumbelina	Golden	300-66
Topsy Turvy Circus	Golden	161
Where Is The Poky Little Puppy	Golden	467

Thomas, Stephen

Pony Who Couldn't Say Neigh, The	TellTale	2543

Thompson, Riley

Woody Woodpecker	Golden	145
Woody Woodpecker	Golden	330
Woody Woodpecker's 'Peck Of Trouble'	TellTale	831

Tierney, Tom

Barbie 'The Big Splash'	Golden	107-86
Barbie On Skates	TellTale	2450-01

Timmins, William

Adventures Of Robin Hood And His Merry Men	Elf	532
Cowboys	Elf	1004
Cowboys	Elf	8341
Cowboys	Elf	8666
Davy Crockett: American Hero	Elf	523
Emmett Kelly In Willie The Clown	Elf	573
Here Comes The Band	DingDong	224
Here Comes The Band	DingDong	DIN 5
Little Cub Scout	Elf	8665
Pony Express	Elf	554
Pony Express	Elf	8344
Super Circus	Elf	503
Wild Bill Hickok And Deputy Marshall Joey	Elf	496
Wild Bill Hickok And The Indians	Elf	570

Totten, Bob

Bugs Bunny's Carrot Machine	Golden	127*
Bugs Bunny, Too Many Carrots	Golden	145*
Cars	Golden	566
Donald Duck, Lost And Found	Golden	D 86
H.R. Pufnstuf	TellTale	2624

Huckleberry Hound And His Friends	Golden	406
Lone Ranger And The Ghost Horse, The	TellTale	2561
Mickey Mouse And The Missing Mouseketeers	Golden	D 57
Peter Pan And The Tiger	TellTale	2616
Porky Pig And Bugs Bunny - Just Like Magic	Golden	146*
Road Runner, The 'A Very Scary Lesson'	Golden	122*
Scooby Doo At The Zoo	TellTale	2570
Wacky Witch	Golden	416
Wacky Witch: The Royal Birthday	TellTale	2546
Winnie-The-Pooh And The Honey Tree	Golden	D116

Turner, Don

Remarkably Strong Pippy Longstocking, The	Golden	123*
Wizard Of Oz, The	Golden	119*

Usher, Peggy

Little Bitty Raindrop	TellTale	875
Little Bitty Raindrop (Second Cover)	TellTale	875

Ushler, John

Gene Autry Goes To The Circus	TellTale	2566
Mickey Mouse And His Space Ship	Golden	D 29
Mickey Mouse And His Space Ship	Golden	D108

Varga, Judith

My Book About God	Wonder	644
Who Lives Here?	Wonder	669

Vaughan, Eillen Fox

Benny The Bus	TellTale	846
Mother Goose	TellTale	825
Whoop-Ee, Hunkydory!	TellTale	884

Vaughn, Frank

Goodbye Tonsils	Golden	327
Tom Corbett's Wonder Book Of Space	Wonder	603
Tom Corbett: A Trip To The Moon	Wonder	713
Wonder Book Of Cowboy's, The	Wonder	640

Vlasaty, J.L.

Wild Animals	Elf	454
Wild Animals	Elf	510
Wild Animals	Elf	8348

Vogel, Ilse-Margaret

1,2,3, Juggle With Me!	Golden	594
Animal Daddies And My Daddy	Golden	576
Bear In The Boat, The	Golden	397
Daisy Dog Wake Up Book	Golden	102*
My Little Dinosaur	Golden	571
When I Grow Up	Golden	578

Wallace, Ivy L.

Jo Jo	Elf	8450
Jo Jo	Elf	8703

Wallace, Lucille

Mother Goose	TellTale	2511
Tom Thumb	Elf	8323
Tom Thumb	Elf	8684
Visit To The Dentist, A	Wonder	732

Walters, Audry

Someplace For Sparky	TellTale	2659

Walz, Richard

Busy Machines	TellTale	2473-42
Emperor's New Clothes, The	Golden	207-66
Jack And The Beanstalk	Golden	207-67
Jack And The Beanstalk	TellTale	2461-51
Johnny Go Round	TellTale	2525
Pied Piper, The	Golden	300-57
Saggy Baggy Elephant No Place For Me	Golden	GBL373
Snoring Monster, The	Golden	208-55

Webbe, Elizabeth

Baby Jesus, The	Elf	8556
Bible Stories: Old Testament	Elf	491
Bible Stories: Old Testament	Elf	8613
Children That Lived In A Shoe, The	Elf	453
Children That Lived In A Shoe, The	Elf	1024
Children That Lived In A Shoe, The	Elf	8391
Children That Lived In A Shoe, The	Elf	8616
Enchanted Egg, The	Elf	577
Enchanted Egg, The	Elf	8407
Enchanted Egg, The	Elf	8640
Forest Babies	Elf	435
Forest Babies	Elf	546
Forest Babies	Elf	8328
Forest Babies	Elf	8730
Growing Up	Elf	560
Growing Up	Elf	8397
Growing Up	Elf	8634
Johnny And The Birds	Elf	439
Johnny And The Birds	Elf	1008
Johnny And The Birds	Elf	8377
Johnny And The Birds	Elf	8704
Kitten Twins, The	Elf	1014
Kitten Twins, The	Elf	8422
Kitten Twins, The	Elf	8637
Kitten Twins, The	Elf	8722
Little Mailman Of Bayberry Lane, The	Elf	458
Little Mailman Of Bayberry Lane, The	Elf	590
Little Mailman Of Bayberry Lane, The	Elf	8361
Little Mailman Of Bayberry Lane, The	Elf	8729
Magic Wagon, The	DingDong	222
Magic Wagon, The	DingDong	DIN 6
Muggsy, The Make-Believe Puppy	Elf	537
My Flower Book	Elf	8382
My Flower Book	Elf	8679
Noah's Ark	Elf	461
Noah's Ark	Elf	1020

Master Index

1 Is Red	TELLTALE	Animal Daddies And My Daddy	LGB	Baby Moses	TELLTALE
1, 2, 3, Juggle With Me!	LGB	Animal Dictionary	LGB	Baby Raccoon	WONDER
10 Rabbits	WONDER	Animal Friends	LGB	Baby Sister	LGB
101 Dalmations	LGB	Animal Gym, The	LGB	Baby Sister	ELF
12 Days Of Christmas, The	LGB	Animal Jingles	TELLTALE	Baby Susan's Chicken	WONDER
5 Pennies To Spend	LGB	Animal Orchestra	LGB	Baby's Birthday	LGB
ABC	TELLTALE	Animal Paintbook	LGB	Baby's Book	LGB
ABC Book	ELF	Animal Quiz	LGB	Baby's Christmas	LGB
ABC- A Tale Of A Sale	TELLTALE	Animal Quiz Book	LGB	Baby's Day	TREASURE
Abc And Counting Book	WONDER	Animal Show, The	ELF	Baby's Day	WONDER
Abc Around The House	LGB	Animal Stamps	LGB	Baby's Day Out	LGB
Abc Is For Christmas	LGB	Animal Stories	LGB	Baby's First Book	LGB
Abc Rhymes	LGB	Animal Stories	ELF	Baby's First Book	WONDER
Adventures Of Goat	LGB	Animal Train	TELLTALE	Baby's First Book	TELLTALE
Adventures Of Lassie, The	LGB	Animal's Vacation	WONDER	Baby's First Christmas	LGB
Adventures Of Robin Hood And His Merry Men	ELF	Animals And Their Babies	LGB	Baby's First Christmas	WONDER
Aesop's Fables	ELF	Animals Build A House, The	WONDER	Baby's House	LGB
Aesop's Fables	WONDER	Animals' Christmas Eve, The	LGB	Baby's Mother Goose	LGB
Airplanes	LGB	Animals In Mother Goose	TELLTALE	Bambi	LGB
Aladdin	LGB	Animals Of Farmer Jones, The	LGB	Bambi	TELLTALE
Albert's Stencil Zoo	LGB	Animals On The Farm	LGB	Bambi - Friends Of The Forest	LGB
Ali Baba	LGB	Animals' Party, The	WONDER	Bambi's Children	WONDER
Alice In Wonderland	ELF	Animals' Abc	LGB	Bamm-Bamm	LGB
Alice In Wonderland	WONDER	Animals' Merry Christmas, The	LGB	Barbie	LGB
Alice In Wonderland	LGB	Animals' Playground, The	WONDER	Barbie 'A Picinic Surprise'	LGB
Alice In Wonderland Finds The Garden Of Live Flowers	LGB	Annie Oakley	LGB	Barbie 'Soccer Coach'	LGB
Alice In Wonderland Meets The White Rabbit	LGB	Annie Oakley Sharpshooter	LGB	Barbie 'The Big Splash'	LGB
All Aboard	LGB	Are Dogs Better Than Cats?	WONDER	Barbie And Skipper Go Camping	TELLTALE
All In A Day's Work	WONDER	Aren't You Glad	LGB	Barbie On Skates	TELLTALE
All My Chickens	LGB	Aristocats 'A Counting Book,' The	TELLTALE	Barbie,The Baby Sitter	WONDER
Alonzo Purr The Seagoing Cat	TELLTALE	Aristocats, The	LGB	Barker The Puppy	LGB
Alphabet From A-Z, The	LGB	Around The World Cutout Book	WONDER	Barney 'Sharing Is Caring'	LGB
Alphabet Rhymes	TELLTALE	Arthur's Good Manners	LGB	Bartholomew The Beaver	ELF
Alphabet Walks	ELF	Astronut And The Flying Bus	WONDER	Beach Day	LGB
Alvin's Daydream	LGB	Babar And Father Christmas	WONDER	Beany And Cecil Captured For The Zoo	TELLTALE
Alvin's Lost Voice	WONDER	Babar The King	WONDER	Beany And His Magic Set	TELLTALE
Amanda's First Day Of School	LGB	Babes In Toyland	LGB	Beany Goes To Sea	LGB
Amos Learns To Talk: The Story Of A Little Duck	ELF	Baby Animal Friends	WONDER	Bear Country	TELLTALE
Amy's Long Night	TELLTALE	Baby Animals	LGB	Bear In The Boat, The	LGB
And So To Bed	TELLTALE	Baby Brown Bear's Big Bellyache	LGB	Bear's Surprise Party	EAGER READ
Andy	TELLTALE	Baby Bunny, The	WONDER	Bears' New Baby, The	LGB
Andy And Betsy At The Circus	TELLTALE	Baby Chipmunk, The	DINGDONG	Beauty And The Beast	LGB
Angel Child	ELF	Baby Dear	LGB	Beauty And The Beast	TELLTALE
Animal Abc	TELLTALE	Baby Elephant, The	WONDER	Beauty And The Beast 'The Teapot's Tale'	LGB
Animal Abc Book	ELF	Baby Farm Animals	LGB	Beaver Valley	TELLTALE
Animal Alphabet	LGB	Baby Fozzie Visits The Doctor	LGB	Bedknobs & Broomsticks	LGB
Animal Babies	LGB	Baby Goes Around The Block	TELLTALE	Bedknobs And Broomsticks - A Visit To Naboombu	TELLTALE
Animal Counting Book	LGB	Baby Huey	WONDER	Bedtime Book, The	TELLTALE
Animal Crackers	TELLTALE	Baby Jesus Stamps	LGB	Bedtime Stories	ELF
		Baby Jesus, The	ELF	Bedtime Stories	LGB
		Baby Listens	LGB		
		Baby Looks	LGB		

Busy Saturday Word Book	TELLTALE	'The Big Cheese Caper'	LGB	Copycat Colt, The	WONDER
Busy Timmy	LGB	Chip, Chip	LGB	Corey Baker Of Julia And His Show And Tell	TELLTALE
But, You're A Duck	LGB	Chipmunks' Abc	LGB	Corkey's Hiccups	LGB
Butterfly 'A Story Of Magic'	TELLTALE	Chipmunk's Merry Christmas, The	LGB	Corky	LGB
Buzzy Beaver	TELLTALE	Chitter Chatter	TELLTALE	Count All The Way To Sesame Street	LGB
Buzzy The Funny Crow	WONDER	ChittyChitty BangBang	LGB	Count The Baby Animals	WONDER
Cabbage Patch Kids 'Xavier's Birthday Surprise!'	LGB	Choo Choo Train, The	WONDER	Count To Ten	LGB
Calling All Cowboys	WONDER	Choo-Choo, The Little Switch Engine	ELF	Count's Poem, The	TELLTALE
Campbell Kids At Home, The	ELF	Christmas Abc	LGB	Counting Book, The	WONDER
Campbell Kids Have A Party, The	ELF	Christmas Bunny, The	LGB	Counting Rhymes	LGB
Camping Trip With The Range Rider, A	WONDER	Christmas Carols	LGB	County Mouse And The City Mouse, The	LGB
Can You Guess? (Guess What)	WONDER	Christmas Favorites	WONDER	Cousin Matilda And The Foolish Wolf	TELLTALE
Cap That Mother Made, The	ELF	Christmas In The Country	LGB	Cow And The Elephant, The	LGB
Captain Kangaroo	LGB	Christmas Is Coming	WONDER	Cow In The Silo, The	WONDER
Captain Kangaroo 'Tick Tock Trouble'	TELL-TALE	Christmas Manger, The	LGB	Cow Went Over The Mountain, The	LGB
		Christmas Puppy, The	WONDER	Cowardly Lion, The	WONDER
Captain Kangaroo And The Beaver	LGB	Christmas Songs And Stories	WONDER	Cowboy Abc	LGB
Captain Kangaroo And The Panda	LGB	Christmas Story, The	LGB	Cowboy Eddie	ELF
Captain Kangaroo And The Too-Small House	TELLTALE	Christopher And The Columbus	LGB	Cowboy Mickey	LGB
		Christopher's Hoppy Day	TELLTALE	Cowboy Stamps	WONDER
Captain Kangaroo's Picnic	TELLTALE	Chritopher John's Fuzzy Mittens	TELLTALE	Cowboys	ELF
Captain Kangaroo's Surprise Party	LGB	Churkendoose, The	WONDER	Cowboys And Indians	LGB
Captain Kangaroo	LGB	Cinderella	ELF	Cozy Little Farm, The	TREASURE
Car And Truck Stamps	LGB	Cinderella	LGB	Cozy Little Farm, The	WONDER
Cars	LGB	Cinderella	TREASURE	Cradle Rhymes	TELLTALE
Cars And Trucks	LGB	Cinderella	WONDER	Crosspatch	ELF
Casper And Friends 'boo-o-s On First'	LGB	Cinderella	TELLTALE	Crusader Rabbit	WONDER
		Cinderella's Friends	LGB	Crybaby Calf	ELF
Casper And Wendy	WONDER	Cindy Bear	LGB	Cub Scouts	LGB
Casper And Wendy Adventures	WONDER	Cinnamon Bear, The	TELLTALE	Curious Little Kitten Around The House	LGB
Casper The Friendly Ghost In Ghostland	WONDER	Circus Abc	LGB		
		Circus Abc	TELLTALE	Custume Party, The	WONDER
Casper, The Friendly Ghost	WONDER	Circus Alphabet	TELLTALE	Daddies	LGB
Cat That Climbed The Christmas Tree, The	LGB	Circus Boy	LGB	Daddies All About The Work They Do	LGB
		Circus Boy And Captain Jack	TELLTALE	Daddy's Birthday Cakes	EDINGDONG
Cat Who Stamped His Feet	EAGER READ	Circus Is In Town, The	LGB	Daffy Duck Space Creature	TELLTALE
Cat's Who Stayed For Dinner, The	WONDER	Circus Mouse	TELLTALE	Daisy Dog Wake-Up Book	LGB
Cats	LGB	Circus Time	LGB	Daktari 'Judi And The Kitten'	TELLTALE
Cave Kids	LGB	Circus Train, The	TELLTALE	Dale Evans And Buttermilk	TELLTALE
Charlie	LGB	City Boy And The Country Horse, The	TREASURE	Dale Evans And The Coyote	LGB
Charmin' Chatty	LGB	City Boy, Country Boy	WONDER	Dale Evans And The Lost Goldmine	LGB
Chatterduck	ELF	Cleo	LGB	Dally	TELLTALE
Cheltenham's Party	LGB	Clip Clop	TELLTALE	Daniel Boone	LGB
Chester, The Little Pony	ELF	Clown Coloring Book	LGB	Daniel In The Lions' Den	LGB
Cheyene	LGB	Clue Club The Case Of The Missing Racehorse	ELF	Daniel The Cocker Spaniel	ELF
Chicken Little	LGB			Daniel's New Friend	TELLTALE
Chicken Little	TELLTALE	Clyde Crashcup And Leonardo	WONDER	Danny Beaver's Secret	LGB
Child's Friend, A	TELLTALE	Cold Blooded Penguin, The	LGB	Darby O'Gill	LGB
Child's Garden Of Verses, A	LGB	Color Kittens, The	LGB	Darkwing Duck, The Silly 'Canine Caper'	LGB
Child's Garden Of Versus, A	WONDER	Colorful Mouse, The	LGB	David And Goliath	LGB
Child's Ten Commandments, A	TELLTALE	Colors	LGB	Davy Crockett 'King Of The Wild Frontier'	LGB
Child's Thought Of God, A	ELF	Colors Are Nice	LGB		
Child's Year, A	LGB	Columbus, The Exploring Burro	TELLTALE	Davy Crockett's Keelboat Race	LGB
Children That Lived In A Shoe, The	ELF	Come And See The Rainbow	WONDER	Davy Crockett: American Hero	ELF
Childs First Picture Dictionary, A	WONDER	Come Play House	LGB	Davy Plays Football	TELLTALE
Chip 'n Dale At The Zoo	LGB	Come Visit My Ranch	WONDER	Davy's Little Horse	ELF
Chip 'n Dale Rescue Rangers		Cookie Monster And The Cookie Tree	LGB		
		Copy-Kitten	ELF		

353

Title	Publisher
Four Little Kittens	ELF
Four Little Kittens	LGB
Four Little Puppies	ELF
Four Puppies	LGB
Four Puppies Who Wanted A Home,The	WONDER
Fox Jumped Up One Winters Night, A	LGB
Fozzie's Funnies	LGB
Fraidy Cat	ELF
Fraidy Cat Kitten,The	WONDER
Franky, The Fuzzy Goat	TELLTALE
Freddy And The Indian	WONDER
Freight Train	ELF
Friendly Book, The	LGB
Friendly Bunny,The	LGB
Frisker	TELLTALE
Frisky, The Black Colt	WONDER
Fritzie Goes Home	LGB
From Tadpoles To Frogs	ELF
From Then To Now	LGB
From Trash To Treasure	LGB
Frosty The Snowman	LGB
Fun For Hunkydory	LGB
Fun With Decals	LGB
Funland Party	ELF
Funny Bunny	LGB
Funny Company, The	TELLTALE
Funny Friends In Mother Goose Land	TELLTALE
Funny Hat, The	ELF
Funny Mixed-Up Story, The	WONDER
Fury	LGB
Fury	TELLTALE
Fury Takes The Jump	LGB
Fuss Bunny	ELF
Fuzzy Dan	TELLTALE
Fuzzy Duckling	TELLTALE
Fuzzy Duckling, The	LGB
Fuzzy Friends In Mother Goose Land	TELLTALE
Fuzzy Joe Bear	TELLTALE
Fuzzy Mittens For Three Little Kittens	TELLTALE
Fuzzy Pet, A	TELLTALE
Fuzzy Wuzzy Puppy, The	TELLTALE
Gandy Goose	WONDER
Garden Is Good, A	ELF
Garfield 'The Cat Show'	LGB
Gaston And Josephine	LGB
Gay Purr-ee	LGB
Gene Autry	LGB
Gene Autry 'Makes A New Friend'	TELLTALE
Gene Autry And Champion	LGB
Gene Autry And The Lost Doggie	TELLTALE
Gene Autry Goes To The Circus	TELLTALE
Gentle Ben And The Pesky Puppy	TELLTALE
Georgie Finds A Grandpa	LGB
Getting Ready For Roddy	TELLTALE
Giant Who Wanted Company, The	LGB
Giant With Three Golden Hairs, The	LGB
Ginger Paper Doll	LGB
Gingerbread Man, The	ELF
Gingerbread Man, The	LGB
Gingerbread Man, The	TELLTALE
Ginghams Backward Picnic, The	LGB
Ginghams, The Ice-Cream Parade	TELLTALE
Giraffe Who Went To School,The	WONDER
Goat That Went To School, The	ELF
Goby Goat And The Birthday Gift	TELLTALE
Golden Book Of Birds, The	LGB
Golden Book Of Fairy Tales, The	LGB
Golden Book Of Flowers, The	LGB
Golden Egg Book, The	LGB
Golden Goose, The	LGB
Golden Sleepy Book, The	LGB
Goliath II	LGB
Good Humor Man	LGB
Good Little, Bad Little Girl	LGB
Good Morning, Good Night	LGB
Good Morning, Good Night	WONDER
Good Night 'A Flocked Book'	TELLTALE
Good Night Fairy Tales	WONDER
Good Night Little Bear	LGB
Good Night, Aunt Lilly	LGB
Good Old Days, The	LGB
Good-By Day, The	LGB
Goodbye Tonsils	LGB
Goodnight Book, The	TELLTALE
Goody Naughty Book	ELF
Goody: A Mother Cat Story	ELF
Goofy And The Tiger Hunt	TELLTALE
Goofy, Movie Star	LGB
Goose Who Played The Piano, The	WONDER
Gordons Jet Flight	LGB
Grand And Wonderful Day, The	LGB
Grandma And Grandpa Smith	LGB
Grandmother Is Coming	EDINGDONG
Grandpa Bunny	LGB
Grandpa's House	TELLTALE
Grandpa's Policemen Friends	TELLTALE
Great Fort, The	TELLTALE
Great Grape Ape At The Circus	ELF
Grover Takes Care Of Baby	LGB
Grover's Guide To Good Manners	LGB
Grover's Own Alphabet	LGB
Grover's Own Alphabet	TELLTALE
Growing Things	EDINGDONG
Growing Up	ELF
Guess What?	WONDER
Guess Who Lives Here	LGB
Gull That Lost The Sea, The	LGB
Gumby And Gumby's Pal Pokey To The Rescue	TELLTALE
Gumby And Gumby's Pal Poky	TELLTALE
Gunsmoke	LGB
H.R. Pufnstuf	TELLTALE
Handy Andy	TELLTALE
Hans Christian Andersen's Fairy Tales	WONDER
Hansel & Gretel	LGB
Hansel And Gretel	ELF
Hansel And Gretel	LGB
Happiest Christmas, The	TELLTALE
Happy	TELLTALE
Happy And Sad, Grouch And Glad	LGB
Happy Birthday	LGB
Happy Birthday Present, The	WONDER
Happy Book,The	TELLTALE
Happy Days	LGB
Happy Family, The	LGB
Happy Farm Animals,The	LGB
Happy Golden Abc, The	LGB
Happy Holidays	ELF
Happy Little Whale, The	LGB
Happy Man And His Dumptruck, The	LGB
Happy Surprise, The	WONDER
Happy Twins, The	ELF
Hat For The Queen, A	EAGER READ
Have You Seen A Giraffe Hat?	TELLTALE
Heckle And Jeckle	WONDER
Heckle And Jeckle Visit The Farm	WONDER
Hector Crosses The River.... With George Washington	WONDER
Hector Heathcoat And The Knights	WONDER
Heidi	LGB
Heidi: Child Of The Mountain	WONDER
Helicopters	LGB
Hello Joe	TELLTALE
Hello, Rock	TELLTALE
Help Mr. Willy Nilly	TREASURE
Helpful Friends,The	WONDER
Helpful Henrietta	ELF
Henny-Penny	TREASURE
Henny-Penny	WONDER
Henrietta And The Hat	TELLTALE
Henry Goes To A Party	TREASURE
Henry Goes To A Party	WONDER
Henry In Lolipop Land	TREASURE
Henry In Lollipop Land	WONDER
Henry The Helicopter	TELLTALE
Here Comes The Band	EDINGDONG
Here Comes The Parade	LGB
Herman And Katnip	WONDER
Heroes Of The Bible	LGB
Hey There It's Yogi Bear	LGB
Hey There It's Yogi Bear!	TELLTALE
Hey, Diddle, Diddle And Other Nonsense Rhymes	ELF
Hi! Cowboy	TELLTALE
Hi! Ho! Three In A Row	LGB
Hiawatha	ELF
Hiawatha	LGB
Hid-Away Puppy	ELF
Hide-And-Seek Duck,The	WONDER
Hide-Away Henry	TELLTALE

Title	Publisher
Hiding Place, The	TELLTALE
Hilda Needs Help!	LGB
Hippety Hop Around The Block	TELLTALE
Hiram's Red Shirt	LGB
Ho-Hum	TELLTALE
Hokey Wolf And Ding-A-Ling	LGB
Home For A Bunny	LGB
Honey Bear Finds A Friend	TELLTALE
Hong Kong Phooey And The Bird Nest Snatchers	ELF
Hong Kong Phooey And The Fire Engine Mystery	ELF
Hong Kong Phooey And The Fortune Cookie Caper	ELF
Hooray For Lassie!	TELLTALE
Hop, Skippy And Jump	TELLTALE
Hop, Little Kangaroo	LGB
Hop-Away Joey	ELF
Hopalong Cassidy And The Bar 20 Cowboys	LGB
Hoppity Hooper Vs Skippity Snooper	TELLTALE
Hoppy The Puppy	WONDER
Hoppy, The Curious Kangaroo	WONDER
Horse For Charlie, A	TELLTALE
Horse For Johnny, A	WONDER
Horses	LGB
House For A Mouse, A	LGB
House My Granpa Built	TELLTALE
House That Jack Built, The	LGB
House That Jack Built, The	WONDER
House That Jack Built, The	TELLTALE
House That Jack Built, The	ELF
House That Popeye Built, The	WONDER
Houses	LGB
How Big	LGB
How Big Is A Baby	TELLTALE
How Can We Get To The Zoo?	TELLTALE
How Does Your Garden Grow?	LGB
How Does Your Garden Grow?	TELLTALE
How Peter Cottontail Got His Name	WONDER
How The Camel Got His Hump: A Kipling "Just So" Story	ELF
How The Clown Got His Smile	WONDER
How The Rabbit Found Christmas	WONDER
How The Rhinoceros Got His Skin: "Just" So Story	ELF
How Things Grow	LGB
How To Be A Grouch	TELLTALE
How To Tell Time	LGB
Howdy Doody And Clarabell	LGB
Howdy Doody And His Magic Hat	LGB
Howdy Doody And Mr. Bluster	LGB
Howdy Doody And Santa Claus	LGB
Howdy Doody And The Magic Lamp	TELLTALE
Howdy Doody And The Monkey Tale	TELLTALE
Howdy Doody And The Princess	LGB
Howdy Doody In Funland	LGB
Howdy Doody's Animal Friends	LGB
Howdy Doody's Circus	LGB
Howdy Doody's Clarabell And Pesky Peanut	TELLTALE
Howdy Doody's Clarabell Clown And The Merry-Go-Round	TELLTALE
Howdy Doody's Lucky Trip	LGB
Huckleberry Hound 'The Big Blooming Rosebush'	WONDER
Huckleberry Hound And His Friends	LGB
Huckleberry Hound Builds A House	LGB
Huckleberry Hound Safety Signs	LGB
Huckleberry Hound The Rainmaker	TELLTALE
Huckleberry Hounds And The Christmas Sleigh	LGB
Huffin Puff Express, The	TELLTALE
Hullabaloo	TELLTALE
Hunchback Of Notre Dame, The	LGB
Hunchback Of Notre Dame, The 'Quasimodo's New Friend'	LGB
Hungry Baby Bunny, The	WONDER
Hungry Lion, The	TELLTALE
Hungry Little Bunny, The	WONDER
Hurry, Scurry	TELLTALE
Hush, Hush, It's Sleepytime	LGB
I Can Do Anything ... Almost	WONDER
I Can Fly	LGB
I Can I Can I Can	WONDER
I Can't Wait Until Christmas	LGB
I Decided	EDINGDONG
I Don't Want To Go	LGB
I Have A Secret	LGB
I Know What A Farm Is	TELLTALE
I Like The Farm	TELLTALE
I Like To Be Little	TELLTALE
I Like To Live In The City	LGB
I Like To See 'A Book About The Five Senses'	TELLTALE
I Live In The City Abc	TELLTALE
I Love My Grandma	TELLTALE
I Love You	WONDER
I Play In The Snow	TELLTALE
I See The Sea	WONDER
I See The Sky	WONDER
I Think About God Two Stories About My Day	LGB
I Think About Jesus	ELF
I Walk To The Park	TELLTALE
I'm An Indian Today	LGB
I'm Not Sleepy	TELLTALE
If I Had A Dog	LGB
In My House	EDINGDONG
In, On, Under, And Through	TELLTALE
Indian Stamps	LGB
Indian, Indian	LGB
Insect Stamps	LGB
Insect We Know	WONDER
It's A Lovely Day	WONDER
It's A Secret	WONDER
It's Fun To Peek	TREASURE
It's Howdy Doody Time	LGB
J. Fred Muggs	LGB
Jabberjaw Out West	ELF
Jack And Jill	ELF
Jack And The Beanstalk	ELF
Jack And The Beanstalk	LGB
Jack And The Beanstalk	TELLTALE
Jack's Adventure	LGB
Jamie Looks	LGB
Jasper Giraffe	TELLTALE
Jean Ellen Learns To Swim	TELLTALE
Jeepers, The Little Frog	ELF
Jenny's New Brother	LGB
Jenny's Surprise Summer	LGB
Jerry And Dr. Dave	TELLTALE
Jerry At School	LGB
Jetsons The Great Pizza Hunt, The	WONDER
Jetsons, The	LGB
Jim Jump	TELLTALE
Jiminy Cricket Fire Fighter	LGB
Jingle Bell Jack	EDINGDONG
Jingle Bells	LGB
Jingle Dingle Book, The	WONDER
Jo Jo	ELF
Johnny And The Birds	ELF
Johnny Appleseed	LGB
Johnny Appleseed	TELLTALE
Johnny Go Round	TELLTALE
Johnny Grows Up	WONDER
Johnny The Fireman	ELF
Johnny's Machines	LGB
Joke On Farmer Al Falfa, A	WONDER
Jolly Barnyard, The	LGB
Jolly Jingles	TELLTALE
Jolly Jumping Man, The	WONDER
Josie And The Pussycats/ The Bag Factory Detour	ELF
Jumpty Dumpty And Other Nursery Rhymes	TELLTALE
Jumpy, Humpy, Fuzzy, Buzzy, Animal Book, The	TELLTALE
Jungle Book, The	LGB
Jungle Book, The	TELLTALE
Just For Fun	LGB
Just Imagine 'A Book Of Fairyland Rhymes'	LGB
Just Like Me	TREASURE
Just Like Me	WONDER
Just Like Mommy, Just Like Daddy	WONDER
Just Watch Me	LGB
Katie The Kitten	LGB
Katy's First Day	TELLTALE
Kermit, Saves The Swamp!	LGB
Kerry, The Fire-Engine Dog	ELF
Kewtee Bear's Christmas	WONDER
Kewtee Bear-Santa's Helper	WONDER
Kitten Twins, The	ELF
Kitten Who Thought He Was A Mouse, The	LGB

Mr. Myer's Cow	EDINGDONG	My Little Book Of Bugs	TELLTALE	Noah's Ark	LGB
Mr. Noah And His Family	LGB	My Little Book Of Cars And Trucks	TELLTALE	Nobody's Puppy	TELLTALE
Mr. Puffer Bill Train Engineer	LGB	My Little Book Of Dinosaurs	TELLTALE	Noel	LGB
Mr. Punnymoon's Train	ELF	My Little Book Of Dogs	TELLTALE	Noises And Mr.Flibberty-Jib	LGB
Mr. Wigg's Birthday Party	LGB	My Little Book Of Farm Animals	TELLTALE	Noisy Clock Shop,The	WONDER
Mr. Wishing Went Fishing	WONDER	My Little Book Of Flying	TELLTALE	Nonsense A B Cs	ELF
Mr. Wizrd's Junior Science Show	ELF	My Little Book Of Horses	TELLTALE	Nonsense Alphabet, The	WONDER
Mr. Rogers Neighborhood 'Henreitta Meets Someone New'	LGB	My Little Book Of Pets	TELLTALE	Not Quite Three	TELLTALE
		My Little Counting Book	TELLTALE	Number 9 The Little Fire Engine	ELF
Mrs. Brisby And The Magic Stone	LGB	My Little Dinosaur	LGB	Numbers	LGB
Mrs. Goose's Green Trailer	WONDER	My Little Golden Animal Book	LGB	Nurse Nancy	LGB
Muggins Becomes A Hero	ELF	My Little Golden Book About Cats	LGB	Nursery Rhymes	LGB
Muggins' Big Balloon	ELF	My Little Golden Book About Dogs	LGB	Nursery Rhymes	TELLTALE
Muggins Mouse	ELF	My Little Golden Book About God	LGB	Nursery Songs	LGB
Muggins Takes Off	ELF	My Little Golden Book Of Cars And Trucks	LGB	Nursery Tales	LGB
Muggsy, The Make-Believe Puppy	ELF			Nutcracker, The	LGB
Mumbly To The Rescue	ELF	My Little Golden Book Of Fairy Tales	LGB	Off To School	LGB
Muppet -Treasure Island	LGB	My Little Golden Book Of Jokes	LGB	Oh, Little Rabbit!	LGB
Mushmouse And Punkin Puss 'The Country Cousins'	TELLTALE	My Little Golden Book Of Manners	LGB	Oh, Look!	TELLTALE
		My Little Golden Calendar	LGB	Old Mac Donald Had A Farm	TELLTALE
Musicians Of Bremen	LGB	My Little Golden Dictionary	LGB	Old Mother Goose And Other Nursey Rhymes	LGB
Muskie And His Friends	WONDER	My Little Golden Mother Goose	LGB		
My A B C Book	WONDER	My Little Golden Word Book	LGB	Old Mother Hubbard	ELF
My Baby Brother	LGB	My Magic Slate Book	LGB	Old Mother Hubbard	LGB
My Baby Sister	LGB	My Own Book Of Fun And Play	TREASURE	Old Woman And Her Pig, The	ELF
My Bible Book	ELF	My Own Grandpa	LGB	Old Woman And Her Pig,The	TELLTALE
My Big Book Of Big Machines	TELLTALE	My Pets	LGB	Old Yeller	LGB
My Big Brother	EDINGDONG	My Poetry Book	WONDER	Ollie Bakes A Cake	WONDER
My Book About God	WONDER	My Prayer Book	ELF	Once I Had A Monster	TELLTALE
My Book Of Dolls	WONDER	My Puppy	LGB	Once There Was A House	WONDER
My Book Of Poems	LGB	My Snuggly Bunny	LGB	Once Upon A Time	WONDER
My Christmas Book	LGB	My Teddy Bear	LGB	Once Upon A Windy Day	TELLTALE
My Christmas Treasury	LGB	My Truck Book	ELF	Once Upon A Wintertime	LGB
My Counting Book	ELF	My Word Book	LGB	One Hundred And One Dalmations	TELLTALE
My Daddy Is A Policeman	EDINGDONG	Name For Kitty, A	LGB	One Of The Family	LGB
My Dolly And Me	LGB	Nancy And Sluggo 'The Big Surprise'	TELLTALE	One Two Buckle My Shoe	TELLTALE
My First Book	LGB	Nancy Plays Nurse	ELF	One Two Three	TELLTALE
My First Book Of Bible Stories	LGB	National Velvet	LGB	One,Two,Cock-A-Doodle-Doo	ELF
My First Book Of Farm Animals	TREASURE	Naughty Bunny, The	LGB	Ookpik, The Actic Owl	LGB
My First Book Of Jesus	ELF	Neatos And The Litterbugs, The	LGB	Open Up My Suitcase	LGB
My First Book Of Jokes	WONDER	Never Pat A Bear	LGB	Oscar's Book	LGB
My First Book Of Planets	LGB	New Baby, The	LGB	Oscar's New Neighbor	LGB
My First Book Of Prayers	TREASURE	New Brother, New Sister	LGB	Our Animal Friends	ELF
My First Book Of Prayers	WONDER	New Friends For The Saggy Baggy Elephant	LGB	Our Auto Trip	ELF
My First Book Of Riddles	WONDER			Our Baby	EDINGDONG
My First Book Of Sounds	LGB	New Home For Snow Ball, A	EAGER READ	Our Flag	LGB
My First Counting Book	LGB	New House In The Forest, The	LGB	Our Puppy	LGB
My Flower Book	ELF	New Kittens, The	LGB	Our World	LGB
My Goldfish	EDINGDONG	New Pony, The	LGB	Our World Of Color And Sound	ELF
My Happy Day: A Word Book	ELF	New Puppy, The	LGB	Out Of My Window	LGB
My Home	LGB	Nibbler	TELLTALE	Outdoor Fun	ELF
My Kindergarten Counting Book	LGB	Night Before Christmas, The	LGB	Outside With Baby	TELLTALE
My Kitten	LGB	Night Before Christmas, The	WONDER	Over In The Meadow	WONDER
My Little Abc	TELLTALE	Night Before Christmas, The	TELLTALE	Owl And The Pussy Cat	LGB
My Little Book About Our Flag	TELLTALE	Nine Friendly Dogs, The	WONDER	Pals	TELLTALE
My Little Book Of Big Animals	TELLTALE	Nine Rabbits And Another	WONDER	Pamela Jane's Week 'A Story About Days Of The Week'	TELLTALE
My Little Book Of Big Machines	TELLTALE	Noah And The Ark	TELLTALE		
My Little Book Of Birds	TELLTALE	Noah's Ark	ELF	Pano The Train	LGB
My Little Book Of Boats	TELLTALE				

361

Sleepytime For Everyone	WONDER	Story Of Jonah, The	LGB	Ten Little Fingers	TREASURE
Slowpoke At The Circus	TELLTALE	Story Of Joseph, The	ELF	Ten Little Fingers	WONDER
Slowpoke, The Lazy Little Puppy	ELF	Story Of Our Flag, The	ELF	Terry Bears Win The Cub Scout Badge,The	TREASURE
Sly Little Bear	LGB	Story Of The Christ Child, The	WONDER	Terrytoon Space Train, The	WONDER
Smart Little Mouse, The	ELF	Storybook For Little Tots	ELF	Tex And His Toys	LGB
Smokey And His Animal Friends	LGB	Storytime Favorites	WONDER	That Donkey	TELLTALE
Smokey Bear 'Saves The Forest'	TELLTALE	Stubby	TELLTALE	That Funny Hat	ELF
Smokey Bear And The Campers	LGB	Stuck In The Tub	TELLTALE	That Puppy	TELLTALE
Smokey The Bear	LGB	Sugar Plum Tree, The	ELF	That's Where You Live	TELLTALE
Smokey The Bear Finds A Helper	LGB	Suitcase With A Surprise, A	EDINGDONG	Theodore Mouse Goes To Sea	LGB
Smoky The Baby Goat	TELLTALE	Summer Friends	WONDER	Theodore Mouse Up In The Air	LGB
Sneezer	TELLTALE	Summer Vacation	LGB	There Are Tyrannosaurs Trying On Pants In My Bedroom	LGB
Snoopy, The Nosey Little Puppy	ELF	Sunny, Honey, And Funny	TELLTALE	There Was Once A Little Boy	WONDER
Snooty	TELLTALE	Super Circus	ELF	Thin Arnold	TELLTALE
Snoozey	TELLTALE	Supercar	LGB	Things I Like	LGB
Snow Storm Surprise	LGB	Superliner United States, The: World's Fastest Liner	ELF	Things In My House	LGB
Snow White	LGB	Superstar Barbie	LGB	Things To Make And Do For Christmas	TREASURE
Snow White	TREASURE	Surpries!	ELF	This Is My Family	LGB
Snow White And Rose Red	ELF	Surprise Doll, The	WONDER	This Is The World	ELF
Snow White And Rose Red	LGB	Surprise For Felix, A	WONDER	This Little Piggy Counting Rhymes	LGB
Snow White And The Seven Dwarfs	WONDER	Surprise For Howdy Doody	TELLTALE	This Magic World	WONDER
Snow White And The Seven Dwarfs	TELLTALE	Surprise For Mickey Mouse	LGB	This Room Is Mine	TELLTALE
Snowball	TELLTALE	Surprise For Mrs. Bunny, A	WONDER	This Way To The Zoo	TELLTALE
Snowman's Christmas Present, The	WONDER	Surprise For Sally	LGB	This World Of Ours	LGB
Snuggles	ELF	Surprise In The Barn	TELLTALE	Three Bears Visit Goldilocks, The	ELF
So Big	LGB	Surprise Party, The	WONDER	Three Bears, The	ELF
So Long	ELF	Susan And The Rain	TELLTALE	Three Bears, The	LGB
So This Is Spring!	WONDER	Susan In The Driver's Seat	LGB	Three Bears, The	TELLTALE
Socks	TELLTALE	Susie's New Stove	LGB	Three Bears, The	TELLTALE
Somebody Forgot	TELLTALE	Swiss Family Duck	TELLTALE	Three Bedtime Stories	LGB
Someplace For Sparky	TELLTALE	Swiss Family Robinson	LGB	Three Billy Goats	LGB
Songs To Sing And Play	WONDER	Sword In The Stone, The	LGB	Three Billy Goats Gruff	TELLTALE
Sonny The Bunny	WONDER	Sword In The Stone, The	TELLTALE	Three Billy Goats Gruff, The	ELF
Sonny The Luck Bunny	WONDER	Tabitha Tabby's Fantastic Flavor	TELLTALE	Three Little Bunnies	ELF
Sorcerer's Apprentice, The	LGB	Tag-Along Shadow	TELLTALE	Three Little Kittens	ELF
Soupy Sales And The Tallking Turtle	WONDER	Tale Of Peter Rabbit, The	TELLTALE	Three Little Kittens	LGB
Space Ship To The Moon	ELF	Tale Of Peter Rabbit, The	LGB	Three Little Kittens And Other Nursery Tales	WONDER
Sparkie-No School Today	TREASURE	Tale Spin 'Ghost Ship'	LGB	Three Little Mice	TELLTALE
Sparky The Fire Dog	ELF	Tales Of Wells Fargo	LGB	Three Little Pigs	LGB
Special Pet, A	TELLTALE	Tall Tree Small Tree	TELLTALE	Three Little Pigs And Little Red Riding Hood	WONDER
Speckles And The Triplets	TELLTALE	Tammy	LGB	Three Little Pigs, The	TELLTALE
Speed Buggy And The Secret Message	ELF	Tarzan	LGB	Three Little Puppies	ELF
Splish Splash, And Splush	TELLTALE	Tawney Scrawney Lion And The Clever Monkey, The	LGB	Three Mice And A Cat	WONDER
Spoon Necklace, The	TELLTALE	Tawny Scrawny Lion	LGB	Three Pigs, The	ELF
Sport Goofy And The Racing Robot	LGB	Tawny Scrawny Lion 'Saves The Day'	LGBLAND	Through The Picture Frame	LGB
Spotted Little Puppy,The	TELLTALE	Taxi That Hurried, The	LGB	Thumper	LGB
Squiffy The Skunk	ELF	Teddy Bear Of Bumpkin Hollow	ELF	Tickety-Tock, What Time Is It?	LGB
Squirrel Twins, The	ELF	Teddy Bear Twins, The	ELF	Tiger's Adventure	LGB
Stacks Of Caps	WONDER	Teddy The Terrier	ELF	Time For Bed	LGB
Steve Canyon	LGB	Teddy's Surprise	TELLTALE	Time For Everything	ELF
Stop And Go (Wheel Book)	LGB	Teena And The Magic Pot	TELLTALE	Timothy Tiger	ELF
Store-Bought Doll, The	LGB	Teeny-Tiny Tale	TELLTALE	Timothy Tiger's Terrible Toothache	LGB
Stories Of Jesus	LGB	Ten Commandments For Children, The	ELF	Timothy Tinker 'The Wonderful Oilcan'	TELLTALE
Stories Of The Christ Child	ELF	Ten Items Or Less	LGB		
Story Of Babar, The	WONDER	Ten Little Animals	LGB		
Story Of David, The	ELF				
Story Of Jesus, The	LGB				

Timothy's Shoes	TELLTALE	Toy That Flew, The	TELLTALE	Uncle Wiggily	LGB
Tin Woodsman Of Oz, The	LGB	Toys	LGB	Uncle Wiggily And His Friends	WONDER
Tiny Dinosaurs	LGB	Train Coming	TELLTALE	Uncle Wiggily And The Alligator	TELLTALE
Tiny Toon Adventures 'Happy Birthday Babs'	LGB	Train Stories	LGB	Uncle Wiggily's Adventures	WONDER
		Trains Stamp Book	LGB	Under Dog	TELLTALE
Tiny Toon Adventures 'Lost In The Funhouse'	LGB	Train To Timbuctoo, The	LGB	Under The Saskatoon Tree	TELTALE
Tiny Toon Adventures 'The Adventures Of Buster Hood'	LGB	Travel	LGB	Underdog And The Disappearing Ice Cream	LGB
		Traveling Twins, The	WONDER		
Tiny Tots 1-2-3	TELLTALE	Treasure Book Of Favorite Nursery Tales	TREASURE	Up And Down Book Staring Ernie And Bert, The	TELLTALE
Tiny, Tawny Kitten, The	LGB			Up In The Attic	LGB
Tip-Top Tree House	TELLTALE	Treasure Book Of Riddles	TREASURE	Valley Of The Dinosaurs	ELF
To Market To Market	WONDER	Trick On Deputy Dog	WONDER	Velveteen Rabbit, The	LGB
To The Store We Go	ELF	Trim The Christmas Tree	LGB	Very Best Home For Me!, The	LGB
Toad Flies High	LGB	Trip In Space, A	ELF	Very Best Of Friends, The	TELLTALE
Toby Bunny's Secret Hiding Place	TELLTALE	Truck That Stopped At Village Small, The	TELLTALE	Very Busy Barbie	LGB
Toby The Rock Hound	TELLTALE			Visit To The Children's Zoo, A	LGB
Toby Tyler	LGB	Trucks	ELF	Visit To The Dentist, A	WONDER
Toby Zebra And The Lost Zoo	TELLTALE	Trucks (2 Paper Model Trucks)	LGB	Visit To The Doctor, A	WONDER
Tom And Jerry	LGB	Trumpet	TELLTALE	Visit To The Hospital, A	WONDER
Tom And Jerry And The Toy Circus	TELLTALE	Try Again, Sally!	TELLTALE	Volksy: The Little Yellow Car	ELF
Tom And Jerry In Model Mice	TELLTALE	Tubby The Tuba	TREASURE	Wacky Witch	LGB
Tom And Jerry In Tom's Happy Birthday	TELLTALE	Tubby Turtle	ELF	Wacky Witch: The Royal Birthday	TELLTALE
		Tubsy And The Picnic Tree (Ideal Doll)	TELLTALE	Wagon Train	LGB
Tom And Jerry Meet Little Quack	LGB			Wait-For-Me-Kitten	LGB
Tom And Jerry's Big Move	TELLTALE	Tuffer	TELLTALE	Waiting For Santa Claus	WONDER
Tom And Jerry's Merry Christmas	LGB	Tuffy The Tugboat	TELLTALE	Waldo, The Jumping Dragon	TELLTALE
Tom And Jerry's Party	LGB	Tuggy The Tugboat	WONDER	Wally Gator	LGB
Tom And Jerry's Photo Finish	LGB	Turtles Turn Up On Tuesday	ELF	Wally Gator 'Guess What's Hiding At The Zoo'	TELLTALE
Tom Corbett's Wonder Book Of Space	WONDER	Tutu The Little Fawn	WONDER		
		Tweety	TELLTALE	Walt Disney Babies 1 To 10 Again	TELLTALE
Tom Corbett: A Trip To The Moon	WONDER	Tweety And Sylvester At The Farm	TELLTALE	Walt Disney World - Big Albert Moves In	TELLTALE
Tom Terrific With Mighty Manfred The Wonder Dog	WONDER	Tweety And Sylvester 'A Visit To The Vet'	TELLTALE		
				Walt Disney's Favorite Stories	LGB
Tom Terrific's Greatest Adventure	WONDER	Tweety And Sylvester 'Picnic Problems'	TELLTALE	Walt Disney's Storytime Book	LGB
Tom Thumb	ELF			Walton's And The Birthday Present, The	LGB
Tom Thumb	LGB	Tweety And Sylvester In 'Birds Of A Feather'	LGB	Walton's The 'Elizabeth And The Magic Lamp'	TELLTALE
Tommy And Timmy	TELLTALE				
Tommy On The Farm	TELLTALE	Tweety Global Patrol	LGB	Water Babies	LGB
Tommy Tractor	TELLTALE	Twelve Dancing Princesses, The	LGB	Water Babies	TELLTALE
Tommy Visits The Doctor	LGB	Twelve Days Of Christmas, The	WONDER	Water, Water Everywhere	WONDER
Tommy's Camping Adventure	LGB	Twenty-Third Psalm, The	ELF	We Help Daddy	LGB
Tommy's Wonderful Rides	LGB	Twilight Tales	ELF	We Help Mommy	LGB
Tonka	LGB	Twins, The	LGB	We Like Kindergarten	LGB
Too Many Kittens	TELLTALE	Two Kittens	TELLTALE	We Like To Do Things	LGB
Too Small Names!	TELLTALE	Two Little Miners	LGB	We Love Grandpa	EDINGDONG
Too-Little Fire Engine, The	WONDER	Two Stories About Chap And Chirpy	TELLTALE	We Talk With God	TELLTALE
Tootle	LGB			We're Busy Charlie Brown	TELLTALE
Tootle And Katy Caboose 'A Special Treasure'	LGBLAND	Two Stories About Kate & Kitty	TELLTALE	Welcome To Little Golden Book Land	LGBLAND
		Two Stories About Lollipop	TELLTALE		
Top Cat	LGB	Two Stories About Ricky	TELLTALE	Whales	LGB
Topsy Turvy Circus	LGB	Two Stories About Wags	TELLTALE	What Am I?	LGB
Tortoise And The Hare, The	ELF	Two Stories About Wendy	TELLTALE	What Am I?	WONDER
Tortoise And The Hare, The	LGB	Two To Twins, The	TELLTALE	What Are You Looking At?	TREASURE
Touch Turtle	LGB	Ugly Dachshund, The	LGB	What Are You Looking At?	WONDER
Town Mouse And The Country Mouse, The	TELLTALE	Ugly Duckling, The	ELF	What Can We Do With Blocks?	WONDER
		Ugly Duckling, The	LGB	What Happened To George?	ELF
Toy Party, The	TELLTALE	Uncle Mistletoe	LGB	What Happened To Piggy?	WONDER
Toy Soldier, The	LGB	Uncle Remus	LGB	What If?	LGB
		Uncle Scrooge 'The Winner'	TELLTALE		

Don't Miss This Golden Opportunity to Add to Your Collection

Price Guide to Holt-Howard Collectibles and Other Related Ceramicwares of the 50s & 60s
by Walter Dworkin

The first-ever price guide devoted to Holt-Howard "Pixie-wares" and similar items from other companies, includes the whimsical items, intended for daily use in the home, featured the heads of impish Pixies on condiment jars of all types, liquor bottles and salt-and-pepper shakers. Historical information on Holt-Howard, full-color photos of almost every piece of the firm's Pixie-ware and current prices for 350 items make this a must-have guide. Softcover
• 8-1/4 x 10-7/8 • 160 pages • 300 color photos
• **HHCK** • **$24.95** • **AVAIL 4/98**

Standard Price Guide to U.S. Scouting Collectibles
ID & Price Guide for Cub, Scout and Explorer Programs
by George Cuhaj

This easy-to-use book is the ultimate guide to Cub Scouts and Boy Scouts collectibles. Detailed descriptions and current market prices in two pricing grades for more than 5,000 items including patches and badges, pins, award medals, handbooks and manuals, medallions, uniforms, storybooks, and unusual items like cameras, games, and calendars. Softcover
• 8-1/2 x 11 • 328 pages • 200+ b&w photos
• 32 color photos • **SCOUT** • **$24.95** • **AVAIL 6/98**

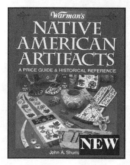

Warman's Native American Collectibles
A Price Guide & Historical Reference
by John A. Shuman III

Join the hottest trend in collecting - Native American artifacts. Gain valuable historical information about handcrafted items including baskets, dolls, totem poles, dishes, pipes, drums, jewelry, beadwork, moccasins, spears, masks, clothing and bags. The items featured in this book range in price from less than $100 into the thousands of dollars, making it a valuable reference guide for both beginning and advanced collectors. Softcover • 8-1/4 x 10-7/8 • 176 pages •
400+ color photos • **NAC1** • **$24.95** • **AVAIL 6/98**

Warman's Antiques & Collectibles Price Guide
32nd Edition
Edited by Ellen Schroy

Continue the tradition with the definitive general price guide to antiques and collectibles, readers will find this book an invaluable part of their library. The 1998 edition contains more than 500 collecting categories with thousands of updated prices and hundreds of photos of the most popular antiques and collectibles including advertising, dinnerware, dolls, firearms, furniture, glassware, jewelry, ceramics, silver, toys and sports.
Softcover • 8-1/4 x 10-7/8 • 640 pages • 600+ b&w photos
• **WAC32** • **$16.95** • **AVAIL 5/98**

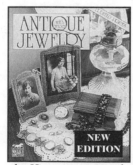

Antique Jewelry with Prices
2nd edition
by Doris J. Snell

Uncover this gem of a guide to antique jewelry, long considered the standard reference in the field. This new edition contains updated prices, information and additional illustrations for hundreds of bracelets, brooches, chains, earrings, lockets, rings, watches and more. Inspect over 100 years of beautiful jewelry, from the Victorian era to the Art Moderne period. Beautiful stones and settings are displayed for you in photos, catalog reprints, and a special color section. Softcover • 8-1/2 x 11 • 160 pages
• 8-page color section • **AJP2** • **$19.95**

krause publications

700 E. State Street • Iola, WI 54990-0001

Visit and order from our secure web site: www.krause.com

Credit Card Calls Toll-Free

800-258-0929 Dept. BGB1

Monday-Friday, 7 a.m. - 8 p.m. • Saturday, 8 a.m. - 2 p.m., CST

Fill Your Shelves With Valuable Hobby Guides

1998 Toys and Prices
5th Edition
by Sharon Korbeck, editor

Journey through the toy collecting market with this accurate, newly updated price guide. Featuring up to three grades of value for more than 18,500 toys manufactured from 1843-1996. Covering 18 categories of toys, including-new this year-western and rock n' roll toys.
Handy carry-along size. Softcover • 6 x 9 • 912 pages • 500 b&w photos • 20 color photos • **TE05** • **$17.95**

1998 Price Guide to Limited Edition Collectibles
3rd Edition
by Mary Sieber, Editor

Uncover updated values for more than 52,000 limited edition figurines, plates, dolls, ornaments, and more in this limited edition "bible." Comprehensive descriptions, 200 photos and 8 pages of full color take the guesswork out of identifying and pricing pieces you want to buy or sell. Nearly 300 manufacturers are represented and experts offer sound advice on the future of your collectibles. Softcover • 6 x 9 • 832 pages • 500 b&w photos • 40 color photos • **LEP03** • **$17.95**

300 Years of Kitchen Collectibles, Antiques and Cookbooks
Identification & Value Guide, 4th Edition
by Linda Campbell Franklin

Whether you collect things that dice, measure, filter or whir, if they belong in the kitchen you'll find them in this guide to three centuries of domestic tools of trade. Listings for more than 7,000 antique items and healthy servings of classic recipes, helpful hints, and fascinating tidbits from 18th , 19th, and 20th century trade catalogs and advertisements. Whet your appetite for homestyle collectibles, then enjoy a full-course feast of Americana in 300 Years of Kitchen Collectibles. Softcover • 8-1/2 x 11 • 640 pages • 1600 illustrations • 5000 illustrations • **KIT04** • **$24.95**

Price Guide to Flea Market Treasures
4th edition
by Harry L. Rinker

Dig deep into this new fourth edition and uncover prices and descriptions for more than 10,000 items you'll likely find at flea markets across the country. Check out the 25 best flea markets in the nation and then put to practice the buying and selling tips that make this a true survival manual. NEW! 50 cutting-edge categories from 35 experts. Softcover • 8-1/4 x 10-7/8 • 356 pages • 700 photos • **FMT4** • **$19.95**

Caring for Your Collectibles — How to Preserve Your Old and New Treasures
by Ken Arnold

Packed with valuable tips on how to clean, store, preserve and display just about every type of fine collectible. Protect your investment for years to come with helpful hints and resource listings. Softcover • 6 x 9 • 208 pages • 90 b&w photos • **CYC** • **$12.95**

Collecting Paper
A Collector's Identification & Value Guide
by Gene Utz

Wraps up more than 15 different categories of papers, from sheet music to autographs to stocks and bonds. Easily identify and value your collectibles with these complete illustrations, descriptions and historical backgrounds from author Gene Utz. Softcover • 8-1/2 x 11 • 222 pages • 372 b&w photos • **PAPE** • **$22.95**

krause publications

700 E. State Street • Iola, WI 54990-0001

Credit Card Calls Toll-Free
800-258-0929 Dept. BGB1
Monday-Friday, 7 a.m. - 8 p.m. • Saturday, 8 a.m. - 2 p.m., CST
Visit and order from our secure web site: www.krause.com